D0849703

Rome's Great Eastern War

Dedication

In loving memory of Geoff Sampson (1947–2019)

Rome's Great Eastern War

Lucullus, Pompey and the Conquest of the East, 74–62 BC

Gareth C Sampson

Pen & Sword
MILITARY

First published in Great Britain in 2021 by
Pen & Sword Military
An imprint of
Pen & Sword Books Ltd
Yorkshire – Philadelphia

ISBN 978 1 52676 268 9

Printed and bound in the UK by CPI Group (UK) Ltd,
Croydon, CR0 4YY.

Pen & Sword Books Limited incorporates the imprints of Atlas,
Archaeology, Aviation, Discovery, Family History, Fiction, History,
Maritime, Military, Military Classics, Politics, Select, Transport,
True Crime, Air World, Frontline Publishing, Leo Cooper, Remember
When, Seaforth Publishing, The Praetorian Press, Wharncliffe
Local History, Wharncliffe Transport, Wharncliffe True Crime
and White Owl.

For a complete list of Pen & Sword titles please contact

PEN & SWORD BOOKS LIMITED
47 Church Street, Barnsley, South Yorkshire, S70 2AS, England
E-mail: enquiries@pen-and-sword.co.uk
Website: www.pen-and-sword.co.uk

Or

PEN AND SWORD BOOKS
1950 Lawrence Rd, Havertown, PA 19083, USA
E-mail: Uspen-and-sword@casematepublishers.com
Website: www.penandswordbooks.com

Contents

Acknowledgements

The first and greatest acknowledgement must go out to my wonderful wife Alex, without whose support none of this would be possible. Next must come Thomas and Caitlin, who always provide a grounding in the real world.

Special thanks go out to my parents, who always encouraged a love of books and learning (even if they did regret the house being filled with books). My father Geoff died recently, and he will be greatly missed by all of us.

There are a number of individuals who through the years have inspired my love of Roman history and mentored me along the way: Michael Gracey at William Hulme, David Shotter at Lancaster and Tim Cornell at Manchester. My heartfelt thanks go out to them all.

A shout goes out to the remaining members of the Manchester diaspora: Gary, Ian, Jason, Sam. Those were good days.

As always, my thanks go out to my editor Phil Sidnell, for his patience and understanding.

It must also be said that as an independent academic, the job of researching these works is being made easier by the internet, so Alumnus access to JSTOR (Manchester and Lancaster) and Academia.edu must get a round of thanks too.

List of Illustrations

Maps & Diagrams

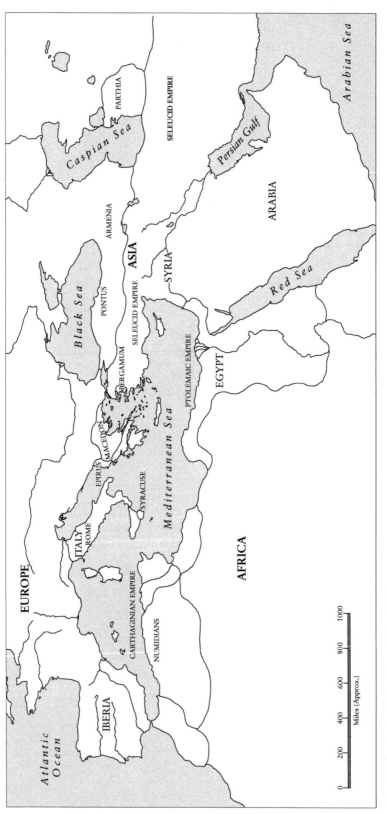

Map 1 The Ancient World in the Mid-3rd Century.

Map 2 The Near East After Apamea.

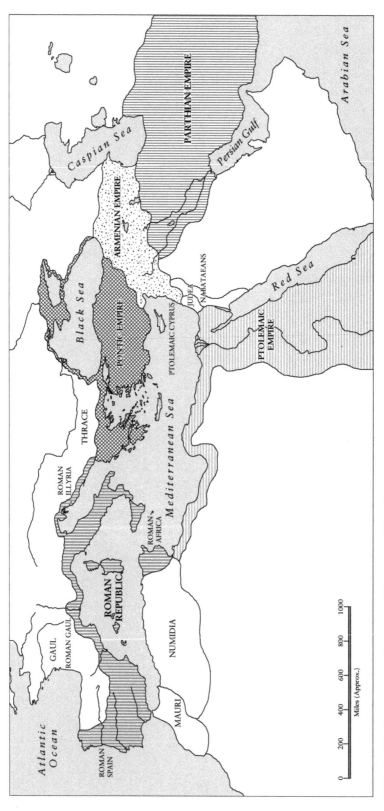

Map 3 The Pontic and Armenian Empires (80s BC).

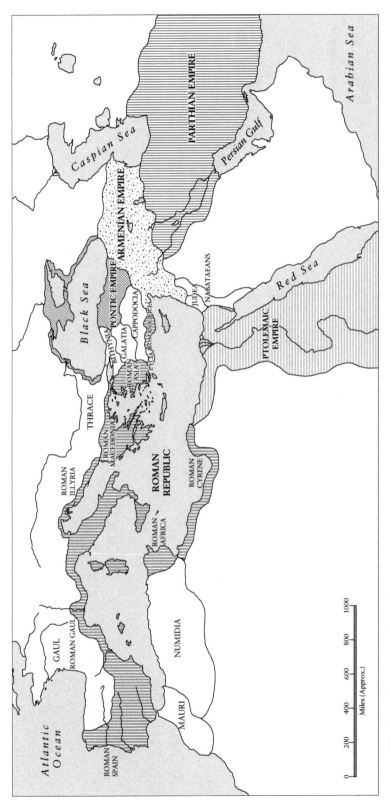

Map 4 The Mediterranean World in 75 BC.

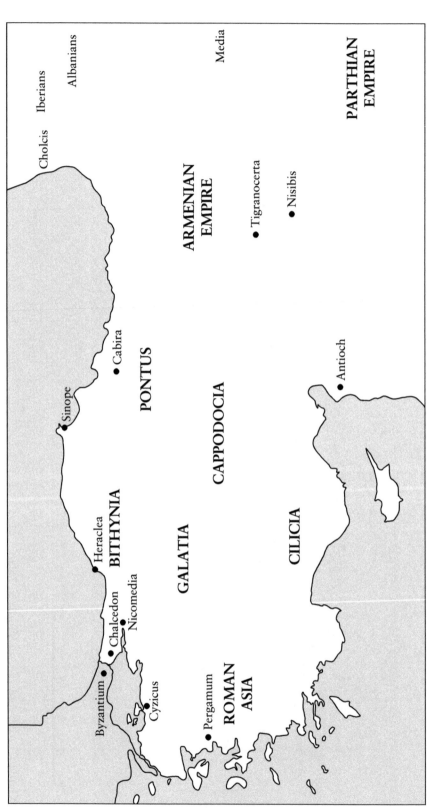

Map 5 Asia Minor.

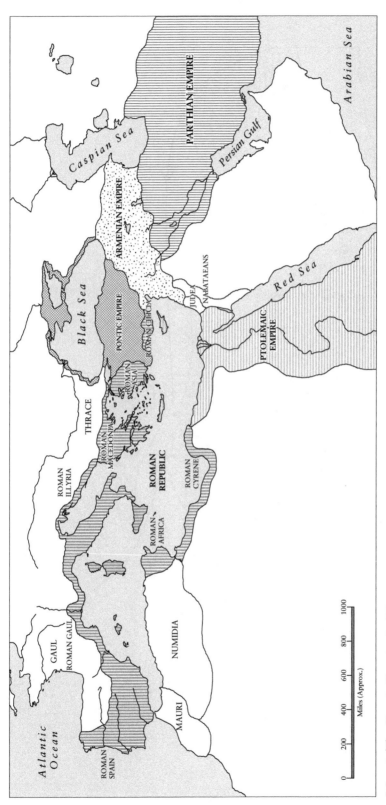

Map 6 The Pontic Empire in 73 BC.

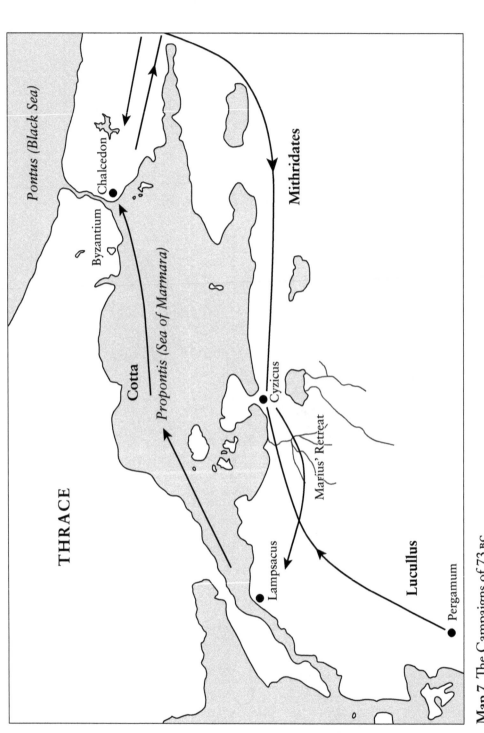

Map 7 The Campaigns of 73 BC.

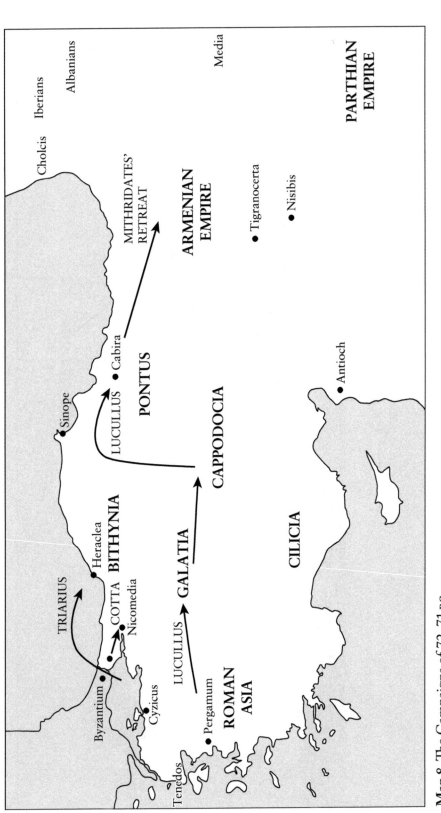

Map 8 The Campaigns of 72–71 BC.

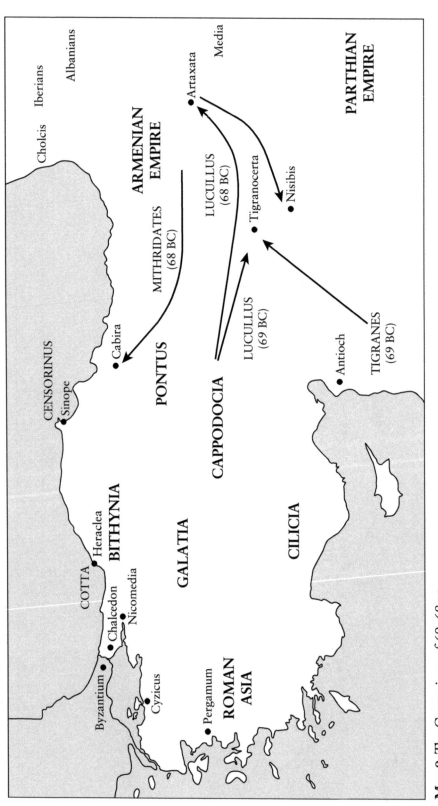

Map 9 The Campaigns of 69–68 BC.

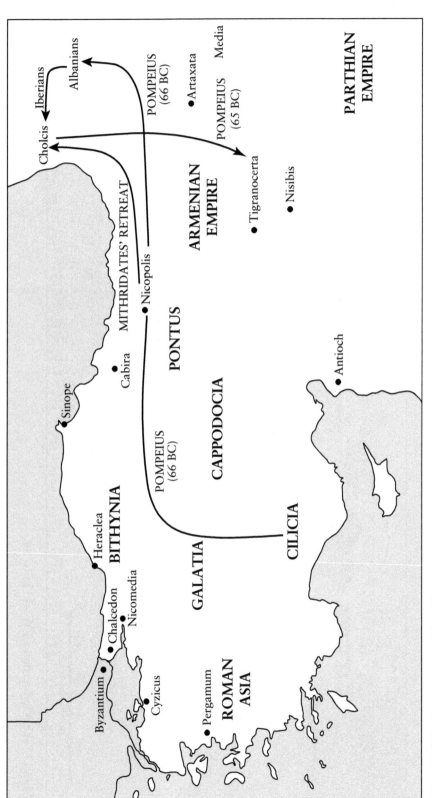

Map 10 The Campaigns of 66–65 BC.

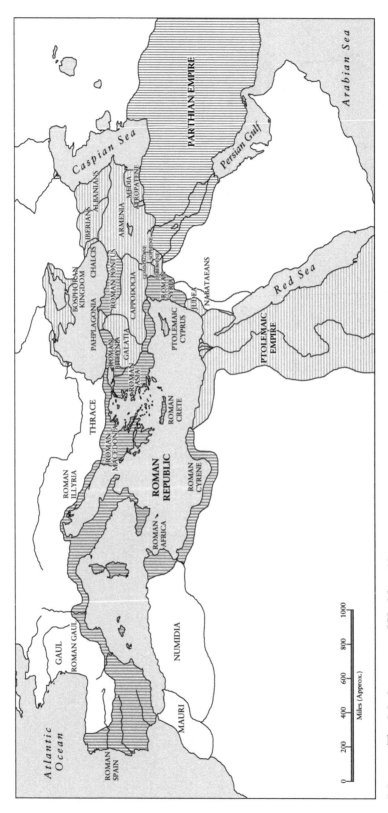

Map 11 The Mediterranean World in 62 BC.

Introduction

The War that Forged Rome's Eastern Empire

In the year that now equates to 74 BC, a war broke out between two of the rival powers vying for control of Asia Minor. This was actually the third war between these antagonists in the last two decades, the first two having ended in stalemates that left their rivalry unresolved. The two belligerent powers were opposites in both their political structures – an oligarchy versus an oriental monarchy – and their geographical heartlands – a power from the West and a native power from Asia Minor. Yet both societies had a common interest in empire building and had empires that stretched across the Mediterranean and the Black Sea, respectively. The two powers in question were the Roman Republic and the Pontic Empire.

What marked out this war from the two that preceded it is not only that it represented the final clash between these two powers, but that it soon escalated into a region-wide war, drawing in the other rival empires of the East, and that at its conclusion the whole of eastern history and the East–West clash of civilizations had been reshaped. As most people will know, the victor was the Roman Republic, but this war represented a massive expansion of their empire, transforming it from a western-based one to one which spanned the Mediterranean and into the Near East. Though Rome had been fighting eastern powers for over a century, prior to this war its physical empire was nothing more than two footholds in Asia Minor (to the east and south). By the end of the war however, Rome's empire stretched from the Crimea to the Red Sea, encompassing all of Asia Minor and the Near East up to the Caucasus and the Euphrates Valley.

The war also marked the penultimate stage in the collapse of the Hellenistic world, forged after the death of Alexander the Great, and saw the extinguishing of the once-mighty Seleucid Empire, along with the newer rising powers of the Pontic and Armenian Empires. Furthermore, it laid the foundations for the clash that came to define the subsequent history of the ancient East, between the empires of Rome and Parthia.

This work will examine the build-up to this war, which soon escalated to involve all the great powers of the East, as well as provide a detailed analysis of the various campaigns and battles fought across a decade-long series of interlocking conflicts. This will cover the key Battle of Tigranocerta, one of Rome's greatest victories in the East, as well as the Roman triumphs at Cyzicus, Cabira and Artaxata.

The work will also attempt to redress the imbalance that exists in studies of this period, and this war in particular. Most commonly, this war has been labelled the Third Mithridatic War, a title that contains two serious flaws. The first weakness is that it limits the scope of the clash to being between Rome and Pontus, reducing it to merely being the final of the 'best of three' wars between the two states. Yet this title does not explain how a war over a contested kingdom on the Bosphorus/Black Sea coast led to Roman armies overrunning the East, from the Caucasus in the north to Judea in the south. Like many wars, the original reason for the conflict soon became lost as more and more powers were drawn into the war, from the Armenian, Seleucid and Parthian Empires, to the Kingdom of Judea and the tribes of the Caucasus and Arabia. Thus I have abandoned this limited title of the Third Mithridatic War in favour of one that more encompasses the far greater scope of the conflict; hence the Great Eastern War of 74–62 BC.

The second reason for the abandonment of the traditional title lies in the distorting nature of the ancient and modern historiography on the subject, which has an unhealthy obsession with just one of the protagonists; namely the King of Pontus, Mithridates VI. Throughout Roman historiography (both ancient and modern), Rome is frequently faced with an almost endless series of mythologized opponents – almost like supervillains in popular fiction – from Hannibal to Jugurtha to Mithridates, men who rise up to oppose the seemingly unlimited advance of Rome, are initially victorious but then inevitably overwhelmed. Whilst events in the ancient world were determined to a great degree by the personalities of generals and kings, too great a focus on the individual comes at the cost of understanding the wider factors at play. Furthermore, excessive focus on just one of the individual protagonists distorts our understanding of the war itself and forces us to only view events in terms of how they relate to that person. Thus everything is seen through the lens of Mithridates, which is a misleading way to view this crucial war.

Of equal, if not greater, importance in this war is the Armenian Emperor Tigranes II (the Great), who at this time was the far more powerful ruler than his father-in-law. Yet Tigranes – perhaps because he sought accommodation after his defeat, rather than a heroic death – did not provide the necessary dramatic element to rate as a major opponent of Rome, despite the fact that his defeat was of far more significance to the history of the Near and Middle East.

Thus, the work that follows will detail the history of the war between the various great powers of the ancient world, and where necessary will acknowledge the contribution of all of the various protagonists, from the key leaders – Lucullus, Pompeius Magnus, Mithridates and Tigranes – to the lesser ones, such as the Parthian Emperor Phraates III, whilst equally focusing on the various factors that brought them into conflict and sustained it for over a decade. We will also analyse the consequences of the war which saw the creation of a new world order in the Near and Middle East, forever changing its history.

Timeline of the Great Eastern War

Notes on Roman Names

All Roman names in the following text will be given in their traditional form, including the abbreviated first name. Below is a list of the Roman first names referred to in the text and their abbreviations:

A.	Aulus
Ap.	Appius
C.	Caius
Cn.	Cnaeus
D.	Decimus
K.	Kaeso
L.	Lucius
M.	Marcus
Mam.	Mamercus
P.	Publius
Q.	Quintus
Ser.	Servius
Sex.	Sextus
Sp.	Spurius
T.	Titus
Ti.	Tiberius

Part I

Rome and the Hellenistic East –
From Periphery to Hegemony (323–74 BC)

Chapter 1

Rome and the Rise and Fall of the Hellenistic World Order (323–80 BC)

The clear danger of studying the background to the war which broke out in the Near East in 74 BC, and which would engulf virtually all the kingdoms and empires of the region, is to judge it simply from the perspective of Rome, a task made easier by the bulk of the surviving sources for these conflicts being Roman. Thus it is easy to construct a narrative that Roman expansion was inevitable and that the foes whom they faced were merely the latest in a long line of 'enemies of Rome', who rose up, were at first successful, but were ultimately defeated.

Yet as always, the reality is a far more complicated picture, and this war saw Rome finally immerse itself into the heart of the ancient world after centuries of trying to avoid such entanglements. The danger in studying Roman history in isolation is that we ignore events in the wider ancient world, and furthermore invert the centre of attention, making Italy and the Western Mediterranean the centre of events rather than the periphery, as it was for much of Rome's existence.

Rome and the Eastern World – On the Periphery (to 338 BC)

Across the ancient world we can see three clusters of civilizations rising and falling: China and India, which fall outside the scope of this work, and then the Mediterranean/Middle East region, within which Rome developed. Founded on the western side of Italy, Rome found itself in the very periphery of the 'civilized' world, which had its heartlands in an arc from the Nile to Mesopotamia. Reading early Roman history (though written much later), we find annual struggles between kingdoms and cities no more than a few miles apart, with very little reference to events in the wider world. In many respects this was reciprocated, with very few people in the wider world seeming to care what was taking place in 'barbarian' territories on the very edges of civilization.

Yet whilst Rome was still being ruled by its kings, the ancient world was reshaped when the world's first mighty empire was created in the Middle East. In the mid-sixth century BC, Cyrus the Great created the largest empire the ancient world had seen when he overran Media, Mesopotamia and Lydia, thereafter ruling a vast territory that stretched from the Indus to the Mediterranean. By the time the city of Rome had founded its Republic, this empire had expanded to include Egypt and had crossed into mainland Europe (namely Thrace).

With the Roman Republic only twenty years old, the mighty Persian Empire decided to continue its annexation of the Mediterranean and expand in a limited way into mainland Greece. Victory for the Greeks (at Marathon) was merely an annoyance to the King of Kings in Persepolis. Ten years later, the full resources of the Persian Empire were thrown at the upstart city-states in Greece, which by the end of 480 BC had been conquered as far as the Isthmus of Corinth, with Athens being burnt. Had Greece fallen at this point, the victorious Persian monarch Darius would have soon expanded across the Adriatic and added Italy and Sicily to his kingdom. In contrast, Rome at this point was locked into a war with its major rival, the Etruscan city of Veii, just 10 miles away.

As is well known, the Greeks were able to defeat the Persians and drive them out of mainland Greece, thus saving both themselves and their neighbours from being absorbed into Darius' universal empire. With Greece acting as a buffer between Italy and the Persian Empire, territories such as Rome were free to continue their local squabbles. Though the Persian threat had receded, Rome still found itself in part of a wider Mediterranean system, with events elsewhere continuing to shape its fortunes. For at least the previous century, the greatest power in Italy were the Etruscans, yet in 474 BC, they suffered a major defeat at the Battle of Cumae at the hands of Hiero I of Syracuse. This setback and subsequent Gallic incursions over the Alps into the Po Valley reduced and then broke Etruscan power and domination over northern and central Italy, allowing other local powers to try to fill the vacuum.

For the rest of the fifth century, Rome continued its local struggles, especially with Veii, all confined within central western Italy, hampered by its own internal dissensions. In the wider world, Persia shrugged off its reversal on the very western edge of its empire but began to be affected by Athenian attacks on its possessions around the Eastern Mediterranean coastline. No serious threat to the empire emerged, especially when the Greek states fell into a decades-long war between the rival powers of Athens and Sparta. By 415 BC, this war spilled out of mainland Greece and into the Western Mediterranean with the attempted Athenian conquest of Syracuse, one of the leading powers in Sicily (the other being the Carthaginians of North Africa). The Athenian defeat at Syracuse in 413 BC ended this brief conjoining of worlds, by which time Rome had the upper hand in its war with Veii.

Athens was to fall to Sparta in 404 BC, whilst Veii finally fell to Rome in 396 BC. Rome's triumph was short-lived though, as the Gallic tribes – whose expansion into northern Italy had done so much to end Etruscan power – began migrating further south into central Italy and famously defeated a Roman army at the Battle of Allia, subsequently sacking Rome itself in c.390/386 BC. Rome was able to recover from this destruction and rebuild both its armies and nascent empire – such as it was, confined to Latium – much as Athens was able to shake off its defeat to Sparta and recover some of its former glory.

Events to the south of Rome, however, showed the Italian peninsula's involvement in the wider power struggles of the ancient world. In the period 390–386 BC, Dionysius I, the tyrant of Syracuse, had invaded and conquered much of southern Italy, adding it to his greater Syracusan Empire. Dionysius then used southern Italy as a launch pad to invade Epirus across the Adriatic Sea and place a puppet ruler on the throne.[1] Though Dionysius' empire soon crumbled, it showed the danger that Rome faced from across the Greek world. Had it remained, Dionysus' empire would have fought any rival trying to create a powerbase in Italy.

As it was, Dionysius' empire collapsed, barely impinging on Rome and its wars in Latium. Whilst Rome rebuilt and continued its local expansion, the Persian Empire continued to dominate the ancient world, occasionally interfering in Greek matters, though never militarily. The Western Mediterranean continued to be dominated by the wars of Carthage and Syracuse in Sicily, with neither gaining a permanent upper hand and thus being able to expand further northwards into Italy, as Dionysius had.

It was in mainland Greece that the next major change to the world order originated. Athens' defeat in 404 BC was followed within a generation by that of Sparta in 371 BC at the Battle of Leuctra at the hands of the city-state of Thebes. Yet the Theban state was never able to turn its brief military supremacy into anything more lasting, and was soon exhausted. It was into this vacuum that a new power emerged, the Kingdom of Macedon. Macedonia was a region to the north of mainland Greece, sandwiched between Greece proper and Thrace, with its borders fully exposed to the tribes of Central Europe. Like Rome, it had been on the periphery of the Greek world and slowly trying to establish itself as a regional power. But unlike Rome, it found itself directly in the path of Darius' expansion of the Persian Empire and swiftly capitulated, becoming part of his empire. Xerxes' defeat saw Macedonia recover its freedom, but it too spent the whole of the fifth century fighting off tribal incursions, attacks from Thrace and Athens' colonization of its coastline.

Like Rome, Macedon's expansion in its own region was slow but also had the potential to amass far more human resources than its rival powers, if only they could be harnessed. Within a generation, both Rome and Macedon were able to do just that, the key factor in their sudden rise to supremacy in their own (for now) separate worlds. In Macedon's case it was primarily down to one man, King Philip II, who forged the various regions under nominal Macedonian control in one unified and centralized state, with strongly defended borders and a large army. Trained under Theban commanders, but with far greater resources than Thebes could ever muster, Philip created the most powerful kingdom in Greece. Once he had secured his northern borders, he set his sights on dominating the weakened powers of central and southern Greece. This process culminated in 338 BC at the Battle of Chaeronea, where a Macedonian army defeated the combined forces of Athens, Thebes and a host of smaller cities. With this victory, Philip now stood as master of Greece, a position no other had achieved.

By coincidence, 338 BC was also a milestone in Roman history, as it saw Rome's victory in the war against the Latin League which had begun in 343. Up to this point, Roman power in Latium had come through domination of the Latin League of city-states. Inevitably, the cities of the League attempted to throw off Roman hegemony, which resulted in five years of war and their eventual defeat. However, the victorious Romans decided to institute a new system. The Latin League was dissolved, and in its place a new system was created, with three central pillars: treaties, colonies and citizenship.

Each defeated city was to have a direct treaty with Rome, which left it with its own language, laws and customs, but bound to Rome in matters of military and foreign policy. Prime farming land was confiscated from the defeated, with colonies created for Rome's excess population, thereby creating a Roman bastion in foreign territory. Finally, a new graded citizenship system was created, with Roman citizenship (the highest) being granted to individuals and communities. Further grades of Latin and Italian citizenship, each with lesser privileges in Roman law, were also extended, again not on a geographic basis, but with grants to individuals, clans and communities.

Of these three pillars, it was the citizenship and the treaties that laid the foundations of Rome's future greatness: the treaties stated that each defeated city would send Rome their troops to fight in Roman armies, thus allowing Rome to move beyond a citizen army and tapping into the wider manpower of Italy. This, combined with subordinating the local elites into the Roman system – via citizenship and access to the Roman political system – gave Rome the tools needed to expand from a city-state into a regional power.

Rome and the Eastern World: Expansion and Defence (338–229 BC)

Rome and Macedon, having created a solid base for expansion, set about overturning the ancient world order. Philip set his sights on the ancient world's only superpower, the Persian Empire, which though territorially the same as in Darius' day, had been riven by internal rebellions (most notably Egypt), weak emperors and conspiracies within the ruling dynasty. Persian Emperor Artaxerxes III, who had recovered Egypt, died in 338 BC from suspected poisoning. With the loss of a strong rival leader, Philip judged the time right to attack what he judged to be a vulnerable Persia. Unfortunately for him, he too was assassinated in 336 BC just as his campaign was in its early stages.

He was famously succeeded by his son Alexander III, better known as Alexander the Great. In just over five years, Alexander spectacularly overturned two centuries of history when he defeated and conquered the Persian Empire, replacing it with an Alexandrian one which spanned from the Adriatic to the Indus.

Consequently, Rome once again suddenly found itself with no buffer between the dominant universal empire and its own region. One of the ancient world's greatest 'what ifs' will always be what would have happened if Alexander the Great hadn't died at such a young age? Given his thirst for conquest and the desire for empire, his attention would surely soon have turned westwards towards the tempting targets of Sicily and Carthage, with the conquest of Italy (and Rome) a by-product.

Though Rome had laid the foundation for its future greatness, at the time it was contesting a three-decade-long war against its greatest rival for domination of Italy, the Samnite Federation. Rome, controlling just the western half of central Italy, would have been no match for the armies of Alexander. Livy himself, in one of history's earliest works on counterfactual history, devoted time to consider the clash between Rome and Alexander,[2] but Livy's Rome was one that had enjoyed three centuries of further development, not the Rome of the late fourth century BC. Yet once again, the threat to Italy (and Rome) from a universal empire in the east dissipated before being realized. Alexander died at the age of 32, and his new universal empire died with him, fracturing into a lengthy war between his various successor generals.[3]

The wars of the successors created a new regional world order, with three mighty empires emerging from the decades of conflict: the Macedonian Empire controlling Greece, the Ptolemaic Empire controlling Egypt and the Seleucid Empire controlling from Asia Minor to Bactria. More importantly, however, for the future of the ancient world, the various wars they fought meant that they ignored the Western Mediterranean, which allowed two states in particular to flourish: those of Carthage and Rome. In the 290s BC, Rome fought its greatest war yet against an alliance of Italian races led by the Samnites, in what is referred to as the Third Samnite War (298–290 BC). The title of the war is again misleading, as it was victory in this clash that gave Rome control over the bulk of Italy, leaving only the Gauls in the north and the Greeks in the south as rivals.

Rome naturally expanded towards the richer and urbanized southern Italy, which led to the first major eastern intervention in Italy, when Pyrrhus, King of Epirus – a Hellenistic kingdom which sat on the Adriatic Sea, and thus between Rome and Macedon – invaded Italy.[4] Though the Greeks of southern Italy appealed for his aid in fighting the Romans (as they had done on several previous occasions against different Italian foes), Pyrrhus was far more interested in carving out a new empire for himself to match those of the great Hellenistic powers, stretching through southern Italy to Sicily. Thus, with an alliance with both Macedon and the Ptolemaic Empire, who provided him with additional military resources, a Hellenistic ruler finally decided to teach the new upstart power in Italy a lesson.

It is important to note that Pyrrhus was not the first Greek king to cross into Italy; he was actually following a well-established precedent.[5] He was, however, the first to try to carve out an empire, though even in that he was following the precedent set over 100 years earlier by Dionysius of Syracuse (see above). More importantly, he was the first Greek general to face Rome.

Greek intervention in Italy stretched back to 334 BC, when King Alexander of Epirus – a brother-in-law of Alexander the Great himself – arrived in Italy for a campaign to protect the Greek cities of southern Italy from the raids of their neighbouring Italian states. In this period, these enemies did not include Rome and the two parties actually concluded a non-aggression pact, which included a Roman naval exclusion from the Gulf of Otranto. King Alexander's campaign, though initially successful, ended with his betrayal and death. He was followed in 303 BC by Cleonymus of Sparta and in 298 BC by Agathocles of Syracuse, neither of whom made any lasting impression on the region.[6]

Rome's first encounter with the wider powers of the Hellenistic East showed both their strengths and their weakness. Whilst Pyrrhus soundly defeated Roman armies at Heraclea in 280 BC and again at Asculum in 279 BC, the Romans were able to call upon the superior manpower resources of their Italian allies and deploy new armies in the field, whilst Pyrrhus' losses could not be replaced (thus we get our 'Pyrrhic victory', a success that is not worth its cost). Finding the prospect of defeating Rome in a war too much for his limited resources, Pyrrhus set his sights on defeating the West's other rising power, Carthage, and thus invaded Sicily to 'free' them from the Carthaginians.

In this new endeavour, however, the pattern was repeated, with Pyrrhus being able to defeat the Carthaginians in battle, and be proclaimed King of Sicily, but the war with Carthage continuing. Very quickly, the Sicilians chafed under his 'liberation' and by 275 BC, both Pyrrhus and his forces were exhausted. He withdrew to Italy, where a third battle with Rome (at Beneventum) saw the tables turned and a Roman victory. Leaving a garrison in Tarentum, Pyrrhus retreated to mainland Greece, where he was briefly able to become King of Macedon before being killed during a siege.

With Pyrrhus withdrawn, the Romans soon annexed the Greek states of southern Italy, including Tarentum, once it had lost its Epirote garrison. Likewise, the Carthaginians were able to sweep through Sicily once again, gaining control of the greater portion of the island (but never Syracuse). Though never commanding the resources of one of the great Hellenistic empires, Pyrrhus was considered to be one of the finest generals of his day. Yet his wars with Carthage and Rome showed that whilst both powers could be defeated in battle, neither could easily be defeated in a war. In Rome's case, the clashes exposed its generals to the fighting styles of the finest armies of Greece. It also brought home to them the much-anticipated dangers from across the Adriatic.

It seems that Pyrrhus' defeat soon brought Rome to the attention of the wider Hellenistic powers, and the sources record a diplomatic mission from the Ptolemaic Empire (which had originally backed Pyrrhus) in 273 BC.[7] Rome was now tentatively entering the wider Hellenistic world, yet the major powers were still more concerned with their jockeying for power in the Eastern Mediterranean and the Near East and the wars that frequently broke out there.[8]

With control of the whole of Italy – except the Gallic north, considered at this time to be part of Gaul – Rome was now a considerable power in its own right. Yet the greatest danger to its dominance did not emanate from the East, but from the rising power of Carthage to the south. Carthage had spent much of its history trying to conquer Sicily, and the expulsion of Pyrrhus had seen it nearly succeed, with the vast majority of the island under its control, along with the islands of Sardinia and Corsica, which took the Carthaginian Empire alongside the Italian coast. Rome's annexation of southern Italy meant the two rising empires shared a border for the first time.

With neither power showing a willingness to tolerate a rival and with both empires expanding towards each other, inevitably it was only a few years after Rome gained control of southern Italy that the First Romano-Punic War broke out in 264 BC. As Pyrrhus had shown, neither power proved easy to defeat in war, but after two decades of conflict the Romans were finally able to wear down the Carthaginians and emerge victorious. Consequently, it was Rome who emerged with control of the bulk of Sicily (though as always Syracuse remained an independent state). Sardinia and Corsica soon followed into Rome's orbit.

With control of their southern and western borders secure, Rome's attention soon turned to Gallic-controlled northern Italy, with a series of wars against the Ligurians in the north-west of Italy. Carthage, by contrast, turned to rebuilding its shattered economy and military, beginning with the conquest of the tribes of Spain, which proved remarkably effective. With success in their wars in the north, the thoughts of the Roman oligarchy soon turned to the one border that concerned them: namely the Adriatic.

Rome and the Eastern World – Expansion (229–188 BC)

The collapse of Epirus in the years after the death of Pyrrhus created a power vacuum, the most obvious manifestation of which was the growth of piracy and the rise of the Illyrian tribes. A new power emerged in the form of the Ardiaean Kingdom, led by King Agron, who had been intervening in wars in Greece at the time. Rome thus faced a new and aggressive kingdom on its shores once more. Yet once again, events presented an opportunity to the Roman oligarchy which they grateful accepted. Agron died in 231 BC, his wife thereafter ruling the kingdom. Furthermore, his ally, King Demetrius II of Macedon, was killed fighting an invasion of tribesmen from Europe. Thus, both kingdoms had lost their leaders and were vulnerable.

Wasting no time, Rome launched its first invasion of the East and attacked the Ardiaeans, defeating them and establishing a protectorate over the Illyrian coastline. Whilst this was not Greece proper, it was Roman expansion into the Hellenistic world and would have set alarm bells ringing in the courts of the great powers. For Rome, this move secured its eastern border by gaining control of the Adriatic, not only stopping the piracy, but – more importantly in the minds of the Roman elite – stopping anyone using the Adriatic as a springboard to invade Italy, as Pyrrhus had done, not that anyone was contemplating such a move. Though the Roman power-brokers certainly felt more secure, Macedon would have felt the opposite. The Ardiaeans had been an ally of Macedon and a buffer between the two powers. Whilst Illyria had no permanent Roman military presence, it would clearly be a source of antagonism between the two states. A Second Illyrian War followed in 219 BC, again taking advantage of the recent death of a Macedonian king, Antigonus III, two years previously.[9]

Between these two wars, however, the Romans renewed their war of conquest in northern Italy against their most consistent foe, the Gallic tribes. Ever since the tribes had crossed the Alps in the fifth century and swept aside the Etruscans, Italy north of the River Po was part of Gaul and tribal Europe. As the sacking of Rome had shown, these tribes represented a clear (if infrequent) threat to Rome and its control of Italy. Having confidently secured their southern, eastern and now western borders (at least in their own minds), the Roman oligarchy set their sights on extending their control to the Alps. These campaigns culminated in one of Rome's greatest ever victories at the Battle of Telamon in 225 BC, ending the Gallic threat to Rome (at least from within Italy) and taking Roman control to the Alps.[10]

However, whilst Rome may have thought it had secured its northern border, it was soon proved to be wrong. Whilst the Roman elite believed that their previous wars had brought them peace and security, not to mention glory and wealth, all they had actually achieved was to store up further trouble for themselves. Two powers in particular, Carthage and Macedon, were determined to challenge Roman dominance and pay them back for earlier losses. In the west, the Carthaginians had forged a new empire in Spain, giving them what they believed to be an equal manpower resource to fight another war and destroy Rome as a power. In the east, the new Macedonian king, Philip V, wanted to drive Rome back across the Adriatic and recover Macedonian dominance in Illyria.

Thus, within a five-year period, Rome found itself at war with Carthage in the west, with the Second Romano-Punic War (218–201 BC), and Macedon in the east, with the First Romano-Macedonian War (214–205 BC), with an alliance between Carthage and Macedon set on Rome's destruction. Of the two wars, the most famous is that against Carthage, where the Carthaginian general Hannibal made a mockery of Rome's 'secure' northern border by marching an army from Spain and invading Italy. Like Pyrrhus before him, Hannibal inflicted defeats on Rome (most notoriously at the Battle of Cannae in 216 BC, one of Rome's greatest ever defeats[11]) but could not break the Roman alliance and manpower system. Ultimately, Hannibal was kept impotent in Italy, whilst Rome set about reducing the Carthaginian Empire in Spain before the decisive Roman victory in North Africa at the Battle of Zama in 202 BC.

Though far less well known, the Roman war against Macedon had two phases, and the first phase – Philip V's attempted invasion of Italy – equally had the potential to destroy Rome. Here, Roman control of the Adriatic proved critical, with Philip attempting to seize control of it and then dominate Illyria by land, but being beaten back by the Roman fleet and land forces. The second phase of the war was fought in mainland Greece and the Aegean, and saw the foundations laid for Rome's longer-term expansion. Seeking to divert Philip away from Illyria and the Adriatic, Rome agreed alliances with Macedon's enemies in Greece and the wider Hellenistic world, most notably the Aetolian League of city-states and the Kingdom of Pergamum.[12] With Rome's allies doing the fighting in mainland Greece, the Roman navy, stationed at Corcyra, began attacks on Greek cities.

By 205 BC, with Rome victorious in the west and Philip holding the upper hand in Greece, the two sides agreed a peace, allowing Rome to finish off Carthage. However, with all the key issues remaining unresolved, this would prove nothing more than a respite. By 201 BC, Rome emerged from the Second Romano-Punic War victorious, with Carthage totally defeated. Rome had conquered both Carthaginian Spain and Syracuse (something the Athenians and Carthaginians had failed to do), and Carthage was reduced to a city-state, surrounded by a strengthened Roman ally, the Kingdom of Numidia.

With victorious armies and generals at their disposal, the Senate decided that, after a four-year gap, the time had come to settle matters with Macedon. Though the Roman People actually rejected the Senate's suggestion for war, the oligarchy was not to be denied and the People agreed at the second time of asking. Roman armies were now to be deployed on mainland Greece for the first time. The Second Romano-Macedonian War (200–196 BC) culminated in the Battle of Cynoscephalae in 197 BC, where the Roman legion faced and defeated the Macedonian phalanx, making a decisive statement to the Hellenistic world. In 196 BC, Rome famously declared the Greek states to be free, albeit under Roman protection. [13]

The following year, the Romans demonstrated their intent by going to war with Sparta, under King Nabis, who was attempting to extend Spartan power over his neighbours. Though on paper this was a clash between two of the ancient world's greatest military powers, Sparta by this point was a faded city-state, trading on its glorious past and no match for the might of Rome. Nevertheless, the war allowed the Romans to make a point, crushing one of Greece's most famous military states to show the other Greeks that Rome would not tolerate disruptions to the peace it had installed. Having made their point, once again the Roman armies withdrew back across the Adriatic.

Though Rome had destroyed Carthage and defeated Macedon, this merely presented an opportunity for another of the Hellenistic rulers, namely Antiochus III (the Great). Throughout the third century BC, the endless rounds of wars between the Seleucid and Ptolemaic Empires for control of the Near East had left both powers weakened.[14] The Seleucid Empire began a decline brought about by its unwieldy size and a series of weak kings. In particular, the eastern provinces of Bactria and Parthia had revolted and gained their independence (*c*.247 BC).[15] The Parthian rulers used this as a springboard for their conquest of the neighbouring Seleucid provinces to begin their own empire.[16]

All of this changed in 222 BC when Antiochus III came to the Seleucid throne. A superb general and leader, Antiochus rebuilt the Seleucid Empire to the height of its power, recovering Seleucid control over the majority of Asia Minor and the Near East and extending the Seleucid Empire back to the Indus, annexing both Parthia and Bactria once more.[17] By the 190s BC and the Second Romano-Macedonian War, Antiochus had defeated the Ptolemaic Empire and was in the process of dismembering its overseas possessions on the Mediterranean coast. Antiochus had even discussed with Philip an alliance to conquer Egypt.[18]

Thus, by 196 BC, the Hellenistic world order was on the verge of collapse: Macedon had been defeated by Rome (an upstart power from the West, as they were seen), whilst Egypt had been defeated by Antiochus. In Antiochus' mind, all that stood between him and recreating Alexander the Great's universal empire was Rome. This mindset would have been encouraged by the presence at the Seleucid court of none other than Hannibal himself, which did not endear Antiochus to the Roman oligarchy.

The stage was therefore set for a clash between the ancient world's two leading powers in the Romano-Seleucid War (192–188 BC).[19] Again the war between the two powers falls into two phases. The first phase saw Antiochus invade Greece, allied to Rome's former ally, the Aetolian League, which culminated in 191 BC at the Battle of Thermopylae – site of a much better known clash some 300 years previously – with Antiochus now in the Spartan role and Rome in the Persian one. The battle ended with a similar outcome, namely a victory for the attacking army, forcing Antiochus to escape and retreat back to Asia Minor. Unsurprisingly, the Aetolian League soon came to terms, bringing to an end their power in Greece.

The second phase of the war saw Roman forces cross from Greece into Asia Minor for the first time and culminated in the Battle of Magnesia (190 BC), where the Seleucid army fared no better than the Macedonian one and the Romans gained a comprehensive victory. With no other option, Antiochus came to terms and the subsequent Treaty of Apamea in 188 BC saw him pay a massive indemnity, face restrictions on the size of his army and navy and lose all territories in Asia Minor, which like Greece before it was now 'free' (allowing for the development of kingdoms such as Pontus).[20] Apamea marks the turning point in the Hellenistic world order and capped an extraordinary decade when both Macedon and the Seleucid Empire were defeated by the ancient world's remaining superpower, the Roman Republic. Rome again withdrew its forces across the Adriatic, happy to leave its regional allies Pergamum and Rhodes to dominate the region.

Rome and the Eastern World – Domination and Intervention (188–129 BC)

Apamea also marked the beginning of the decline of the Seleucid Empire, though Antiochus IV (see below) made efforts to hold it together. Antiochus the Great died the following year, in 187 BC, in a minor campaign and his successors faced a disintegrating empire, albeit one which continued to arouse Roman suspicion. However, just as Rome's earlier wars brought about unforeseen consequences for them, the same happened on this occasion. Though Rome had no ambitions to acquire territory in the Near East, others did, and the removal of Seleucid power immediately invigorated the Parthians, who regained their independence and began to grow their empire again at the Seleucids' expense. Under a series of aggressive kings, Parthian expansion culminated in the 140s BC with the attack and eventual annexation of the Seleucid heartland of Mesopotamia, and with Mithradates I (the Great) claiming the Persian title of King of Kings and the creation of the Parthian Empire.[21]

We can see that throughout this period, though no Roman armies crossed into the East, the mere threat was enough, and an increasing number of Senatorial commissions or ambassadors were sent to the various powers of Greece and the East to arbitrate between the states or inform them of Rome's views on certain matters. Though these could range from small disputes to more important matters, perhaps the greatest intervention came in 168 BC, when the Senate dispatched a commission to prevent the Seleucid invasion (and annexation) of Ptolemaic Egypt, under Antiochus IV. The actions of C. Popillius Leanas (who held the Consulship in 172 and 158 BC) are infamous: he drew a line in the sand around Antiochus and demanded an answer to the Senate's orders for him to withdraw. Thus a small delegation of Senators forced the Seleucid Emperor and his army to withdraw. Throughout this period we have records of such missions in 186, 185, 184, 183, 175, 174, 173, 172 and 171 BC. Thus we can see a flurry of missions after Apamea and again before the next war in Greece (see below), though our record is by no means complete.[22]

With the Seleucids unwilling to face Rome again, it fell to Macedon to challenge Roman supremacy. Whilst Philip V begrudgingly accepted Roman supremacy in Greece, he steadily rebuilt the Macedonian kingdom. In the war against Antiochus, Philip publicly backed the Romans, preferring their indirect rule to becoming part of Antiochus' new empire. Philip's reticence was not shared by his son, Perseus, however, who took the throne in 179 BC. Inheriting the throne of Alexander the Great whilst being dominated by a 'lesser' civilization from Italy was never going to sit well with the young king, and war inevitably broke out in 171 BC. Although Perseus held off Rome in the early years, the two sides met in a set-piece battle in 168 BC at Pydna, where the Macedonian army was defeated again.

The following year (167 BC) was a catastrophic one for the region. The Kingdom of Macedonia was abolished, with Perseus and his son Alexander spending the rest of their lives in Italy. In its place, the Romans created four Macedonian Republics and closed their mines in order to keep the region economically weak. Just as Rome had made an example of Sparta after the Second Macedonian War, another state was chosen after the Third War, this time the Republic of Epirus, the former kingdom of Rome's old enemy Pyrrhus. Like many Greek states, the Epirotes were split between those who had supported Rome and those who favoured Perseus. Nevertheless, the Senate declared an example was to be made of them; all cities that had declared for Perseus were sacked, with upwards of 150,000 Epirotes enslaved. It was a disaster from which Epirus never recovered.

The immediate aftermath of the Third Romano-Macedonian War saw Roman intervention in the Near East hit a peak. The clear danger in the minds of the Roman oligarchy lay in the Seleucid Empire regaining its strength, hence the Roman intervention when Antiochus IV attacked Egypt. Antiochus' death in 164 BC gave the Senate an unparalleled opportunity to act. The heir to the throne was the Seleucid Prince Demetrius, who was a hostage at Rome. Instead of sending him back to rule, Demetrius was kept in Rome and, in 163 BC, the Senate dispatched a commission to install another son of Antiochus (Antiochus V), then just 9 years old, as Seleucid Emperor. The commission also had a second brief, to monitor the state of the Seleucid military, and when it was found to be in contravention of the Treaty of Apamea, they ordered ships to be burnt and elephants to be hamstrung. These actions resulted in a riot and the murder of the Commissioner Cn. Octavius (who had been Consul in 165 BC).

Thus we can see the state of Roman intervention in the Eastern Mediterranean. Nevertheless, Rome soon suffered a setback when Prince Demetrius escaped from Rome and made his way back to the Seleucid Empire, where he soon overthrew Antiochus V (who was murdered) and installed himself as Seleucid Emperor. In retaliation, the Senate conducted an alliance with the rebel Seleucid province of Judea but took no other action, perhaps realizing their overreach. The year 163 BC saw two other eastern commissions (that we are aware of), one to the Ptolemaic Empire to determine a dynastic dispute between Ptolemy VI and VII, and another to Cappadocia to render a judgement on a local matter.

Rome's allies fared little better than its enemies. We have already seen that one of Rome's original Greek allies, the Aetolian League, chafed under Roman 'freedom' and allied with Antiochus III, suffering defeat and ultimately oblivion. In the war against Antiochus, Rhodes had proved to be a staunch Roman ally, particularly in providing naval support. The island state emerged with additional (former Seleucid) territories and became a regional power. Yet by the 160s BC, Rhodes attempted to intervene in the Third Romano-Macedonian War as a neutral arbiter.[23] In the eyes of the Roman oligarchy, there were no neutrals, only friends and enemies, and Rhodes now fell into the latter category. In 164 BC, after narrowly avoiding an outright declaration of war by the Senate, Rhodes lost its territories and its influence, going into long-term decline.

The 140s BC saw two final challenges to the Roman world order from their old enemies: Carthage and Macedon. After the Second Romano-Punic War, Carthage had been reduced to a city-state, surrounded by the Roman client kingdom of Numidia. It was Numidia, led by their King Masinissa, whom Rome had charged to keep Carthage in check, and the next fifty years saw constant low-level raids on Carthage by Masinissa, who built Numidia into one of the Mediterranean's most prosperous kingdoms. Carthage had its hands tied, bound by treaty to refer all disputes to the Senate, which frequently (though not always) came down, unsurprisingly, on the side of Masinissa. By 150 BC, the Carthaginians, believing their treaty with Rome fulfilled, went to war with Numidia to recover some of their independence and end the constant harrying. However, not only did they prove to be no match for the stronger Roman ally, but their attempt at self-defence was seen as an act of aggression by a paranoid Senate, which needed little encouragement to declare war on its former enemy.

Thus the Roman Republic, with an empire stretching from Spain to Greece, went to war with the city-state of Carthage in the Third Romano-Punic War (149–146 BC). The title is far grander than the subsequent war, which was little more than a three-year siege of the city of Carthage itself, which had few military resources to call on, and ended with the total destruction of the city in 146 BC. The aftermath saw the annexation of Carthage's territory as the Roman province of Africa, their first on that continent.

Whilst these events were occurring in North Africa, similar disruption to the Roman-imposed order was taking place in Macedon. The 150s BC saw the emergence of a pretender to the Macedonian throne in the form of Andriscus, who easily overthrew the deliberately weak Macedonian Republics and briefly reunified the Kingdom of Macedon. Clearly, this was a challenge that Rome would not ignore, and armies were immediately dispatched, sparking off the Fourth (and final) Romano-Macedonian War (150–148 BC). With Macedon a shell of its former glory, like Carthage, the outcome was inevitable; by 148 BC, Andriscus had been defeated at the Second Battle of Pydna. Having ruled Greece indirectly for fifty years, and with the failure of the experiments of the Macedonian Republics, Rome wasted little time in annexing Macedonia as its first province in the East.

With Rome having ended the Second and Third Romano-Macedonian Wars by making an example of a Greek state to drive the point home, the Achaean League of Greek city-states showed a spectacularly poor sense of timing in staging a rebellion against the Roman order in 146 BC, especially with battle-hardened Roman armies still in Macedonia. A short conflict ensued (the Romano-Achaean War), which ended with an inevitable Roman victory and allowed the Romans to commit their usual show of strength – or atrocity, depending on your point of view – when they sacked and destroyed the ancient city of Corinth. Technically, mainland Greece was not turned into a Roman province, but it was to be administered by the Governor of Macedon. The Romans had declared the Freedom of the Greeks in 196 BC; fifty years later, in 146 BC, they ended that 'freedom'.

The year 146 BC not only saw the destruction of the cities of Carthage and Corinth, but the Romans establish their first provinces outside of Italy and Spain, in Greece and North Africa. Intervention and withdrawal had now become occupation, albeit still on a modest scale. The annexation of Macedon, whilst solving one problem, inevitably led to another for the Romans, who now had to defend its porous border with tribal Europe, namely Thrace. Whilst the states of Greece had come to fear, and usually avoid, Roman military strength, the tribes of Thrace had no such qualms, leading to over 100 years of Roman warfare on the Macedonian border, either repelling incursions or raiding ever deeper into Europe themselves. Just as Spain presented a near-annual theatre of warfare for Rome, now the Macedonian border did the same. It was to be another century before the Princeps Augustus brought a solution to the matter, with the annexation of all territories up to the Danube.[24]

With the destruction of Rome's long-standing foes, Carthage and Macedon, focus once again turned on Rome's allies, and in particular two of its longest-standing ones, Pergamum and Numidia. Pergamum, which had been Rome's longest-serving ally in the East, actually became Rome's first territory in Asia Minor. The Attalid Dynasty always maintained their loyalty to Rome and became Asia Minor's leading power, ensuring the passivity of the region and that nothing disputed the Roman-imposed order (after Apamea). In 133 BC, the last king, Attalus III, took his loyalty to an extreme length when, dying without an heir, he willed his kingdom to Rome, it thus becoming Rome's first province in Asia Minor. It must be said that this was something of a posthumous act of spite against his regional enemies, who must have been hoping to profit from the dynasty's demise to annex territory. Instead, they now faced a permanent Roman presence in their region.

Naturally, as the kingdom was one of the richest in the region, Rome did not decline the gift, and although delayed by a rebellion under an Attalid pretender (Eumenes III Aristonicus), soon annexed the kingdom in 129 BC. However, the issue of consequences again came to the fore, Rome using the province as a cash cow when it had actually been the guardian of Rome's interests in the region. With the previous role now removed, the other monarchs of the region saw their chance to expand; one in particular, Mithridates VI of Pontus, who took the throne in 120 BC, used this vacuum to carve out first a Black Sea Empire, and then one in Asia Minor, the latter of which eventually brought him to Rome's attention (see below).

Rome and the Eastern World – Inattention (129–99 BC)

Thus, by 129 BC, Rome had its first territory in Asia Minor, but Rome's presence was an economic not a military one and it had no intention of gaining further territory. The limits of Roman ambitions in the East seemed to have been control of Greece, which provided the oligarchy with the secure buffer between Italy and the rest of the ancient world which they desired. Certainly, Pergamum was too tempting a prize to turn down, but Rome's focus for the next forty years was to wander from the East to other regions.

The world they left behind, certainly in the Near East, was seemingly one of decay, which suited Rome's interests. The surviving two former Hellenistic superpowers, the Ptolemaic and Seleucid Empires, were both in decline and no threat to Roman interests. The Seleucid Empire was locked in a war with the Parthians over Mesopotamia, whilst the Ptolemaic one, although it remained in control of Egypt, Cyrene and Cyprus, had effectively been reduced to a Roman client kingdom. Aside from these two former powers, there were a patchwork of smaller kingdoms stretching from the borders of the Roman province of Asia to the Caspian Sea – Bithynia, Pontus, Galatia, Cappadocia, Commagene and Armenia – all benefiting from the Roman elimination of Seleucid power, as were the Kingdoms of Judea and the Nabataean Arabs in the Middle East (see Map 1).[25]

Further afield lay the Parthian Empire, which aside from a brief mention in Polybius,[26] left no trace in the surviving Roman record of this period. This makes it impossible for us to accurately judge contemporary Roman attitudes to the rising Parthian power in the East. Certainly, in the short term, they would have judged that anything that weakened the Seleucids and prevented their return to regional dominance could only have been a good thing. However, whether anyone in the Senate considered that this conflict could result in the rise of a new 'Persian' Empire in the east, threatening Roman interests, is not known.

As far as the Roman oligarchy were concerned, matters in the East were settled. Macedon provided a secure buffer for Italy, and the province of Asia a record source of revenue. In terms of military action, the Macedonian frontier provided an endless source of campaigns and glory, tinged with the occasional disaster. Thus the oligarchy soon turned their attention to the other frontiers of Rome's growing empire, and in the 120s BC chose to focus on securing their northern border, annexing southern Gaul to secure the land route to Spain and the Balearic Islands to secure the sea route.

Whilst the following decade saw further entrenchment of Rome's Gallic border, it ended with Rome facing the total collapse of its northern border in Gaul and Macedon, along with a war in North Africa with the client kingdom of Numidia, a state which they had done so much to build into a regional power. The subsequent Northern War (113–101 BC) and Romano-Numidian War (112–106 BC) saw Rome's attention tied firmly to Europe and Africa for a decade. Indeed, the Northern War led to one of Rome's greatest ever defeats at the Battle of Arausio in 105 BC, and saw Italy itself invaded by migrating Northern European tribes. These events fall outside the scope of this work and have been covered elsewhere.[27]

Key to this study, however, is the fact that between 129 and 100 BC, Roman attention was firmly focused on the West and not the East, which though not a deliberate policy, was to allow two powerful rivals to emerge in the East, both of whom were to challenge Rome's status as the Mediterranean and Near Eastern superpower. Within a space for four years, two kings came to the thrones of their countries who were to transform their respective states: Mithradates II of Parthia in 124 BC and Mithridates VI of Pontus in 120 BC.

Though Parthia had annexed Mesopotamia, the death of its great ruler Mithradates I (c.132 BC) saw Parthian power temporarily wane, with tribal invasions in the east of their empire and regional challengers in Mesopotamia. Yet with the accession of Mithradates II, this decline was reversed; not only were their previous conquests secured, but their power was extended.[28] Within a decade, the Parthians had defeated Armenia and extended their power into the Caucasus and near to the Black Sea, leaving only a handful of minor buffer states between them and Roman Asia. Further expansion in Northern Mesopotamia saw the Seleucid Empire restricted to the region of Syria and in severe danger of outright annexation to the Parthian Empire, giving them a presence on the Mediterranean. Further campaigns saw the Parthians edging towards the Roman ally of Judea, beyond which lay the riches of Egypt.

Consequently, by 100 BC, when the Romans were able to emerge victorious from the Northern Wars against the tribes of Europe, the Seleucid Empire no longer needed intervention to prevent it being a threat to Roman interests, but instead needed intervention to help it survive. However, Mithradates II was not the only danger to the Roman world order imposed after Apamea. Mithridates VI of Pontus, stymied by the Roman presence in Asia Minor, instead focused his expansionist efforts across the Black Sea and by 100 BC had created a Black Sea Empire which stretched from Pontus in Asia Minor to the Crimea, with significant holding around the Black Sea coast.[29] Thus, Rome found another empire had arisen right on its borders, with only Bithynia and Galatia separating Roman Asia from the Pontic Empire. Mithridates himself had reason to fear the Parthian expansion, which by the 110s BC had annexed the neighbouring Kingdom of Armenia. By the 90s BC, he turned his attention to the handful of independent kingdoms in Asia Minor which now lay sandwiched between the empires of Rome, Pontus and Parthia.

The first person in Rome to seemingly notice this change to the eastern world order was none other than C. Marius. A cunning politician, he had risen to the Consulship and command of the Romano-Numidian War in 107 BC, bringing it to a successful conclusion. The emergency caused by the defeats in the Northern War created an opportunity for Marius, to whom the Senate reluctantly turned, and saw him hold the Consulship continuously between 104 and 100 BC (five in a row). Victories over the tribes at the Battles of Aquae Sextiae in 102 BC and Raudine Plain (Vercellae, 101 BC) the following year saw him hailed as the saviour of Rome. Marius cemented this position by forming a temporary Triumvirate with the politicians Saturninus and Glaucia to dominate Roman politics, though both men were soon discarded and killed by Marius' forces (with the backing of the Senate) late in 100 BC.

Rome and the Eastern World – Intervention and Collapse (98–91 BC)

With the wars in the north and south ended, Marius rightly seemed to have realized that there were growing threats to Rome's eastern settlement rising in the East. Marius therefore went out to Asia to assess the situation, meeting Mithridates VI in person in 98 BC.[30] Unsurprisingly, almost immediately

(96 BC)[31] the Senate dispatched a propraetor to Asia Minor to arbitrate in a dispute between Mithridates VI and the neighbouring King of Bithynia, Nicomedes III. In what was surely not a coincidence, the man sent as commander was none other than Marius' longstanding protégé, L. Cornelius Sulla.

The dispute in question was between two former allies. Mithridates VI of Pontus and Nicomedes III of Bithynia had formed an alliance to dominate the other kingdoms of Asia Minor, with first Galatia and then Cappadocia being overrun by the two kings. Yet by the mid-90s BC, the two men had fallen out and Nicomedes appealed to the Senate and presumably Marius, all of whom felt that the time for inaction was over and that Roman interests and their eastern settlement were in danger. Though the details are scant, open warfare between Pontus and Rome was averted when Mithridates backed down. Sulla's campaign saw another notable event, with the Parthian Emperor Mithradates II sending an envoy to meet Sulla (acting as an envoy of both the Senate and Marius), thereby establishing the first diplomatic contact between the two powers.[32]

Thus by the mid-90s BC, the three great empires of Rome, Pontus and Parthia all stood poised in Asia Minor, waiting to see who would strike first. It was at this point that events elsewhere came to the fore. Within a few years of each other, both the Roman Republic and the Parthian Empire spiralled into decades of civil wars. Rome's was caused by the collapse of its alliance system (created in 338 BC – see above) and internecine conflict across Italy between the various races and peoples. This was by a second phase of civil war between factions of the Roman oligcrahy, and saw Rome itself sacked in 87 BC by a Roman army. Again, these events have been covered elsewhere.[33] Parthia's civil war is far less documented (see Appendix Two), but was seemingly brought about by dynastic clashes within the ruling Arsacid Dynasty which followed the death of Mithradates II in c.92 BC.

Rome and the Eastern World – The Rise of the New Powers (91–80 BC)

Into this vacuum caused by the collapse of Rome and Parthia arose two new powers. The first was none other than Pontus under Mithridates. The second was more surprising, and saw the rise of Armenia, under its new King Tigranes II (the Great), who went from being a Parthian vassal to king of his own Near Eastern empire in just over a decade. In a tumultuous decade (the 80s BC), both kings overturned well over a century of history and forged mighty new empires which between them stretched from the Adriatic to the Black Sea and the Mediterranean to the Caspian (see Map 3).

Of the two, the rise of Mithridates is the most documented, both in the ancient world and the modern. Taking advantage of Rome's seemingly total collapse and limited military presence in the East, he invaded and overran the kingdoms of Asia Minor and the Roman province of Asia in 88 BC, with much bloodshed, and then conquered Greece itself, nominally taking his empire from the Black Sea to the Adriatic and once again placing a hostile enemy on the shores of the Adriatic (though his control of western Greece was limited – see Map 3). Naturally enough, Rome's leaders were not going to accept such a reversal, and command of the impending war fell again to Marius' protégé Sulla. In an infamous (and much written about)[34] situation in Rome in 88 BC, Sulla was betrayed by his old mentor Marius, who seized command of the war itself, only to see Sulla and his consular colleague march on Rome itself and take it by force, sparking off a second phase of the First Roman Civil War.

By 87 BC, Sulla and his army had crossed into Greece to face Mithridates, but a further civil war broke in Rome between the consuls of that year, which saw a new alliance of factions violently seize Rome, headed by none other than Marius. Thus Sulla was outlawed, and Marius received command of the war again.[35] This placed Sulla between two hostile enemies: the Western Roman Republic of Marius and his consular colleague L. Cornelius Cinna and the Eastern Empire of Pontus. Sulla chose to act first and focused on overcoming Mithridates before his enemies from Rome could arrive, defeating the Pontic armies at the Battles of Chaeronea and Orchomenus (86 BC) and driving Mithridates out of Greece.

The seemingly inevitable clash between master and pupil in Greece failed to materialize due to Marius dying early in 86 BC of natural causes (he was over 70), brought about by the exertions of the previous two years. In his place the ruling factions chose L. Valerius Flaccus as commander of the 'official' Roman Mithridatic campaign, from one of the factions' most prominent families. With the Pontic armies being driven from Greece, all three armies (Mithridatic, Sullan and Flaccan) converged on Asia.

The dynamic changed again when Flaccus was murdered in late 86 BC by his deputy, C. Flavius Fimbria, who seized control of the 'official' Roman forces in Asia. The failure of the two Roman armies to cooperate allowed Mithridates to escape. Sulla, having recovered all lost Roman territory and faced with two enemies, chose to focus on his priority, namely the Roman Civil War. He therefore agreed a peace settlement with Mithridates in 85 BC, the Treaty of Dardanus, under which the Pontic Empire returned to its pre-88 BC borders and Mithridates paid an indemnity and supplied additional resources to Sulla for an attack on Italy.

We can clearly see the change in the Roman priorities between the Treaty of Apamea (188 BC) and the Treaty of Dardanus (85 BC), both of which were agreed in Asia Minor. In the former, the Romans had driven Antiochus from Greece, defeated him in Asia and humbled him in the subsequent peace treaty. In the second, the Romans drove Mithridates from Greece, defeated him in Asia but then sought his assistance in attacking political enemies in Italy itself.

Mithridates thereby emerged from the war defeated, but with his empire intact and his reputation enhanced by having inflicted the greatest blow on the Roman Republic in over a century. Before the year was out, Sulla had secured the betrayal of Fimbria's army, with Fimbria himself committing suicide. Wisely – for himself anyway – Sulla chose to leave the Fimbrian legions in Asia (having betrayed their previous two commanders) to guard against any further Mithridatic attacks, under the command of a legate, L. Licinius Murena. He returned to Greece and launched an invasion of Italy in 83 BC, plunging the peninsula into a devastating two-year civil war from which he emerged victorious as Dictator of Rome.

In the meantime, Murena, commanding the Roman forces in Asia, launched an attack on Pontus itself, starting a Second Romano-Pontic War (83–81 BC). Perhaps reflecting the quality of his forces (and his own poor leadership), Murena was defeated in 82 BC and forced to retreat back to Asia, where orders from Rome's new master arrived, halting any hostilities. Thus Mithridates came out of a second war with Rome with a further enhanced reputation, having beaten back a Roman attack. For the Sullan regime in Rome, the ongoing civil war – at the time still raging in Spain, Sicily and Africa – took precedence over matters in the East, which had been restored to the status quo.

Sulla used his control of Rome to forge a new version of the Republic and retired from office, preferring to oversee the running of this reformed system from the background. With civil war still raging in Spain, he clearly had no wish to be distracted from matters in Rome to resurrect the unfinished business of a new Romano-Pontic War. Furthermore, Sulla was revealed to be seriously (and fatally) ill, dying in 78 BC, leaving behind a fragile Republic with internecine conflict still raging in Spain and a new eruption in Italy itself the following year. It would fall to the next generation of the ruling Sullan faction – men such as Pompeius, Crassus and Lucullus – to pick up where Sulla had left off.

However, the Romano-Pontic Wars were not the only conflicts that the East saw, and in many ways were ultimately a sideshow (with the status quo being restored). The same was not the case with the other wars taking place simultaneously, which saw a new dominant force arise in the Near East, the Armenian Empire of Tigranes the Great. Unlike its more recent Hellenistic neighbours, the Kingdom of Armenia dated back to before the Persian Empire, but soon fell prey to the expanding empires of first Persia and then the Seleucids. Like its neighbours, it benefitted from the collapse of Seleucid power in Asia Minor after Apamea, but unlike Pontus found itself attacked and defeated by the rising power of the Parthian Empire in *c.*120 BC. Armenia retained its own monarchy but became a vassal state of the Parthian Empire, and as part of Armenia's submission the Armenian King Tigranes I was forced to send his eldest son, Tigranes, as a hostage to the Parthian court.

Raised as a Parthian prince, Tigranes II was sent back to Armenia upon the death of his father in *c.*96 BC to rule the kingdom in Parthia's name. However, it seems that the impact of being raised at the Parthian court did not have the effect that the Parthian Emperor had hoped for: Tigranes not only retained his desire for his homelands' independence, but learned first-hand the mechanics and benefits of running a great empire. With Mithradates II on the Parthian throne, independence was not achievable, but within five years Mithradates was dead and his successors plunged the Parthian Empire into a lengthy civil war (see Appendix Two). At some point soon afterwards (the details are not clear), Tigranes seized his opportunity and not only succeeded in gaining Armenian independence from the Parthian Empire, but defeated the Parthian armies (garrisons) and annexed the neighbouring kingdom of Media-Atropatené and the territories of Gordyene, Adiabene and Osrhoene, all from the Parthian Empire.[36]

Again due to the lack of surviving sources, we have no details as to how this was accomplished, but we must assume that Tigranes learnt the Parthian art of war at the Parthian court and transformed the Armenian military in preparation. Thus it was Tigranes who was the first person to seize the initiative and take advantage of the sudden collapse of Parthian power. Within a few years he had transformed Armenia from a Parthian vassal to an independent nation with enhanced territory. Further territories in the form of the Kingdoms of Sophene, Commagene and Cappadocia were soon added.

However, it was his next campaign that transformed Armenia from an independent kingdom to a great empire, when in the late 80s BC he invaded and annexed the Seleucid Empire, adding Syria and Phoenicia to his existing territories and creating an empire that stretched from the Caucasus to the Mediterranean (see Map 3). The few surviving sources state that the Seleucids were in the midst of another civil war themselves and the throne was 'offered' to Tigranes. What is more likely is that Tigranes saw this opportunity and took it to accomplish something that neither Rome nor Parthia had managed, namely the annexation of the Seleucid Empire. The timing of such a move was also notable, coming as it seemingly did when Rome's attention was focused on civil war in Italy and the Western Republic (83–81 BC) rather than wider Mediterranean affairs.

To enhance his newly established status as the ruler of the greatest empire in the Near East, he seized the old Persian title of 'King of Kings' from the Parthians and founded a new imperial capital, Tigranocerta,[37] clearly tapping into the vein of Alexander the Great. What the reaction in Rome was to the fall of the Seleucid Empire no longer survives, but as Rome was in the midst of a civil war itself, it was hardly a priority. Nevertheless, a Roman magistrate was dispatched to Cilicia in 80 BC, perhaps with these events in mind (see Chapter Two). However, by the time the civil war had been confined to Spain and the Sullan oligarchy set about surveying the eastern world, they found that a new aggressive empire had arisen.

Clearly the Armenian Empire was a threat to the Roman eastern settlement: not only had Seleucid Syria fallen, but Armenia had begun to expand into Cappadocia and Cilicia (through to what extent is not clear from the surviving sources). The Armenians now had a Mediterranean coastline and were in a position to threaten the Roman ally of Judea, beyond which lay the prize of the Egypt, the wealthiest – and one of the weakest – nations in the ancient world. Furthermore, Tigranes at some point had married a daughter (Cleopatra) of Mithridates VI, meaning the Pontic and Armenian Empires were allied, creating a power bloc that stretched from the Black Sea to Judea (see Map 3).

The rise of the Armenian Empire had effectively obliterated Roman domination of the Near East, which was now restricted to Egypt. This was clearly a challenge that the new Sullan oligarchy in charge of Rome would have to face if they were to restore the position Rome once held.

Chapter 2

The Powderkeg and the Spark: Roman Expansion in the East (80–74 BC)

1. The Ongoing Civil War

It would be fair to say that the East was not the focal point of the Sullan oligarchy's attention in the early 70s BC, indeed if anything it was just the opposite. Though Sulla and his faction had won the campaigns in Italy in 83/82 BC and seized control of the bulk of the Western Republic, the wider civil war itself had not ended. There was a brief point in 81 BC when Sicily and Africa had been conquered by the Sullan faction, spearheaded by Cn. Pompeius, and the return of Spain and the two Gauls had been negotiated with C. Valerius Flaccus, but this unity proved to be short-lived. By 80 BC, Q. Sertorius had returned from Africa and re-invaded Spain, reigniting the civil war in the Western Republic once more.

Based on his control of the bulk of the Roman Republic, Sulla installed himself as Dictator of Rome (resurrecting the ancient office) to reshape the Roman constitution, in an attempt to cure what he saw as the ills that had befallen the Republic in the previous fifty years.[1] Having accomplished this to his satisfaction – accompanied by a slaughter of his enemies, both in Rome and across Italy – he then resigned from public life to take up a position as a guardian or Princeps to oversee his new Republic. However, his death in 78 BC (of natural causes) robbed the Republic of this role, and Italy collapsed into renewed civil war the following year. Though this renewed internecine conflict in Italy was soon extinguished, that in Spain soon escalated, bolstered by Sertorian victories and the survivors of the war in Italy, and soon became the major campaign fought by the Sullan faction. This campaign required the attention of two of the factions' leading figures, Q. Caecilius Metellus 'Pius' (Consul in 80 BC) and Cn. Pompeius 'Magnus'. Thus it was the Western Republic which attracted the bulk of the Senate's attention in these years.

However, any analysis of this period is hampered by a general lack of surviving sources, with the loss of all the annalist historians, especially Livy, as well as Sallust's histories. Furthermore, the sources that do survive for this period are naturally focused on the civil war in the Western Republic and the great figures involved. Nevertheless, we can see that whilst the bulk of Roman military activity was in the West – first in Italy and then Spain – it was not the only theatre of war, and the Eastern Republic did see its fair share of military activity.

2. Roman Campaigns in the Eastern Republic (80–74 BC)

The Illyrian Campaigns (78–76 BC)

As is common with the 70s BC, aside from the wars which featured men who received a biography by Plutarch, we have very little information about the other conflicts of the period. We do know that Rome committed its resources to an Illyrian campaign, which lasted for two years, commanded by a Proconsul, C./Cn. Cosconius. Both Eutropius and Orosius preserve brief coverage of the campaigns, taken from a fuller (though no longer surviving) Livian account:

'Cnaeus Cosconius was sent into Illyricum as Proconsul. He reduced a great part of Dalmatia, took Salonae, and, having made an end of the war, returned to Rome after an absence of two years.'[2]

'The Proconsul Cosconius was allotted the Illyrian War. He wore down and subdued Dalmatia and finally, after two years took by storm and captured the flourishing town of Salonae.'[3]

Cicero also raises the matter in relation to a case of his, writing, 'but it was also made evident by the letters of Caius Cosconius and by the evidence of many witnesses, that a legion in Illyricum had been tampered with'.[4]

Thus, we have very little evidence upon which to base any analysis. Clearly, however, from the fact that the Romans had to conduct a long siege, they were not repelling a tribal invasion (as with Macedonia) but subduing the local cities. It is therefore logical to assume that elements of the region had used the collapse of Roman rule east of the Adriatic to assist their independence, possibly even returning to piracy along the Adriatic coast, requiring Rome to reassert its regional dominance.

The Macedonian/Thracian Campaigns (80–73 BC)

The issue in Macedonia in this period is far clearer, as once again Roman forces were called on to repel tribal incursions over the (arbitrary) Macedonian border. As noted earlier (see Chapter One), by annexing Macedonia, Rome now occupied territory that bordered tribal Europe (the nearest region being Thrace) from the Adriatic to the Aegean, a region that had few natural barriers to defend it.[5] Orosius provides us with an account of the issues, which yet again saw an invasion of Macedonia by the Scordisci, a Thracian tribe with whom Rome had been to war on many prior occasions and who paid no heed to the concept of 'Roman' territory.[6]

Rome had been fighting a major war against tribal incursion into Macedonia and Greece in the mid-80s BC, under L. Cornelius Scipio Asiaticus, when Mithridates had invaded from the east. Asiaticus continued to campaign from 86–84 BC, when he returned to Rome to stand for Consul and take joint lead of the civil war campaign, defending Italy from Sulla. It is not clear in what condition Scipio left the Macedonian border, but we find his civil war opponent – none other than Sulla himself – fighting Thracian tribes in a short campaign upon his return from the Asia, before his attack on Italy.[7]

Tribes like the Scordisci needed little encouragement to cross the porous Macedonian border, probably caring little for whether or not Rome was distracted by military matters elsewhere. Certainly by 81 BC, the Sullan oligarchy felt concerned enough that matters in Macedonia needed firm military action, and one of the Consuls, Cn. Cornelius Dolabella, was appointed to govern Macedonia. We have little detail as to his actions, other than that he returned to Rome in 77 BC to celebrate a triumph; over whom is no longer explicitly recorded, but Cicero lists him along with his successors as having 'well-earned Triumphs'.[8] We must assume that he was fighting against the invading Thracian tribes.

Dolabella was succeeded in 78 BC by another former Consul, Ap. Claudius Pulcher (Consul the previous year), but illness prevented him taking up his command until the following year, when he was appointed Proconsul to lead the campaign. Once he took up his command in Macedonia, more is recorded of his campaigns in various sources:

'It was these tribes that Claudius attempted to drive out from the borders of Macedonia and brought a great deal of troubles on his own head. As a result whilst he was sick at heart and surrounded by worries, he fell ill and died. His successor Scribonius, declined to force the issue with the tribes his predecessors had fought, turned his forces on Dardania instead and captured it.'[9]

'Proconsul Appius Claudius defeated the Thracians in several battles.'[10]

'Through Appius Claudius, a Proconsul, those who used to inhabit Rhodope were conquered.'[11]

'Appius Claudius, on the expiration of his Consulate was sent into Macedonia. He had some skirmishes with different tribes that inhabited the province of Rhodopa, and there fell ill and died. Cnaeus Scribonius Curio, on the termination of his Consulship, was sent to succeed him.

He conquered the Dardanians, penetrated as far as the Danube, and obtained the honour of a Triumph, putting an end to the war within three years.'[12]

Thus, Pulcher scored several skirmishing victories against the Scordisci, reasserting Roman dominance in the region without ending the tribal threat before he died (*c.*76 BC). He was succeeded by C. Scribonius Curio (Consul in 76 BC), who built on Claudius' success and went on the offensive, attacking the Dardani, a Thracian tribe who occupied the western border of Macedonia (and Illyria), equating to modern Kosovo. Again, we only have small excerpts from the sources as to Curio's campaign, but he achieved the major milestone of being the first Roman commander to reach the Danube, apparently crossing it into Dacia:[13]

'At the beginning of spring in the same year, in Macedonia Caius Curio set off into Dardania with all his army, so that he could by all possible means collect the money which had been demanded by Appius.'[14]
'Curio reached Dacia but shrank from its gloomy forests.'[15]

Thus, it seems Claudius had demanded monies from the Dardani, presumably to show their loyalty to Rome, and when it was not forthcoming, attacked and seemingly overwhelmed them, though the Roman advance was a temporary measure and no permanent movement of the Macedonian border was contemplated. Curio campaigned in Thrace until his recall in 72 BC, when he returned and celebrated a Triumph, and the campaign continued under a new commander, M. Terentius Varro Lucullus (Consul in 73 BC), the fourth Proconsular commander in a row (see Chapter Four).

Nevertheless, Curio's campaign is an important one, as what started out as a defence of Rome's most porous border soon expanded into a major campaign of expansion which saw Roman armies reach the Danube. Though no fresh territories were added, it did show that the Sullan faction was in an expansive move, endorsing Curio's extended command and his advancement well beyond the remit of defending Macedonia. Given the ongoing civil war in Spain, it seemed that the Senatorial oligarchy welcomed any chance to take pride in Roman martial endeavours and expansion, as seen by four consuls taking up the command. This expansionist attitude is important to understand in the context of the Eastern War that was to follow.

The Reconquest of Asia Minor

If we turn our attention further to the east and Asia Minor, we find ongoing military activity at the start of this period. As we have seen (Chapter One), after driving Mithridates from Greece, Sulla (and Fimbria) confronted him in Asia and pushed him back into Pontus, recovering the Roman province. With Sulla's priority being the ongoing First Civil War, he left Asia under the command of L. Licinius Murena, supported by the Fimbrian legions. However, it seems that whilst Mithridates had withdrawn from the Roman province of Asia he was still fighting a war by proxy, having supported a number of pirate forces operating in the region, encouraging them to attack a weakened Asian province. Appian writes:

> 'The province of Asia had her fill of misery. She was assailed openly by a vast number of pirates, resembling regular fleets rather than robber bands. Mithridates had first fitted them out at the time when he was ravaging all the coasts, thinking he could not long hold these regions. Their numbers had then greatly increased, and they did not confine themselves to ships alone, but openly attacked harbours, castles, and cities. They captured Iassus, Samos, and Clazomenae, also Samothrace.'[16]

Murena had to contend with a growing pirate problem as well as a province devastated by the bloodshed of the Mithridatic conquest. As we have seen, to compound matters, Murena launched an attack on what he presumed to be a weakened Mithridates, but was beaten back in what was a short-lived Second Romano-Pontic War (83–81 BC) (see Chapter One). Murena was aided in ruling Asia by a certain L. Licinius Lucullus, a staunch Sullan loyalist, acting as his proquaestor. Murena was unsurprisingly recalled to Rome in 81 BC by Sulla, leaving Lucullus in Asia. Murena's replacement was a M. Minucius Thermus, who reached Asia in either late 81 or early 80 BC. During Thermus' governorship (most likely in early 80 BC), we have interesting notes in several surviving sources of the culmination of a military campaign in Asia, namely the reconquest of Mytilene, a city on Lesbos, off the Asian coast:

> 'Finally, Mytilene in Asia, the only city still in arms after the defeat of Mithridates, was captured and destroyed.'[17]
>
> 'During the rest of the campaign he enjoyed a better reputation, and at the storming of Mytilene Thermus awarded him the civic crown.'[18]

The Mytilenian campaign is an interesting one as it shows continuing resistance to Rome, despite the defeat of Mithridates. We have no other references to

Roman campaigns to pacify the region, and it is possible that this campaign was related to the ongoing piracy problem noted by Appian. Nevertheless, it does show that Rome still needed to pacify the region to return it to the state it had been prior to the First Romano-Pontic War.

Furthermore, the siege of Mytilene is noteworthy for two of the other Romans involved. Firstly, it may well have been commanded by the Roman proquaestor, L. Licinius Lucullus, who after the siege ended was soon recalled to Rome, where he was elected as Aedile for 79 BC, with a Praetorship soon following (most likely in 78 BC), putting him on the pathway for a campaign for the Consulship. The second man involved was a young Roman aristocrat, fighting in his first campaign, C. Iulius Caesar, who was awarded the honour of a civic crown, given for those who excelled in battle.

The Cilician Campaigns (80–74 BC)

There were also significant campaigns in Asia Minor itself. During this period, Roman territory in Asia had reverted to the pre-88 BC border (see Map 1) and was comprised of a considerable swathe of lands stretching from the eastern Aegean seaboard into the interior (the former Kingdom of Pergamum). Whilst the Roman province of Asia was well-defined and efficiently organized (and taxed), Rome also had an interest in a strip of the southern coast, running from their province of Asia to south of the Taurus Mountains. This was composed of the regions of Lycia, Pamphylia and Cilicia, though Cilicia was not actually an organized Roman province as yet, more a vague coastal protectorate, much as Illyria had been. The key change in this period is that from the late 80s/early 70s BC, eastern Cilicia now bordered the new Armenian Empire, though exactly where the frontier lay cannot be determined from the surviving sources.

Aside from its strategic position, where Asia Minor meets the Middle East, Cilicia held little of value for Rome, and was a constant source of irritation, namely on account of it being the principal base for piratical activity in the Eastern Mediterranean. The region itself, both through its geography (isolated rocky coastlines) and lack of central political authority, with their being no coherent kingdom ruling it, leant itself to be a pirate haven.

Furthermore, the Romans themselves inadvertently allowed the pirates to flourish by removing or restricting the influence over the region of the major naval powers: Rhodes, the Seleucids and the Ptolemies (see Chapter One).[19] This naturally created a void, which Rome itself had no intention of filling, allowing the pirates to flourish. Rome had finally acknowledged the issue in 102 BC when it appointed Praetor M. Antonius[20] to a command against the pirates of the region, which despite Antonius' subsequent Triumph, proved to be nothing more than temporary respite. The chaos of the wars of the 80s BC would have done nothing to restrict the pirates, and if anything would have boosted their numbers and opportunities.

It seems that the Sullan regime in Rome recognized this, and in 81 BC, another Praetor, Cn. Cornelius Dolabella, was appointed to a proconsular command in Cilicia, presumably at the behest of, or agreement of, Sulla himself. Dolabella served from 80–79 BC, but no details have been preserved as to his campaigns or the size of the force. Presumably, this campaign had the secondary (or perhaps primary) aim of placing a Roman army in Cilicia just after, or perhaps during, Tigranes' annexation of the Seleucid Empire (see Chapter One). The surviving sources we have for this are few and unclear, so the campaign may have been a fact-finding mission and a show of Roman strength, albeit one which showed that Rome could not prevent the Seleucid Empire (such as it was) falling to Tigranes.

What details that are preserved are due to the fact that a certain C. Verres served as his Proquaestor during the campaign and was accused (and convicted by Cicero) of looting a number of cities and temples during his command. Cicero's comment on Verres' appointment does afford us one nugget of information, namely that Verres' predecessor as Dolabella's Quaestor (a C. Publicius Malleolus) was killed whilst serving in Cilicia, thus giving us one glimpse of the Roman fighting there:

> 'They will declare to you that Caius Verres has behaved himself like a most infamous pirate in regard to that fleet which was built against pirates.'[21]

Dolabella's campaign appears to have also met with limited success, and he returned to Rome, where he was successfully prosecuted for his own greed and rapacity as commander and promptly went into a disgraced exile. In point of fact, the Senate seems to have escalated the importance of the Cilician campaign due to the appointment of one of the Consuls of 79 BC (P. Servilius Vatia 'Isauricus') to the command. One of Vatia's junior officers was a certain C. Iulius Caesar. Thus, not only had the campaign been upgraded to a consular one, but it has left a greater impression on the surviving sources, most notably those who drew from Livy, notably the Periochae, Eutropius and Orosius:

> 'The former Consul Publius Servilius set about Cilicia and Pamphylia in a terrible fashion through his eagerness to subdue them, and almost destroyed them altogether. He also captured Lycia, besieging, and destroying its cities. In addition to this he crossed Mount Olympus,

razed Phasis to the ground, sacked Corycus and combing the flanks of Mount Taurus, where it borders on Cilicia, he broke the Isaurians in battle and brought them under Roman control. He was the first Roman to march an army through the Taurus Mountains and open up a road through them. In the third year of the war he received the name Isauricus.'[22]

'Publius Servilius, an energetic man, was sent, after his consulate, into Cilicia and Pamphylia. He reduced Cilicia, besieged and took the most eminent cities of Lycia, amongst them Phaselis, Olympus, and Corycus. The Isauri he also attacked, and compelled to surrender, and, within three years, put an end to the war. He was the first of the Romans that marched over Mount Taurus. On his return, he was granted a Triumph, and acquired the surname of Isauricus.'[23]

'Publius Servilius was sent against them, and, although with his heavy and well-equipped ships of war he defeated their light and elusive brigantines, he won a by no means bloodless victory. Not content, however, with having driven them off the seas, he overthrew their strongest cities, full of spoil collected over a long period, Phaselis, Olympus and the city of the Isauri, the very stronghold of Cilicia, from which, conscious of the greatness of his achievement, he assumed the title of Isauricus.'[24]

'Near the mountain ridges of the Taurus lies the piratical stronghold of Zenicetus, I mean Olympus, both mountain and fortress, whence are visible all Lycia and Pamphylia and Pisidia and Milyas; but when the mountain was captured by Isauricus, Zenicetus burnt himself up with his whole house. To him belonged also Corycus and Phaselis and many places in Pamphylia; but all were taken by Isauricus.'[25]

'The Proconsul Servilius, who had been dispatched to a pirate war, obtained Pamphylia, Lycia, and Pisidia.'[26]

'Servilius, a Proconsul, having been dispatched to a bandit war, subjugated the Cilicians and the Isaurians, who had allied themselves with pirates and seagoing marauders, and first established a road through Mount Taurus; and he celebrated a Triumph over the Cilicians and Isaurians and thus received the *cognomen* Isauricus.'[27]

'One man, Publius Servilius, took more captains of pirates alive than all our commanders put together had done before. Was any one at any time denied the enjoyment of being allowed to see a captive pirate? On the contrary: wherever Servilius went he afforded everyone that most delightful spectacle, of pirates taken prisoners and in chains. Therefore, people everywhere ran to meet him, so that they assembled not only in the towns through which the pirates were led, but from all neighbouring towns also, for the purpose of seeing them. And why was it that that Triumph was of all Triumphs the most acceptable and the most delightful to the Roman People? Because nothing is sweeter than victory. But there is no more certain evidence of victory than to see those whom you have often been afraid of, led in chains to execution.'[28]

Thus we can see that Vatia, unlike his predecessor, looked upon the campaign as a chance for military glory, rather than quick profit; as well as defeating the pirates, he chose to establish a permanent Roman presence in the region and expand their territory inland to effectively create the province of Cilicia.[29] The timing of this sudden desire to annex Cilicia should perhaps be seen in the Armenian context rather than just the piratical one. Having annexed Syria and Cappadocia, the next logical region to be targeted by Tigranes would have been Cilicia, especially to protect his newly won control of the Eastern Mediterranean trade routes from piracy. Consequently, despite the ongoing civil war in the Western Republic, we see signs that the Sullan oligarchy recognized the danger of a rival power growing in the East, and though they couldn't overturn Tigranes' conquests, they took steps to ensure that he expanded no further into Asia Minor.

Nevertheless, despite the glorious write-up Vatia received in the Roman sources for this period (and transmitted for posterity), the additional *cognomen* ('Isauricus') and the Triumph, subsequent historians questioned his success in quelling the actual pirate menace, which by 75 BC had reached the coast of Italy itself:

'Murena had attacked them, but accomplished nothing worth mention, nor had Servilius Isauricus, who succeeded him.'[30]

If anything, as Magie points out, the high point of Vatia's command – the war against, and conquest of, the Isauri – would have actually distracted Vatia from the prime goal of destroying the pirates.[31] This adds weight to the suspicion that the pirates were an excuse for the conquest of the inland region, to secure it from the expanding Armenian Empire. Nevertheless, the campaign does show that even with the Senate's (and the sources') focus on the civil war in the Western Republic, Rome was militarily active in the Eastern Mediterranean and paying more attention to the new balance of power that had emerged.

3. The Spark – The Bithynian Question (75 BC)

Despite the Roman expansion in Cilicia, Asia Minor remained split between three expanding empires – the Roman, Pontic and Armenian – a powderkeg situation itself. Whilst Pontus and Armenia were allies, there were clearly unresolved issues between Mithridates and Rome, ruled by the heirs of Sulla, who would have regarded Mithridates' continued existence as unfinished business, looking to erase the stain of the Treaty of Dardanus. Furthermore, there would have been tensions between Rome and Armenia over the latter's expansion into the Near East and threat to Judea and Egypt. It was Rome and Pontus who, perhaps unsurprisingly, were the first to clash, a conflict engineered by a dying man, Nicomedes IV of Bithynia.

A Poisoned Legacy – Nicomedes IV and Bithynia

Sandwiched between these expanding empires were a patchwork of small and medium-size kingdoms – most notably Bithynia – Galatia and Cappadocia, all of which had been overrun by either the Pontic or Armenian Empire in the previous decade. These remaining states lived a perilous existence stuck between three rapacious and expanding empires, with their very existence solely dependent on the balance of power between the other three empires. Throughout history there have been many regions which have found themselves stuck between rival empires and which, when faced with a dynastic crisis, became so weak that they plunged their rivals into war. In this particular case, the weak link proved to be Bithynia, under the rule of King Nicomedes IV.

Bithynia was a Hellenistic state which lay on the north-western coast of Asia Minor, bordering the Sea of Marmara (see Map 1). It had fallen under the rule of first the Persian Empire and then that of Alexander the Great, but soon asserted its independence in the early third century BC during the various wars that broke out in the aftermath of the death of Alexander. Like many of the kingdoms of Asia Minor finding themselves on the very western fringes of the Seleucid Empire, they were able to maintain their independence. The smaller kingdoms of Asia Minor had always had to maintain their independence sandwiched between two great powers. In the third century BC, it was between Macedon and the Seleucids, and now in the first century BC it was between the Roman and Pontic/Armenian Empires.[32]

The rise of Rome initially benefited the Bithynians, with Macedon humbled, followed by the defeat of Antiochus the Great and the Treaty of Apamea, which ensured the exclusion of the Seleucid Empire from Asia Minor. Yet the following years saw the rise of the Roman-backed Kingdom of Pergamum,[33] which in 133 BC became a direct Roman province, bringing

Rome right up to the borders of Bithynia. The reigns of the last two Bithynian kings, Nicomedes III (*c.*127–94 BC) and Nicomedes IV (*c.*94–74 BC), came to exemplify this tension between the Roman and Pontic rivals. Nicomedes III was a contemporary of Mithridates VI of Pontus and became a staunch ally, with the pair of them conspiring to carve up the other Asian kingdoms in the late second century, first with Paphlagonia and then Cappadocia.[34] Yet Nicomedes III became worried about his erstwhile ally's intentions, and near the end of his life moved towards becoming a Roman ally, intending to use them as a counterweight to the Pontic threat.

The death of the old king presented Mithridates with an opportunity, which he seized when he invaded and overran Bithynia in 90 BC, forcing Nicomedes IV to flee to Rome. A temporary restoration was undermined by the collapse of the Roman Republic into the First Civil War (91–70 BC), which saw Bithynia overrun once more, becoming a province of the Pontic Empire. Mithridates' defeat at the hands of Sulla saw the restoration of the status quo in 84 BC and an independent Bithynia, but one which was now clearly a Roman client.

By 75 BC, Nicomedes IV was dying and without a direct male heir, a situation which posed an existential threat to Bithynian independence. His impending mortality forced him to make a decision. Knowing that his kingdom would soon be extinguished by either Rome or Pontus, he chose to spite his old enemy Mithridates one last time, bequeathing his kingdom to the Senate and People of Rome.

Although this may seem a strange act, it was the third time Rome had been bequeathed an entire kingdom and all its peoples. The first came in 133 BC, when Attalus III of Pergamum, then Asia Minor's most powerful kingdom, died without an heir and named the People of Rome, his old ally, as his heirs (see Chapter One). Attalus' move was both strategic and spiteful, knowing that without it, his enemies would have invaded and carved up his kingdom amongst themselves. Now he had ensured that his enemies would forever have a Roman presence on their doorstep, thereby endangering their own existence.

The second time such a bequest occurred had relevance for the events of 75 BC, and concerned the Ptolemaic Kingdom of Cyrene, which had been bequeathed to Rome in 96 BC by its dying ruler Ptolemy Apion. Whilst the Romans had jumped at the chance to annex a wealthy kingdom of Asia Minor, they had not done so with Cyrene on the North African coast, which had languished in quasi-independence for twenty years. Yet in 75 BC, the Roman Republic was sufficiently recovered from destruction of the ongoing civil war that it felt bold enough to expand, as we have already seen with Servilius Vatia's campaigns reaching their peak. Thus the Senate agreed that it was time to annex Cyrene as a Roman province, and the Quaestor P. Cornelius Lentulus Marcellinus was instructed to transform it into a Roman province. It was against this background that at some point during 74 BC,[35] Nicomedes IV died and his will was presented to the Senate.

It must be pointed out, however, that, unhelpfully, the exact year that Nicomedes died – and thus the whole chronology of the early years of the war – is disputed. Due to the paucity of the surviving sources for this period, and their focus on the civil war in Spain, there is no certain date for when Nicomedes died and thus which year the war broke out. McGing presents the best synthesis of the ancient sources on this problem.[36] For this work, we take the opinion that Nicomedes died in early 74 BC, with hostilities not breaking out until the winter of 74/73 BC.

Rome and Bithynia (74 BC)

Unlike Cyrene, Bithynia represented another wealthy eastern state, with an excellent position guarding the entrance to the Bosphorus and the trading routes to and from the Black Sea. Furthermore, it would bring Roman territory right to the borders of Pontus and prevent Mithridates from adding Bithynia to a resurrected Pontic Empire. Consequently, Rome lost no time in agreeing to turn the kingdom into a province. Perhaps showing the urgency that the Senate gave the matter, they did not dispatch a fresh commander from Rome to handle the task, as they had done with Cyrene, but instructed the incumbent Governor of Asia, a certain M. (Iunius) Iuncus, to proceed swiftly to Bithynia and ensure a smooth transition.

We are not told outright of any active opposition to this move, though there were two rival claimants to the throne, a daughter of Nicomedes and an individual who claimed to be a son.[37] However, Iuncus seems to have been able to secure control of Bithynia without incident. By the end of the year we find him in Bithynia, where he was visited by a young Roman noblemen, C. Iulius Caesar, who had just been freed from piratical captivity and had attacked and seized his former captors.[38] Regrettably, we have no other details of Iuncus' campaign, but from later events we must assume that he left the bulk of the Asian (Fimbrian) legions in Asia itself, and thus only took a small force with him.

Nevertheless, it seems clear that by the end of 74 BC, Bithynia had been secured for Rome and was being turned into a Roman province. However, given the paucity of Roman forces in Bithynia and the unknown stance of the Pontic King Mithridates, we can question just how secure Rome's latest acquisition actually was. Certainly, Rome had seized the initiative, but Iuncus and Roman Bithynia were terribly exposed.

Waiting for Mithridates (74 BC)

The few surviving sources we have for Nicomedes' bequest only cover the matter briefly. It is far from clear whether Mithridates knew that Nicomedes was close to death and, more importantly, whether he knew the contents of his will. It may have been that Mithridates did know of Nicomedes' illness and was readying himself to take possession of the kingdom when he found out that it had been bequeathed to Rome. However, as the sources state, even though Nicomedes had no legitimate son of his own, there seems to have been relatives who staked a claim to the throne,[39] so there would have been no guarantee that Nicomedes would have taken such a bold step. Having found out that Rome would inherit the kingdom, Nicomedes would have had to pause his own plans and create a new strategy.[40]

The Bithynian bequest brought matters to a head and forced Mithridates' hand, as presumably Nicomedes knew it would. Clearly, matters had not been settled from the first two Romano-Pontic Wars, with both empires blocking each other's expansion. Although Mithridates had been defeated militarily in the first war, the conflict only ended with a negotiated settlement and he emerged with his original empire intact. Thus Mithridates faced an unwelcome choice: a renewed war with Rome, which he may well have been contemplating at some point, but now at a time that was not of his choosing, or wait and not contest the Roman annexation of Bithynia.

In retrospect, it may seem outlandish that Mithridates believed that his Pontic Empire could defeat the might of the Roman Republic. Yet such a view ignores the situation at the time. The Republic was still fighting a vicious and bloody civil war, which had seen all central authority collapse, and although it had regained some of its strength, Rome was still potentially weak. Mithridates himself had shown just how fragile Rome's control of the East was when he had overrun all of Asia Minor and Greece, and these fragilities still remained.

Furthermore, as events in the East had shown, the mighty and seemingly unstoppable Parthian Empire had also collapsed into internecine strife and had given the Armenians, under Tigranes, the chance to forge a new empire at their expense. Thus the westward expansion of Rome, like the eastward expansion of Parthia, was not inevitable or inexorable, and could indeed have been stopped or even reversed. The region had witnessed first-hand the inexorable rise of the seemingly unstoppable Persian, Macedonian and Seleucid Empires, and had also seen their decline. So even though the timing of the war would not have been of his choosing, Mithridates would have believed that he stood a chance of winning and driving Rome back to the west.

The alternative would have been to bide his time and wait for a more opportune moment, but would that moment ever have come? The clear military focus of Rome at that moment was in the West, not the East. Yet if the Senatorial forces were victorious and the civil war extinguished, then he would have to face the full force of Rome rather than a distracted one. Furthermore, it would be a Republic bolstered by the wealth of Bithynia, which could have hosted Roman legions right on his borders. Rome would also have access to the Bithynian ports on the southern shores of the Black Sea, jeopardizing Mithridates' control of the region and its trade routes.

Feeling that he could not allow Rome to permanently annex Bithynia and bring its empire to his borders, towards the end of 74 BC Mithridates clearly determined that war now was preferable. If he waited then the moment would be lost, so he set about amassing his forces for the forthcoming conflict. Appian contains a wealth of detail on Mithridates' preparations (see below). It is notable that he did not immediately launch a surprise attack on Bithynia in response to Iuncus' annexation, but built up both his forces whilst attempting to forge a broader coalition. Clearly Mithridates felt that whilst an immediate attack on Bithynia would seize the initiative, the war with Rome would not be a short one so moving precipitously would endanger his longer-term chances of victory. Appian tells us Mithridates mobilized the full resources of his Black Sea empire:

'The remainder of the summer and the whole of the winter he spent in cutting timber, building ships, and making arms. He distributed 2,000,000 medimni of grain along the coast. Besides his former forces he had for allies the Chalybes, Armenians, Scythians, Taurians, Achaeans, Heniochi, Leucosyrians, and those who occupy the territory about the river Thermodon, called the country of the Amazons. These additions to his former strength were from Asia.

'From Europe he drew of the Sarmatian tribes, both the Basilidae and the Iazyges, the Coralli, and those Thracians who dwelt along the Danube and on the Rhodope and Haemus mountains, and besides these the Bastarnae, the bravest nation of all. Altogether Mithridates recruited a fighting force of about 140,000 foot and 16,000 horse. A great crowd of road-makers, baggage carriers, and sutlers followed.'[41]

A Coalition of the Unwilling

Yet Mithridates found that his enthusiasm for a decisive war against Rome was not shared by his neighbours. As detailed previously (Chapter One), there were three other major empires in the East at this time: the Armenian,

Parthian and Ptolemaic. Of the three, the weakest was the Ptolemaic Empire (now reduced to Egypt and Cyprus), which was a long-term, if somewhat reluctant, Roman ally. With Rome acting as the guarantor of Ptolemaic independence, especially in the face of the encroaching Armenian Empire, they could be swiftly ruled out as potential allies.

Of the two remaining empires, the most dominant was that of Armenia, under the rule of Mithridates' son-in-law Tigranes the Great. Tigranes had carved out a Middle Eastern empire, annexing the Seleucid Empire and chunks of the Parthian Empire. Yet despite their alliance, followed by Tigranes' recent aggressive moves against Cappadocia and a Roman counter in Cilicia, Tigranes chose not to be involved in the aggressive war against Rome. Instead, Tigranes followed a policy of non-aggression against Rome, one which would backfire quite spectacularly. Even with their encroachment into Cilicia, Rome was not the immediate threat to Armenia that it was to Pontus, and a war in the west would detract from Tigranes' campaigns to secure his new eastern conquests in Syria and Phoenicia and his expansion towards Judea. It seems that Tigranes was more than happy for Mithridates to act as a proxy, with the Pontic and Roman Empires wearing each other out in a war of attrition, allowing him to secure his existing gains and potentially pick off any weak pickings (Cappadocia or Cilicia).

The final power was that of Parthia, the largest of the eastern empires and the self-proclaimed inheritor of the Macedonian, Seleucid and Persian Empires. Yet, as has been discussed earlier, just as Rome had collapsed into internal strife, so had Parthia, and at the same point (*c.*88 BC), with the ending of central Arsacid authority (see Appendix Two). By the mid to late 70s BC, the Parthian Emperor Sinatruces, who appears to have been involved in the outbreak of the civil war, seems to have defeated the majority of his rivals and secured the throne (though there may have been one rival, Arsaces XVI, still fighting – see Appendix Two). Furthermore, Tigranes had taken advantage of the Parthian collapse to annex the westernmost provinces of their empire, as well as the long-term Parthian goal of Seleucid Syria. Thus, Parthia was in no condition to send armies to fight Rome in Asia, and had every reason to stay neutral and hope that the Armenian Empire would become entangled with Rome. Again, it was a policy which would have mixed results for the Parthians.

Thus, Mithridates found that, whilst he probably had the best wishes of the three other eastern empires (including the Ptolemies) for his forthcoming clash with Rome, he received no concrete support.

Eastern War and Civil War

Paradoxically, whilst Mithridates found no willing allies amongst the eastern powers, he did find them amongst the Romans themselves. Though the First Civil War had been extinguished in the East, with Sulla's defeat of Cinnan commander C. Flavius Fimbria, the war was still being fought in the West, though now confined to Spain (since the death of Lepidus in Italy in 77 BC). During his dictatorship, rather than pursue a policy of reconciliation, Sulla had pursued his enemies with a bloody ruthlessness, murdering hundreds and outlawing their families. Whilst this brought temporary stability in Rome, it ensured a lasting legacy of bitterness and a desire to fight on. In Spain, anti-Sullan forces centred on a commander named Q. Sertorius, a junior-ranking officer of the Marian-Cinnan faction, but one with a gift for military and political leadership. In Italy, opposition centred on the Consul M. Aemilius Lepidus (father of the Triumvir). Lepidus' defeat and death in 77 BC saw the survivors of his forces flee to Spain and join Sertorius, who became the leader of the anti-Sullan faction of the First Civil War.

Yet, whilst Spain was the one remaining theatre for the civil war, exiles from the various anti-Sullan factions were seemingly scattered throughout the empire. Two men in particular seem to have been lying low in the East: L. Magius and L. Fannius, both junior officers in the army of C. Flavius Fimbria, who had lost his army to Sulla in Asia in 84 BC (see Chapter One). What they had been up to in the intervening years is far from clear, though latterly both seem to have taken to the seas (probably in piracy) and had forged links with Sertorius in the West, though they were independent of him.[42]

In the majority of the surviving sources, it is Sertorius who sends these two men as emissaries to Mithridates in order to forge an alliance, yet Orosius (presumably based on Livy's account) presents the opposite case:

'Two refugees from Fimbria's army, Fannius and Magius joined Mithridates and on their advice Mithridates sent envoys to Spain and made a pact with Sertorius.'[43]

With Mithridates determined on a war with Rome in the East, they seemingly saw an opportunity to revenge themselves on the Sullan faction in Rome and, probably more importantly, restore their own fortunes. Thus, Fannius and Magius became brokers between the two leaders fighting the Sullan faction in control of Rome, and an alliance was brokered between East and West:

'However, a treaty was actually made and ratified with oaths. Mithridates was to have Cappadocia and Bithynia, Sertorius sending him a general and soldiers, while Sertorius was to receive from Mithridates three thousand talents and forty ships.'[44]

Thus, Mithridates gained a Roman ally, although the benefit of this alliance was more political than martial. Even without this alliance, the bulk of Rome's best soldiers and generals (Pompeius and Metellus Pius) were in Spain fighting Sertorius. Furthermore, the few troops that would have arrived would have been dwarfed by the size of Mithridates' own forces from his Black Sea Empire, and were no substitute for a sizeable Armenian or Parthian contingent. Mithridates did receive one tangible political asset in the arrival of a figurehead for his eastern campaign: M. Marius, sent by Sertorius from amongst the exiled Roman Senators in Spain.

Frustratingly, none of the surviving sources state what M. Marius' connection was to the Roman general and civil war faction leader C. Marius (himself uncle of C. Iulius Caesar). We know that Marius' son had already been killed in the civil war, as had his one clearly attested nephew (M. Marius Gratidianus). Yet our knowledge of Marius' family is poor, and this man could easily have been another nephew. Nevertheless, he was clearly linked with the fallen leader of the anti-Sullan faction and Mithridates now had a figurehead to lead his campaign. It would be wrong to say that it was Marius fighting Rome and not Mithridates, but Mithridates had now blurred the lines between outright foreign invader and participant in Rome's civil war. There would have been enough blurring of the lines between the two to make many think twice. Throughout Rome's First Civil War, the local rulers had tended to remain neutral rather than pick the wrong side, and if Mithridates could tap into that neutrality then it would give him an advantage.

Aside from this, Mithridates now had three Roman commanders in his army able to brief him on Roman tactics and likely strategies. Furthermore, both Magius and Fannius had served in the army of C. Flavius Fimbria, the bulk of which was still stationed in Asia and formed Rome's main defensive strength in Asia Minor. Fimbria's army had originally been drawn up for C. Marius to command, before his unexpected death by natural causes. Mithridates must have harboured every hope that his Roman officers would be able to subvert the Roman forces that faced him in Asia.

He also now had a treaty with the exiled Roman Senate in Spain, which guaranteed his claim on Bithynia and Cappadocia, though not Roman Asia. Appian also adds the provinces of Paphlagonia and Galatia into the mix.[45] Thus, Mithridates could go into battle claiming a Roman general as a figurehead and a Roman agreement that Bithynia and Cappadocia were his to conquer, all of which would further muddy the waters politically, if not provide any material assistance on the battlefield.

The Die is Cast (74–73 BC)

Though the bulk of the Senate's attention will have been focused on the stalemate in Spain and the worry over Pompeius (who had threatened to return to Rome with his army and secure the reinforcements he needed), some thought must have been given to the Bithynian issue. The Senate had certainly moved quickly to secure Bithynia, and had done so seemingly without any immediate Pontic retaliation. Nevertheless, a passage of Cicero alludes to the size of the build-up of Mithridates' forces and that it wouldn't have gone unnoticed:

> 'But Mithridates employed all the time which he had left to him, not in forgetting the old war, but in preparing for a new one; and, after he had built and equipped very large fleets, and had got together mighty armies from every nation he could, and had pretended to be preparing war against the tribes of the Bosphorus, his neighbours.'[46]

So it seems that Mithridates attempted to disguise his military build-up through a pretence that his campaign was going to be against the tribes of the Crimea region. Presumably, he was aided in this attempted deception by his Roman contacts, who could use their networks of family and friends both in Asia and perhaps Rome itself. There would have been many in Asia and Rome who hoped that this build up was not a prelude to war with Rome, given their commitments in the Western Republic and Macedonia, and perhaps there was a willingness to believe this deception.

Certainly, we hear of no Roman military build-up in the East. Rome's leading eastern general, P. Servilius Vatia, was actually returning to Rome this year to celebrate a Triumph for his campaign, his successor being a L. Octavius (Consul in 75 BC). Rome thereby withdrew its most seasoned eastern general on the eve of the war. Furthermore, any thoughts of Octavius being in position to face any Mithridatic counterattack were disrupted when Octavius unexpectedly died (seemingly of natural causes) during 74 BC.

With his forces assembled and judging the time to be right, Mithridates launched his second invasion of Roman territory, this time into Bithynia. Again the exact timing for this invasion had not been retained by our few surviving sources, but it seems to have been in the spring of 73 BC (through again the year is open to debate – see above). Appian preserves what purports to be a fragment of his speech on the eve of the invasion:

'At the beginning of spring Mithridates made trial of his navy and sacrificed to Zeus Stratius in the customary manner, and also to Poseidon by plunging a chariot with white horses into the sea. Then he hastened against Paphlagonia with his two generals, Taxiles and Hermocrates, in command of his army. When he arrived there, he made a speech to his soldiers, eulogistic of his ancestors and still more so of himself, showing how his kingdom had grown to greatness from small beginnings, and how his army had never been defeated by the Romans when he was present. He accused the Romans of avarice and lust of power "to such an extent," he said, "that they had enslaved Italy and Rome itself".

'He accused them of bad faith respecting the last and still existing treaty, saying that they were not willing to sign it because they were watching for an opportunity to violate it again. After thus setting forth the cause of the war he dwelt upon the composition of his army and his apparatus, upon the preoccupation of the Romans, who were waging a difficult war with Sertorius in Spain, and were torn with civil dissensions throughout Italy, "for which reason," he said, "they have allowed the sea to be overrun by pirates a long time, and have not a single ally, nor any subjects who still obey them willingly. Do you not see," he added, "some of their noblest citizens (pointing to Marius and the two Luciuses) at war with their own country and allied with us?"

'When Mithridates had finished speaking and exciting his army, he invaded Bithynia.'[47]

Thus, early in 73 BC, the phoney war ended and the fighting began, with a Mithridatic blitzkrieg into a poorly defended Roman Bithynia. A war which began as a regional conflict over a small independent nation sandwiched between two empires was, over the subsequent decade, to expand out of all proportion to become an all-out war between the great powers of the East, which saw the extinguishment of three empires, the revival of a fourth and the establishment of a new empire in the East.

Part II

The Early Campaigns –
The Pontic and Civil Wars (74–71 BC)

Chapter 3

The Pontic Invasion of Bithynia and Asia (73 BC)

1. Roman Forces and Commanders

Roman Forces in Asia Minor (73 BC)

At the start of 73 BC, Roman forces in Asia Minor were split across their three provinces. The smallest force was in Bithynia itself, under the command of the Proconsul of Asia, M. Iuncus, and his legate Q. Pompeius Bithynicus. We are not told the size of the force he took from Asia to secure Bithynia, but the indications are that the bulk of the legions stationed in Asia remained behind, so we must assume that it was nothing more than a token force to defend the Proconsul.

The legions stationed in Asia had been there since the end of the First Romano-Mithridatic War, and were the two legions left behind by Sulla when he returned to the Western Republic (see Chapter One). As Plutarch himself points out, this longevity of service had both positive and negative aspects:

> 'All these had long been spoiled by habits of luxury and greed, and the Fimbrians, as they were called, had become unmanageable, through long lack of discipline. These were the men who, in collusion with Fimbria had slain Flaccus, their Consul and general, and had delivered Fimbria himself over to Sulla. They were self-willed and lawless, but good fighters, hardy, and experienced in war.'[1]

The third Roman force in the region was perhaps the most promising: the legions fighting in Cilicia formerly under P. Servilius Vatia Isauricus in his pacification of the region (see Chapter Two). These forces (though again the exact size is unknown) were battle-hardened but without any of the disciplinary problems that the Fimbrian legions seemingly possessed, being freshly levied and not having fought in the First Civil War.

Thus, despite civil war still raging in the Western Republic, the Eastern Republic was far from defenceless and had two armies stationed there: one in Asia, to the west of Bithynia and defending the approach to Greece, and one to the south in Cilicia which could push northwards into Pontus if required. However, Bithynia itself lay virtually defenceless.

Further afield, Rome was fighting a significant campaign in Thrace, with the Macedonian legions engaged in the seemingly never-ending defence of the province and its porous borders from the neighbouring tribes of mainland Europe. Again, whilst we have little detail of the campaign, we do know that Rome was finally on the offensive and had not only repelled the attacks on Macedonia, but had pushed into Thrace itself, fighting the Dardani.

Whilst these wars in defence of Macedonia were frequent occurrences, there are two particular aspects to note. The first is that Scribonius had command of five legions:[2] a notable-sized Roman army given the ongoing commitments in Spain. This meant, however, that with the army operating deep into Thrace, they would not be available to reinforce Roman interests in Asia or even defend Greece if required.

Roman Commanders in Asia Minor (74–73 BC)

The situation with the Roman commanders in Asia Minor is far from simple, and is compounded by our lack of sources for the period. We know that in 74 BC, Asia was commanded by the proconsul M. Iuncus, who seems to have personally led the annexation of Bithynia. Iuncus, however, disappears from our surviving narrative; we do not even know if he was in Bithynia when Mithridates invaded or had returned to Rome upon the termination of his command.[3]

In terms of Cilicia, we have a clearer picture, thanks to the campaigns of P. Servilius Vatia 'Isauricus' from 78–74 BC. Having achieved the conquest of a portion of Cilicia and created a Roman bastion in the face of an encroaching Armenian Empire, he returned to Rome in early 74 BC to celebrate a Triumph. Interestingly, despite the success of Servilius' conquests, Cilicia remained a proconsular command and one of the Consuls of 75 BC (L. Octavius) was dispatched. We have already analysed the issue surrounding Servilius' campaigns, ostensibly to subdue the Cilician pirates, but more likely to block any Armenian encroachment. Certainly, Octavius' focus did not seem to have been the pirate problem, given that the Senate shortly created a special *imperium* for command against the pirates of the Mediterranean. As this command was designated in 75 BC before the death of Nicomedes, it cannot have been connected to events in Bithynia. Presumably, the Senate intended to keep legions in their newly acquired province to ensure its subjugation and as a bastion against Armenian expansion and the loss of the Seleucid Empire.

At this point, in mid-74 BC, Octavius was clearly the most senior Roman commander in Asia Minor, and it would have fallen to him to command the war against Mithridates, but for two subsequent events. The most obvious one is Octavius' death, at some point in 74 BC, which at best we could speculate was in the middle of the year. He was certainly alive when the Consuls of 74 BC were assigned their provinces. It is these subsequent assignments that muddy the issue somewhat. As well as keeping Octavius in the proconsular command in Cilicia, the Senate created a new proconsular command in Bithynia (its first).

The tactical thinking behind designating Bithynia as a proconsular command for 73 BC was obvious. Bithynia had only just been annexed, was held by a token force under a junior commander and was potentially faced with a massive invasion from its neighbour, Pontus. Thus, command of any potential Romano-Pontic War fell to one of the Consuls of 74 BC, M. Aurelius Cotta, the first Proconsul of Bithynia. Under the normal rules of the Sullan Senate, Cotta would only take up his command at the start of 73 BC, when Iuncus would presumably return to the province of Asia. We are not aware of any designated replacement for Iuncus in the province of Asia for 73 BC.

We know that Cotta hailed from a long-standing plebeian consular family (the first Consul coming in 252 BC), though not of the top rank of Senatorial families; they did not see a Consul every generation (only in 144 and 119 BC). He was the middle of three brothers, the eldest preceding him in the consulship the previous year and the youngest (Lucius) some ten years later (65 BC).

Far more is known about the background of elder brother C. Aurelius Cotta, who was an ally of the Tribunes M. Livius Drusus (Tribune in 91 BC) and P. Sulpicius (88 BC). The elder Cotta was exiled from Rome by the Tribune Q. Varius Severus (90 BC), but clearly chose the winning side of the First Civil War having thrown in his lot with Sulla. The family prospered under the Sullan Republic, as seen by having two brothers in a row as Consuls in 75 and 74 BC. Our lack of surviving sources robs us of information on their military service, though an Aurelius Cotta was defeated by Sertorius in a naval engagement off Spain in 80 BC, but we do not know which brother it was. We also have no knowledge of where he served his praetorship (c.77 BC). Thus, Cotta is an unknown entity to us, especially in terms of his military experience, but that does not mean that the Senate viewed him as such.

The Sullan Senate intended that it would be Octavius and Cotta who would command any potential Pontic War, with Cotta (as Proconsul of Bithynia) in command. As stated above, this situation was disrupted by two outside elements: the unexpected death of Octavius and the attitude and politicking of his eventual replacement, L. Licinius Lucullus. During 74 BC, Lucullus was the other Consul, along with Cotta, yet despite his extensive military experience in the East (eee Chapter One), he was not appointed to the Bithynian command, instead receiving Cisalpine Gaul. This decision does seem an unusual one and may hint at some underlying tensions within the Sullan oligarchy. At this point, war with Pontus was not a certainty, but given the historic issues associated with the command of the First Pontic War, perhaps Lucullus not getting the command and it going to a lower-profile figure was not surprising.

Command of the First Romano-Pontic War had originally been awarded to Sulla by the Senate, but this had been overturned in a supreme piece of political opportunism by Sulla's mentor, C. Marius, who used a Tribune to transfer the command to himself. This in turn caused Sulla (importantly supported by his consular colleague) to march his army on Rome and seize power, restoring the command to himself, sparking off another bloody round in Rome's First Civil War.

With that same civil war still raging in Spain, and Lucullus being a noted adherent of Sulla, perhaps more moderate members of the Sullan oligarchy (which was never a homogenous body) felt that an eastern command, potentially against Mithridates himself, would be a step too far. There is also the possibility that several other powerful figures would have had their eye on any potential war against Mithridates, so advocated a minor figure to have the command initially until they were ready (and here we are thinking either Pompeius Magnus or Crassus, both young and ruthless).

Yet Octavius' demise threw the Senate's careful plans into disarray and opened up an opportunity. We have only one line from Plutarch that refers to Octavius' death, with no additional details:

'At this time there came tidings of the death of Octavius, the Governor of Cilicia.'[4]

Frustratingly we do not know whether he died of natural causes, was murdered or killed in battle, though natural causes seems the most likely. Given the tensions in the region and a potential war with Pontus (of which Cotta was still the lead commander), Octavius' demise represented an opportunity for many in the Senate. Plutarch himself sums up the situation when he says, 'There were many eager applicants for the province.'[5]

It was this opportunity that Lucullus seized. Using the lesson from Rome's recent political history, he saw that it was an opportunity not only to command in Cilicia rather than Cisalpine Gaul, but to take charge of any potential war itself. Again we are hampered by a lack of detailed chronology of the events of this year, but the outline remains.

Like his colleague Cotta, Lucullus hailed from a middle-ranking consular family (the earliest being 151 BC), but unlike Cotta far more is known of

Lucullus, with two biographies surviving to this day.[6] His fate was forever intertwined with L. Cornelius Sulla, with whom he fought in the First Civil War against the Italian rebels and for whom he became Quaestor (*c.*88/87 BC). He served extensively under Sulla in Greece and then Asia Minor in the latter's fight against Mithridates. Lucullus stayed in the East, originally under the command of Murena, eventually returning in 79 BC after the fall of Mitylene (see Chapter One). A praetorship soon followed in 78 BC and a pro-praetorian command in Africa (77–76 BC). Again this command of a backwater province, with no chance of taking part in a major campaign such as in Spain, Macedonia or Cilicia, may well be an indication of a loss of political momentum. Nevertheless, he was able to secure a consulship for 74 BC. This was followed however by another less than inspiring proconsular command, in Cisalpine Gaul, to succeed his colleague's brother, C. Aurelius Cotta (Consul in 75 BC) no less.

Throughout the year, Lucullus had been actively involved in the main Roman domestic political dispute of the period, the agitation for the restoration of the full powers of the Plebeian Tribunate, which had been curtailed by Sulla.[7] Lucullus had firmly planted himself on the side of his former mentor and the hard-line Sullan faction by opposing the Tribune L. Quinctius in his move for the full restoration of the tribunate's powers, especially that of unrestricted legislation.[8]

The great irony here is that commanders prior to these restrictions found the most convenient method of securing a command was to have a Tribune propose the necessary legislation in the Tribal Assembly, regardless of the Senate's decision, as happened in 88 BC. With this avenue denied him, Lucullus clearly used other moves to secure the vacant command of Cilicia. Unfortunately for us, our surviving sources are frustratingly vague on how he achieved it. To make matters more complicated, Velleius clearly believes that Lucullus was appointed Proconsul of Asia (but only at the end of his Consulship),[9] seemingly backed up by Memnon.[10] Certainly, we see Lucullus talking charge of the Fimbrian legions during the early stages of the war (see below).

Plutarch, who provides the fullest account, focuses on Lucullus' acquisition of the Proconsulship of Cilicia and does not mention Asia. He does, however, detail the shadowy figure of Cornelius Cethegus, who emerges from Plutarch's text as a major political powerbroker in the Senate. Interestingly, Plutarch refers to him as a 'popular leader' (δημαγωγόν),[11] comparing him to the Tribune Quinctius.[12] Initially, Lucullus too had opposed Cethegus' otherwise unknown activities, but seemingly changed his mind when he needed his help. With Cethegus swung to his side, this change of command from Cisalpine

Gaul to Cilicia (likely along with Asia) was accomplished, clearly without the opposition of the Senate but in a manner which is no longer recorded. We certainly hear of no Tribunician legislation (even with Senatorial blessing) this year. Again, all we have is Plutarch's vague passage:

'... but all were unanimous and prompt in putting into his hands the Mithridatic War, assured that no one else could better bring it to a triumphant close.'[13]

Thus it appears that Lucullus overturned not one but two of the Senate's decisions, and not only got himself command in Cilicia (with the largest Roman army in Asia Minor) but also seemingly secured the governorship of Asia and its legions. So whilst his colleague Cotta was the Roman commander in Bithynia, the likely target of any Pontic attack, it was Lucullus who had control of all of Rome's military forces in Asia Minor. We must also consider that the surviving sources are writing with the benefit of hindsight, so to them it was at this point that Lucullus was appointed commander of the war against Pontus. In reality, war had not yet been declared by either side and Lucullus was merely securing himself prime position should it do so.

These changes meant that towards the end of 74 BC, there were possibly no senior Roman commanders in Asia Minor. Under the Sullan constitution, Consuls were expected to serve their year in office before leaving for a province, and even though an invasion may have been suspected, no Pontic forces had crossed into Bithynia. Even if Cotta had already left Rome, he may not have been in place by the end of the year. Thus potentially we have a scenario of both Lucullus and Cotta (Proconsuls for 73 BC) still in Rome and Octavius dead, leaving the Governor of Asia (and now Bithynia), M. Iuncus, as the only Roman commander in Asia Minor. The timing of a Pontic attack on Bithynia, before any new commanders arrived, would therefore have been a tempting proposition for Mithridates, especially as he had Roman commanders on his own staff, presumably keeping him abreast of events in Rome.

2. The Mithridatic Invasion and the Cottan Campaign (73 BC)

When it came, Mithridates launched his invasion of Bithynia with a two-pronged land and naval assault. The best source for this early campaign is the Greek writer Memnon:

'Mithridates assembled another large army and 400 triremes, together with a considerable number of smaller ships, including fifty-oar ships and *kerkouroi.* He sent Diophantus Mitharus with a force to Cappadocia, to establish garrisons in the cities and, if Lucullus marched towards Pontus, to confront him and prevent him from advancing further. Mithridates took with him an army of 150,000 foot-soldiers, 12,000 cavalry and 120 scythed chariots, as well as an equal number of workmen. He advanced through Paphlagonia Timonitis into Galatia, and nine days later arrived in Bithynia. Lucullus ordered Cotta to sail to the harbour of Chalcedon with all his ships.'[14]

Facing these overwhelming numbers were a small garrison in Bithynia, several legions in Asia and a number of legions to the south in Cilicia. Thus Mithridates was able to sweep through central Asia Minor with very little resistance, with his main army marching through Paphlagonia and Galatia into Bithynia. Furthermore, a secondary army advanced into Cappadocia (presumably with Armenian blessing), thereby securing all the independent kingdoms of Asia Minor and immediately re-establishing the Pontic Empire of the 80s BC (see Map 5).

Given the size of his army, it is hardly surprising that we hear of no resistance from the local rulers, who were all awaiting the arrival of Roman armies. Memnon is correct to state that securing Cappadocia would secure his southern flank, not from Lucullus, but from the Roman legions in Cilicia, commanded by an unnamed deputy following the death of Octavius the previous year. At the same time as Mithridates swept through the client kingdoms of Asia Minor, his Black Sea fleet moved down the Bithynian coastline:

'Mithridates' navy sailed past Heracleia; it was not admitted into the city, but the Heracleians provided supplies when they were asked for them. While the sailors and inhabitants were mingling together, as was natural, Archelaus, the commander of the navy, seized Silenus and Satyrus, two distinguished Heracleians, and did not release them until he had persuaded them to provide five triremes to assist in the war against the Romans. As a result of this action, as Archelaus had contrived, the people of Heracleia were regarded as enemies by the Romans.'[15]

In short time, Mithridates had seized the prize of Bithynia, from both land and sea, before the Romans had time to check his advance. We hear of no Roman resistance in Bithynia, garrisoned as it can only have been by a small force, possibly still commanded by M. Iuncus. In fact we hear the opposite, and that Mithridates seems to have been welcomed by the locals:

'Then he [Mithridates] burst into Bithynia, and not only did the cities there receive him again with gladness, all Asia suffered a relapse into its former distempered condition, afflicted, as it was, past bearing by Roman money-lenders and tax-gatherers.'[16]

The Roman tax-gathering system had been a longstanding source of resentment in Asia and a source of support for Mithridates' invasion in 88 BC, when he massacred the Italian tax collectors. The Roman tax-collection system in Asia was indeed notorious and dated back to C. Sempronius Gracchus (Tribune from 123–121 BC). The Roman government, usually via the Censors, held auctions where cartels of Roman businessmen (belonging to the equestrian order) bid to pay for the rights to collect Roman taxes in Asia and paid the Roman treasury upfront. Their profit came from the ability to squeeze more than they bid, and paid to the Roman state, from the locals, all the time backed up by the threat of the Roman army for any 'acts of rebellion'. By this period, the system had been in place in Asia for nearly fifty years and the Bithynians must have been fearful of the same system being extended to them.

The few Roman forces in Bithynia must have seen little support from the locals and would not have been able to mount an effective resistance, so we must assume that they chose to retreat in the face of a land and sea invasion, presumably to the coastal cities, such as Chalcedon. Furthermore, it seems that the Fimbrian legions of Asia, did not advance from their province but remained, presumably to guard Asia and await the arrival of a new commander. This allowed Mithridates time to consolidate his gains before the arrival of additional Roman forces under the Consul M. Aurelius Cotta. Plutarch provides us with a passage describing the policy of Mithridates and the role of the Roman general M. Marius, which most likely dates from this period:

'Accordingly, a general was sent to Asia by Sertorius, one of the Senators who had taken refuge with him, Marcus Marius. He was assisted by Mithridates in the capture of certain cities of Asia, and when he entered them with fasces and axes, Mithridates would follow him in person, voluntarily assuming second rank and the position of a vassal. Marius gave some of the cities their freedom, and wrote to others announcing their exemption from taxation by grace of Sertorius, so that Asia, which was once more harassed by the revenue-farmers and oppressed by the rapacity and arrogance of the soldiers quartered there, was all of a flutter with new hopes and yearned for the expected change of supremacy.'[17]

We must assume that Cotta arrived in early 73 BC, though we are not told how many forces he had with him, and unusually he did not seem to reinforce himself with the Fimbrian legions of Asia. Nevertheless, Cotta seems to have made straight for Bithynia and occupied a forward position in the Greek coastal city of Chalcedon, situated on the Bosphorus Straits, opposite Byzantium and guarding the entrance to the Sea of Marmara and the Aegean beyond. This would act as a bulwark against a Mithridatic thrust into Thrace or a naval move into the Aegean

Appian tells us that Chalcedon acted as a focal point for Roman refugees from the region.[18] Clearly outnumbered on both land and sea, Cotta took up a defensive position with the intention of checking Mithridates' momentum, preventing him from sweeping into Roman Asia and allowing a build-up of Roman forces, including the Fimbrian legions in Asia and the legions in Cilicia. Plutarch, in his biography of Lucullus, ascribes Cotta's advance to his jealousy of Lucullus himself, eager to steal his glory:

'While Lucullus was thus occupied, Cotta, thinking that his own golden opportunity had come, was getting ready to give battle to Mithridates. And when tidings came from many sources that Lucullus was coming up, and was already encamped in Phrygia, thinking that a triumph was all but in his grasp, and desiring that Lucullus have no share in it, he hastened to engage the king.'[19]

Such an attitude may well have been present in the contemporary Roman sources, or even accounts sent back to Rome by Lucullan supporters, eager to blacken his rival's name even further. They clearly overlook the fact that no commander would rush to engage such an overwhelming force with so few numbers in his own army. Furthermore, it was Cotta who was the Proconsul of Bithynia and it was his province that was being invaded, so it was down to him to be the first to reach Bithynia and potentially face Mithridates.

Though the Romans may have been expecting a Mithridatic invasion at some point, they seem to have been taken by surprise at the exact timing. Given their troop dispositions, there was no way to stem Mithridates' invasion and conquest of Bithynia, which meant the clear tactical requirement was to block his advance before he overran Asia, leaving the way open for an invasion of an underdefended Greece. This would especially be the case if Lucullus was still struggling to restore order in the Fimbrian legions of Asia or, alternatively, hadn't even reached the province yet.

On the other hand, although Mithridates' initial campaign had been a total success – catching the Romans off-guard and netting him Bithynia, Galatia and Cappadocia – he now found himself facing an old problem: time. Unlike in the First Romano-Mithridatic War, the Romans already had a military presence in Asia Minor itself, though moderate, and now the arrival of Cotta prevented Mithridates from driving the Romans completely out of Asia Minor. The Pontic king faced a stark choice: either sit back and consolidate, but allow the Romans time to build up even more forces in the region for a counterstrike, or continue to press his advantage and try to deny the Romans the time they needed. He gambled on continuing his lightning campaign, choosing to attack Cotta in Chalcedon by land and sea.

There is some confusion in the sources over whether Mithridates split his army. Orosius states clearly that he does – 'Mithridates dispatched the generals Marius and Eumachus against Lucullus'[20] – yet followed it up by stating that it was these two generals who attacked Cotta at Chalcedon. Plutarch does at one point have Marius in the east of the Roman province of Asia, in Phrygia, along with Mithridates himself (see below). The surviving sources (and their forebears) seem confused about the splitting of Mithridates' army. It does, however, make sense that Mithridates dispatched his Roman commander into a Roman province to stir up rebellion there, along with a portion of his army, whilst he pursued the subjugation of Bithynia and the attack on the main Roman resistance led by the Consul M. Aurelius Cotta.

The Battle of Chalcedon (73 BC)

It was at the city of Chalcedon in Bithynia that Cotta chose to make his stand and stop the Mithridatic advance. Whilst Mithridates could have chosen to ignore the smaller Roman force there and thrust southwards into Asia proper, his whole strategy would have been endangered, for two reasons. Firstly, Cotta was effectively guarding the exit from the Black Sea and stopping Mithridates' navy, which he would need to reduce the coastal cities of Asia, from keeping his army resupplied and eventually crossing the Aegean. Secondly, had he pressed on into Asia he would have left Roman (though mostly allied) forces to his rear which could harry his land supply lines, reconquer Bithynian cities and eventually trap him between two armies. Thus, it was clear that Chalcedon had to fall. Furthermore, defeating a Roman Consul – albeit one with a meagre force – would have been a definite boost to the morale of his campaign and another blow of the myth of Roman invincibility. Mithridates therefore launched a massive land and naval assault on Chalcedon.

We have a number of accounts of the initial battle between Rome and Pontus, the most complete being Plutarch, Appian and Memnon. We don't have any numbers for the Roman and allied forces at Chalcedon, but given that we know the Fimbrian legions were still in Asia, we must assume that Cotta was heavily outnumbered and facing the bulk of Mithridates' invasion force. We do know, however, that bolstering his meagre forces were contingents from the neighbouring allied cities (such as Cyzicus – see below). Nevertheless, Cotta arranged his forces in defence of the city, which acted as a bastion, and arranged a naval and land defence. The sources tell us the bloody outcome of the one-sided clash:

'The navies of Rome and Pontus met in battle by the city of Chalcedon, and a battle also broke out on land between the king's army and the Romans; the generals of the two sides were Mithridates and Cotta. In the land battle the Bastarnae routed the Italians and slaughtered many of them. There was a similar outcome in the naval battle, and on one and the same day the land and sea were covered with the bodies of dead Romans. In the naval battle 8,000 men were killed and 4,500 were captured; in the land battle 5,300 of the Italians were killed, and out of Mithridates' army about 30 Bastarnae, and 700 others. Everyone was cowed by this success of Mithridates.'[21]

'The Romans from all directions flocked to Cotta at Chalcedon. When Mithridates advanced to that place Cotta did not go out to meet him because he was inexperienced in military affairs, but his naval prefect, Nudus, with a part of the army occupied a very strong position on the plain. He was driven out of it, however, and fled to the gates of Chalcedon over many walls which greatly obstructed his movement. There was a struggle at the gates among those trying to gain entrance simultaneously, for which reason no missile cast by the pursuers missed its mark. The guards at the gates, fearing for the city, let down the gate from the machine. Nudus and some of the other officers were drawn up by ropes. The remainder perished between their friends and their foes, holding out their hands in entreaty to each.

'Mithridates made good use of his success. He moved his ships up to the harbour the same day, broke the brazen chain that closed the entrance, burned four of the enemy's ships, and towed the remaining sixty away. Nudus offered no resistance, nor Cotta, for they remained shut up inside the walls. The Roman loss was about 3,000, including Lucius Manlius, a man of Senatorial rank. Mithridates lost twenty of his Bastarnae, who were the first to break into the harbour.'[22]

'But he [Cotta] was defeated by sea and land, lost sixty vessels, crews and all, and four thousand foot-soldiers, while he himself was shut up in Chalcedon and besieged there, looking for relief at the hands of Lucullus.'[23]

'Mithridates dispatched the generals Marius and Eumachus against Lucullus. They quickly mustered a great army and met Publius Rutilius [Nudus] at Chalcedon, killing him along with most of his army.'[24]

All sources agree that Mithridates was victorious on both land and sea, inflicting heavy losses on the Romans (3,000 according to Appian, 4,000 from Plutarch and over 13,000 in Memnon). If we are to believe Appian, then Cotta did have a contingent of Italian soldiers with him, which he must have brought from Italy. The high number of Roman casualties appears to have stemmed from the land force being routed and entry to the city being barred, resulting in its almost total destruction. In Appian, the Roman commander P. Rutilius Nudus is one of the only men to survive the battle, whilst in Orosius he is killed.

The only remaining Roman force in Bithynia had been comprehensively defeated. Thus, Cotta himself may well have been able to hold out in Chalcedon, but it was nothing more than an isolated pocket of Roman resistance, unable to slow Mithridates' invasion force. Just as important as the military aspect was the psychological one, with Mithridates adding another victory over Roman forces (no matter how woeful) and demonstrating to all the weakness of the Roman position, whilst enhancing his own legend.

Nevertheless, whilst he had achieved his principal goals of destroying the Roman army in Bithynia, opening up the Bosphorus to his navy and demonstrating his superiority over the Romans once more, the city of Chalcedon itself did not fall. Mithridates chose to lay siege to the city with a portion of his land and naval forces, but interestingly he chose to press on and advance into Asia. Furthermore, the Roman Consul M. Aurelius Cotta was still alive, though bottled up and unable to pose a threat to Mithridates' flank.

As we have said throughout this discussion, the chronology in 73 BC is difficult to reconstruct and one gets the sense that the various events have been compressed together. Principally, this involves the timings of the campaigns of Cotta and Lucullus, and where Lucullus was when Cotta was defeated at Chalcedon. Memnon has him already in Asia, camped by the Sangarius (the modern Sakarya), as does Plutarch (but camped in Phrygia). Appian, however, does not directly state this, and presents a break in his narrative between the defeat of Cotta at Chalcedon and a discussion on the arrival of Lucullus in Asia, by which time Mithridates was engaged in a siege (see below).[25] The location of Lucullus is important, as it allows us to judge Mithridates' subsequent campaign.

The Invasion of Asia (73 BC)

Having defeated Cotta and Nudus at Chalcedon in Bithynia, our sources are split as to the events that happened next. The narratives of Memnon and Appian move onto the siege of Cyzicus, a major city in the Roman province of Asia on the coast of the Sea of Marmara. Having destroyed the meagre Roman land and sea forces at Chalcedon, this attack would mark a logical move, with Mithridates invading the Roman province of Asia from Bithynia by moving south-westwards down the Marmaran coastline, allowing him to operate in concert with his navy. Plutarch adds an interesting snippet of information about Cyzicus and its role in the Battle of Chalcedon:

'But in the meantime, Mithridates planned a blow at Cyzicus, which had suffered terribly in the battle near Chalcedon, having lost three thousand men and ten ships.'[26]

From this it seems that Cotta did indeed draw upon the military assistance of the cities of Asia in his move to block Mithridates' advance. The losses Cyzicus suffered, if we are to believe Plutarch, would make the city an even more attractive target, with the Pontic monarch believing it to be weakened. Yet two problems remain with this analysis. The first comes in the form of a bizarre episode in Plutarch's narrative, which comes between the Chalcedon and Cyzicus campaigns:

'With these words, he [Lucullus] led his army against Mithridates, having thirty thousand foot-soldiers, and twenty-five hundred horsemen. But when he had come within sight of the enemy and seen with amazement their multitude, he desired to refrain from battle and draw out the time. But Marius, whom Sertorius had sent to Mithridates from Spain with an army, came out to meet him, and challenged him to combat, and so he put his forces in array to fight the issue out. But presently, as they were on the point of joining battle, with no apparent change of weather, but all on a sudden, the sky burst asunder, and a huge, flame-like body was seen to fall between the two armies. In shape, it was most like a wine-jar, and in colour, like molten silver. Both sides were astonished at the sight and separated. This marvel, as they say, occurred in Phrygia, at a place called Otryae.'[27]

Aside from the timely appearance of a celestial body, perhaps a comet entering the atmosphere, we have to question what the two armies were doing in Phrygia at all, as it lay to the extreme east of the Roman province of Asia in the Anatolian plains. Prior to this event Mithridates was at Chalcedon on the western coast, and following it he was back on the western coast at Cyzicus. We have to ask ourselves why both armies would quit the coast and their supply lines to march into the interior, fail to give battle, and then both march back to the coast. There are three logical answers.

The first is that this was a made-up story by Plutarch, or one of his sources, to include the heavenly intervention episode. The second is the possibility that this did happen, but Plutarch has the timing of the event incorrect and that it happened later. The third is the possibility that it was not Mithridates and Lucullus, but Marius who had struck off from the main Mithridatic army to subdue the western part of Asia and was intercepted by a portion of the Roman army, either from Asia or Cilicia. In any event, we should not include it in our main campaign, which saw the two key participants fighting on the Asian coastline. The situation is best summed up by Eutropius:

'Cotta, being defeated by him in a battle near Chalcedon, was even forced into the town, and besieged there. But Mithridates, having marched from thence to Cyzicus ...'[28]

Having dealt with this Plutarchian excursion into the supernatural, there still remain questions about the whole timing of the Cyzicus campaign itself. In theory, attacking the city remains both logical and understandable, given the need of Mithridates to reduce the key cities of Asia, gain ports on the coastline for resupply from the Black Sea and advance southwards into Asia, whilst being protected by his navy. Yet it is the timing of Mithridates' attack which is the most curious element and brings us back to the question of where Lucullus was, *vis-à-vis* the Chalcedon campaign.

If we are to believe Plutarch and Memnon, then Lucullus was in Asia, with his army fully mobilized and able to march on Mithridates. Yet when faced with this key obstacle to his whole invasion campaign – the only remaining Roman army in western Asia Minor and all that stood between him and overturning the whole region – Mithridates chose not to give battle, against what still must have been a numerically inferior force and one of questionable quality, but instead to lay siege to a city and allow himself to be trapped between it and a Roman relief army. Mithridates must have believed that the city would fall quickly, given its earlier losses, yet to attempt this in the face of a supposedly advancing Roman army defies common sense, especially as he hadn't chosen to besiege Chalcedon himself, which held a Roman Proconsul.

Here it is interesting to juxtapose the accounts of Plutarch and Memnon, who have Lucullus in Asia and in command of a fully mobilized army, with that of Appian, who has an interesting break in his narrative between the two battles (Chalcedon and Cyzicus). In Appian's account, the defeat of Cotta is followed by the arrival of Lucullus and the assembly of his army. Only then does he move to attack Mithridates, who is already engaged in the siege of Cyzicus. Both this account and Plutarch's provide a sense of the time it would have taken for Lucullus to prepare his campaign to fight Mithridates, both in terms of unifying the three separate elements of his army and the time taken to quell the rebellion in Asia. The only difference is that Plutarch places these events before Chalcedon, whereas Appian seems to place them afterwards.

This again harks back to the problem of when Lucullus left for Asia. If it was at the same time as Cotta, though unlikely, then Lucullus was indeed mobilized by the time Mithridates was victorious at Chalcedon and thus ready to fight him immediately, making the attack on Cyzicus all the stranger to understand; why did Mithridates not move on Lucullus at once? Yet the alternative perhaps makes more sense, that Lucullus arrived at some point after Cotta (having been appointed later), and thus still had to spend time assembling his army and quelling the rebellions in Asia before he was ready to face Mithridates. Thus, Mithridates did not turn his back on a Roman army, but wanted to reduce the coastal cities before Lucullus had time to gather his forces and be ready for battle. Mithridates' aim would have been to seize control of Cyzicus long before facing Lucullus. As it turned out, this was a grave miscalculation.

The Lucullan Campaign (73 BC)

As we have stated, whenever Lucullus arrived in Asia, he was faced with two problems. Firstly, he needed to assemble an army capable of stopping Mithridates, having only had time to bring one legion with him from Italy. Secondly, he faced a province with a significant rebellion in progress (if we are to believe Plutarch):

'… but all Asia suffered a relapse into its former wretched condition, afflicted, as it was, past bearing by Roman money-lenders and tax-gatherers. These were afterwards driven off by Lucullus; harpies that they were, snatching the people's food; but then he merely tried, by admonishing them, to make them more moderate in their demands, and laboured to stop the uprisings of the towns, hardly one of which was in a quiet state.'[29]

Again, of great interest is the question over the role of the Fimbrian legions of Asia. Throughout this period, they are conspicuous by their absence. Cotta arrived in Asia but did not use them to fight Mithridates at Chalcedon, nor did their presence prevent the rebellions breaking out in Asia. Under normal circumstances, having two battle-hardened Roman legions within a week's march would make most cities think twice, as is later seen by Lucullus being able to quell the rebellions in a short period, however 'laboured'.

We can only draw two conclusions. Firstly, their discipline was indeed so poor that prior to Lucullus' arrival they had neither the inclination nor ability to fight either Mithridates or rebellious cities. The other alternative is that they were not in the province but had been transferred to Servilius Vatia in Cilicia. This latter possibility would give Lucullus' desire to gain the Cilician proconsulship more weight, it being the only one with any military forces in Asia Minor. However, the fragment of the speech of C. Aurelius Cotta (75 BC) preserved by Sallust seems to rule this out when he refers to separate armies in Asia and Cilicia.[30] Nevertheless, key to Lucullus' campaign was the creation of a new Roman army, which we are told was comprised of three different elements:

> 'Lucius Lucullus, who had been chosen Consul and general for this war, led one legion of soldiers from Rome, joined with it the two of Fimbria, and added two others, making in all 30,000 foot and 1,600 horse.'[31]
>
> '... having thirty thousand foot-soldiers, and twenty-five hundred horsemen.'[32]

Thus Lucullus had five legions in total, an interesting mix of men from different regions and with differing levels of experience. The most experienced would have been the two Fimbrian legions stationed in Asia for over a decade. Whilst on the one hand they had experience in fighting Mithridates' forces and knew the region, on the other they had not fought in nearly a decade (unless they were transferred to Cilicia), were apparently notorious for their lax discipline and had originally been commanded by the faction leaders opposed to Sulla, both of whom they betrayed (L. Valerius Flaccus, murdered in 85 BC, and C. Flavius Fimbria, in 84 BC).

Aside from the Fimbrian legions, we are told that Lucullus brought one legion from Italy, presumably freshly raised, but one which may well have been composed of veterans from previous civil war campaigns, possibly even former Sullan veterans. The final two legions are something of a mystery, only joining Lucullus in Asia. Here we have two possibilities. The first is that they were freshly levied from the local communities of Asia and thus had little in the way of fighting experience. The other possibility is of course that they were the Cilician legions, formerly commanded by Servilius Vatia (and then

L. Octavius). Given Lucullus' Proconsulship of Cilicia (as well as Asia), the tactical necessity of combining all Roman forces in the region to counter Mithridates' invasion force and the curious absence of the Cilician legions from the narrative of the war, then it would make more sense that these last two legions were the Cilician ones, who had travelled westwards to meet the summons of their new commander.

Having assembled his army, Lucullus was faced with several tactical options, most of which are detailed by Plutarch, albeit through the voices of others.[33] His tactical decisions would have had to take into account the following elements: rebellions across Asia, a possible Marian splinter force in western Asia, the main Mithridatic army to his north, his colleague being besieged in Chalcedon and the path being open to Pontus itself. Our few surviving sources do not allow us a definitive judgement on whether Lucullus quelled the rebellions across Asia or sent a force into Phrygia to confront Marius, though the latter does seem likely.

Although there were many options open to him, he rightly saw that the key to the campaign lay in neutralizing Mithridates himself. In terms of the rebellions, he only needed to quell those in western part of the province and keep his supply lines open and his route north clear. Any cities still in rebellion, or even the smaller army of Marius, could be dealt with after the main threat had been neutralized. Likewise, there was no tactical advantage in relieving Chalcedon, which lay beyond Mithridates' army and whose loss would now make little difference. Nor would a thrust into Pontus be of any use, as the key to Mithridates' Pontic Empire was not the infrastructure, but the man himself, and he was closer to hand.

Thus Lucullus gambled on facing Mithridates himself in a direct battle, even though he was outnumbered. If he defeated the Pontic king, then the tide of the war would turn. Furthermore, his decision was made easier by Mithridates' actions; rather than press towards him and face him in open battle, he became embroiled in a protracted (and some would say unnecessary) siege at Cyzicus. With such a stroke of fortune, Lucullus' mind was made up and he pressed northwards to face Mithridates.

The Siege of Cyzicus (73 BC)

As we have seen, the key to Mithridates' campaign to date had been the speed of his attack, sweeping across Asia Minor and securing Bithynia before the Romans had time to muster an effective response. Yet if we can borrow the modern analogy of a blitzkrieg policy, then Cyzicus seems to have been his Stalingrad, tying down his army in a long siege and allowing a relief army to entrap him. Cyzicus was a long-established city, dating back to at least the eighth century BC, which occupied what was originally an island off the Marmaran coast. By this period, the island had become connected to the mainland by a narrow isthmus, but it was still a highly defensible position (not unlike the island city of Tyre in the Middle East). The best description of the city comes from Strabo:

> 'Cyzicus is an island in the Propontis, being connected with the mainland by two bridges; and it is not only most excellent in the fertility of its soil, but in size has a perimeter of about five hundred stadia. It has a city of the same name near the bridges themselves, and two harbours that can be closed, and more than two hundred ship-sheds. One part of the city is on level ground and the other is near a mountain called Arctonoros.'[34]

Key to understanding this campaign is why Mithridates chose to invest so many of his resources into taking the city, discarding his tactical advantage in terms of the Roman forces in Asia, rather than face Lucullus in a set-piece battle, where he could bring his numerical advantage to bear? This allowed Lucullus to catch him with his army totally embroiled in a protracted siege, which steadily weakened his forces.

Though strategically desirable, Cyzicus was hardly vital to the whole campaign, and certainly was of far less importance than taking Chalcedon. It did not control the exit to the Aegean, and could have easily been bypassed by land and sea with little risk, especially if we are to believe Plutarch's report of the Cyzican losses at Chalcedon. It is possible that Mithridates was looking for a suitable base for winter quarters for his army and navy, as it was autumn when the siege started. Yet the geography of the city meant that Mithridates was unable to bring his huge numerical advantage to bear, which led to a policy of 'doubling down', with an increasingly frantic effort to capture Cyzicus before Lucullus could take to the field. If we are to believe Strabo and Plutarch, then Mithridates committed huge numbers of men to the siege:

> '... for when the king [Mithridates] unexpectedly came over against them with one hundred and fifty thousand men and with a large cavalry [force], and took possession of the mountain opposite the city, the mountain called Adrasteia, and of the suburb, and then, when he transferred his army to the neck of land above the city and was fighting them, not only on land, but also by sea with four hundred ships, the Cyziceni held out against all attacks, and, by digging a counter-tunnel,

all but captured the king alive in his own tunnel; but he forestalled this by taking precautions and by withdrawing outside his tunnel.'[35]

'Mithridates was besieging Cyzicus both by land and sea, having encompassed it with ten camps on the land side, and having blockaded with his ships by sea the narrow strait which parts the city from the mainland.'[36]

Against the 'one hundred and fifty thousand' of Mithridates' army, Plutarch says Lucullus only had 'thirty thousand foot-soldiers, and twenty-five hundred horsemen'.[37] Mithridates was either unwilling or unable to break the siege and turn to face the advancing Lucullus on open ground, so Lucullus was able to draw the Roman army up to the rear of Mithridates' forces. Lucullus determined that his best course of action was to use Mithridates' numbers against him. An army of such a vast size required a huge amount of food and fodder to remain in position, so Lucullus decided to starve the Pontic king into submission:

'When he learned from deserters that the king's army contained about 300,000 men and that all his supplies were furnished by foragers or came by sea, he said to those around him that he would presently reduce the enemy without fighting, and he told them to remember his promise. Seeing a mountain well suited for a camp, where he could readily obtain supplies, and could cut off those of the enemy, he moved forward to occupy it in order to gain a victory by that means without danger. There was only one narrow pass leading to it, and Mithridates held it by a strong guard. He had been advised to do so by Taxiles and his other officers.'[38]

It seems that the use of Roman agents now backfired on Mithridates, as the Roman legate L. Magius appears to have switched sides once again (back to the Romans) and told Mithridates that the Fimbrian legions would soon desert Lucullus. By the time Mithridates found that the legions had not joined him, Lucullus had taken up a fortified position at Mithridates' rear, effectively cutting him off. Appian tells us:

'He [Mithridates] allowed the Romans to go through the pass unmolested and to fortify the great hill on his front. When they had possessed themselves of it, they were able to draw supplies from their rear without difficulty. Mithridates, on the other hand, was cut off by a lake, by mountains, and by rivers, from all provisions on the landward side, except an occasional supply secured with difficulty; he had no easy way out and he could not overcome Lucullus on account of the difficulty of the ground, which he had disregarded when he himself had the advantage. Moreover, winter was now approaching and would soon interrupt his supplies by sea.'[39]

Mithridates, by a mixture of stubbornness and treachery, found his massive army trapped by a force one-fifth its size, sandwiched between the walls of Cyzicus and the Romans at his rear and increasingly short of supplies. Faced with this dilemma, Mithridates appears to have doubled down yet again and launched a massive series of assaults on Cyzicus, from both land and sea, using a range of siege weapons, as detailed by Appian.[40] He felt that if he could secure the city then he could use it as a base for the winter and defend it against Lucullus. Yet even if he had taken the city, it would not have been able to support an additional 150,000 mouths to feed and he would have continued to find himself bottled up.

Time and again, Mithridates refused to give battle and attempt to crush the smaller Roman army, continuing to follow a policy which only ensured that his position worsened every day until it became self-fulfilling. Had he chosen to immediately break off the siege and face (and possibly defeat) Lucullus' army, then in all likelihood the Cyzicans would have come to terms. Yet the sight of the Roman army merely emboldened the defenders to hold out.[41] With the onset of winter – including snow falls, if we are to believe Plutarch – Lucullus' policy of entrapment continued to squeeze Mithridates' army, as Plutarch reveals:

> 'Mithridates, as long as his generals deceived him into ignorance of the famine in his army, was vexed that the Cyzicenes should successfully withstand his siege. But his eager ambition quickly ebbed away when he perceived the straits in which his soldiers were involved, and their actual cannibalism. For Lucullus was not carrying on the war in any theatrical way, nor for mere display, but, as the saying is, was "kicking in the belly", and devising every means for cutting off food.'[42]

Florus also reports that pestilence broke out in the Pontic camp.[43] Facing the inevitable, Mithridates admitted defeat and made plans to evacuate as much of his army as he could, given the circumstances. He staged a two-fold withdrawal, by land and sea. In a siege, the least useful elements of his army were ironically normally his most valuable: his cavalry, which originally numbered more than 12,000 men. Furthermore, cavalry were especially vulnerable in a famine situation, with the horses requiring just as much fodder as the men, whilst being an obvious target for consumption themselves. But now the cavalry, being the fastest element of the army, would lead a breakout of Lucullus' encirclement and make direct for Bithynia for the winter. Mithridates showed his ruthless side and ordered the other elements of the besieging army who would find no room in the naval evacuation, 'the beasts of burden, and those of his foot-soldiers who were disabled',[44] to join the cavalry.

Clearly, these injured men and beasts would not have been able to outrun the encircling Roman army, so we must assume that they were to be sacrificed to the Romans to slow them down and allow the more valuable cavalry to escape.

Battle of Rhyndacus (73 BC)

The cavalry and other elements chosen to break out by land were initially successful and moved through the Roman encirclement, perhaps utilizing the cover of darkness and poor weather. Yet Lucullus, having no intention of allowing key elements of the Pontic army to live to fight another day, set off in pursuit, catching them as they attempted to cross the River Rhyndacus (the modern Mustafakemalpasha) to the south-east of Cyzicus:

> 'On learning of this, Lucullus returned to his camp while it was still night, and early in the morning, in spite of a storm, took ten cohorts of infantry and his cavalry, and started in pursuit, although snow was falling and his hardships were extreme. Many of his soldiers were overcome with the cold and had to be left behind, but with the rest he overtook the enemy at the river Rhyndacus and inflicted such a defeat upon them that the very women came forth from Apollonia and carried off their baggage and stripped their slain. Six thousand horses and fifteen thousand men were captured, besides an untold number of beasts of burden. All these followed in the train of Lucullus as he marched back past the camp of the enemy.'[45]
>
> 'As his horses were not useful here and were weak for want of food and had sore hoofs, he sent them by a roundabout way to Bithynia. Lucullus fell upon them as they were crossing the river Rhyndacus, killed a large number, and captured 15,000 men, 6,000 horses, and a large amount of baggage.'[46]
>
> 'Lucullus followed him and, in the ensuing fighting, he utterly defeated the Pontic army. In a short time he killed many tens of thousands, and he took 13,000 prisoners.'[47]

Thus, the Romans won their first victory of the war, attacking a portion of the Pontic army which was in retreat and obviously not set for a battle. Lucullus thereby destroyed the majority of Mithridates' cavalry.

Unnamed Battle (73 BC)

Orosius has a second battle occurring shortly after this one. He only devotes a sentence to the battle itself, and it may even have been part of the main battle:

'After this Fannius, who had allied himself with Mithridates, and Metrophanes, the king's praetor, were defeated by Mamercus. They fled to Mysia with 2,000 cavalry.'[48]

This is the only reference we have to Lucullus' legate Mamercus and we have no other details other than that Fannius, one of the two Romano-Pontic leaders, survived and was able to extract 2,000 horsemen, though how many were lost is not recorded. Regrettably, Orosius then goes on to devote more narrative space to Fannius' journey back to Cyzicus.

The Naval Withdrawal (73 BC)

Having dispatched several elements of his army to the south, Mithridates attempted to withdraw the bulk of his forces by sea, of which he still had command. Yet this effort too met with disaster, though we have several accounts of how his misfortunate played out:

'Mithridates was now resolved upon the speediest possible flight, but with a view to drawing Lucullus away, and holding him back from pursuit, he dispatched his admiral, Aristonicus, to the Grecian sea. Aristonicus was just on the point of sailing when he was betrayed into the hands of Lucullus, together with ten thousand pieces of gold which he was carrying for the corruption of some portion of the Roman army. Upon this, Mithridates fled.'[49]

'The crafty king, who had had experience of Roman avarice, ordered that gold and money should be scattered in their path by his flying troops in order to delay his pursuers. His flight by sea was no more fortunate than by land; for a tempest which arose in the Black Sea attacked his fleet of more than a hundred ships laden with material of war, and shattered them with such terrible loss as to produce the effect of a naval defeat and make it appear as if Lucullus, by some compact with the waves and storms, had handed over the king to the wind to be defeated.'[50]

'Various disasters occurred as he boarded the triremes, because the men who were still waiting to board them grasped the ships and hung onto them, both the ships which were already full and the ones which remained. So many men did this that some of the ships were sunk and others were capsized.'[51]

The attempted naval withdrawal was a disaster, beset by bad weather and treachery, both of which were to be expected. In terms of the elements, the sources have already stated that winter had arrived and the Marmaran Sea had become rough. With regards to the human factor, Mithridates had already suffered the betrayal of Magius, one of his Roman lieutenants, earlier in the siege, though interestingly we are not given the identity of these new betrayers. With Mithridates' army composed of so many nationalities, including Romans, it is hardly surprising that many would be willing to change sides when the tide had so clearly turned against him. Memnon presents us with the picture of the aftermath as the troops who were not able to retreat by land or sea perished in their quarters:

> 'When the citizens of Cyzicus saw this, they attacked the Pontic camp, slaughtered the exhausted troops who were left there and pillaged everything that had been left in the camp.'[52]

Battle of Granicus-Aesepus (73 BC)

Despite the shambolic nature of the withdrawal, it seems that Mithridates himself was able to escape Cyzicus by sea, along with a portion of his army. Nevertheless, aside from the casualties there remained a significant portion of his army who weren't able to take to the ships and thus attempted to break through the Roman encirclement by land before the Pontic camp was attacked, seemingly led by the Roman general M. Marius. Memnon numbers this force as 30,000 strong, the same size as Lucullus' own army, albeit now without any cavalry.

This remnant of the Pontic army, choosing to retreat rather than give battle, headed southwards along the Asian coast, further into Roman territory, perhaps to link up with the remains of the Pontic fleet. Alternatively, with Marius in command, they may have been hoping to reach safety in a city that had rebelled against Roman rule. Lucullus pursued them, catching up with them in the vicinity of the rivers Granicus and Aesepus – the former being the site of a famous victory by Alexander the Great in 334 BC, a fact that would not have been lost when Lucullus came to announcing his victory back in Rome. It would seem, given the overwhelming nature of the victory and the casualties inflicted, that the ensuing battle was more a case of Lucullus cornering the Romano-Pontic army as it was retreating across the rivers than it turning to fight. We have various sources as to the course of the battle:

> 'He [Mithridates] appointed Hermaeus and Marius to lead the foot-soldiers, with an army of over 30,000 men, while he made his way back

by sea. Lucullus pursued the army as far as the river Aesepus, where he surprised it and killed a great number of the enemy.'[53]

'Soon afterwards, he [Lucullus] attacked and defeated Marius, putting him to flight. In this battle, more than 11,000 of Marius' troops are said to have been killed.'[54]

'Upon this, Mithridates fled to the sea, and his generals of infantry began to lead the army away. But Lucullus fell upon them at the river Granicus, captured a vast number of them, and slew twenty thousand.'[55]

'Lucullus followed him and dealt him so heavy a blow that the rivers Granicus and Aesepus ran with blood.'[56]

Lucullus was therefore able to defeat and destroy a significant portion of Mithridates' land army, killing up to 20,000, though a significant portion commanded by M. Marius survived and fled to the city of Lampsacus. Marius' survival allowed the 'civil war' aspects of this conflict to continue.

The Asia Minor Campaign (73 BC)

The battles of the Cyzicus campaign were not the only Roman victories that year. As detailed above, Mithridates seemed to split his forces into two sections, commanding the bulk himself and sweeping into Asia via the northern coastline, whilst a second force was dispatched into central and eastern Asia. This other army has clearly caused confusion amongst the surviving sources, as we have seen with Plutarch's narrative on the conflict with Marius being interrupted by a celestial body in Phrygia.

It is Appian who provides a brief, but revealing, narrative as to the activities of this second army, whose size is unknown. With the Romans under Lucullus focusing on western Asia, the east of the province was left undefended, as was, seemingly, Cilicia, adding weight to the Cilicia legions having been summoned to Asia by Lucullus:

'While these things were transpiring at Cyzicus Eumachus, one of Mithridates' generals, overran Phrygia and killed a great many Romans, with their wives and children, subjugated the Pisidians and the Isaurians and also Cilician. Finally Deiotarus, one of the Tetrarchs of Galatia, drove the marauder away and slew many of his men. Such was the course of events in and around Phrygia.'[57]

'Deiotarus, the king of the Galatians, killed the king's prefects in battle.'[58]

'Deiotarus, one of the tetrarchs of Gallograecia, crushed the deputies of Mithridates who tried to transfer the war to Phrygia.'[59]

These sources reveal that this army penetrated into the eastern part of the Roman province of Asia and then moved further south-east into the freshly subdued lands of the Isaurians, presumably hoping to spur them into rebellion, and thence into Cilicia. Given the language, we must assume that this was more of a large raiding force than an army of conquest, but nonetheless, it exploited the absence of Roman forces in an attempt to prise these territories away from Rome and into the sphere of the expanding Pontic Empire.

As we see, however, it was not the Roman forces that defeated these invaders but those of the Roman client ruler Deiotarus of Galatia. Though we hear of no immediate Galatian resistance to the invading Pontic armies at the start of the year, with Mithridates himself suffering at Cyzicus, it seems that Deiotarus was spurred into action and made a clear demonstration – no matter how late – of his pro-Roman credentials, safe in the knowledge that he was backing the winning side. There may well have even been a role for a certain young Roman aristocrat, namely C. Iulius Caesar, whose biography in Suetonius includes the following:

'He then proceeded to Rhodes, but as Mithridates was devastating the neighbouring regions, he crossed over into Asia, to avoid the appearance of inaction when the allies of the Roman People were in danger. There he levied a band of auxiliaries and drove the king's prefect from the province, thus holding the wavering and irresolute states to their allegiance.'[60]

Though there is no further detail in Suetonius, the terminology used – once translated – does strike a chord between the two incidents. Thus, Caesar may well have been present in the force led by Deiotarus which defeated this second Pontic army.

Summary

As we can see, the latter part of this year's campaigns saw both invading Pontic armies destroyed. It appears that this campaign was clearly a case of the general who made the least mistakes winning the conflict. On paper, Mithridates' forces severely outnumbered Lucullus' legions, yet he was never able to bring them to bear in open battle. The whole campaign, as with the war, turned on the siege of Cyzicus, with Mithridates becoming totally bogged down in a siege which saw his army pinned down, encircled, starved and pestilence-ridden. With the onset of winter, Mithridates ordered a fragmented three-pronged retreat, each element of which met with disaster. The whole campaign centred on Mithridates' gamble that he could reduce Cyzicus before Lucullus could march north, a gamble he lost.

Despite this gamble, and despite the uncertain timescales involved, credit must be given to Lucullus, who saw his opportunity and advanced north to entrap Mithridates at Cyzicus rather than wait for him further south. His policy of 'tightening the noose' around Mithridates' army, though seemingly unpopular with his forces, totally negated Mithridates' superior numbers and led to the destruction of an army which massively outnumbered his own. Even allowing for the usual exaggeration one finds in the sources, the siege of Cyzicus and subsequent botched retreat must go down as one of the greatest military catastrophes in history, certainly on a par with the Napoleonic retreat from Moscow or German losses at Stalingrad:

> 'It is said that out of the whole horde of camp-followers and fighting men, not much less than three hundred thousand perished in the campaign.'[61]
> 'He [Mithridates] is said to have lost more than 300,000 men through starvation and disease in this siege.'[62]

Both of the more recent disasters had the same effect as that of Mithridates, the destruction of a huge army which led to a swing in the balance of a wider war.

Chapter 4

The Roman Invasion of
Bithynia and Pontus (72–71 BC)

As with the whole of the early years of the Romano-Pontic War, the surviving sources we have do not maintain a coherent chronological framework for the campaigns that followed the Roman victory at Cyzicus, even leading to uncertainty over which year certain events took place. Yet we can nevertheless piece together the key events.

Events in Rome and Beyond (73 BC)

Despite his remarkable military success during the previous year, perhaps the greatest potential threat to Lucullus came from Rome itself. Having initially been sidelined when it came to provincial commands, and having used political chicanery to secure command of the Mithridatic campaign, the clear danger he now faced was having his command prorogued and being replaced by another commander. Yet it seems that the political alliance he had put together the previous year to gain the command was still in place in Rome, and was able to secure the election as Consul of his younger brother, M. Terentius Varro Lucullus, for 73 BC.[1] So throughout 73 BC he had a dependable ally in Rome and was highly unlikely to be replaced in his command. As it happened, towards the end of the year, Marcus Lucullus was appointed to command in Macedonia, replacing C. Scribonius Curio in the wars with the tribes of Thrace, thereby securing Lucius Lucullus' western flank.

As always, overshadowing the war in the East was the ongoing civil war in the Western Republic, with Cn. Pompeius slowly winning an attritional campaign against Q. Sertorius. Aside from the wars against the Thracian tribes, the other major campaign was in the Mediterranean with the continuing anti-pirate campaign of M. Antonius, whose focus had shifted to the Eastern Mediterranean and the island of Crete. Back in Rome, domestic focus had shifted from the political battle to restore the powers of the Tribunate of the Plebs, as spearheaded by C. Licinius Macer, to the repeated Roman military failures to defeat what had started as a minor slave revolt in Capua in southern Italy, headed by a Thracian named Spartacus.

The Naval War (73–72 BC)

Having successfully broken the siege of Cyzicus, Lucullus briefly occupied the city, which acted as a temporary headquarters whilst he planned the next moves of the campaign. His colleague Cotta, meanwhile, was still based in Chalcedon, and likely still under siege. With the onset of winter and the destruction of the bulk of Mithridates' army, the war shifted its focus to the sea, where Mithridates still held an advantage.

The surviving Pontic land forces from the Battle of Granicus had seemingly been able to seek refuge at the Greek port of Lampsacus (see Map 2), along with the Roman general M. Marius, where they were being besieged by Lucullus. Yet Mithridates' control of the seas allowed him to dispatch a portion of his remaining fleet to rescue the remnants of his army, as Appian recorded:

> 'Mithridates sent ships for those who had taken refuge in Lampsacus, where they were besieged by Lucullus, and carried them away, together with the Lampsaceans themselves. Leaving 10,000 picked men and fifty ships under Marius (the general sent to him by Sertorius), and Alexander the Paphlagonian, and Dionysius the eunuch, he sailed with the bulk of his force for Nicomedia. A storm came up in which many of both divisions perished.'[2]

We are not told how many were rescued, but given that he left behind 10,000 troops as a rearguard, the surviving portion of his army must have been in the tens of thousands.

Pontic Attacks on Perinthus and Byzantium (73–72 BC)

Following his withdrawal from Cyzicus and Lampsacus, it seems that Mithridates did not retreat back into the Black Sea straightaway, but attempted to secure another coastal city to spend the winter. We only have two passing references to this, from Memnon and Eutropius: 'Mithridates recovered as best he could and besieged Perinthus but failed to take it and crossed back over to Bithynia';[3] and 'at last [Lucullus] pursued him [Mithridates] to Byzantium'.[4]

It therefore seems that Mithridates made one final attempt – or two, if we accept that Eutropius hasn't confused Perinthus for Byzantium – to secure another coastal city to act as a forward base for the winter, this time on the western shore of the Bosphorus, where Lucullus' army could not reach him. Having failed to take Cyzicus after a long siege, and with his army in tatters, it would seem that Mithridates was relying on the element of surprise to take this city (or cities) by storm, but once that failed, he did not invest much time or effort in the matter and retreated back into the Black Sea.

Thus, whilst Mithridates had been comprehensively defeated at Cyzicus, he was still able to evade capture and retreat back to his newly won territory. Furthermore, whilst Mithridates himself retreated, he left behind M. Marius in joint command of a portion of his forces still in the Hellespont, to harry the Roman forces and deny them control of the entrance to the Black Sea, the crossroads of his empire. It was a classic case of the Romans being dominant on land, but the Pontic forces controlling the seas.

Lucullus' Naval Strategy (72 BC)

This move highlighted to Lucullus the key weakness of his campaign: naval power, which had allowed Mithridates to escape his defeat in Asia and spirit away a portion of his army. In many ways this brings to mind events from the First Romano-Pontic War, when Fimbria had Mithridates trapped in the city of Pitane, only for the lack of Roman naval support (commanded by Lucullus himself) to apparently allow Mithridates to escape.[5]

Obviously, the figure of Mithridates was critical to the war; capture Mithridates, and his army and empire would dissolve, thereby ending the war. Mithridates had snatched a victory from defeat and Lucullus had lost his chance to end the war quickly, tainting his victory at Cyzicus.

Lucullus' priority therefore had to be the assemblage of a fleet with which to challenge Mithridates' (and now Marius') domination of the Sea of Marmara and the Black Sea, a task not made easier by the command of M. Antonius with his *imperium* over the Mediterranean and its naval resources. Again, although we have the narratives of Plutarch, Appian and Memnon, none present us with an accurate chronology for the subsequent events of the naval campaign. We are clear that Lucullus did indeed assemble a fleet, but not how long it took him, as Appian merely says, 'he collected a fleet from the Asiatic province and distributed it to the generals serving under him'.[6] We must assume that it took several months to gather the necessary ships into a serviceable fleet.

Having assembled a fleet, Lucullus took the offensive, splitting the fleet in three between himself and two of his commanders, C. Valerius Triarius and an unknown officer, named only as Barba. Each force was to have a different objective. Lucullus, who must have had the largest portion of the new fleet, set himself the task of tracking down and defeating this Pontic fleet commanded by M. Marius, which seems to have left the Hellespont and moved into the Aegean and down the Asia Minor coast. Memnon states that the Pontic fleet had two objectives, to ally with the pirate fleets of Crete fighting M. Antonius and the civil war forces of Sertorius in Spain, thus creating a wider anti-Sullan/Roman front.[7]

Of the other two Roman commanders, the one we know least about is the man known only in the sources as Barba, though it is believed he was a Cassius Barba.[8] We have no further information on his background, but a line in Memnon indicates that Barba arrived in Asia with fresh forces: 'Then Barba arrived at the head of a large force of Italians.'[9] The other commander, C. Valerius Triarius, can be identified with a man who held the Quaestorship in 81 BC and a Praetorship in 77 BC,[10] making him a firm (albeit junior) supporter of Sulla. He took part in the civil war campaign of 77 BC when he defended Sardinia against M. Aemilius Lepidus, after the latter's failed attack on Rome. Whilst Lucullus took the bulk of the Roman fleet into the Aegean in pursuit of Marius, Barba and Triarius were tasked with securing control of the Bithynian coast and capturing the remaining cities that were either loyal to Mithridates or held by his garrisons.

The Campaigns of Triarius and Barba

Although we have no chronology for the actions of Triarius and Barba, two of the main sources for this period – Appian and Memnon – do preserve an outline of their campaigns (see Map 7):

> 'Triarius sailed to Apamea, captured it, and slew a great many of the inhabitants who had taken refuge in the temples. Barba took Prusias, situated at the base of a mountain, and occupied Nicaea, which had been abandoned by the Mithridatic garrison.'[11]
>
> 'Triarius the Roman general advanced and started to besiege Apamea; the citizens of Apamea resisted as much as they could, but finally they opened their gates and let the Romans in. The Roman army also captured the city of Prusa, which lies at the foot of the Asian Mount Olympus. From there Triarius took his army to the city of Prusias by the sea. When Triarius arrived there, the inhabitants of Prusias drove out the Pontic soldiers and willingly let him in.
>
> 'From there Triarius went on to Nicaea, where Mithridates had placed a garrison. But the Pontic soldiers realised that the inhabitants of Nicaea were inclining towards the Romans, and so they withdrew at night towards Mithridates at Nicomedeia; after that the Romans gained control of the city without a fight.'[12]

Thus, both commanders were able to secure at least four key western Bithynian cities, from the ports of Apamea and Prusias on the Sea of Marmara to the inland cities of Prusias and Nicaea. As the sources highlight, both Prusias and Nicaea were taken without a fight, with the Pontic garrisons either fleeing or being expelled, highlighting that the locals and even Mithridates' remaining forces had seen which way the war was turning. Thus, the Roman commanders had been able to secure the Sea of Marmara for Rome and carve out a zone of control of the border between Asia and Bithynia.

The Civil War in the Eastern Republic: Lucullus, Marius and the Battle of Tenedos (72 BC)

Whilst his commanders were securing the Sea of Marmara, Lucullus chose to pursue the Pontic fleet commanded by M. Marius, which had moved into the eastern Aegean, most likely to link up with the pirate fleets of the region in an anti-Roman alliance. Lucullus, it seems, based himself in the region of the Troad and awaited intelligence on the exact whereabouts of Marius' fleet; news which came from the city of Ilium, where a portion of the Pontic fleet had anchored.[13] Lucullus then brought his fleet to engage what must have been a numerically inferior portion of the Pontic navy:

'… there came certain men from Ilium, with news that thirteen of the king's galleys had been seen off the harbour of the Achaeans, making for Lemnos. Accordingly, Lucullus put to sea at once, captured these, slew their commander, Isodorus, and then sailed in pursuit of the other captains, whom these were seeking to join.'[14]

'At the harbour of the Achaeans, Lucullus captured thirteen of the enemy's ships.'[15]

Having overwhelmed the smaller Pontic fleet, Lucullus found out from his prisoners that the main fleet of Marius was heading for Lemnos and so set out to confront them, leading to a decisive naval battle at the island of Tenedos, for which we have numerous sources:

'He overtook Marius and Alexander and Dionysius on a barren island near Lemnos and dashed at them in a contemptuous manner. They stoutly held their ground. He checked his oarsmen and sent his ships toward them by twos in order to entice them out to sea. As they declined the challenge, but continued to defend themselves on land, he sent a part of his fleet around to another side of the island, disembarked a force of infantry, and drove the enemy to their ships. Still they did not venture out to sea, but hugged the shore, because they were afraid of the army of Lucullus. Thus they were exposed to missiles on both sides, landward and seaward, and received a great many wounds, and after heavy slaughter took to flight.

'Marius, Alexander, and Dionysius the eunuch were captured in a cave where they had concealed themselves. Dionysius drank poison which he had with him and immediately expired. Lucullus gave orders that Marius be put to death, since he did not want to have his triumph graced by a Roman Senator, but he kept Alexander for that purpose. Lucullus sent letters wreathed with laurel to Rome, as is the custom of victors, and then pressed forward to Bithynia.'[16]

'They chanced to be lying at anchor close to shore, and drawing their vessels all up on land, they fought from their decks, and sorely galled the crews of Lucullus. These had no chance to sail round their enemies, nor to make onset upon them, since their own ships were afloat, while those of their enemies were planted upon the land and securely fixed. However, Lucullus at last succeeded in disembarking the best of his soldiers where the island afforded some sort of access. These fell upon the enemy from the rear, slew some of them, and forced the rest to cut their stern cables and fly from the shore, their vessels thus falling foul of one another, and receiving the impact of the ships of Lucullus. Many of the enemy perished, of course, and among the captives there was brought in Marius, the general sent from Sertorius. He had but one eye, and the soldiers had received strict orders from Lucullus, as soon as they set sail, to kill no one-eyed man. Lucullus wished Marius to die under the most shameful insults.'[17]

'Afterwards Lucullus engaged the same Marius in a naval battle and sank or captured 32 of the king's ships and a great number of merchantmen. Many of those whom Sulla had proscribed perished here.'[18]

'But the king [Mithridates] heard that the Pontic navy had been defeated in two sea battles, which it had fought with Lucullus near Tenedos and in the Aegean.'[19]

'Do you think that that naval battle at Tenedos, when the enemy's fleet were hastening on with rapid course and under most eager admirals towards Italy, full of hope and courage, was a trifling engagement; an insignificant contest?'[20]

'Ours is the glory which will be for ever celebrated, which is derived from the fleet of the enemy which was sunk after its admirals had been slain, and from the marvellous naval battle off Tenedos: those trophies belong to us, those monuments are ours, those triumphs are ours.'[21]

There is clearly some confusion in the sources as to which of the two battles was which. Both Appian and Plutarch agree on a smaller battle off the coast of Ilium and then a much larger battle off Lemnos, though neither use the name Tenedos. Cicero, with his customary literary excess, names Tenedos as a great victory for Lucullus, but provides no useful details, though the implication is that it was the one Lucullus fought with Marius. Memnon seems to refer to the Battle of Tenedos twice, firstly fought by Lucullus and then again fought by Valerius Triarius, even though he had been in Bithynia when Lucullus fought this naval battle. The battle Triarius fought was not in the Aegean, but the Sea of Marmara, and has erroneously been labelled as Tenedos.[22]

Despite the confusion in our sources, the outcome was clear and decisive; the Pontic fleet had been destroyed, and M. Marius and a number of Roman civil war figures were killed. Marius' plan to continue the civil war in the East had been crushed, as had Mithridates' scheme to join with the other anti-Roman forces in the Mediterranean. Just as Lucullus had driven Mithridates back into Bithynia by land, now he removed his control of the sea and drove the war back into the Sea of Marmara and the Black Sea.

Lucullus, never slow in singing his own praises, wrote to the Senate of his naval victories, which may well have been where Cicero got his information from on the dangers to Italy from the Marian fleet. Furthermore, when the Senate voted him a subsidy to raise a fleet, Lucullus turned this down:

'And so it happened that the boastful speech of Lucullus to the Senate brought no divine retribution down upon him. When, namely, that body was ready to vote three thousand talents to provide a fleet for this war, Lucullus blocked the measure by writing a letter, in which he made the haughty boast that without any such costly array, but only with the ships of the allies, he would drive Mithridates from the sea.'[23]

Cotta, Triarius and the Siege of Nicomedeia (72 BC)
Whilst Lucullus was fighting the Romano-Pontic navy in the Aegean, his fellow commander Cotta, who still technically held the command in Bithynia, was freed from his siege at Chalcedon. We are given no timeline for this, nor exactly what happened, but there are two references to it:

'He [Lucullus] rescued his colleague [Cotta] from a siege, after he had been defeated by king Mithridates and had taken refuge in Chalcedon.'[24]
    'Sent against Mithridates, he freed his colleague Cotta from the blockade at Chalcedon.'[25]

Interestingly, the two sources differ on the timescale of the rescue and neither provides any detail on the method. The de viris illustribus suggests that the rescue came before the siege of Cyzicus, though as detailed previously (see Chapter Three), that would have been highly unlikely, with Lucullus having to bypass Mithridates at Cyzicus and then loop back again, and without naval control of the Sea of Marmara. Far more likely is the order presented in the inscription to Lucullus (and thus contemporary), where the rescue comes after the victories on land and sea. What is not recorded is whether Lucullus personally commanded the relief, though it is more likely that he ordered either Triarius or Barba to break the siege and rescue his unfortunate colleague.

Once freed from Chalcedon, Cotta – still legally the Roman commander in Bithynia – set about making up for lost time and took the offensive, though whether he was reinforced is not clear. Nevertheless, he was able to move deeper into Bithynia (though we are not told the size of his force) and advanced on the Bithynian capital of Nicomedia, where Mithridates had been wintering. Whilst we are not specifically told when this occurred, we do know from Memnon that it happened at the same time as Lucullus' naval campaign. Here he was reinforced by Valerius Triarius, and the two commanders prepared to lay siege to Mithridates. Yet again, however, Mithridates chose flight and was able to flee the city before it was placed under a tight Roman cordon:

> 'Cotta wanted to make amends for his earlier failures, and advanced from Chalcedon, where he had been defeated, to Nicomedeia, where Mithridates was staying. He camped 150 stades from the city but was reluctant to join battle. Without waiting to be summoned, Triarius hastened to join Cotta, and when Mithridates withdrew inside the city the Roman army prepared to besiege it from both sides. But the king heard that the Pontic navy had been defeated in two sea battles, which it had fought with Lucullus near Tenedos and in the Aegean, and he did not think that he was strong enough to withstand the Roman army which confronted him. Therefore he embarked his forces and sailed up the river.'[26]

Plutarch presents a slightly different version and makes it all about Lucullus, having airbrushed Cotta out of his account altogether here, substituting a previously unknown legate named Voconius:

> 'Lucullus hastened in pursuit of Mithridates himself. For he expected to find him still in Bithynia under the watch and war of Voconius, whom

he had dispatched with a fleet to Nicomedeia that he might intercept the king's flight. But Voconius was behindhand, owing to his initiation into, and celebration of, the mysteries in Samothrace, and Mithridates put to sea with his armament, eager to reach Pontus before Lucullus turned and set upon him.'[27]

We can square these two accounts by having Lucullus dispatching Voconius to free Cotta and accompany him to attack Mithridates at Nicomedia. It is also possible that Voconius is none other than Valerius Triarius, and that the name has been corrupted over the centuries. Nevertheless, the key element is that Mithridates was able to retreat from Bithynia and back into his heartland of Pontus, abandoning his Bithynian conquests to the Romans, though there may well have been token garrisons left behind. However, as the sources detail, Mithridates did not escape scot-free, once again being hit by a storm:

'He was overtaken, however, by a great storm, which destroyed some of his vessels and disabled others. The whole coast for many days was covered with the wrecks dashed upon it by the billows.'[28]

'As Mithridates was sailing to Pontus, a second tempest overtook him and he lost about 10,000 men and sixty ships, and the remainder were scattered wherever the wind blew them. His own ship sprang a leak and he went aboard a small piratical craft although his friends tried to dissuade him. The pirates landed him safely at Sinope.'[29]

Mithridates' remaining forces having been further depleted, the king was lucky to escape back to Pontus. We must presume that Mithridates' retreat allowed the Romans to reoccupy the Bithynian capital of Nicomedia. Interestingly, Memnon (of Heracleia) introduces a story that during his retreat, Mithridates was able to recapture the Bithynian port of Heracleia (see Map 2) through the treachery of its ruler, allowing him to install a garrison and use it as a staging post.[30]

The Reconquest of Asia Minor (72 BC)
Again, we do not know how much time elapsed between Cotta and Triarius recapturing Nicomedia and the arrival of Lucullus from the Aegean, though it could have been anything from a few weeks to a month. Once the two Proconsuls had reunited, they set about planning the retaking of the other client kingdoms of the regions which had been invaded and annexed (however briefly) to the Pontic Empire – notably Galatia and Cappadocia – with an eye to then invading Pontus itself.

Here it would be interesting to understand what Cotta and Lucullus' initial brief from the Senate actually was when they were given their respective commands, and whether it extended to invading Pontus itself. Cotta would most likely have been charged with recovering Bithynia (a task now mostly complete), but Lucullus probably had the wider goal of defeating Mithridates. As Mithridates was still in the field, albeit in Pontus, then this would have allowed Lucullus the license to invade the Pontic Empire (Pontus itself and its Black Sea territories), with an eye to outright annexation. In many respects, the failure to capture Mithridates allowed Lucullus the opportunity/excuse to widen the war into one of conquest and not simply the defence and recovery of existing Roman provinces, a fact which undoubtedly was not lost on him. Plutarch does state that Lucullus was advised to bring the war to a conclusion, now that Mithridates had been defeated and Bithynia recaptured, writing, 'Though many now advised Lucullus to suspend the war, he paid no heed to them.'[31]

Lucullus had clearly decided that Roman control of Asia Minor would never be secure until Mithridates himself had been defeated and killed or captured, and his Pontic Black Sea Empire dismantled. To that end, he set about not only recapturing the client kingdoms of Asia Minor but invading Pontus itself. According to Memnon, Lucullus split the Roman forces into three, between himself, Cotta and Triarius, with the latter two being given supporting roles whilst he took the bulk of the Roman army and invaded Galatia and Cappadocia:

'Lucullus, Cotta and Triarius, the commanding generals of the Romans, came together at Nicomedeia, and set off to invade Pontus. But when they heard about the capture of Heracleia – they did not know it had been betrayed, but thought that the whole city had changed allegiance – they decided that Lucullus should march with most of the army through the inland districts into Cappadocia, in order to attack Mithridates and his entire kingdom; that Cotta should attack Heracleia; and that Triarius should gather the naval forces around the Hellespont and Propontis, and lie in wait for the return of the ships which Mithridates had sent to Crete and Spain.'[32]

Thus, once again, Cotta was given a subordinate task, whilst Lucullus resumed command of the main Romano-Pontic War. The statement on Triarius' role is an interesting one, as the general assumption is that the Pontic fleet was destroyed at Tenedos, which Memnon refers to (albeit not by name) earlier in his text, when Mithridates was at Nicomedia. Yet Memnon then goes on to describe another naval battle between Triarius and a Pontic fleet:

'Shortly before this, Triarius set off from Nicomedeia with the Roman fleet to confront the Pontic triremes which, as has been said previously, had been sent out to Crete and Spain. He learnt that they were withdrawing to Pontus, after losing many ships which had been sunk in storms and in various battles. He intercepted the remaining ships and fought a battle against them near Tenedos, in which he had 70 triremes and the Pontic navy had just under 80. When the two sides met, the king's ships offered some resistance to start with, but later they were completely routed, and the Roman navy won a decisive victory. And so the entire naval force, which had sailed out to Asia with Mithridates, was destroyed.'[33]

Clearly, Memnon has labelled the wrong battle as the naval engagement was fought in the Sea of Marmara, not the Aegean, but that does not mean that the whole incident is a duplicate. It is entirely possible that Lucullus only destroyed a part of the remaining Pontic fleet commanded by Marius, whilst another portion had attempted to reach Sertorius in Spain.

Once again, we are at the mercy of our surviving sources, who gloss over the reconquest of Bithynia, Galatia and Cappadocia in order to record the Roman invasion of Pontus. This may well have been the result of there being little to record in the way of military action. The local cities and rulers would all have thrown in their lot with the advancing victorious Roman army, and Mithridates, in all likelihood, would have withdrawn his remaining garrisons, or they would have already pulled back to Pontus. As we have already noted (see Chapter Three), Deiotarus of Galatia had defeated the main Pontic army of the region the year previously.

We must assume that Galatia and Cappadocia fell easily back under Roman control, allowing Lucullus to plan his invasion of Pontus. As stated, we do not know the timescale for how long this reconquest took, but we can suppose that it cannot have taken more than a few months, meaning that Lucullus was poised to invade Pontus by the late spring or early summer of 72 BC.

However, the reconquest of Bithynia held one major stumbling block, namely the Pontic garrison of Heracleia on the Black Sea coast (see Map 2). The city had recently had a Pontic garrison installed by Mithridates to cover his retreat, and the Proconsul M. Aurelius Cotta had been tasked with its recapture. On the face of it, this should have been a relatively simple task, given that the garrison of just 3,000 were now stranded in a Roman-dominated Bithynia, with Rome in naval control of the southern Black Sea, and with the city having been captured by a ruse, aided by some elements in the city. Unsurprisingly, given that it was his home city, Memnon produced a detailed account of the Roman siege.[34]

With an initial assault having failed, Cotta laid the city under siege, and was soon joined by Triarius to complete a naval blockade. From Memnon's description, however, the Pontic garrison was supported by a sizeable number of Heracleians, who seem to have been split between pro-Roman and pro-Pontic parties, along with a large contingent of neutrals, we must assume. According to Memnon, the city held out for over two years, and was not captured until early 70 BC. Even then the fall of the city was accomplished by treachery, not by force of arms.

With starvation and disease breaking out – the garrison thereby losing over a third of its strength – the Pontic commander, Connacorex, struck a deal with Triarius, in which he would betray the city in return for the safe withdrawal of the surviving Pontic forces. According to Memnon, neither man trusted the Roman Proconsul Cotta, keeping him in the dark over the deal. With the gates opened by the retreating Pontic garrison, the Roman forces of Triarius sacked the city, with those of Cotta joining later in the day, the two groups nearly coming to blows over the plunder. Seemingly to make up for lost time, Cotta took charge of the looting of the city, after which he ordered large parts of it to be burnt, actions which brought censure when he eventually returned to Rome (see Chapter Seven). Thus the final reconquest of Bithynia would take several years to complete, though the bulk of the country was securely in Roman hands by mid-72 BC.

The Invasion of Pontus (72 BC)

Whilst the siege of Heracleia was being fought, Lucullus was advancing through Galatia, with an invasion of Pontus his intention. Again due to the paucity of our sources, we do not know exactly when he invaded, or where he invaded, but he seems to have pushed through into Pontus from Galatia, heading north to the rich coastal cities, the heart of the Pontic kingdom.

Plutarch purports to outline Lucullus' strategy, which was to reduce Mithridates' powerbase in Pontus by capturing all the rich cities and eventually forcing him into battle. However, Mithridates, having seen an army of several hundred thousand destroyed the previous year, did not immediately have the resources to face Lucullus in open battle. He needed time to assemble a fresh army from his Black Sea Empire, time which it seems Lucullus was more than willing to give him. It would appear that Lucullus wanted Mithridates to gather a new force and then face him in battle, so that he could deliver the 'knockout' blow, defeat the king and either capture or kill him.

Consequently, the campaigns for the rest of the year were ones of submission, with no major clashes taking place. Plutarch reports that Lucullus' army complained that he was allowing too many cities to surrender rather than take them by storm:

> 'But when Lucullus merely wasted and ravaged the country with cavalry incursions, which penetrated the Themiscyra and the plains of the river Thermodon, his soldiers found fault with him because he brought all the cities over to him by peaceable measures; he had not taken a single one by storm, they said, nor given them a chance to enrich themselves by plunder.'[35]

Nevertheless, the army got their wish and several of the coastal cities were placed under siege, notably Amisus and Themiscyra (see Map 7), which as with Heracleia proved to be difficult cities to take:

> 'Lucullus moved to the front with the prestige of victory, subduing everything in his path and subsisting on the country. Lucullus laid siege to Amisus and also to Eupatoria, which Mithridates had built alongside of Amisus and named after himself and where he had fixed the royal residence.
> 'With another army Lucullus besieged Themiscyra, which is named after one of the Amazons and is situated on the river Thermodon. The besiegers of this place brought up towers, built mounds, and dug tunnels so large that great subterranean battles could be fought in them. The inhabitants cut openings into these tunnels from above and thrust bears and other wild animals and swarms of bees into them against the workers.'[36]

Mithridates himself had originally landed at Amisus after his flight from Nicomedia, but had shifted his base of operation to the city of Cabira in the interior of Pontus (see Map 2), where he set about creating a new army to fight off the Roman invasion. Appian provides us with a flavour of his preparations:

> '... he sent appeals to his son in law, Tigranes the Armenian, and his son, Machares, the ruler of the Cimerian Bosphorus, that they should hasten to his assistance. He ordered Diocles to take a large quantity of gold and other presents to the neighbouring Scythians, but Diocles took the gold and the presents and deserted to Lucullus.'[37]

Mithridates, now clearly no longer in the ascendency, was suffering from an unwillingness of others to become involved in facing Rome. Tigranes, the ruler of the Armenian Empire – then the region's greatest superpower – was clearly not willing to get drawn into a war with Rome (ironically, as it turned out). Though he expressed continued friendship, Armenian armies were not forthcoming. As we have seen, others openly defected to the Roman cause.

Mithridates spent the remainder of 72 BC creating a new army in Pontus, and by winter had amassed 40,000 infantry and 4,000 cavalry, a far cry from the size of his 'grand army' of 74–73 BC. Lucullus and Mithridates both seemed happy to prepare for a major battle in the following spring.

The Second Front – The Thracian War of M. Lucullus (72–71 BC)

The Romans had been fighting a war in Thrace since 80 BC, yet it was this year that the two wars combined. As detailed earlier (see Chapter Two), the Roman campaign to defend Macedonia from the Thracian tribes had expanded into a war of aggression, with Roman armies crossing into Thrace to face the tribes in their homelands, most notably the Dardani. The first commander was Cn. Cornelius Dolabella (Consul in 81 BC), who fought well enough to earn a Triumph between 80 and 78 BC, but no details are recorded. He was succeeded by Ap. Claudius Pulcher (Consul in 79 BC), who campaigned in 77 and 76 BC, drove the tribes back from Macedonia and then pushed on into Thrace. His replacement was C. Scribonius Curio (Consul in 76 BC), who, between 75 and 73 BC, took Roman armies as far as the Danube for the first time, and even beyond into Dacia (see Chapter Two).

In 72 BC, a new commander took his place, none other than the Proconsul M. Terentius Varro Lucullus, L. Lucullus' younger brother (having been adopted into a different Roman Senatorial family). Thus, 72 BC saw one Lucullus commanding a force in Asia and the other doing so in Thrace. Whilst Dolabella and Claudius had focused on campaigning in the western parts of Thrace, near to the Macedonian/Illyrian border, Curio had pushed further north, towards the Danube and Dacia. M. Lucullus shifted the campaign to the east of Thrace and pushed towards the Black Sea, the heart of the Pontic Empire.

As is to be expected from a lesser campaign in the 70s BC, we have few details preserved in our surviving sources. The fullest account comes from Eutropius (based on Livy), but we also hear of it from Ammianus:

'The other Lucullus, who had the management of affairs in Macedonia, was the first of the Romans that made war upon the Bessi, defeating them in a great battle on Mount Haemus; he reduced the town of

Uscudama, which the Bessi inhabited, on the same day in which he attacked it; he also took Cabyle, and penetrated as far as the river Danube. He then besieged several cities lying above Pontus, where he destroyed Apollonia, Calatis, Parthenopolis, Tomi, Histros, and Burziaone, and, putting an end to the war, returned to Rome.'[38]

'After these came General Lucullus, who was the first of all to encounter the savage tribe of the Bessi and in the same onslaught overcame the Haemimontani in spite of their stout resistance. While he threatened that region, all parts of Thrace passed under the sway of our forefathers, and in this way, after dangerous campaigns, six provinces were won for the Republic.'[39]

It seems that the Senate had determined to subdue all the neighbouring tribes of Thrace, from the Dardani and Scordisci in the west to the Bessi, who were the principal enemies that Lucullus fought. The surviving sources state this was the first time that the Romans had fought the Bessi, so this can hardly have been a campaign to retaliate against invading tribes, as the war had started out being. Principally, the campaign was to assert Roman dominance over the whole region – without actually taking any territory – and thus safeguard Macedonia and Greece.

As later events showed, Mithridates had in his army a large contingent of Thracians, who defected to fight for the Romans.[40] Though the sources do not state to which tribes these Thracians belonged, it would be tempting to speculate that Mithridates would have recruited from those nearest the Black Sea, possibly even the Bessi, and thus Lucullus' thrust into eastern Thrace had the secondary aim of dissuading the Thracian tribes from supplying mercenary forces to the Pontic Empire.

Eutropius states that Lucullus pushed on and reached the western Black Sea coast, where he attacked and sacked the Greek colony cities of Apollonia, Calatis, Parthenopolis, Tomi, Histros and Burziaon.[41] Strabo records that Apollonia was sacked and its most precious artwork, a huge statue of Apollo, was looted and taken to Rome:

'The greater part of Apollonia was founded on a certain isle, where there is a temple of Apollo, from which Marcus Lucullus carried off the colossal statue of Apollo, a work of Calamis, which he set up in the Capitolium.'[42]

These attacks on the Greek cities of the Black Sea made little strategic sense in terms of defending Macedonia from Thracian tribes. However, the Black Sea coastline was part of the Pontic Empire – although what degree of control

Mithridates had over them is unclear – so this second part of Lucullus' campaign, which lasted from late 72 into 71 BC, was clearly the opening up of a second front, with M. Lucullus attacking the Pontic Empire in the Black Sea whilst his brother attacked Pontus proper.

Given the number of cities sacked, this would not only have hurt the economy of the Pontic Empire, but would have been a massive psychological blow, with a Roman army emerging from the wilderness of Thracian Europe and destroying poorly defended cities. Furthermore, it showed the inhabitants of the Pontic Empire on the Black Sea that Mithridates could not defend them; they were vulnerable to Roman power and would pay for their ruler's war with Rome.

Having reached the western coast of the Black Sea, and presumably now being able to link up with L. Lucullus' Roman fleets, it may have been M. Lucullus' plan to continue to march around the coastline to the Crimean heartland of the northern Pontic Empire. If so, he was only prevented from doing so by the escalation of a crisis in Italy, the slave revolt of the Thracian Spartacus, which caused the Senate to recall M. Lucullus in 71 BC.

Had this not interrupted them, Roman forces would have been able to attack the heartland of the Pontic Empire and destroy Mithridates' overseas powerbase, thereby possibly ending the Romano-Pontic War far earlier than it did. Nevertheless, Rome had shown that Pontus' previously untouchable Black Sea Empire was now vulnerable, which may have contributed to the region's decision to break away from Mithridates (see Chapter Five).

Events in Rome and Beyond (72 BC)

Away from the wars of the East – both in Asia Minor and Thrace – Roman military efforts were meeting with mixed success. In the Mediterranean, M. Antonius, despite having been invested with a superior command, was continuing his ineffective campaigns against the pirate forces based on Crete.

Further to the west, the civil war in Spain had ended after nearly a decade. Although the Senatorial forces of Pompeius and Metellus Pius had been making steady progress against Sertorius, the war was only brought to a conclusion by an act of treachery. As was an all-too-common occurrence during the First Civil War, Sertorius was murdered by a subordinate, in this case M. Perperna, an exiled commander from the army of Lepidus.

The murder of Sertorius demoralized the remnants of his Romano-Spanish forces, and Perperna proved to be far less of an able commander; before the year was out, he had been defeated, captured, and murdered by Pompeius, ending the war in Spain.[43] Though Pompeius had to remain in Spain over the winter to reassert full Roman control over the two Spanish provinces, this now left one of Rome's most ambitious, restless and ruthless commanders seeking further campaigns and glory.

However, by the winter of 72 BC, all Rome's wars had faded into the background in terms of the Senate's attention to a military crisis on their very doorstep: the Slave War in Italy. What had started as an escape by a group of gladiators from a training school in Capua had grown into a full-blown revolt, fuelled by the devastation and dispossession caused by the First Civil War. A number of Roman commanders had been sent against what they assumed was a 'rag tag' collection of slaves, only to be defeated by a well-drilled force. Every defeat brought more recruits to the slave army.

This culminated in the defeat of the two Consuls of 72 BC, L. Gellius Publicola and Cn. Cornelius Lentulus Clodianus. Whilst Pompeius is often considered to be the most ruthless and ambitious Roman commander of this period, there was another rival for that title, a man who had forged an identical path in the First Civil War, having raised a private army and thrown in his lot with Sulla: M. Licinius Crassus. Crassus' military career had culminated in the Battle of the Colline Gate in 82 BC, where his victory on the right wing had given Sulla not just victory, but control of Italy. At that point his career had diverged from that of Pompeius; whilst Pompeius continued to fight in the civil war campaigns in Sicily, Africa, Italy and Spain, Crassus concentrated on building a powerbase in Rome, amassing considerable wealth and political power. This process culminated in the Senate turning to him, even though he had only held a Praetorship, to save the Republic and command the armies against Spartacus.[44]

The War in Pontus (71 BC)

Far away from events in Italy, Lucullus and Mithridates were preparing for a showdown in Pontus. If anything, the Senate's attention being focused on the chaos in Italy was of benefit to Lucullus, as it allowed him to continue as commander of the Romano-Pontic War without interruption. However, Lucullus cannot have been happy that his brother had been recalled from the Black Sea coast as a consequence, nor that Pompeius had concluded his campaigns in Spain. Lucullus had clearly been aware that Mithridates was raising a fresh army in Pontus, but far from disrupting him, Lucullus seemed happy to allow the king time to prepare. It is clear that Lucullus considered it far better to bring Mithridates to battle, where he could defeat and capture or kill him, than allow him to flee Pontus and have to chase him across the Black Sea or further into the Middle East.

Receiving reports that Mithridates had assembled his army at Cabira, Lucullus left a subordinate, L. Licinius Murena, in charge of the siege of

Amisus and marched the bulk of the Roman army eastwards, over the mountains that separated the coast from Cabira. What followed was not the major set-piece battle that either side had probably expected, but a series of minor clashes, which together proved to be decisive. Mithridates had also been aware of Lucullus' advance and made plans to harry him as he crossed the mountains, but these plans backfired:

> 'When spring came Lucullus marched over the mountains against Mithridates, who had stationed advanced posts to hinder his approach, and to start signal fires whenever anything important should happen. He appointed a member of the royal family, named Phoenix, commander of this advance guard. When Lucullus drew near, Phoenix gave the fire signal to Mithridates and then deserted to Lucullus with his forces.'[45]

The First Battle of Cabira (71 BC)

Having crossed the mountains unopposed, Lucullus marched his army towards Cabira, where Mithridates had drawn his army up to face him. We are told that the Pontic army was 40,000–50,000 strong (40,000 infantry and either 4,000[46] or 8,000[47] cavalry), but we do not know the size of the Roman army. We only have brief details from Plutarch and Appian of the truncated battle that ensued:

> 'Crossing the River Lycus and advancing into the plain, he [Mithridates] offered the Romans battle. A cavalry fight ensued, and the Romans took to flight. Pomponius, a man of some note, having been wounded, was taken prisoner, and led into the presence of Mithridates, suffering greatly from his wounds. When the king asked him if he would become his friend provided he spared his life, Pomponius answered: "Yes, indeed, if you come to terms with the Romans; otherwise I must remain your enemy." Mithridates was struck with admiration for him and did him no harm.'[48]

> 'Lucullus now passed over the mountains without difficulty and came down to Cabira but was beaten by Mithridates in a cavalry engagement and retreated again to the mountain. Pomponius, his master of horse, was wounded and taken prisoner and brought to the presence of Mithridates. The king asked him what favour Pomponius could render him for sparing his life. Pomponius replied, "A great one if you make peace with Lucullus, but if you continue his enemy, I will not even consider your question."'[49]

Unfortunately, the surviving ancient sources chose to focus on the virtue of Pomponius in defeat rather than the details of how the reverse came about. Although the Romans had been beaten, it is clear that the two main armies were never brought to bear against one another. From what we are told, it was only the opposing cavalry forces that met in battle, with the Roman horsemen utterly defeated and their commander captured. We must assume that the Roman cavalry were some distance ahead of the bulk of Lucullus' infantry, as he had time to turn and retreat into the mountains when he learned of the setback.

The clash ended with Mithridates retaining control of the plain and the Roman army in the foothills. We are told that Mithridates continued to offer battle, but Lucullus wisely refused.[50] Temporarily, the momentum of the war had turned, Mithridates again having the upper hand. Shortly afterwards, however, Lucullus was able to move his army from the mountains without having to face Mithridates' cavalry:

'Lucullus hesitated about going down directly to the plain since the enemy was so much superior in horse, nor could he discover any way around, but he found a hunter in a cave who was familiar with the mountain paths. With him for a guide he made a circuitous descent by rugged paths over Mithridates' head. He avoided the plain on account of the cavalry and came down and chose a place for his camp where he had a mountain stream on his front. As he was short of supplies, he sent to Cappadocia for corn, and in the meantime had frequent skirmishes with the enemy.'[51]

Though Lucullus had been able to extricate his army from the mountains, he feared facing Mithridates on the plain due to his lack of cavalry. He also found himself with supply issues, being on the wrong side of the mountains. What ensued seems to have been a stalemate, with Lucullus unwilling to commit to a full-scale battle and his position being strong enough that Mithridates could not attack without suffering heavy losses. In the days that followed, it seems there were a number of clashes between the sides:

'[The Romans] in the meantime had frequent skirmishes with the enemy. Once when the royal forces were put to flight, Mithridates came running to them from his camp and, with reproachful words, rallied them to such good purpose that the Romans became terrified in turn and fled up the mountain side with such swiftness that they did not know for a long time that the hostile force had desisted from the pursuit, but each one thought that the fleeing comrade behind him was an enemy, so great was the panic that had overtaken them. Mithridates sent bulletins everywhere announcing this victory.'[52]

'Now neither commander had any intention of hazarding an engagement at once. But we are told that while some of the king's men were chasing a stag, the Romans cut them off and confronted them, whereupon a skirmish followed, with fresh accessions continually to either side. At last, the king's men were victorious. Then the Romans in their camp, beholding the flight of their comrades, were in distress, and ran in throngs to Lucullus, begging him to lead them, and demanding the signal for battle. But he, wishing them to learn how important, in a dangerous struggle with the enemy, the visible presence of a prudent general is, bade them keep quiet. Then he went down into the plain by himself, and confronting the foremost of the fugitives, bade them stop, and turn back with him. They obeyed, and the rest also wheeled about and formed in battle array, and in a short time routed the enemy and drove them to their camp.'[53]

'After they had joined up with the others, at first the two sides tested each other in skirmishes almost every day, and then there were two cavalry battles, in the first of which the Romans were victorious, and in the second the men of Pontus won.'[54]

Despite these clashes, neither side committed to a full-scale battle. To force Lucullus' hand, Mithridates tried to cut him off from his supply lines from Cappadocia, engaging in a policy of harrying the Roman supply trains. Whilst this was a sound tactic, it led to two further clashes between Pontic and Roman forces, the latter of which was to prove surprisingly decisive.

The Second Battle of Cabira (71 BC)
We only have Plutarch as a source for the second battle between Lucullus and Mithridates:

'After this, Sornatius was sent with ten cohorts to get supplies of grain. Being pursued by Menander, one of the generals of Mithridates, he faced about, joined battle, and routed the enemy with great slaughter.'[55]

As nothing else survives in our ancient sources, we have very little to analyse. Given that the Romans had refused to engage in a full-scale battle due to the superior numbers of the Pontic cavalry, it is surprising that the Romans were able to score such a decisive victory. All we can assume is that the Pontic force became overconfident, perhaps overstretching and allowing themselves to be ambushed by the Romans, who, under Sornatius, seem to have effectively taken their pursuers by surprise. Presumably the Pontic force contained a cavalry element, but once they were driven off then Sornatius was able to deploy the more effective Roman infantry in close-order combat. Whatever the case, it showed that if the Romans could level the terms, then they could defeat the Pontic army.

The Third Battle of Cabira (71 BC)

It seems that Mithridates and his generals did not learn the lessons of the previous skirmish, soon after attacking another Roman supply column:

'And again, when [M. Fabius] Hadrianus was sent out with a force to procure an abundance of grain for the soldiers, Mithridates did not look on idly, but dispatched Menemachus and Myron, at the head of a large body of cavalry and footmen. All these, it is said, except two, were cut to pieces by the Romans. Mithridates tried to conceal the extent of the disaster, pretending that it was a slight matter, and due to the inexperience of his generals. But when Hadrian marched pompously past his camp, convoying many waggons laden with grain and booty, a great despair fell upon the king, and confusion and helpless fear upon his soldiers.'[56]

'It was his [Mithridates'] great object to cut off Lucullus' supplies, which were drawn from Cappadocia alone, but when his cavalry came upon the advance guard of the convoy in a narrow defile, they did not wait till their enemies had reached the open country. Consequently their horses were useless in the narrow space, where the Romans hastily put themselves in line of battle across the road. Aided, as foot-soldiers would naturally be, by the difficulties of the ground, they killed some of the king's troops, drove others over precipices, and scattered the rest in flight. A few of them arrived at their camp by night, and said that they were the only survivors, so that rumour magnified the calamity which was indeed sufficiently great.'[57]

It is only thanks to Appian that we understand the nature of this Roman victory. Once again, Mithridates sought to maximize his advantage and sent a cavalry-heavy force against the Romans. Yet the Roman commander, M. Fabius Hadrianus, perhaps learning from the previous battle, sought to utilize the terrain to negate the influence of the Pontic cavalry and thus fight an infantry battle, where the superiority of the Roman legionary once again proved decisive.

Though this was hardly the anticipated clash between the great Roman and Pontic armies, it proved to be the decisive battle of the Pontic campaign. Its effects were magnified far beyond the scale of the Pontic defeat and panic set into Mithridates' army, amplified, it seems, by indecision at the top:

'[Mithridates and his commanders] decided, therefore, to remain where they were no longer. But when the king's servants tried to send away their own baggage first, and to hinder the rest from going, the soldiers at once got angry, pushed and forced their way to the exits of the camp, and there plundered the baggage and slew the men in charge of it. There it was that Dorylaüs, the general, with nothing else about him but his purple robe, lost his life for that, and Hermaeus, the priest, was trampled to death at the gates.'[58]

'Mithridates heard of this affair before Lucullus did, and he expected that Lucullus would take advantage of so great a slaughter of his horsemen to attack him forthwith. Accordingly he fell into a panic and contemplated flight, and at once communicated his purpose to his friends in his tent. They did not wait for the signal to be given, but while it was still night each one sent his own baggage out of the camp, which made a great crush of pack animals around the gates.

'When the soldiers perceived the commotion, and saw what the baggage carriers were doing, they imagined every sort of absurdity. Filled with terror, mingled with anger that the signal had not been given to them also, they demolished and ran over their own fortification and scattered in every direction over the plain, helter-skelter, without orders from the commanding general or any other officer. When Mithridates heard the disorderly rush he dashed out of his tent among them and attempted to say something, but nobody would listen to him. He was caught in the crowd and knocked from his horse but remounted and was borne to the mountains with a few followers.'[59]

'As the war dragged on, Lucullus sent some men to Cappadocia to fetch supplies, and when Taxiles and Diophantus heard of this, they sent off a force of 4,000 infantry and 2,000 cavalry to attack and plunder the men who were bringing back the supplies. But when the two forces clashed, the Romans had the upper hand, and after Lucullus sent reinforcements to his side, it turned into a complete rout of the barbarians. In their pursuit of the fleeing barbarians the Roman army reached the camp of Diophantus and Taxiles and proceeded to mount a fierce assault on them. The Pontic army withstood the attack for a while, but then they all gave way, with their generals being the first to turn to flight. The generals went to Mithridates as the messengers of their own defeat; and a large number of the barbarians were killed.'[60]

Once again, we see a mixture of patience and luck being responsible for Lucullus' success in this campaign; wise enough to hold off providing Mithridates with a set-piece battle where the king could deploy his superior numbers of cavalry, and then wearing him down. Yet it was a very fine line between success and ignominious failure. Lucullus' decision to allow Mithridates the chance to build a fresh army, followed by a rash attack across the mountains, nearly resulted in the destruction of the Roman army.

Firstly, he lost his cavalry contingent in the opening clashes of the campaign and nearly found himself stranded in the mountains. He was then nearly starved into submission, with insufficient supplies and a highly vulnerable supply chain. It was only due to the superior skills of his two legates, Sornatius and Fabius Hadrianus, that the Romans were able to inflict defeats on the attacking Pontic forces and cause the panic that led to the collapse of Mithridates' army. Lucullus was clearly a lucky general.

If we are surprised at the speed with which the Pontic army collapse, we must remember that it was a hastily assembled one, composed of many peoples from the wider Pontic Empire and its allies. The army lacked both cohesion and experience, with the best of Mithridates' forces falling at the siege of Cyzicus in 73 BC. The Romans had scored two, apparently bloody, morale-boosting victories and shown that in a straight infantry clash the Pontic army was no match. All that held the Pontic army together was loyalty to its general, the near-mythical Mithridates, and when his resolve looked to be wavering, various sections of the army lost the only thing that held them together: belief in their leader.

As detailed in Plutarch and Appian, the Pontic army collapsed into a rout, aided by Lucullus taking advantage of this stroke of good fortune and sending the remnants of his cavalry to attack the fleeing army. Eutropius provides the following assessment of Pontic casualties (presumably taken from Livy):

> 'In a second battle, near the city [of] Cabira, where Mithridates had assembled a vast army from all parts of his kingdom, thirty thousand of the king's chosen troops were cut in pieces by five thousand of the Romans, and Mithridates was put to flight and his camp plundered.'[61]

However, once again, this decisive victory in battle could not be translated into a victory in the wider war as the main prize eluded Lucullus, Mithridates being able to evade pursuit and flee eastwards, first to Comona, before leaving

Pontus behind him altogether. Mithridates, along with 2,000 cavalry, sought refuge with his son-in-law, the Emperor Tigranes II (the Great), in the hitherto neutral Armenian Empire.

Summary

So the year ended with a near-complete Roman victory: Bithynia had been recovered (apart from Heracleia), Mithridates had again been defeated, and the heartland of his empire – the Kingdom of Pontus – had been captured (all but a handful of cities). In every respect bar one, Lucullus had fulfilled his objectives when he took command of the war. The one outstanding issue was that of Mithridates himself, who had again escaped capture. This presented Lucullus with both a problem and an opportunity.

The king had never been reconciled to Roman rule in Asia Minor and would always remain a threat, in both symbolic and practical terms. For the last twenty years, he had presented himself as an opponent of Roman expansion in the East, someone who always escaped defeat on the battlefield to remain a thorn in Rome's side. His continued freedom elevated him to a 'quasi-mythical' figurehead of defiance to Rome. In practical terms, although he had lost the heartland of his empire, he still possessed resources across the Black Sea, particularly in the Crimea, from which he could draw a fresh army in an attempt to recapture his kingdom. There was also the danger that he could raise fresh forces from the other powers of the Near and Middle East, namely the Armenian and Parthian Empires.

Yet the failure to capture the king himself, though irksome for Rome as a whole, presented Lucullus with a great opportunity. Despite having come close to losing the Pontic campaign in 71 BC, Lucullus now stood as the victor, the restorer of Roman rule in Asia Minor, at the head of an experienced Roman army. Had Mithridates been captured, then the war would indeed be over, and Lucullus would have to return to Rome – admittedly to a hero's welcome – thereby ending his greatest military command and foreshadowing his retirement. Mithridates' continued freedom allowed Lucullus the opportunity to extend the war, and thus his command and opportunity for even greater glory.

Part III

Escalation – The Armenian & Pontic Wars (70–66 BC)

Chapter 5

A New Aggression: Lucullus and the Romano-Armenian War (70–69 BC)

Events at Rome – The End of the First Civil War (71 BC)

Whilst Lucullus had defeated Mithridates and all but conquered Pontus, the focus of the Senate and People of Rome was far nearer home. During 71 BC, what seemed at the time to be an existential threat to the Republic, posed by the slave army of Spartacus, was ended in comprehensive fashion by the Proconsul M. Licinius Crassus. This again highlighted the military talent of Crassus which he had shown in the civil war campaigns. His victory coincided with the triumphant return of Cn. Pompeius Magnus from his success in the civil war in Spain. That victory, together with Lucullus' defeat of M. Marius, meant that there was a brief lull in the ongoing civil war. But this interlude looked likely to be only a short one, with two victorious Roman armies now stationed in Italy (in defiance of Sulla's blueprint for a stable Republic), commanded by two of Sulla's most ambitious and unscrupulous lieutenants. Having endured twenty years of Roman generals and their armies marching on Rome itself, the Senate and People must have been bracing themselves for what came next.

In the short term, however, both were to be pleasantly surprised, though many came to regret the longer-term implications. Pompeius and Crassus, both having seen the bloodshed of the preceding twenty years and having both lost fathers – and in Crassus' case an elder brother – to the fighting in 87 BC,[1] realized that by combining their forces they could seize effective control of the Republic, and thus was born the Duumvirate. With two Roman armies camped outside the city, along with both men's political connections – not to mention money and popularity with the People – the two ran as a joint ticket for the Consulships of 70 BC on a programme of political reform. The result was inevitable, and the Duumvirate of Pompeius and Crassus prepared to take control of Rome and the Republic.

Away from Rome's internal conflict, the two other major campaigns in the Eastern Republic also drew to a conclusion in 71 BC. In Macedonia and Thrace, Lucullus' brother, M. Terentius Varro Lucullus, had to cut short his campaign against the Thracian tribes and return to Italy when he was recalled to assist the confrontation with Spartacus, though in the end his forces were not needed. This gave him the opportunity to celebrate a Triumph for his success against the Bessi. Despite his recall, his campaigns had been successful, and the neighbouring tribes pacified – at least in the short term – meaning that no fresh commander was sent to continue the war.

Rome was far less successful in the campaign against the pirates of the Eastern Mediterranean, with M. Antonius badly defeated off Crete and forced to come to terms. Perhaps fortunately for Antonius, an ignominious and disgraced return to Rome was averted when he died in the region, presumably of natural causes. This defeat earned him the ironic title of Creticus, meaning 'conqueror of Crete'. Aside from his own personal failure, despite the Senate creating an extraordinary command in terms of its remit and powers, the pirate problem not only remained but, if anything, had been made worse by their recent success. Another Roman general would be required to take up the challenge.

The Fall of Pontus (71/70 BC)

With the collapse of the remaining Pontic army and the flight of King Mithridates, Lucullus was able to spend the rest of 71 BC reducing the remaining northern Pontic cities, in particular ending the sieges of Cabira, Amisus and Sinope:

'Then Lucullus advanced to Cabira with his entire army and surrounded the city; he gained control of the walls after the barbarians agreed to surrender under a truce. From there he went to Amisus and tried to persuade the inhabitants to come to terms with the Romans, but as they did not listen to him, he moved away and began to besiege Eupatoria. There he pretended to conduct the siege negligently, in order that he might lull the enemy into the same attitude of negligence, and then achieve his object by mounting a sudden attack. The result was as he expected, and he captured the city by this stratagem. Lucullus suddenly ordered his soldiers to bring up ladders, when the defenders were paying little attention because they expected nothing of the sort, and he sent the soldiers up the ladders to the top of the walls. In this way Eupatoria was captured, and it was immediately destroyed. Shortly afterwards Amisus was captured in a similar fashion, the enemy mounted its walls with ladders. Many of the citizens of Amisus were slaughtered immediately, but then Lucullus put an end to the killing. He restored the city and its territory to the remaining citizens and treated them considerately.'[2]

Memnon also presents a detailed account of the fall of the coastal city of Sinope,[3] which was eventually taken in a bloody siege after the treachery of its Pontic commander. However, during the siege the defenders were able to score a victory at sea over a small Roman naval force:

'Meanwhile Censorinus, the Roman admiral in command of 15 triremes which were bringing corn from the Bosporus to the Roman army, halted near Sinope. Cleochares, Seleucus and their associates sailed out against him with the triremes at Sinope. In the ensuing naval battle, under the command of Cleochares, they defeated the Italians and seized the transport ships for their own use.'[4]

The Pontic victory, however, was short-lived as the city fell to Lucullus, with great slaughter. This was soon followed by the capture of the city of Amaseia, leaving Lucullus as master of Pontus. His fellow Proconsul Aurelius Cotta and his legate Valerius Triarius were also finally able to capture Heracleia (as detailed in Chapter Four). The Pontic commander Connacorex, who had betrayed the city, attempted to continue his resistance by capturing the cities of Tius and Amastris, but these were soon recaptured by Triarius without a fight, though Connacorex once again was able to sail away. In early 70 BC, Aurelius Cotta set off for Rome, along with his cargo of booty seized from Heracleia:

'Cotta, after acting as described above, sent the infantry and cavalry to Lucullus, dismissed the allies to their homelands, and set off home with the fleet. Some of the ships which were carrying the spoils from Heracleia were sunk by their weight not far from the city, and others were forced into the shallows by a northerly wind, so that much of their cargo was lost.'[5]

Having subdued northern Pontus, Lucullus turned his attention to the southern part of the kingdom, also known as Lesser Armenia, though we only have brief details via Plutarch and Eutropius:

'After subduing the Chaldaeans and the Tibareni, he occupied Lesser Armenia, reducing its fortresses and cities.'[6]
'Armenia Minor, also, of which he had taken possession, was wrested from him.'[7]

Consequently, by early 70 BC, the whole of Pontus had fallen to Rome, which only left Pontus' overseas empire, centred on the Bosphoran Kingdom in the

Crimea. Though the territory lay on the other side of the Black Sea, it was a rich kingdom, and as such a potential haven for Mithridates. However, a military solution no longer became necessary when the regent of the kingdom, one of Mithridates' own sons, Machares, sent emissaries to Lucullus offering to betray his father. A deal was soon agreed, and Machares and the overseas Pontic Empire changed sides, becoming an ally of Rome, a deal sealed with a present of a gold crown to Lucullus.

Not only had Pontus been overrun, but the appearance of a Roman army on the shores of the Black Sea in early 71 BC, and the destruction of the Greek cities on the western coast by Lucullus' brother, would have further influenced the Bosphoran Kingdom's decision to split from the Pontic Empire and become a client state of Rome. This defection was soon followed by suppliers of grain from one of the ancient world's most productive food-producing regions.

Having conquered Pontus and disremembered its empire, Lucullus returned to the Roman province of Asia, which he set about reorganizing, including its finances, tackling the ever-present issue of debt. In doing so he set himself against the interests of the equestrian cartels which held the contract to collect the Asian taxes, who objected to his reforms. Plutarch tells us:

'In the first place, he ordered that the monthly rate of interest should be reckoned at one per cent, and no more; in the second place, he cut off all interest that exceeded the principal; third, and most important of all, he ordained that the lender should receive not more than the fourth part of his debtor's income, and any lender who added interest to principal was deprived of the whole.'[8]

The equestrian cartels, who stood to lose out in these reforms, tried to bring charges against Lucullus in Rome, via unnamed Tribunes, an attempt which seemingly failed due to Lucullus' political base in Rome and his new status as the victor over Mithridates. Yet Lucullus' reform programme in Asia was merely a distraction from the war's one remaining burning question: what to do about Mithridates?

Mithridates and the Armenian Question (70 BC)

As we have seen, having been defeated at Cabira, Mithridates fled eastwards into the Armenian Empire, ruled by his son-in-law, Tigranes II (the Great). This presented both Lucullus and Tigranes with a major diplomatic headache. Though Mithridates loomed large in the Roman psyche – both at the time and ever since – he did not command the greatest superpower in the Near or Middle East at the time. That position fell to Tigranes.

Tigranes had used the two previous decades to transform the small Hellenistic state of Armenia into the pre-eminent power of the Near East, with an empire stretching from the Caspian to the Mediterranean (see Map 3). During this process, he annexed the second of the formerly 'great' Hellenistic empires, that of the Seleucids, and defeated his former overlords the Parthian Empire. With the Seleucids annexed and the Parthians humbled, only two other empires lay in his path: to the south lay the rich but weak Ptolemaic Empire of Egypt (a Roman client), whilst to the west was Rome.

In geopolitical terms, Mithridates was a useful ally of Tigranes, and his Pontic Empire an effective buffer client state protecting the Armenian Empire's western flank from the ever-expanding empire of Rome. In Tigranes' eyes, the Third Romano-Pontic War would keep Rome busy whilst he consolidated his rule in the Near East. Our lack of surviving sources, especially native ones, does not allow us to view the war through Tigranes' eyes, nor whether he thought of using the conflict to make a move on the Roman allied state of Egypt, the pre-eminent prize of the Near East.

What does survive (albeit in a much later source) is a Roman view of the Armenian Empire, with a speech reported by Plutarch as coming from the mouth of Lucullus himself. Whilst we must exercise extreme caution with accurately reported speeches of this nature found in our surviving sources, it does seem to encapsulate the Roman view at the time, especially given the absence of Armenia as a superpower by Plutarch's time:

'And it is only a few days' journey from Cabira into Armenia and over Armenia there sits enthroned Tigranes, King of Kings, with forces which enable him to cut the Parthians off from Asia, transplant Greek cities into Media, sway Syria and Palestine, put to death the successors of Seleucus, and carry off their wives and daughters into captivity.

'This king is a kinsman of Mithridates, his son-in-law. He will not be content to receive him as a suppliant but will make war against us. If we strive, therefore, to eject Mithridates from his kingdom, we shall run the risk of drawing Tigranes down upon us. He has long wanted an excuse for coming against us and could not get a better one than that of being compelled to aid a man who is his kinsman and a king. Why, then, should we bring this to pass and teach Mithridates, when he does not know it, with what allies he must carry on war against us? Why help to drive him, against his wish and as a last resource, into the arms of Tigranes, instead of giving him time to equip himself from his own resources and get fresh courage? Then we shall fight with Colchians and Tibareni and Cappadocians, whom we have often overcome, rather than with Medes and Armenians.'[9]

On the face of it, this is an exhortation by Lucullus not to allow Mithridates to escape Pontus and provide the Armenian Emperor with an excuse to intervene. On the other hand, the Romans clearly viewed the Armenian Empire as a threat and we can see the common Roman view that an aggressive neighbouring power must be readying themselves to attack them, an opinion held since at least the time of the Hellenistic King Pyrrhus, if not Alexander the Great himself.[10]

As stated before, nothing survives in our sources which details the Roman relationship with the new Armenian Empire, which had clear overlapping interests not only in Cilicia, but with the Roman clients of Cappadocia, Judea and Egypt. In the short term, however, if the Romans – and Lucullus in particular – viewed the Armenian Empire as a threat, both to their overlordship of Asia Minor and the prize of Ptolemaic Egypt, then here was an opportunity to do something about it.

Lucullus' Dilemma – Escalation or Negotiation

For Lucullus, such a move offered diplomatic, political and military difficulties. In diplomatic terms, Rome was not at war with Armenia, and Tigranes had not committed any offensive acts against Rome and was keeping Mithridates at arm's length. This fed into the political arena at Rome, as it stretched to breaking point Lucullus' remit when being awarded his command to defeat Mithridates. By all counts bar one, the war was over: Mithridates had been defeated, Bithynia recovered, Pontus conquered and the Black Sea Pontic Empire was now an ally. Yet Mithridates had not been captured or killed, and whilst he lived, he was a clear danger to Rome. Furthermore, at the back of Lucullus' mind must have been the fact that the two Consuls in Rome were Pompeius and Crassus, Rome's two most ruthless and opportunistic politicians, and neither were friends of his.

Militarily, Lucullus had been outnumbered by Mithridates but had prevailed when the far larger Pontic army had been destroyed at the siege of Cyzicus. Although Lucullus had defeated the Pontic king at the Battles of Cabira, even that had been a close-run thing and his forces were now depleted. An attack on Pontus was one thing, but an assault on the Armenian Empire – the dominant power of the region – was another matter altogether.

Thus, in the short term, Lucullus attempted to use the diplomatic route and sent various emissaries to the Armenian court seeking to have Mithridates returned. Plutarch details at some length the diplomatic mission, being led Lucullus' brother-in-law, Ap. Claudius Pulcher.[11] At the time, Tigranes was actually campaigning in Phoenicia, but agreed to accept the Roman embassy, attempting to slow them down and dazzle them with his might. When the two men finally did meet, Pulcher delivered Lucullus' ultimatum in blunt fashion, and got an equally direct response:

> 'Appius, however, was not frightened or astonished at all this pomp and show, but as soon as he obtained an audience, told the king plainly that he was come to take back Mithridates, as an ornament due to the triumph of Lucullus, or else to declare war against Tigranes.'[12]
>
> 'However, he [Tigranes] replied to Appius that he would not surrender Mithridates, and that if the Romans began war, he would defend himself.'[13]

Matters had not been helped by the usual Roman 'talent' of not observing the diplomatic niceties, and in particular Lucullus' refusal to address Tigranes by his full title:

> 'He was vexed with Lucullus for addressing him in his letter with the title of King only, and not King of Kings, and accordingly, in his reply, would not address Lucullus as Imperator.'[14]

Although Appius' embassy consequently returned to Roman territory laden down with gifts, in terms of its main prize, it did so empty-handed, shifting the onus back onto Lucullus.

Tigranes' Dilemma – The Shadow of Rome

Yet for all his show of defiance, Tigranes too had been given an unwelcome headache by the arrival of his fugitive father-in-law and kept him at arm's length for as long as possible:

> 'Mithridates had stayed in the region of Armenia for a year and eight months, and still had not come into the presence of Tigranes. Then Tigranes felt obliged to grant him an audience; he met him in a splendid parade and gave him a royal welcome.'[15]

However, having received Rome's ultimatum, Tigranes was forced to determine what his strategic objectives were in this situation. Any hopes he harboured of Mithridates driving Rome out of Asia Minor had spectacularly failed; indeed the reverse had been achieved, actually drawing Rome further into Asia Minor. Pontus having fallen meant that Roman territory now bordered that of the Armenian Empire.

Tigranes only had three options. Firstly, he could acquiesce to Rome's demands and surrender his father-in-law. Yet for the new King of Kings to meekly submit to an order from a foreign (Western) power would be to damage his authority and undermine his newly won empire, even though it may avoid a military confrontation. The opposite solution was war with Rome. He had a vastly numerically superior force and would be fighting in or near his homeland, whereas the Romans would be fighting on the eastern fringes of their empire and with a smaller army.

But Tigranes' grip on his own newly forged empire was not yet secure, and the Parthians especially would be looking to regain the upper hand, not to mention rebels from within the recently conquered states. Furthermore, whilst he may take the upper hand in the early stages of the war, Tigranes fully understood that the Senate would send reinforcements to the East to ensure their martial reputation, especially now that the Roman Civil War had ended and ambitious commanders were available.

The third option was for the problem to disappear; in other words, Mithridates to absent himself from Armenian territory and thereby remove the object of the quarrel between the two powers. Were it not his father-in-law, then a simple assassination – or murder made to look like suicide – may well have been considered. A simpler solution would be to send Mithridates on his way, yet there were not many destinations to choose from. Egypt was a Roman ally, as was the Bosphoran Kingdom, whilst Parthia was hardly friend to Tigranes and would not want to get involved. Therefore, Tigranes chose to meet with Mithridates and try to resolve this situation, which was a distraction from his own agenda of empire-building.

Lucullus' Gamble – Escalation into the Unknown

Whilst both Tigranes and Lucullus had the same problem, it is clear that of the two men, only one had the luxury of time; namely Tigranes, who, as absolute monarch of the Armenian Empire, was under no pressure to bring the matter to a conclusion. The same could not be said of Lucullus, and in fact the opposite was true. His command in Asia was now entering its fifth year, and with military operations drawing to a conclusion in Pontus, even his allies would have to admit that the war was over.

Lucullus would have known that he faced pressure to return home, especially with Pompeius and Crassus having temporarily seized control of the Republic. Yet to return home now, without the prize of Mithridates, would severely tarnish his victory. No matter that he had defeated Mithridates at Cyzicus and Cabira, saved Asia, recovered Bithynia and conquered Pontus, he had been dispatched by the Senate and People to stop Mithridates himself.

Coming back without the man, dead or alive, would ultimately have been deemed a failure and tarnished the pinnacle of his career.

Given the lack of a solid chronological structure in our surviving sources, we don't have a timescale for Appius' embassy to Tigranes: when it was sent, how long it took or when it returned. We must assume that Lucullus dispatched it early in 70 BC, and that it would not have arrived back until late autumn. Lucullus cannot have been surprised by Tigranes' response; the new King of Kings was hardly a common provincial ruler likely to be cowed by the threat of Roman force. He would have understood that Tigranes would play for time and try to draw matters out. With winter approaching, and clearly expecting a recall to Rome, Lucullus faced his moment of destiny and took the only decision that a Roman aristocrat and general could take when faced with the choice of war or failure; he chose war, and spent the winter preparing for an assault on the Armenian Empire in early 69 BC.

This was a major escalation in the conflict, with Lucullus choosing to attack the leading superpower in the Middle East. It was a major gamble on Lucullus' part, both politically and militarily. In political terms, whilst there would have been few amongst the Roman elite who would not have relished the prospect of attacking Rome's new rival in the region – especially the two outgoing consuls, Pompeius and Crassus – but this was a serious extension of his remit and one that would have left him dangerously exposed. Whilst, as the commander appointed by the Senate and People to prosecute the war against Mithridates, he had the power to take the war in any direction he chose, but attacking a rival power which had committed no overtly aggressive act against Rome would leave him open to a charge of abusing his power. There had indeed been many Roman commanders charged with fighting 'illegal' wars.

Here we must try to analyse Lucullus' objectives in going to war with the Armenian Empire. In military terms, he was vastly outnumbered by the Armenian army, not to mention the fact that no Roman army had ever crossed so far east, stretching his supply lines to the extreme. The empire he faced was the pre-eminent military power in the Near East and was undertaking a fifteen-year campaign of expansion. We must assume that, at best, Lucullus was planning a punitive campaign against Tigranes to convince him to hand over Mithridates, backed up, if not by the actual numbers on the ground, then the threat of future Roman intervention. Here we can think back to Popillius Laenus in 168 BC, who faced down the Seleucid Emperor Antiochus IV with no army at all. Yet given the geography and the massive military disparity, this was a huge gamble that Lucullus was taking, jeopardizing both his political career and his very life.

Tigranes' Complacency – War by Proxy

Whilst Lucullus had clearly decided on war with the Armenian Empire, by contrast, Tigranes seems to have sought no outright confrontation, but rather chose to act through an agent and returned to his policy of backing Mithridates in fighting Rome. Though Mithridates had burnt through the resources of his own empire, Tigranes decided to rebuild his army and send him back to Pontus to continue the fight:

> 'After they had spent three days in secret talks, Tigranes entertained Mithridates at a magnificent banquet, and sent him back to Pontus with 10,000 cavalrymen.'[16]

This would not only resurrect the war in Pontus and keep the Romans tied down, but give Tigranes 'plausible deniability' when it came to answering the charge of harbouring an enemy of Rome. Mithridates would no longer be in Armenian territory. On the face of it, this was a sound plan by Tigranes, to fan the flames of the Romano-Pontic War, without taking overtly hostile action against Rome.

Yet the subtleties of this plan may well have suited the more Machiavellian world of Hellenistic politics. Tigranes clearly underestimated the ambition of Rome, and in particular Lucullus. Even if Lucullus had not already decided on war, having Mithridates reappear in Pontus with 10,000 fresh cavalry would clearly point towards Tigranes' involvement, now that Mithridates had no resources of his own to call on.

Tigranes failed to understand the danger he was in and chose to continue with what was a failing policy; backing Mithridates against Rome, whilst he continued to focus on strengthening his own empire. He clearly thought that by dismissing the Roman envoy and sending Mithridates back into Pontus, the matter was at an end, at least in the short term. It was to prove a dramatic miscalculation. We are told that when the Roman invasion came, Tigranes had returned to campaigning against the Seleucid claimant Cleopatra II Selene, so the Armenian Empire was left under-defended in terms of a clash with Rome, something which Lucullus must have banked upon.

The Roman Invasion of Armenia (69 BC)

We are not told whether Lucullus kept abreast of Tigranes' movements in the winter of 70/69 BC, but given the gamble he was taking, it is more than likely that he was, so we can assume that Lucullus knew Tigranes had travelled south and diverted his attention away from the dispute with Rome. Tigranes had given Lucullus an opportunity to make an incursion into Armenia proper whilst Tigranes – and we must presume the bulk of his army – was further south in Phoenicia. We have a number of surviving passages which give us the size of the army that Lucullus took with him and sum up the endeavour he was undertaking and the mood of his men:

'He therefore left Sornatius there as guardian of Pontus, with six thousand soldiers, while he himself, with twelve thousand footmen and less than three thousand horse, set out for the second war. He seemed to be making a reckless attack, and one which admitted of no saving calculation, upon warlike nations, countless thousands of horsemen, and a boundless region surrounded by deep rivers and mountains covered with perpetual snow. His soldiers, therefore, who were none too well disciplined in any case, followed him reluctantly and rebelliously.'[17]

'Advancing through Cappadocia, whose ruler Ariobarzanes was his ally, Lucullus unexpectedly crossed the river Euphrates and brought his army up to the city in which he had heard that Tigranes kept his concubines, along with many valuable possessions. Lucullus also sent a detachment of his men to besiege Tigranocerta, and another force to attack the other important settlements.'[18]

'After the sacrifices had been performed, he marched with two legions and 500 horse against Tigranes.'[19]

'[Lucullus] proceeded by forced marches through the territory of King Ariobarzanes up to the river Euphrates, where it forms the border between Cappadocia and Armenia. And although he had some barges, which had been constructed secretly during the winter ...'[20]

Thus having garrisoned Pontus, which now potentially faced a renewed rebellion from Mithridates, Lucullus used the allied kingdom of Cappadocia as a launchpad for an invasion of the Armenian Empire with little over two legions. Clearly, with this size of army, Lucullus was not planning a war of conquest, but we must assume that it was a punitive expedition; a demonstration of Roman might to bring Tigranes to heel in the matter of Mithridates. The only positive aspects of an army of this size were that it could move quickly and required far less provisioning than a larger force. Given Tigranes' presence in the south of his empire, the obvious target of this punitive campaign seems to have been his new imperial capital, the recently founded city of Tigranocerta, built in the Hellenistic fashion and named after himself. By attacking Tigranes' capital, Lucullus would have been showing the king that Rome should not be trifled with, but he needed to capture the city and retreat before Tigranes marched north.

We know from a passage of Plutarch that Lucullus attacked very early in the year, as it talks about crossing a Euphrates swollen by winter floods.[21] Thus we can see Lucullus again utilizing the element of surprise to catch Tigranes and his empire off-guard. Plutarch provides us with his route, across the Euphrates and into Sophene, then across the Tigris and into Armenia proper.

The First Battle (69 BC)

Tigranes was far south in Phoenicia laying siege to the coastal city of Ptolemais, occupied by the Seleucid claimant Cleopatra II Selene, who still held out against his rule. Both Appian and Plutarch record that Tigranes was shocked when news was brought to him that Lucullus had invaded Armenia; if we are to believe Appian or Plutarch, he actually executed the messenger, although the method is disputed:

'No one told Tigranes that Lucullus was advancing, for the first man who brought this news he hanged, considering him a disturber of the morale of the cities.'[22]

'Since the first messenger who told Tigranes that Lucullus was coming had his head cut off for his pains, no one else would tell him anything, and so he sat in ignorance while the fires of war were already blazing around him, giving ear only to those who flattered him and said that Lucullus would be a great general if he ventured to withstand Tigranes at Ephesus, and did not fly incontinently from Asia at the mere sight of so many myriads of men.'[23]

Tigranes continued to hand the initiative to Lucullus by his inaction, but having recovered from his shock (and considerable loss of face), Josephus records that he was forced to break off the siege.[24] Yet to disengage his army, secure his position in the region and then march northwards would all take time. He therefore dispatched a trusted general, Mithrobarzanes, to march north with a light force – which still outnumbered the Romans – to intercept Lucullus before he could attack Tigranocerta:

'He was sent at once against Lucullus with three thousand horsemen and a large force of infantry, under orders to bring the general alive, but to trample his men under foot.'[25]

He also sent orders to another general, Mancaeus, to defend Tigranocerta itself whilst he himself marched northwards, gathering an even larger army than the one he had with him in Phoenicia. Despite the delays in accepting the news, Tigranes must have then acted quickly as the force he dispatched was able to intercept Lucullus before he reached Tigranocerta, though we are not given any further details as to Lucullus' progress. Plutarch details the subsequent first battle of the war, while Appian merely records the outcome:

> 'Now, part of the army of Lucullus was already preparing to go into camp, and the rest was still coming up, when his scouts told him that the Barbarian was advancing to the attack. Fearing lest the enemy attack his men when they were separated and in disorder, and so throw them into confusion, he himself fell to arranging the encampment, and Sextilius, the legate, was sent at the head of sixteen hundred horsemen and about as many light and heavy infantry, with orders to get near the enemy and wait there until he learned that the main body was safely encamped. This was what Sextilius wished to do, but he was forced into an engagement by Mithrobarzanes, who boldly charged upon him. A battle ensued, in which Mithrobarzanes fell fighting, and the rest of his forces took to flight and were cut to pieces, all except a few.'[26]

> 'Lucullus, at his first encounter with Mithrobarzanes, defeated him and put him to flight.'[27]

Thus the first victory of the Romano-Armenian War went to Rome and Lucullus' legate, a man known only as Sextilius. Aside from being told that it was Mithrobarzanes who launched a surprise attack on the Roman force, we have no other details. We must assume that, despite the superior numbers, the death of the Armenian commander caused his force to flee, handing Rome a victory.

The Siege of Tigranocerta and the Second and Third Battles – A Question of Sources

After this first battle, our surviving sources differ in their narratives of the next phase of the campaign. In Plutarch, which is the more detailed account, Lucullus had not yet reached Tigranocerta before Mithrobarzanes' force intercepted him. This raises questions about when Tigranes was informed of Lucullus' invasion and how quickly the Roman army was moving, if Tigranes was able to receive the news, prevaricate and dispatch Mithrobarzanes, who still had time to march north to Armenia.

In Appian's account, Lucullus' legate Sextilius is then sent to lay siege to Tigranocerta whilst Lucullus and the main army remain some way off. Plutarch, however, has two further battles taking place before the Romans reached Tigranocerta, one of which involved Sextilius. Memnon does not have the first battle, but agrees with Appian that the Roman army divided, with one contingent besieging Tigranocerta. Neither Appian nor Memnon have the clash between Tigranes and Lucullus' legate Murena (see below), but both include the encounter between the Roman besieging army (Sextilius is named in Appian) and a relief column sent to rescue Tigranes' harem from Tigranocerta.

We may marry up these varying accounts if we equate the force of Arabs in Plutarch's version with the rescue mission in Appian's and Memnon's accounts. We can thereby say that after the first battle, Sextilius was dispatched to begin the siege of Tigranocerta and the second battle took place there, as detailed below:

'Sextilius [was sent] to hold in check a large body of Arabs which was drawing near the king's [city]. At one and the same time Sextilius fell upon the Arabs as they were going into camp, and slew most of them.'[28]

'[Tigranes] sent an army to the city in which his concubines were kept. When this army arrived at the city, the archers prevented the Romans from leaving their camp and they sent away the concubines and the most valuable items during the night. But at daybreak the Romans and Thracians attacked bravely, and there was a widespread slaughter of the Armenians. The number of Armenians captured was no less than the number killed; but the convoy which they had sent ahead reached Tigranes safely. Thus the main Armenian force was destroyed but the city was evacuated of the people and items, Tigranes treasured the most.'[29]

'Sextilius shut up Mancaeus in Tigranocerta, plundered the palace outside the walls, drew a ditch around the city and tower, moved machines against them, and undermined the wall. While Sextilius was doing this, Tigranes brought together some 250,000 foot and 50,000 horse. He sent about 6,000 of the latter to Tigranocerta, who broke through the Roman line to the tower, and seized and brought away the king's concubines.'[30]

It is unclear why Plutarch chose to label the force sent by Tigranes as Arabs, especially as Memnon has them as Armenians, with a force of archers, whilst Appian says they were mostly composed of cavalry, which would make sense for a rescue force. Nevertheless, whilst the rescue mission was successful, the bulk of the force was wiped out by Sextilius and the siege continued.

The other interesting aspect is Memnon's reference to the composition of the Roman force, being both Roman and Thracian. Dio later adds that the Thracians were mercenaries who were previously in the employ of Mithridates but had changes sides, though we are not told when this happened (presumably during the conquest of Pontus).[31] It would be interesting to know if Plutarch's and Appian's account of the Roman forces under Lucullus in Armenia included these Thracian allies, as this may well inflate the total number of men Lucullus had with him.

The third battle presents us with something of a problem, not in terms of whether it took place, but in who the Romans were fighting. The fundamental problem is that Plutarch seems to have Tigranes in his capital Tigranocerta at the start of Lucullus' invasion:

'Upon this, Tigranes abandoned Tigranocerta, that great city which he had built, withdrew to the Taurus, and there began collecting his forces from every quarter.'[32]

This contradicts the two works of Josephus, who has Tigranes and a sizeable portion of his army in Phoenicia at the siege of Ptolemais. Furthermore, Plutarch's account would have us believe that Tigranes fled his capital to gather his army. This does not account for why he sent a rescue column (mentioned in Appian and Memnon) to the city to evacuate his harem. Thus we must discount Plutarch's statement that Tigranes was in Armenia in the vicinity of Tigranocerta, as he was in fact returning north from Phoenicia. We can then view the following battle, found only in Plutarch, as being a skirmish between Lucullus' legate L. Licinius Murena and a force of Armenians led by a commander of Tigranes, not the king himself:

'Lucullus, however, gave him no time for preparation, but sent out [L. Licinius] Murena to harass and cut off the forces gathering to join Tigranes, and Murena, following hard upon Tigranes, seized his opportunity and attacked the king as he was passing through a rough and narrow defile with his army in long column. Tigranes himself fled, abandoning all his baggage, many of the Armenians were slain, and more were captured.'[33]

It was only after this battle that Lucullus himself joined Sextilius in the siege of Tigranocerta. Here Lucullus had taken another gamble and faced a race against time. He had to take the city before Tigranes assembled his grand army and marched to Tigranocerta to face Lucullus. As Appian has no less a figure than Mithridates point out, this was potentially a reversal of the situation in 73 BC when Mithridates' army and whole campaign was destroyed by his refusal to break of the siege of Cyzicus (see Chapter Three), allowing

Lucullus to advance and surround him.[34] If Tigranes was able to assemble a numerically superior army and march on Lucullus whilst the siege was still underway, Lucullus would face the stark choice of fight or flight; the first posing a military risk, the second a political one.

Backlash at Rome

To make matters worse, whilst Lucullus was facing military danger in Armenia, he was in political danger in Rome, as his invasion of Armenia – a significant escalation in the war – allowed his enemies the chance to undermine him, utilizing the newly restored office of the Tribunate of the Plebs.

> '... while the popular Tribunes at Rome raised an outcry against him, and accused him of seeking one war after another, although the city had no need of them, that he might be in perpetual command and never lay down his arms or cease enriching himself from the public dangers.'[35]

His political enemies could claim that he had engineered a crisis to ensure he remained in perpetual command of an army, with all the association of civil war and bloodshed which this entailed, especially from a protégé of the Dictator Sulla. Yet whilst these attempts seem to have come to nought, they nevertheless were a clear warning sign.

The critical omissions from this narrative of events in Rome are the two recently retired Consuls, Cn. Pompeius Magnus and M. Licinius Crassus, both of whom had eschewed foreign commands to remain in Rome. It has been argued elsewhere that this unusual move by the two men was to ensure that they were well placed to safeguard the reforms they had introduced the year before, and thus 'police' the new Republic which they had created.[36] Though both men would have relished the chance at commanding a major war against Rome's rivals in the East, their priority had to be stability at Rome. However, this did not mean that they would pass up the chance to undermine a rival if the opportunity presented itself.

Nevertheless, the lack of overt references to the two men and the fact that these attempts were brushed off by Lucullus' allies shows that there was as yet no real effort on the part of either Pompeius or Crassus to unseat Lucullus. Their priorities lay closer to home, and there would also have been an element of giving Lucullus' enough rope with which to hang himself. The most likely outcomes of Lucullus' invasion were his defeat and death – which would have to be avenged by a new commander – an ignominious retreat, which could be used to finish him off politically, or the start of a long drawn-out war, command of which would still be available when either man adjudged matters in Rome to be sufficiently settled that they were able to take up the post themselves.

The Battle of Tigranocerta (69 BC) – The Armies

For Lucullus, the gamble had not paid off and Tigranocerta had not fallen by the time Tigranes assembled a larger army and marched to relieve the siege of his capital. Plutarch dates the clash to 6 October, which means that even if Lucullus had not moved immediately on Tigranocerta, the city had still held out against him throughout the spring and summer of 69 BC, allowing Tigranes all that time to assemble his army (if we are to believe Plutarch's dating).

Tigranes already had a sizeable army for the siege of Ptolemais, but had dispatched 8,000 cavalry in two columns, to intercept Lucullus and rescue his harem. Nevertheless, it was a sensible tactic on Tigranes' part to gather an even larger force if he was to face the Romans in battle for the first time. Given that he expended so much effort to rescue his harem from Tigranocerta, he seemed to show little faith in the resistance of his capital. Having rescued them, he was now seemingly under no pressure to rush to relieve the city. The fact that it still held out by the time his army had assembled and moved to intercept Lucullus must have been a bonus.

It is always possible that the delay in Tigranes gathering his army and moving to relieve Tigranocerta was down to a reticence to actually fight Rome, despite the provocation. Whilst he clearly expected to massacre Lucullus and his force, he would have been acutely aware that to do so would be to irrevocably plunge the Armenian Empire into war with Rome, and he could expect retaliation, led no doubt by either Pompeius or Crassus. Whilst there is no record of it in our surviving sources, the king may well have been giving Lucullus the time and space to abandon the siege and return to Roman territory. Only when the campaigning season was drawing to a close did Tigranes choose to make the decisive move and attack a Roman army.

The arrival of Tigranes' army – which vastly outnumbered the Roman (and allied) one – seemingly heralded the failure of Lucullus' gamble. His invasion of Armenia had clearly not brought Tigranes to heel over the matter of Mithridates, nor cowed the 'King of Kings' in any way. He now faced the might of the Armenian army, the most successful eastern army of its day, with a smaller force which was still engaged in a siege, and had no capital nor hostages to bargain with.

Interestingly, Plutarch actually names his source for the size of the Armenian army, namely the letter that Lucullus himself sent to the Senate describing his victory, though it is unlikely he ever viewed this first-hand and thus took it from a secondary (and unknown) source:

'For he was in command of twenty thousand bowmen and slingers, and fifty-five thousand horsemen, of whom seventeen thousand were clad in mail, as Lucullus said in his letter to the Senate; also of one hundred and fifty thousand heavy infantry, some of whom were drawn up in cohorts, and some in phalanxes; also of road-makers, bridge-builders, clearers of rivers, foresters, and ministers to the other needs of an army, to the number of thirty-five thousand. These latter, being drawn up in array behind the fighting men, increased the apparent strength of the army.'[37]

Appian joins Plutarch in this estimate but actually goes further, saying, 'Tigranes brought together some 250,000 foot and 50,000 horse.'[38]

Nevertheless, we have to question the validity of the size of the Armenian army: some 250,000 (300,000 in Appian). Memnon, a native and earlier source, gives a much smaller figure:

'Tigranes collected an army of 80,000 men and went down to Tigranocerta, in order to lift the siege and drive away the enemy.'[39]

It seems that Plutarch and Appian preserve Lucullus' vast inflation of his opponent's numbers when informing his allies (and enemies) in the Senate, whereas Memnon seems to tap into a more local tradition. Even if we accept that Tigranes had 80,000 men in his army, that is still more than four times the number Lucullus had available. Plutarch goes on to provide us with a flavour of the nature of the Armenian army:

'But when the Armenians and Gordyeni joined him with all their hosts, and the kings of the Medes and Adiabeni came up with all their hosts, and many Arabs arrived from the sea of Babylonia, and many Albanians from the Caspian sea, together with Iberians who were neighbours to the Albanians; and when not a few of the peoples about the river Araxes, who are not subject to kings, had been induced by favours and gifts to come and join him …'[40]

Even if we allow for the usual Plutarchian flourishes, this passage does emphasize the multinational flavour of Tigranes' army, pulling elements from all sections of his empire, which had seemingly taken at least six months. The inequality in numbers was exacerbated by Lucullus choosing to continue the siege of Tigranocerta, thus having to split his army and leave behind a force to carry on the attack:

'Murena, with six thousand footmen, he left behind in charge of the siege; while he himself, with twenty-four cohorts, comprising no more than ten thousand heavy infantry, and all the horsemen, slingers, and archers, to the number of about a thousand, set out against the enemy.'[41]

If we are to believe Plutarch – and here we know he was using Lucullus' own exaggerated account of the battle – Lucullus faced an army of 80,000 with just 10,000 infantry and less than 1,000 cavalry, archers and slingers. Perhaps one of the most interesting aspects of Lucullus' army is his use of slingers. Whilst these were a standard feature of eastern armies, it was not a common Roman tactic, but was famously used some thirty years later in 38 BC by the Roman commander Ventidius when facing the Parthians at the Battle of Gindarus.[42] Their presence here shows Lucullus had interwoven native elements into his army, revealing a tactical flexibility that was not seen at the Battle of Carrhae (53 BC).[43]

Lucullus, his gamble of attacking Tigranocerta not having paid off, apparently now faced the might of the Armenian army – being heavily outnumbered by at least seven to one if we accept Lucullus' own numbers – whilst backed up against a city he was besieging. Aside from the issue of the end of his career had he turned and retreated, in military terms, he would have had to fall back with a huge army giving chase and harrying him all the way, making the destruction of the Roman army more than likely. Once Tigranes had arrived at Tigranocerta, the die was cast as far as Lucullus' options were concerned.

Interestingly, if we are to believe Plutarch, then Mithridates – who seems to have returned in Pontus – sent messengers, including his general Taxiles, urging Tigranes not to attack the Roman army but to starve it into submission, though the tone of Plutarch's account smacks strongly of hindsight.[44] If there was a reticence on Tigranes' part, it was due to anxiety over the next Roman invasion, not the current one. In any event, his role as the new 'King of Kings' would hardly permit him to suffer the indignity of allowing a Roman army to attack his capital unchallenged, and it is this pressure that may have finally forced his hand.

The Battle of Tigranocerta – Plutarch

What followed was portrayed in Roman histories as one of the most stunning victories by a Roman army against a numerically superior foe, and was certainly Rome's greatest victory to date in the East. Seemingly against all odds, Lucullus pulled off what even the less pro-Roman sources describe as a crushing victory.

Plutarch presents the most detailed account, which again may come directly (or indirectly) from Lucullus' own account (see battle plan below):

'Now, the Armenian army lay to the east of the river. But as the stream takes a turn to the west at the point where it was easiest to ford, and as Lucullus led his troops to the attack in that direction first, and with speed, he seemed to Tigranes to be retreating.'[45]

'And so, with much tumult and confusion, his [Tigranes'] multitude formed in battle array, the king himself occupying the centre, and assigning the left wing to the King of the Adiabeni, the right to the King of the Medes. In front of this wing also the greater part of the mail-clad horsemen were drawn up.'[46]

'Saying this, and bidding his men be of good courage, he [Lucullus] crossed the river, and led the way in person against the enemy. He wore a steel breastplate of glittering scales, and a tasselled cloak, and at once let his sword flash forth from its scabbard, indicating that they must forthwith come to close quarters with men who fought with long range missiles, and eliminate, by the rapidity of their onset, the space in which archery would be effective.

'But when he saw that the mail-clad horsemen, on whom the greatest reliance was placed, were stationed at the foot of a considerable hill which was crowned by a broad and level space, and that the approach to this was a matter of only four stadia, and neither rough nor steep, he ordered his Thracian and Gallic horsemen to attack the enemy in the flank, and to parry their long spears with their own short swords.

'Now the sole resource of the mail-clad horsemen is their long spear, and they have nothing else whatsoever, either in defending themselves or attacking their enemies, owing to the weight and rigidity of their armour; in this they are, as it were, trapped. Then he [Lucullus] himself, with two cohorts, hastened eagerly towards the hill, his soldiers following with all their might, because they saw him ahead of them in armour, enduring all the fatigue of a foot-soldier, and pressing his way along. Arrived at the top, and standing in the most conspicuous spot, he cried with a loud voice, "The day is ours; the day is ours, my fellow soldiers!"

'With these words, he led his men against the mail-clad horsemen, ordering them not to hurl their javelins yet, but taking each his own man, to attack the enemy's legs and thighs, which are the only parts of these mail-clad horsemen left exposed. However, there was no need of this mode of fighting, for the enemy did not await the Romans but, with loud cries and in most disgraceful flight, they hurled themselves and their horses, with all their weight, upon the ranks of their own infantry, before it had so much as begun to fight, and so all those tens of thousands were defeated without the infliction of a wound or the sight of blood.

'But the great slaughter began at once when they fled, or rather tried to fly, for they were prevented from really doing so by the closeness and depth of their own ranks. Tigranes rode away at the very outset with a few attendants and took to flight. Seeing his son also in the same plight, he took off the diadem from his head and, in tears, gave it to him, bidding him save himself as best he could by another route.

'The young man, however, did not venture to assume the diadem, but gave it to his most trusted slave for safe keeping. This slave happened to be captured, and was brought to Lucullus, and thus even the diadem of Tigranes became a part of the booty. It is said that more than a hundred thousand of the enemy's infantry perished, while of the cavalry only a few, all told, made their escape. Of the Romans, on the other hand, only a hundred were wounded, and only five killed.'[47]

Battle Plan

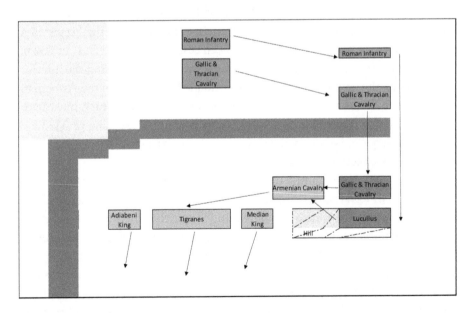

What are we to make of this battle, where a small Roman army comprehensively defeated the army of the strongest of the eastern empires? Firstly, we need to be extremely sceptical of the losses, which again seem to have been taken from Lucullus' own account, to be read back in Rome: five Roman dead contrasted to 100,000 Armenian dead. As we have stated earlier, the size of the Armenian army is likely to have only been 80,000 at most, and the narrative of the battle states that the cavalry turned and fled, doubtless inflicting casualties on the infantry they rode into. The bulk of the Armenian casualties thus seem to have been caused by their own cavalry and the infantry stampede that followed.

We can see that key to Lucullus' tactics were a Romano-Thracian cavalry attack on the Armenian cavalry on the right flank, delaying them long enough for the Roman infantry to climb to the top of this hill and then attack the Armenians at close quarters. Lucullus led this infantry assault himself, engaging the Armenian cavalry at close range and thus negating the advantage of their long spears. We must question Plutarch's earlier assertion – again probably based on Lucullus himself – that the Romans had less than 1,000 cavalry for the flanking attack to hold the Armenian cavalry until the Roman infantry could close the gap.

At the heart of Lucullus' battle plan was seemingly another massive gamble, namely that by going on the offensive, even with a vastly smaller number of troops, he could fight the battle on his own terms and not give Tigranes the luxury of time to deploy his superior numbers. In leading from the front – or certainly near it – one gets the feeling that Lucullus opted for a 'do or die' strategy, that would either result in a Roman victory, taking the attack to a startled enemy, or his own death, having been easily surrounded and cut down.

What is clear is that Tigranes and his forces were not expecting the inferior side to attack the greater. The two major strategic blunders from the Armenian side were the failure to station a garrison on the hill itself – which must have been next to the Armenian right wing, commanded by the King of Media – and the subsequent failure by the right wing to counter-attack Lucullus when they saw he had secured the hill.

Lucullus seemingly gambled everything on a swift 'knock out' attack on the Armenian cavalry, denying them space and fighting at close quarters, and then routing them into the oncoming Armenian infantry. Once again, Lucullus' gamble paid off, and the Armenian cavalry found themselves taken by surprise and facing Roman infantry at close range, fighting the type of battle that the Romans excelled at. With no one seemingly to co-ordinate the cavalry, Tigranes himself being in the centre, they routed, then the topography of the battlefield – the hill being behind them and to their right, and the river to their front – funnelled them into the bulk of the Armenian infantry.

The Battle of Tigranocerta – The Other Sources
Appian presents a variation on the battle.

'Lucullus saw a hill favourably situated in the rear of Tigranes. He pushed his horse forward from his own front to worry the enemy and draw them upon himself, retiring as they came up, so that the Armenians should break their own ranks in the pursuit. Then he sent his own infantry around to the hill and took possession of it unobserved. When he saw the enemy pursuing as though they had won the fight, and scattered in all directions, with their entire baggage train lying at the foot of the hill, he exclaimed, "Soldiers, we are victorious," and dashed first upon their baggage carriers.

'These immediately fled in confusion and ran against their own infantry, and the infantry against the cavalry. Presently the rout was complete. Those who had been drawn a long distance in pursuit of the Roman horse, the latter turned upon and destroyed. The baggage train came into collision with others tumultuously. They were all packed together in such a crowd that nobody could see clearly from what quarter their discomfiture proceeded. There was a great slaughter.'[48]

As we can see, there are significant variations in this version, the first being that Lucullus was mounted whereas Plutarch has him on foot. Though the rest of the account largely tallies, the key variant is that the Armenian cavalry were drawn out of position by a feint, then broke discipline and ranks and charged after the Romans. With the cavalry seemingly out of the picture, the Roman infantry attacked the baggage train – though what it was doing set between the Armenian cavalry and infantry is not explained – which then was routed into the Armenian infantry.

Appian takes this unlikely scenario further by having the vastly inferior number of Roman (and presumably Thracian) cavalry turn and somehow massacre the full force of the Armenian cavalry, which vastly outnumbered them, and which to that point had been chasing them. Whilst Appian has preserved the basics of the battle, he – or his source – has muddled the details significantly.

Given the status of the victory (in Roman eyes at least), Frontinus devotes a small discussion of it in his *Stratagems*, where he emphasises the swift and decisive attack of Lucullus:

'At Tigranocerta in Greater Armenia, Lucullus, in the campaign against Mithridates and Tigranes, did not have above 15,000 armed men, while the enemy had an innumerable host, which for this very reason was unwieldy. Taking advantage, accordingly, of this handicap of the foe, Lucullus attacked their line before it was in order, and straightway routed it so completely that even the kings themselves discarded their trappings and fled.'[49]

A second discussion summarizes the battle as found in Plutarch, with emphasis on the taking of the hilltop and the flanking attack on the cavalry which broke them:

'When Lucullus was planning to fight Mithridates and Tigranes at Tigranocerta in Greater Armenia, he himself swiftly gained the level top of the nearest hill with a part of his troops, and then rushed down upon the enemy posted below, at the same time attacking their cavalry on the flank. When the cavalry broke and straightway threw the infantry into confusion, Lucullus followed after them and gained a most notable victory.'[50]

Memnon also preserves an account, which, though presenting far less detail of the battle, confirms one crucial element; that Lucullus routed the Armenian army on the right wing:

'Immediately he routed the enemy's right wing; and then the troops next to them gave way, and so on until the whole army was in flight. A dreadful and unstoppable panic seized the Armenians, and inevitably this was followed by the destruction of their army. Tigranes handed over his diadem and emblems of power to his son and fled to one of his fortresses.'[51]

Orosius offers brief details, but places the Armenian casualties at 20,000, which seems a far more sensible figure:

'[Lucullus] came to battle with Mithridates and Tigranes outside the city of Tigranocerta. He killed a great number of the enemy with his tiny band; for 20,000 men are said to have been slaughtered in the battle. Tigranes threw away his diadem and tiara to avoid being recognised and fled accompanied by scarcely 150 cavalry.'[52]

Festus, meanwhile, places Lucullus' army at 18,000 strong, whilst Tigranes had 7,000 cavalry in his force:

'[Lucullus] with 18,000 Romans, conquered Tigranes, the Armenians' king, with 7,000 armoured horsemen and 2,000 archers.'[53]

Eutropius, however, goes further than anyone and has Tigranes' army at an incredible 700,000:

'... the king himself, who advanced against him [Lucullus] with six hundred thousand cavalry, and a hundred thousand archers and other troops, he so completely defeated with a force of only eighteen thousand, that he annihilated a great part of the Armenians.'[54]

The Fall of Tigranocerta (69 BC)

The immediate aftermath of the battle saw Lucullus resume his siege of Tigranocerta, which he needed to capture before the onset of winter. Here, Lucullus' victory reaped its most immediate reward when the city, which had seemingly held out all year, fell to him by treachery, inspired no doubt by the Roman success, but again in a manner which is disputed by the various surviving sources:

'When Mancaeus beheld this defeat from Tigranocerta, he disarmed all of his Greek mercenaries because he suspected them. They, in fear of arrest, walked abroad or rested only in a body, and with clubs in their hands. Mancaeus set upon them with his armed barbarians. They wound their clothing around their left arms, to serve as shields, and fought their assailants courageously, killed some, and shared their arms with each other. When they were sufficiently provided with weapons, they seized some of the towers, called to the Romans outside, and admitted them when they came up. In this way was Tigranocerta taken, and the immense wealth, appertaining to a newly built and nobly peopled city, plundered.'[55]

'But in the city of Tigranocerta, the Greeks had risen up against the Barbarians and were ready to hand the city over to Lucullus; so he assaulted and took it. The royal treasures in the city he took into his own charge, but the city itself he turned over to his soldiers for plunder.'[56]

'Nevertheless he did seize Tigranocerta when the foreigners living in the city revolted against the Armenians; for the most of them were Cilicians who had once been carried off from their own land, and these let in the Romans during the night. Thereupon everything was plundered, except what belonged to the Cilicians.'[57]

'Lucullus returned to Tigranocerta and pressed the siege more intently, until Mithridates' generals in the city gave up all hope and surrendered the city to him in return for their own safety.'[58]

Summary

Despite the gamble Lucullus took in invading the Armenian Empire with such a small force, in the short term this paid off handsomely, earning the Romans their first victory over the previously unstoppable Armenians, defeating the 'King of Kings' and sacking his capital. Lucullus had fought the most successful eastern campaign by any Roman general to date, defeating Mithridates twice, recovering Bithynia, conquering Pontus, defeating Tigranes and humbling the mighty Armenian Empire. Yet it was from this pinnacle of success that both Rome's position and that of Lucullus himself began to deteriorate.

Chapter 6

Snatching Defeat –
From Victory to Collapse (68–67 BC)

The Backlash at Rome (69 BC)

As Plutarch alludes to, Lucullus would have wasted no time in informing the Senate of his great victory, suitably embellished as we have seen. Yet to many in the Senatorial oligarchy, there was only one thing worse than a Roman general that failed in battle, and that was one that was too successful. Time after time, from the Scipios to Marius, the families that made up Rome's ruling class would always unite to try to stop one of their own from becoming too powerful. In this case, many would have been giving Lucullus enough rope with which to hang himself, and when news of his spectacular victory emerged, the backlash would have started. The only explicit reference we can find to this is in a fragment of Dio, whose narrative picks up immediately after the Battle of Tigranocerta:

'While they were thus engaged, Lucullus did not follow up Tigranes, but allowed him to reach safety quite at his leisure. Because of this he was charged by the citizens, as well as others, with refusing to end the war, in order that he might retain his command a longer time. Therefore they at this time restored the province of Asia to the Praetors.'[1]

To many in Rome it would have seemed that no matter how many victories Lucullus achieved, the war itself seemed to continue, and if anything kept escalating. Neither Mithridates nor Tigranes had been captured, and there was talk of the Parthian Empire being sucked into the conflict (see below). We begin to see support for Lucullus ebbing away, and the Senate or Assembly – it is not clear which – begin to reduce the scale of Lucullus' command. As Dio reports, it was soon after Tigranocerta and receipt of the news of his victory that the province of Asia was stripped from his command. Whilst this was of little practical loss to Lucullus, it was clearly a warning to him. Again, we have no details as to the roles in this of Rome's two leading men, Pompeius and Crassus.

Following on from his loss of Asia, for the following year of 68 BC it was determined that the province of Cilicia, which had been the backbone of

Lucullus' bid to take command of the Romano-Pontic War, would also be removed from him and passed over to one of the Consuls for 68 BC, Q. Marcius Rex. Little is known of Marcius Rex, other than that he came from a plebeian consular family, which like many others only came to prominence in the office-holding lists in the aftermath of the Second Punic War. Their first and only consulship prior to 68 BC came in 118 BC. It is tempting to speculate that Marcius must have been a supporter of Pompeius, both to gain the consulship in the aftermath of his and Crassus' constitutional settlement and to be trusted with a caretaker role of an eastern command. As it was, Marcius was to have an extraordinary year as Consul, with his colleague L. Caecilius Metellus dying early in the year, soon followed by his replacement, a (Servilius?) Vatia. This left Marcius Rex in the almost unique position of ruling alone as Consul for the majority of the year.

The loss of the province of Cilicia, on top of Asia the previous year, raises questions as to what command Lucullus was left with, as these two provinces formed the basis of his original command. The paucity of surviving sources and our reliance on much later Imperial writers such as Appian and Plutarch means that we have little left on Republican details such as the formalities of Lucullus' command. With both Asia and Cilicia having been given to other commanders, we must assume that at some point, not recorded in our surviving sources, Lucullus received command in either or both Bithynia and Pontus. We know that Cotta returned to Rome in 70 BC, and Lucullus may well have been named his successor to bolster his powerbase. Lucullus may have been granted command in Pontus (though not yet a province) prior to his invasion in 72 BC, again to underpin the military reality. Whatever the case, by 68 BC, Lucullus still had more than sufficient political support to finish the war.

Lucullus' Dilemma

No matter how splendid a victory, one battle does not a war make. Even though Lucullus had stated to the Senate that he had destroyed an army of several hundred thousand men, killing the majority of them, the reality was far more prosaic. Closer to the truth would have been Memnon's figure of a defeated army of 80,000, along with Orosius' figure of 20,000 dead. To the 'King of Kings', with an empire stretching from the Caspian to the Mediterranean, such losses could easily be replaced.

Here we need to re-examine Lucullus' campaign objectives. He had invaded Armenia seemingly in pursuit of the fugitive Pontic King Mithridates; at the very least to force Tigranes to break off his support for him, and at best hand him over. In the short term this policy had reaped the rewards of a splendid victory and a successful sacking of the Armenian capital. Yet as the fires of

Tigranocerta were dying down, the stark dilemma that faced Lucullus was what he should do next.

Whilst he may have hoped that defeating Tigranes and sacking his capital would force the Armenian Emperor to make terms with Rome, in reality the opposite was true. During the last fifteen years, Tigranes had carved out the largest empire in the Near East, defeating both the Seleucids and the Parthians. This nascent empire was still new and depended upon the myth of Tigranes' own invincibility and the idea that his rise was inevitable, both of which came to a shuddering halt at Tigranocerta. If Tigranes was to keep his new empire and his new title, then he had not only to continue the fight against Rome, but be seen to have won it. For Tigranes, this war was now a matter of survival.

If we examine Lucullus' position, then there were some hard truths hiding behind the exultation he received for his victory. Both opposing commanders were still free, and Tigranes still had the whole resources of the Armenian Empire to draw upon. Lucullus' own force was less than 20,000-strong and was in enemy territory, albeit with secure lines of supply to the client kingdom of Cappadocia. His bid for Tigranes to stop supporting Mithridates and hand him over had now completely failed, ironically as a result of his own success, and like many of his opponents in Rome, there may have been some doubt in his mind as to how he was going to end this war.

This thought would have been reinforced by the notion that his time in command was running out. His command was now nearing the end of its sixth year, the emergency had clearly passed, and his enemies and rivals were circling what was now the greatest opportunity for an eastern command in nearly a century. This had been driven home by the loss of the provinces of Asia and Cilicia, and Lucullus must have been wondering how long it would be before either Pompeius or Crassus felt secure enough to move to sieze the command themselves. Lucullus needed to end the war quickly and return to Rome as the conquering hero.

The Romano-Armenian War – Escalation

The Battle of Tigranocerta and the ending of the siege came late in 69 BC, which meant that Lucullus' thoughts had to turn to where he was going to spend the winter months. Despite having established a bridgehead in Armenia, he found it prudent to retreat back to Cappadocia, a friendly state with plentiful supplies where he could regroup and plan his next moves. Over the winter, his campaign to secure Roman control of the region was theoretically boosted by a slew of ambassadors coming to him for the various minor powers of the region, all seemingly professing their loyalty to him and to Rome:

'The kings of the Arabs came to him, with proffers of their possessions, and the Sopheni joined his cause. The Gordyeni were so affected by his kindness that they were ready to abandon their cities and follow him with their wives and children, in voluntary service.'[2]

'He furthermore received Antiochus, King of Commagene, a part of Syria near the Euphrates and the Taurus, and Alchaudonius, an Arabian chieftain, and others who had made overtures to him.'[3]

'After this, suppliant ambassadors came to Lucullus from almost all the East.'[4]

Whilst these professions of loyalty seem to have impressed Plutarch, it is doubtful they did so with Lucullus himself. At that moment, the greatest danger to these kingdoms had been Tigranes, so most would have welcomed his defeat and have been happy to profess insincere protestations of loyalty to the man who beat him. Yet as Lucullus would have been fully aware, these kings and ambassadors only maintained their independence by 'swaying in the wind', and would soon switch loyalties back to Tigranes if it looked like he was gaining the upper hand. Furthermore, diplomatic embassies from the minor powers would not determine the outcome of the war; it was envoys from the courts of Pontus, Armenia and Parthia that would prove crucial.

Whilst Lucullus was forced to withdraw for the winter, in Armenia his worst fears were confirmed when Mithridates, who had been recalled when the Romans invaded, joined Tigranes. Between them, Tigranes and his father-in-law forged an active alliance to defeat the Romans, with Tigranes putting the resources at the Armenian Empire under the command of Mithridates:

'However Mithridates went to Tigranes and restored his spirits, reclothing him in royal apparel, no less splendid than before. Mithridates already had a considerable force, and he encouraged Tigranes to collect another army, so that he could once again strive for victory. Then Tigranes put Mithridates in overall command, trusting in his nobleness and intelligence, because he seemed most capable of maintaining a war against the Romans.'[5]

Having no option but to commit to an all-out war with Rome, we are told that Tigranes and Mithridates spent the winter months gathering a new army:

'Now Tigranes and Mithridates traversed the country collecting a new army, the command of which was committed to Mithridates, because Tigranes thought that his disasters must have taught him some lessons.

'Mithridates manufactured arms in every town. The soldiers he recruited were almost wholly Armenians. From these he selected the bravest to the number of about 70,000 foot and half that number of horse and dismissed the rest. He divided them into companies and cohorts as nearly as possible according to the Italian system and turned them over to Pontic officers to be trained.'[6]

Once again, Mithridates found himself in command of a substantial army, which meant that Lucullus' main policy aim – to isolate Mithridates – had failed resoundingly, and the Romans (and thus Lucullus) faced the prospect of another phase in this ongoing war.

The Shadow of Parthia

It was at this juncture, after the Roman victory at Tigranocerta and the renewed alliance between Mithridates and Tigranes, that the war threatened to escalate even further as the two kings sent ambassadors to the Parthian court, bearing a letter from Mithridates to the Parthian Emperor. Although one of the major powers of the Near and Middle East, the Parthian Empire had been in decline for a generation due to the outbreak of a (poorly recorded) civil war some time between 91 and 88 BC following the death of the Parthian monarch Mithradates II (see Appendix Two). What followed was up to thirty years of warfare between rival claimants to the throne from various branches of the ruling Arsacid family.

Unlike the Roman Civil War, however, we have no narrative sources for the internecine conflict and thus no clear details, which has led to this period being known as a Parthian Dark Age. Basic questions such as who the rival claimants were and for how long they were fighting have to be reconstructed from various fragmentary sources and surviving coin hoards. We have evidence of a number of rival Parthian emperors in this period: Sinatruces (c.92–69/68 BC), Gotarzes I (c.91–87 BC), Mithradates III (c.87–80 BC), Orodes I (c.80–75 BC) and even an otherwise unknown Arsaces XVI (c.78/77–62/61 BC) (see Appendix Two).

By the mid to late 70s BC, the Parthian Emperor Sinatruces, who appears to have been involved in the outbreak of the civil war, seems to have defeated the majority of his rivals and secured the throne (though there may have been one rival, Arsaces XVI, still fighting), thereby bringing a degree of stability to the Parthian Empire. In c.69/68 BC, he was succeeded by his son Phraates III, who it has been argued continued to fight a mysterious challenger, the unknown Arsaces XVI, and it seems that it was only by around 61 BC that the Parthian Civil War had been brought to a conclusion.

It was this internal conflict which had weakened the Parthian Empire to such an extent that their former vassal, Tigranes, was not only able to declare Armenia's independence, but defeat the Parthians and occupy a portion of their north-western territories. Tigranes had gone further and annexed a weakened Seleucid Empire, which had been a long-term strategic aim of the Parthians themselves, and had usurped the title of 'King of Kings', which the Arsacid monarchs had claimed for themselves as the inheritors of the old Persian Empire. Consequently, it must have been galling for Tigranes to seek the assistance of his former rulers who were now subordinate to him. This most likely explains the fact that the letter to the Parthian Emperor was written by Mithridates and not Tigranes. Sallust in his (now lost) *Histories* presents us with what he claims was the actual text of the letter, translated from the original into Latin and again now into English (see Appendix Three).

In short, the letter is an appeal by Mithridates for Parthian military assistance in a grand coalition of the eastern powers against Rome. At the heart of the letter is Mithridates' assessment of the ever-expanding power of Rome, which he said would threaten even the Parthian Empire before too long, and that it was better for Parthia to stand against the Romans now, as part of a wider alliance, than have to face them alone. The letter, and embassy, was received by the newly enthroned Emperor Phraates III, who had only recently inherited the Parthian crown from his father Sinatruces.

Unsurprisingly, Mithridates and Tigranes' appeal to Phraates did not result in Parthian military assistance or a grand alliance. The current threat to the Parthian Empire was not from the distant Roman Republic, but the neighbouring Armenian Empire, which even held former Parthian territory, though apparently Tigranes offered to return those conquered lands as part of any agreement. Furthermore, the Parthian Empire was still weak from the twenty years of fighting, and there may still have been an ongoing civil war.

It seems that Phraates then sent an embassy to Lucullus, informing him of the request from Mithridates and Tigranes, presumably to begin negotiations for his neutrality. This resulted in Lucullus also sending emissaries to the Parthian court, the first time any Roman had done so, and only the second formal diplomatic contact between the two powers. Phraates clearly had no intention of sending military aid to either side, but was content to let both powers wear each other down and then take advantage to at least recover his lost provinces, if not annex the whole Armenian Empire. Whilst Phraates entered into secret agreements with both sides, he remained firmly neutral. Interestingly, Plutarch believes that Lucullus was planning to attack the Parthian Empire itself, thereby predating the First Romano-Parthian War by over a decade:

'Accordingly, when Lucullus was apprised of this, he determined to ignore
Tigranes and Mithridates as exhausted antagonists, and to make trial of
the Parthian power by marching against them, thinking it a glorious
thing, in a single impetuous onset of war, to throw, like an athlete, three
kings in succession, and to make his way, unvanquished and victorious,
through three of the greatest empires under the sun.'[7]

According to Plutarch, Lucullus was only prevented from attacking Parthia
by a rebellious army, which threatened mutiny rather than invade. However,
here we must inject a note of realism. Even if Lucullus believed the Parthian
Empire to be weak – certainly weaker than the Armenian one – the main
threat was clearly the Armenian army of Tigranes, which stood between
him and Parthia itself. Lucullus' enemies in Rome would have happily made
accusations that he was intending to widen the war yet again and attack
Parthia. However, Lucullus' objectives were clear: rebuild his forces and await
the renewed assault of the Mithridatic-led Armenian army.

Rome and the Eastern Mediterranean (69–68 BC)
Throughout 69 BC, Lucullus' campaigns were not the only ones in the East
involving Rome, with the Senate making a renewed effort to deal with the
pirate problem that had been plaguing the Mediterranean. The last attempt
had ended dismally in 72/71 BC when the Proconsul M. Antonius Creticus
(father of the Triumvir) had been defeated at Crete by the pirate fleets.

In 69 BC, the Senate – presumably with the blessing of Pompeius and
Crassus – determined that Crete would once again be declared a proconsular
province, despite nominally being part of the Ptolemaic Empire. When his
colleague Q. Hortensius Hortalus refused the command, it fell to the other
Consul, Q. Caecilius Metellus, who undertook the campaign with the military
zeal usually associated with his family. Thus, as Lucullus was preparing to
face Mithridates and Tigranes in Armenia, Metellus was planning a Roman
assault on the island of Crete, showing Rome's expanding reach across the
Near East.

The Armenian Campaign of 68 BC
The curious element of the campaigns of 68 BC is the seeming absence of any
activity from either side in the early stages of the year, at least any noted in
our surviving sources. Both Plutarch and Dio comment that it was the height
of summer before Lucullus advanced into Armenia once more, though Dio
blames the weather.

'Lucullus entered upon his campaign when summer was already at its height, since in the spring it had been impossible to invade the enemy's country because of the cold.'[8]

'[Lucullus] marched once more against Tigranes, it being now the height of summer.'[9]

We have no reason to distrust Dio's assertion, and it may well be that the spring of 68 BC was colder than normal, though this rarely slowed down a Roman invading army, especially one which had such secure supply line. Aside from the weather, however, there may have been two additional factors in Lucullus' delay in taking to the field. The first of these relates to a mutiny in the Roman army:

'Accordingly he sent orders to Sornatius and his fellow commanders in Pontus to bring the army there to him, as he intended to proceed eastward from Gordyené. These officers had already found their soldiers unmanageable and disobedient, but now they discovered that they were utterly beyond control, being unable to move them by any manner of persuasion or compulsion. Not only that, they roundly swore that they would not even stay where they were, but would go off and leave Pontus undefended.'[10]

Plutarch relates this incident to the alleged plan to attack Parthia, yet it was more likely that this was a general mutiny upon being mustered to invade Armenia once more. Although Plutarch (and his sources) ascribe it to a growth of decadence and luxury, it must be acknowledged that the war was now in its seventh year, with no obvious end in sight, and in fact seemed to be escalating year-on-year. There may have been undercurrents of the soldiers trying to force a change in commander, and there must have been rumours – if not outright agitation – that Pompeius was eager to take charge. Lucullus consequently had to contend with a mutinous army over the winter of 69/68 BC and into the early spring; Plutarch does not state how long it took Lucullus to restore discipline.

The second factor in the delay was that the dynamic of the war had changed once again, and Lucullus would be facing an Armenian army commanded by Mithridates. Thus, he may have been waiting to see if Mithridates and Tigranes would be taking any offensive action, such as invading Roman-occupied Pontus. It seems that only when he determined that the two kings were not taking the offensive, but were sitting back and waiting for him to invade, that he obliged them.

It appears that Mithridates was sticking to his strategy of not directly engaging the Romans, but drawing them further into Armenia and stretching their supply lines. Plutarch, along with Dio, sums up the early part of the campaign:

'However, he [Lucullus] descended from the mountains, routed the Armenians who twice or thrice ventured to attack him, and then plundered their villages without fear, and, by taking away the grain which had been stored up for Tigranes, reduced his enemy to the straits which he had been fearing for himself. Then he challenged them to battle by encompassing their camp with a moat, and by ravaging their territory before their eyes; but this did not move them, so often had they been defeated. He therefore broke camp and marched against Artaxata, the royal residence of Tigranes, where were his wives and young children, thinking that Tigranes would not give these up without fighting.'[11]

'He [Lucullus] devastated a part of their land, purposing to draw the barbarians imperceptibly into battle while defending it; but when even then they made no move, he marched against them.'[12]

Mithridates seemed to be taking a leaf out of the Roman book and adopting Fabian tactics[13] of refusing to give battle. Plutarch reports that there were clashes, but these can have been little more than skirmishes. Again, this would have served two purposes. Firstly, whilst Mithridates and Tigranes might have had the superior numbers, these would have been freshly levied troops, and the very number of them may have been a disadvantage when faced with an opposition of battle-hardened veterans, well used to acting as a coherent force. Furthermore, the more time Mithridates had to train his new army, the better. Secondly, Mithridates and Tigranes would have been well aware of the Roman mutiny over the winter and the pressure Lucullus was facing at Rome, both of which would have been alleviated by a Roman victory and the death or capture of Mithridates.

Yet whilst Mithridates, having already lost his own empire, could sustain this tactic, it seems that when faced with the loss of a second capital, Tigranes was not so steadfast and overruled his ally, determining to attack the Romans to save his old capital. This resulted in the Battle of Artaxata.

The Battle of Artaxata (68 BC)
Having been made aware of the Roman intentions – and Lucullus would not have wanted it to be a secret – Tigranes marshalled the Armenian army in front of the city of Artaxata, with the river between him and Lucullus. Once

again, as he had at Tigranocerta, Lucullus decided to attack the enemy head-on in an effort to negate their superior numbers and put the quality and nerve of the Armenian (and allied) soldiers to the test. Plutarch preserves a detailed account of the battle, while Dio's is more cursory:

'When Lucullus marched against this city, Tigranes could not suffer it quietly, but put himself at the head of his forces, and on the fourth day encamped over against the Romans, keeping the river Arsania between himself and them, which they must of necessity cross on their way to Artaxata.

'Thereupon Lucullus sacrificed to the gods, in full assurance that the victory was already his, and then crossed the river with twelve cohorts in the fore, and the rest disposed so as to prevent the enemy from closing in upon his flanks. For large bodies of horsemen and picked soldiers confronted him, and these were covered by Mardian mounted archers and Iberian lancers, on whom Tigranes relied beyond any other mercenaries, deeming them the most warlike.

'However, they did not shine in action, but after a slight skirmish with the Roman cavalry, gave way before the advancing infantry, scattered to right and left in flight, and drew after them the cavalry in pursuit. On the dispersion of these troops, Tigranes rode out at the head of his cavalry, and when Lucullus saw their splendour and their numbers, he was afraid.

'He therefore recalled his cavalry from their pursuit of the flying enemy, and taking the lead of his troops in person, set upon the Atropateni, who were stationed opposite him with the magnates of the king's following, and before coming to close quarters, sent them off in panic flight. Of three kings who together confronted the Romans, Mithridates of Pontus seems to have fled most disgracefully, for he could not endure even their shouting.

'The pursuit was long and lasted through the whole night, and the Romans were worn out, not only with killing their enemies, but also with taking prisoners and getting all sorts of booty. Livy says that in the former battle a greater number of the enemy, but in this more men of high station were slain and taken prisoners.'[14]

'In this engagement the opposing cavalry gave the Roman cavalry hard work, but none of the foe approached the infantry; indeed, whenever the foot-soldiers of Lucullus assisted the horse, the enemy would turn to flight. Far from suffering any injury, however, they kept shooting back

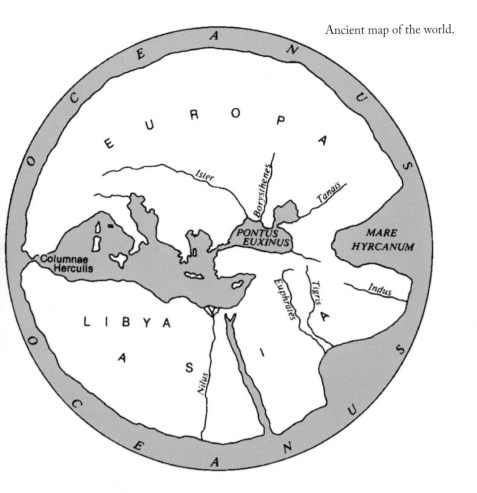

Ancient map of the world.

Possible bust of C. Marius.

Bust of L. Cornelius Sulla.

Bust of Cn. Pompeius Magnus.

Possible bust of M. Licinius Crassus.

Bust of C. Iulius Caesar.

Possible coin issued by Lucullus.

Bust of Antiochus III.

Bust of Mithridates VI.

Modern statue of Tigranes II.

Coin of Mithradates II of Parthia.

Coin of Sinatruces of Parthia.

Coin of Phraates III of Parthia.

Coin of Tigranes II of Armenia.

Coin of Nicomedes IV of Bithynia.

Coin of Pharnaces II of the Bosphorus Kingdom.

Coin of Aretas III of the Nabataean Kingdom.

at those pursuing them, killing some instantly and wounding great numbers.'[15]

The second battle of the Romano-Armenian War thus followed a similar pattern to the first: Roman attack, Armenian collapse and flight. Unlike Tigranocerta, we are not given numbers for the armies involved, nor the casualties, but Plutarch (quoting Livy) states that the collapse was a total one, with a number of high-status casualties on the Armenian side.

Once again, the key problem for Lucullus was that neither Tigranes, nor more importantly Mithridates, were amongst these 'high status' casualties, meaning that the war was far from over. Furthermore, the loss seems to have convinced Mithridates that defending Armenia was a lost cause and so, eluding the Roman pursuit, he managed to regroup his forces, changed direction and invaded Pontus. Lucullus did not seem to be aware of this, continuing with his conquest of the Armenian provinces. It appears that, once again, the Romans were not able to take the city of Artaxata, due to a relapse of the mutinous spirit in the Roman army, a matter which Plutarch refers to:

'And yet Lucullus plied them with entreaties, calling upon them to possess their souls in patience until they had taken and destroyed the Armenian Carthage, the work of their most hated foe, meaning Hannibal.[16] But since he could not persuade them, he led them back, and crossing the Taurus by another pass, descended into the country called Mygdonia, which is fertile and open to the sun, and contains a large and populous city, called Nisibis by the barbarians, Antioch in Mygdonia by the Greeks.'[17]

The Siege of Nisibis and the Counterattack (68 BC)

While the Romans failed to take Artaxata, they instead focused on a greater prize, the city of Nisibis in northern Mesopotamia, which had been taken from the Parthians. Nisibis, which later featured heavily in the Romano-Parthian and Romano-Persian Wars, held two attractions for Lucullus. Firstly, it held a royal treasury, guarded by one of Tigranes' brothers, Gouras. Seizing the royal treasury would go some way to quelling his mutinous troops. Secondly, the city would provide him with winter quarters, rather than having to march a mutinous army all the way back to Cappadocia or Gordyené. Furthermore, the city lay close to the border of the Parthian Empire, which would allow Lucullus the chance to spend the winter monitoring the situation with Parthia and Phraates III, his tentative ally.

However, whilst the city soon fell (Dio[18] provides the best account), Lucullus had made a serious tactical error. Though his move made sense for the reasons stated above, it totally neglected that fact that both Mithridates and Tigranes were still on the loose. Although their army had been defeated and routed, Plutarch stated that the numbers killed were not as high as at Tigranocerta, so a significant force remained in the field. Whilst these forces did not seem large enough to attack Lucullus' main Roman army, they were still of such a size to allow both kings to take the offensive, which is just what they did:

'Nisibis, then, he captured as described, but he lost many districts of Armenia and of the other countries around Pontus. For Tigranes had not aided Nisibis, believing that it could not be captured, but had hurried to the places just mentioned to see if he could secure them ahead of Lucullus, while the latter was occupied around Nisibis. Then sending Mithridates back home, Tigranes himself entered his own district of Armenia. There he was opposed by Lucius Fannius, whom he surrounded, however, and besieged, until Lucullus learned of it and sent assistance.'[19]

So whilst Lucullus was planning on wintering in the south of the Armenian Empire, Tigranes was still at large further to the north and was able to mount an attack on a Roman garrison. We are not told where in Armenia this occurred, but it showed the continuing weakness of Lucullus' position; he had twice heavily defeated the Armenian army, but was seemingly no nearer bringing the war to a successful conclusion. Plutarch's talk of Hannibal may have been a deliberate attempt to draw a parallel between the two men, both being successful in battle but ultimately unable to defeat their enemy. Whilst it seems that Lucullus was able to send reinforcements to Fannius in time to break the siege and drive off Tigranes, Lucullus was soon to find out that he had once again been outmanoeuvred by Mithridates, who re-invaded his Roman-occupied kingdom of Pontus, opening up a second front of the war.

The Pontic Campaign of 68 BC

Lucullus' failure to follow up his victory at Artaxata had handed the advantage to Mithridates and Tigranes. Though he had been defeated in battle once again – a battle that he did not wish to fight – Mithridates seems to have quickly realized the flaw in the Roman campaign; namely not retreating to Pontus but wintering in Armenia. Whilst that kept a Roman presence in Armenia and left them able to respond to any move by Parthia, it neglected Pontus, which was manned by just a handful of garrisons, allowing Mithridates to take what forces he could muster and try to regain his recently conquered kingdom:

'Mithridates hastened to what was left of his own kingdom of Pontus, taking with him 4,000 of his own troops and as many more that he had received from Tigranes.'[20]

We are not told how many Romans still occupied Pontus, but they can't have been more than garrison-strength at key cities, the bulk of the army being with Lucullus in Armenia. The most senior Roman commander in Pontus was Lucullus' legate, M. Fabius Hadrianus. Dio, along with Appian, preserves an account of Mithridates' ensuing campaign, though Plutarch chooses to gloss over it and focus on disaffection within the Roman army:

'Meanwhile Mithridates had invaded the other Armenia and the neighbouring districts. Here he fell upon and destroyed many of the Romans, to whom he appeared unexpectedly as they were wandering about the country, while others he killed in battle; and thereupon he promptly recovered most of the districts.'[21]

In just a few short months, Mithridates was able to significantly undermine the Roman conquest of Pontus, overturning years of Roman effort, highlighting the superficial control they had of the region and the limited number of troops they had available. The lack of Roman forces in the region can be seen from Dio's account of the key clash between Fabius and Mithridates, with Fabius having to rely on Thracian mercenaries and freed slaves, being let down by both.

The Unnamed Battle (68 BC)

We have few details for this battle between Fabius and Mithridates, only that it occurred in Pontus late in 68 BC and resulted in a Roman defeat:

'For the Thracians, who had formerly served as mercenaries under Mithridates but were then with Fabius, and the slaves present in the Roman camp gave them valiant assistance. For the Thracians, when sent ahead by Fabius to reconnoitre, did not bring back to him any reliable report, and later, when he was proceeding in rather careless fashion and Mithridates suddenly fell upon him, they joined in the attack on the Romans; and at the same time the slaves, to whom the barbarian king had proclaimed freedom, took a hand in the affair.

'They would have destroyed the Romans utterly had not Mithridates, who, although over seventy years old, was in the battle, been struck by a stone while leading a bold attack against the enemy. This caused the barbarians to fear that he might die; and while they halted battle on that account Fabius and others were able to escape to safety.'[22]

'Mithridates made haste and attacked Fabius, who had been left in command by Lucullus, put him to flight, and killed 500 of his men. Fabius freed the slaves who had been in his camp and fought again an entire day, but the battle was going against him until Mithridates was struck by a stone on the knee and wounded by a dart under the eye and was hastily carried out of the fight. For many days thereafter his forces were alarmed for his safety, and the Romans were quiet on account of the great number of wounds they had received.'[23]

The Siege of Cabira (68 BC)

Although Fabius was defeated, he did not seem to lose many men, and with having to use freed slaves, he probably did not have a large force to begin with. The injury to Mithridates allowed Fabius to withdraw and regroup, but clearly the Roman position in Pontus was crumbling. Fabius was able to retreat to the city of Cabira, which was promptly besieged by Mithridates, hoping to eliminate the last major Roman presence in Pontus.

The complete collapse of Roman rule in Pontus was not averted by Lucullus – wintering in Mesopotamia at Nisibis – but by another of Lucullus' legates, C. Valerius Triarius, who was last recorded in charge of the Roman fleet in the Aegean in 69 BC. It would appear that Triarius had previously been given orders to assemble reinforcements for Lucullus in the Roman province of Asia – though technically Asia was no longer under Lucullus' command – and march them to join him in Mesopotamia. We do not know Triarius' exact route, as the direct route from Asia to Mesopotamia would go via Cilicia or Cappadocia, not Pontus, but at some point after Mithridates' invasion he was made aware of events and diverted his army into Pontus and towards Cabira:

'Fabius was subsequently shut up and besieged in Cabira but was rescued by Triarius. The latter was in that vicinity on his way from Asia to Lucullus; and upon learning what had happened he collected as large a force as was possible in the circumstances and so alarmed Mithridates, who supposed he was advancing with the full strength of the Roman army, as to make him withdraw before ever he came in sight.'[24]

Hearing of the approach of another Roman army, Mithridates seems to have abandoned the siege of Fabius in Cabira – no doubt wary of being caught in another siege, as happened at Cyzicus – and retreated eastwards into the mountains, choosing to make a stand at the city of Comana. Triarius gave pursuit and the two sides met in battle.

The Battle of Comana (68 BC)

As is common, we have two slightly contradictory accounts of the battle that followed:

> 'At this Triarius took courage, and pursuing the king as far as Comana, whither he had retired, won a victory over him there. Mithridates was encamped on the opposite side of the river from the point which the Romans were approaching and was anxious to join battle with them while they were worn out from the march. Accordingly, he advanced to meet them himself, and also directed that at the crisis of the battle others should cross by another bridge and attack them. But although he held his own in the struggle for a long time, he was not only deprived of the reinforcements but seriously embarrassed besides by the collapse of the bridge across which many were hastening and crowding all at once.'[25]
>
> 'Triarius, the other general of Lucullus, now came with his own army to the assistance of Fabius and received from the latter his forces and authority. He and Mithridates not long afterward joined battle, during which a tempest of wind, the like of which had not been known in the memory of man, tore down the tents of both, swept away their beasts of burden, and even dashed some of their men over precipices. Both sides then retreated.'[26]

Dio, usually the more reliable source, describes the battle as a Roman victory, despite Mithridates attacking first, whereas Appian depicts the clash as a draw on account of the stormy weather. The important aspect to note is that neither side was destroyed, and both took to the field again early in the following year. Both sides retreated to consolidate their positions, Triarius in northern Pontus and Mithridates in the Pontic region of Lesser Armenia. Consequently, the Pontic campaign of 68 BC ended in a stalemate, with Triarius salvaging the Roman occupation of Pontus and averting a disaster, but Mithridates still active in the region.

As the sixth full year of the war drew to a conclusion, a final victory seemed further away than ever for the Romans. Whilst the Armenian army had been defeated for a second time, neither Mithridates nor Tigranes had been captured and both were still active in the field. Furthermore, Lucullus was faced with a mutinous army in Armenia and allowed Mithridates to open up a second front back in Pontus, which saw him nearly reconquer his former kingdom and unravel years of Roman advances. The total collapse of the Roman war effort was only averted by the timely arrival of Triarius, who was able to check the momentum of Mithridates. Had Pontus fallen once more to Mithridates, then Lucullus would have found himself cut off in Mesopotamia.

The Backlash in Rome – the Pompeian Masterplan (68/67 BC)

Lucullus having already tried the patience of a number of the Senate and People of Rome, we cannot be surprised that this latest round of disasters – a mutinous army and the near loss of Pontus – provoked a backlash in Rome. After six full years of warfare, and despite a string of victories, Lucullus was no nearer capturing Mithridates and bringing the war to a conclusion. The previous year had seen Lucullus stripped of the provinces of Asia and Cilicia, leaving him only with Bithynia and Pontus. Now, early in 67 BC, a Tribune proposed that Lucullus' two remaining provinces be stripped from him and, along with part of his army, transferred to the Consul M. Acilius Glabrio.

The Tribune in question was A. Gabinius, a known supporter of former Consul Cn. Pompeius 'Magnus'. During 69 and 68 BC, Pompeius and his former colleague M. Licinius Crassus had both remained in Rome, most likely to ensure that their constitutional reforms, which had reshaped the Republic, would be protected. One of these reforms was to restore the full powers of the office of the Tribunate of the Plebeian Order, which despite its lowly position possessed the power to initiate legislation in the assemblies on any subject they wished. These powers had been severely curtailed when Sulla seized Rome in 82 BC.

With the Tribunate restored, and judging the time to be right, Pompeius – possibly with the tacit backing of Crassus – had Gabinius propose, and eventually pass, two laws on foreign affairs. The first was to strip Lucullus of the command of Bithynia and Pontus, and thus command of the Pontic and Armenian Wars. These, however, were not transferred to either Pompeius or Crassus, but to an inexperienced commander (and possibly another supporter of Pompeius), M. Acilius Glabrio, who was Consul in 67 BC.[27] For Pompeius, this was nothing more than installing a caretaker in command, whilst he dealt with a far more serious problem – at least to the People of Rome – namely the pirate issue in the Mediterranean.

In an attempt to curtail this growing menace to trade and the supply of food to Italy and Rome, the Senate had granted M. Antonius a superior command (*imperium infinitum*) over the forces of the Mediterranean, but he had been defeated by the pirates of Crete. In response, Q. Caecilius Metellus had been dispatched to Crete to deal with the immediate problem, and though he had defeated the pirates based there and had begun to subdue the whole island, the wider problem remained.

Gabinius' second law on foreign affairs was to grant Pompeius another *imperium infinitum* over the forces of the Mediterranean. This command went further than any before, giving Pompeius a number of wider powers, such as command of the Mediterranean for three years, extending 50 miles inland from any coastline, the right to raise a fleet of up to 500 ships and draw upon public funds as he wished. Effectively, Pompeius was given (temporary) control of the Republic's military and instructed to deliver Rome from the scourge of the pirates.

Unfortunately for any study of the ongoing wars in the East, the majority of the attention in our surviving sources focuses on Gabinius' pirate bill and not the eastern command bill. Not only was the pirate bill controversial, but it was only passed after much violence in the Assemblies, representing a return to the Tribunician dissensions of the pre-civil war period. By contrast, we have few references to the first of Gabinius' bills, on the command of the Pontic and Armenian Wars, the principal one being Plutarch, though we do have a contemporary source in Cicero:

'In their disaffection, they received the greatest support from the popular leaders at Rome. These envied Lucullus and denounced him for protracting the war through love of power and love of wealth. They said he all but had in his own sole power Cilicia, Asia, Bithynia, Paphlagonia, Galatia, Pontus, Armenia, and the regions extending to the Phasis, and that now he had actually plundered the palaces of Tigranes, as if he had been sent, not to subdue the kings, but to strip them. These were the words, they say, of Lucius Quintus, one of the Praetors, to whom most of all the People listened when they passed a vote to send men who should succeed Lucullus in the command of his province. They voted also that many of the soldiers under him should be released from military service.'[28]

'[Lucullus] being compelled by your orders, because you thought, according to the old principle of your ancestors, that limits ought to be put to length of command, discharged a part of his soldiers who had served their appointed time and delivered over part to Glabrio.'[29]

Lucullus was accused of prolonging the war and profiting handsomely from it, whilst his soldiers suffered. It would seem that the mutinous elements of his army were able to pass their disaffection to friends and supporters in Rome. With the weight of this testimony, the resources of Pompeius and the very fact that the war was dragging into an eighth year – with no end in sight and Mithridates still in the field – there would have been little that Lucullus' supporters could do to prevent this transfer.

We are not told when Lucullus heard of this news, though it seems to have been before he left Nisibis for the Pontic campaign of 67 BC. Nevertheless, Lucullus faced more immediate problems. Plutarch's biography chooses to focus on the mutinies which again wracked the Roman army quartered at Nisibis during the winter of 68/67 BC. These were seemingly centred on the veterans in Lucullus' army who had been part of the notorious Fimbrian legions in the Roman Civil War in the 80s BC.

These men had been sent to the East to fight both Mithridates and Sulla by the Cinnan regime in Rome, under the command of L. Valerius Flaccus, but had mutinied and murdered Flaccus at the instigation of his deputy, C Flavius Fimbria. These legions subsequently betrayed Fimbria to Sulla, who wisely chose to leave them stationed in the East, both to act as a deterrent to Mithridates and quite frankly to be rid of them and their unreliability in future civil war battles. Not only were they complaining of their long service and the seemingly endless war in the East, but according to the sources they were being stirred up by Lucullus' brother-in-law, P. Claudius (Clodius) Pulcher, in a mixture of personal enmity and political ambition.[30]

The Pontic Campaign (67 BC)

Despite the grave situation in Pontus and Armenia, with both Mithridates and Tiridates still at large, Rome chose not only to replace the commander, but to discharge a significant portion of the Roman army in the field, which as we shall see did nothing to quell their mutinous mood. Nevertheless, when news reached Lucullus in Nisibis that Mithridates had invaded Pontus and defeated Fabius, he seemingly set about mobilizing the army to return to Pontus the following spring. When he also learned that Triarius had secured Pontus and driven Mithridates eastwards, Lucullus was presented with an opportunity to finish the Romano-Pontic War once and for all. If he could march his army north-westwards towards Pontus and Mithridates, then he could trap his erstwhile foe between himself and Triarius' army further west.

Lucullus was able to convince his men to march with him back to Pontus, their only alternative being to remain in Nisibis or to desert, but they were far from home. Whether they would fight when they got there was another matter. However, Mithridates was well informed as to Lucullus' movements; we are told of another exiled Roman Senator, named Attidius, who was still with Mithridates, though later attempted to betray him.[31] Mithridates, faced with being trapped between two Roman armies, could either stand his ground and fight or flee. Typically, Mithridates chose to gamble and fight, which given the increasing chaos affecting the Romans offered an unparalleled opportunity to recover all he had lost. He determined to bring the smaller of the two Roman armies, that of Triarius, to battle and defeat him before Lucullus arrived from Mesopotamia. He further seems to have sent word to Tigranes to join him with whatever forces he could muster in an attempt to drive the Romans from Pontus and Armenia.

The Battle of Zela (67 BC)

This strategy resulted in a major Mithridatic victory at Zela in Pontus, which is well covered by our surviving sources, Dio's being the most detailed:

'Mithridates encamped opposite Triarius near Gaziura, with the purpose of challenging and provoking him to battle; in particular, he not only took his own exercise but also drilled the army in plain sight of the Romans. His hope was to engage and vanquish Triarius before Lucullus should come up, and thus recover the rest of his realm. But when the other did not stir, he sent some men to Dadasa, a stronghold where the Romans' baggage was deposited, in order that his opponent might at least go to its defence and so be drawn into conflict.

'And thus it came about. Triarius, who feared the numbers of Mithridates and was awaiting Lucullus, whom he had sent for, was remaining quiet for the time; but when news came of the siege of Dadasa, and the soldiers in their fear for the place were becoming excited and were threatening that if no one would lead them forth they would go to the rescue at their own bidding, he reluctantly left his position. As he was now moving forward, the barbarians fell upon him, surrounded and overwhelmed by their numbers those near at hand, and then riding around, killed those who had fled into the plain not knowing that the river had been directed into it.

'They would have destroyed them utterly, had not one of the Romans, pretending to belong to the allied force of Mithridates (for, as I have related, he had many of his troops equipped in the same manner as the Romans), approached the king, as if wishing to communicate something, and wounded him. To be sure, the fellow was immediately seized and put to death; but the barbarians were so excited over the occurrence that many of the Romans escaped. Mithridates, accordingly, was having his wound cured; and suspecting that there were others also of the enemy in the camp, he held a review of the soldiers, as if for a different purpose, and then ordered them to retire hastily every man to his own tent. In this way he detected the Romans and cut them down while they were left there by themselves.'[32]

Appian and Plutarch, meanwhile, tell us:

'The fight continued for a long time doubtful, until the king made a powerful charge on that division of the enemy that was opposed to him and decided the battle. He broke through their ranks and drove their infantry into a muddy trench, where they were unable to stand and were slaughtered. He pursued their horse over the plain and made the most spirited use of the stroke of good luck until a certain Roman centurion, who was riding with him in the guise of an attendant, gave him a severe wound with a sword in the thigh, as he could not expect to pierce his back through his corselet. Those who were near immediately cut the centurion in pieces.

'As soon as Mithridates came to himself he reproved those who had recalled the army from the fight and led his men again the same day against the camp of the Romans. But they had already fled from it in terror. In stripping the dead there were found 24 Tribunes and 150 Centurions. So great a number of officers had seldom fallen in any single Roman defeat.'[33]

'It is said that over seven thousand Romans fell, among whom were a hundred and fifty Centurions, and twenty-four Tribunes; and their camp was captured by Mithridates.'[34]

The Romans suffered their first major reverse in the Pontic and Armenian conflict and their heaviest defeat in the East to date, with some 7,000 men killed, along with the majority of their officers. Both Plutarch and Appian represent a long-standing Roman tradition that blames the default squarely on the rashness of the Roman commander, in this case Triarius, who is said to have unwisely attacked Mithridates rather than wait for Lucullus. Dio, however, has Triarius' hand being forced by Mithridates launching a feint, with his attack on the Roman baggage train, and by the mutinous actions of Triarius' own troops, fearful of losing their possessions and wealth.

Having been spurred into action against Triarius' wishes, the Roman army – whose strength is unknown – walked into an ambush by the forces of Mithridates. Nevertheless, the battle appears to have been in the balance until Mithridates himself led a charge on the Roman lines. The Roman casualties seem to have been so heavy due to Mithridates driving the Romans onto a pre-prepared killing ground. Dio talks of Mithridates having flooded the plain by directing a river into it, whilst Appian mentions a 'muddy trench'. Once the Roman army had been broken, rather than being able to retreat, they were cornered in boggy terrain and slaughtered by the Pontic-Armenian cavalry. Triarius' army, which must have been at least two legions, was utterly destroyed, with the few survivors (including Triarius himself) fleeing in the direction of Lucullus' advance.

The Roman Hiatus

Mithridates had completely turned the tables on Lucullus, who now found himself in danger of being trapped between two armies as news reached him of the imminent arrival of Tigranes and his forces (of unknown number). According to Plutarch, Lucullus attempted to repeat Mithridates' tactic of defeating the nearest force before the other could arrive, but to no avail:

'But Lucullus, coming up a few days afterward, hid Triarius from the search of his infuriated soldiers. Then, since Mithridates was unwilling to give fight but lay waiting for Tigranes, who was coming down with a large force, he determined to anticipate the junction of their armies, and march back to meet Tigranes in battle.'[35]

Dio goes further and states that not only would Mithridates not be drawn into battle, but that a third force arrived on the scene, one led by Mithridates I of Media-Atropatené, son-in-law of Tigranes:

'At this juncture Lucullus arrived, and gave some the impression that he would conquer Mithridates easily and soon recover all that had been let slip; nevertheless, he accomplished nothing. For Mithridates, entrenched on the high ground near Talaura, would not come out against him, and the other Mithridates from Media, the son-in-law of Tigranes, fell suddenly upon the Romans while they were scattered, and killed many of them; also the approach of Tigranes himself was announced, and there was mutiny in the army.'[36]

Lucullus' plan to trap Mithridates had not only failed, but he himself now faced being trapped between three opposing forces. Nevertheless, Lucullus theoretically still held the advantage, as his forces were the superior in number – he had with him the bulk of the Roman army – and he had defeated both of his major opponents in open battle on at least four occasions, at Cyzicus,

Cabira, Tigranocerta and Artaxata. Yet his army had been in mutinous mood throughout the winter and now found itself facing a hard fight against three armies, rather than the anticipated easier task of surrounding and trapping Mithridates.

Furthermore, it seems that the army now knew that Lucullus had been replaced as commander and a significant portion of the army – the Fimbrian legions – had been discharged from service. Lucullus' army, feeling they had nothing to gain from attacking Tigranes, refused to fight, with an outright mutiny breaking out:

> 'But while he was on the way thither, the Fimbrian soldiers mutinied and left their ranks, declaring that they were discharged from service by decree of the People, and that Lucullus no longer had the right to command them, since the provinces had been assigned to others.'[37]

> 'But they rejected his advances, and threw their empty purses down before him, bidding him to fight the enemy alone, since he alone knew how to get rich from them. However, at the request of the other soldiers, the Fimbrians were constrained to agree to remain during the summer; but if, in the meantime, no enemy should come down to fight them, they were to be dismissed. Lucullus was obliged to content himself with these terms, or else to be deserted and give up the country to the barbarians. He therefore simply held his soldiers together, without forcing them anymore, or leading them out to battle.'[38]

> 'When Lucullus was already encamped near Mithridates, the proconsul of Asia sent heralds to proclaim that Rome had accused Lucullus of unnecessarily prolonging the war, and had ordered that the soldiers under him be dismissed, and that the property of those who did not obey this order should be confiscated. When this information was received the army disbanded at once, all but a few, who remained with Lucullus because they were very poor and did not fear the penalty.'[39]

Thus, in the middle of a war against an alliance of three Eastern kings, the Roman war effort collapsed, with the army mutinying and refusing to fight or follow a commander who had been replaced. Lucullus attempted to salvage the situation by making contact with the new Roman commander of Cilicia, Q. Marcius Rex, who was crossing Asia Minor with three legions:[40]

> 'Lucullus, then, was in perplexity, both for these reasons and because Marcius Rex, Acilius' predecessor, who was on his way to Cilicia, his destined province, had refused a request of his for aid.'[41]

'As for Marcius, the pretext which he gave for not assisting Lucullus was that his soldiers refused to follow him. Instead, he went to Cilicia, where he received one Menemachus, a deserter from Tigranes, and also Clodius, who had left Lucullus out of fear because of the occurrence at Nisibis.'[42]

We therefore have the extraordinary situation of both a Roman army and a fellow Roman commander refusing to follow Lucullus' lead, and ignoring the Pontic and Armenian forces that were roaming the region. Amazingly, in the middle of the war, the Romans turned around and withdrew from central and northern Asia Minor, ceding it to Mithridates and Tigranes, who could probably not believe their good fortune. It appears that Lucullus marched the remaining Roman army into Galatia and held there for the winter and the arrival of the new Roman commander, M. Acilius Glabrio.

Mithridates Ascendant

In just one campaign, the Roman war effort collapsed and the whole momentum of the war swung back in the favour of Mithridates and Tigranes. With the Roman army refusing to give battle or even hold onto their newly conquered possessions, Mithridates and Tigranes had the rest of the year to regain their losses and build up their forces once again.

The remainder of the year was spent in a surreal situation, with both sides studiously ignoring the other. Mithridates spent the year recovering his Kingdom of Pontus, whilst Tigranes rebuilt the strength of Armenia, though details are not recorded. Towards the end of the year, the two monarchs felt secure enough to invade Cappadocia once more and annex the kingdom, driving King Ariobarzanes into Roman exile again.[43] Throughout all this, one Roman army and its (powerless) commander sat in Galatia, doing nothing, whilst another remained in Cilicia, also inert. Although Pontus and Cappadocia fell to the kings, it seems Bithynia remained in Roman hands, as did the allied Kingdom of Galatia.

Lucullus' Final Pontic Campaign (67–66 BC)

There is a passing reference in Appian that hints that Lucullus may not have been as passive as the other sources imply:

'[Mithridates] had an army selected from his own forces, of 30,000 foot and 3,000 horse, stationed on his frontier; but since Lucullus had lately devastated that region there was a scant supply of provisions, and for this reason many of his men deserted.'[44]

This suggests that whilst Lucullus no longer had the forces to attack the Pontic or Armenian armies, he still mounted raids on the southern Pontic border region, destroying crops and livestock and thereby reducing Mithridates' ability to operate in it. If this is the case, then it shows Lucullus making the most of his now limited military resources and doing what he could to slow Mithridates down until Rome, under a new commander, was in a position to retake the offensive.

Summary

An extraordinary year ended with the clock reset as though the last four years of fighting had not taken place. The Romans held Asia, Bithynia, Galatia and Cilicia, whilst Mithridates held Pontus and Cappadocia and Tigranes the Armenian Empire. The Roman victories at Tigranocerta and Artaxata had been wasted by the collapse of the Roman war effort, with mutinous armies and changes of commanders all placing their own interests (or those of their patrons) ahead of those of the Republic. For Lucullus it was a disastrous end to the greatest command he would hold.

Though ultimately undone by a mutinous army and the loss of his command in the Roman Assembly, it must be said that Lucullus was to a great extent the master of his own downfall. He stood guilty of failing to translate overwhelming victories on the battlefield into a successful conclusion to the war. A parallel for this can be found in the Romano-Numidian War of 112–105 BC, with Q. Caecilius Metellus 'Numidicus' victorious in battle but unable to end the war as the Numidian King Jugurtha constantly eluded him. It was this inability to capture Mithridates that allowed the war to continue year after year and if anything intensify, while dragging in the neighbouring powers of the Armenian and possibly the Parthian Empire. This prospect of a seemingly never-ending war undermined Lucullus in the Senate and before the People.

Added to this general failure came the mistake of wintering in Mesopotamia and seemingly focusing more on Parthia than on Mithridates and Tigranes. After the victory at Artaxata, he knew that both kings were still in the field, yet chose to place himself at the other side of the Near East, leaving central Asia Minor largely undefended and virtually inviting one or both to march westwards, away from the main Roman army and into Pontus. Lucullus was also ultimately the architect of the disastrous campaigns of late 67 and early 66 BC, underestimating the tactical ability of his opponents and overestimating the strengths of his own subordinates. Thus, the winter of 67/66 BC found the Romans set back several years in their war effort, and the alliance of Mithridates and Tigranes – at least temporarily – in the ascendancy.

Yet Rome's war effort had merely been paused, with Roman armies in Galatia and Cilicia defending Roman territory (though not that of certain of their allies it seems), awaiting the arrival of a new commander who could bring fresh impetus to the war. Technically that commander was M. Acilius Glabrio, who was taking his time in arriving in Asia Minor – perhaps deliberately so.

However, there was more than one Roman force operating in Cilicia. Whilst formal command of the province fell to Q. Marcius Rex with his three legions, none other than Cn. Pompeius Magnus was active in the region. Having received command across the Mediterranean, Pompeius wasted no time in carving the region up into various theatres of operation, each with its own commander, and had within the year isolated and defeated each of the pirate forces at sea and then captured their bases on land.

Uncoincidentally, Pompeius reserved for himself the Eastern Mediterranean and the pirate fleets operating off the Cilician coast. His campaign culminated in victory at the Battle of Coracesium, where the Roman navy destroyed the largest pirate fleet and then captured its base on the Cilician coast. The year 67 BC ended with Pompeius victorious in the long-standing war against the pirates and conveniently already stationed in Cilicia, only a short march away from Mithridates and Tigranes.

Chapter 7

A Fresh Impetus – The Pompeian Campaign (66 BC)

The Non-Existent Campaigns of M. Acilius Glabrio

Having ceded the initiative to Mithridates and Tigranes through the self-inflicted chaos of 67 BC, with mutinies and changes of leadership, it was imperative that the new Roman commander, M. Acilius Glabrio, proceed to Bithynia as fast as possible to take up command, reorganize the Roman army and start to apply pressure once again on Mithridates. Glabrio found himself in command of the most prestigious Roman war in the East for a generation. However, the situation was far from clear politically.

We know little of Glabrio himself. He came from a long-established Plebeian consular family, which hailed from the new wave of families who came to prominence in the wake of the Second Punic War, their first Consulship being 191 BC. Though a further Consulship followed in 154 BC, the family's fortunes seemed to have waned; the next generation did not reach the Consulship and appear to have gone no further than the Tribunate.[1] We can conclude that this is another case of a family's fortunes being revived by choosing the winning side of the First Civil War.

More importantly, we know nothing of Glabrio's prior military record. We see that he was elected Praetor in 70 BC, the same year that the Duumvirate of Pompeius and Crassus were elected Consuls and seized temporary control of the Republic. To be elected that year would strongly indicate that he was a supporter of one of those two leading men, and his subsequent career would suggest that he was an adherent of Pompeius and most likely served under him, probably in Spain.

Despite – or more likely because of – his solid but undistinguished background, Glabrio was rapidly elevated to the Consulship, being elected in 68 for 67 BC. Pompeius and Crassus both chose to stay in Rome in 69 and 68 BC to ensure no one overturned their constitutional reforms. Whilst the Duumvirs could not totally control who was elected each year, they could ensure that no one reached the Consulship who was outright opposed to them. Given Glabrio's rapid elevation from Praetor to Consul, we can detect a powerful patron supporting him.

This suggests that the choice of Glabrio to command the Pontic and Armenian campaigns of the Eastern War was not based upon military merit, but political usefulness. Glabrio was merely a militarily competent 'caretaker' commander, to ensure that Lucullus was removed and not replaced by anyone of note until such time as his patron could assume command of the war. With that in mind, the non-existent campaign of Glabrio makes sense, in political terms, if not in military ones. Rather than hasten to Bithynia and Galatia to take up command of the Roman armies from Lucullus, Glabrio apparently took his time reaching Asia Minor. He actually went no further than Bithynia, which meant that Lucullus was still in day-to-day command of the Roman army wintering in Galatia. This also meant that Mithridates and Tigranes' effort to rebuild their respective kingdoms went further unchecked throughout the beginning of 67 BC.

The Culmination of the Pompeian Masterplan

Roman political and military policy in this period were clearly under the influence of two men: Cn. Pompeius Magnus and M. Licinius Crassus. In 71 and 70 BC, the two men had united their considerable powerbases – military, political and economic – and seized control of the Republic through their joint election as Consuls, bringing an end to the First Civil War. They spent their year in office reshaping the Republican constitution, which had been revised throughout the civil war, and created a new version of the Republic (effectively the Pompeian-Crassan one). During the years which immediately followed their Consulship, both men chose to remain in Rome to make sure that their new Republican constitution was bedded in.

Though both men were accomplished military commanders, it was Pompeius who seemed to define himself by martial success and thus would have been constantly on the lookout for new and 'glorious' military opportunities. Paradoxically, Lucullus' failure to bring an end to the Eastern War had allowed it to escalate, expanding to encompass the Armenian Empire and entangling the Parthian one, making it an enticing opportunity to an ambitious Roman commander. Any war that involved the empires of the East would immediately bring connotations of the great Macedonian king, Alexander the Great, still an icon for any military leader of the ancient world.[2]

Yet interestingly, Pompeius held off seizing the opportunity offered by the Eastern War to play a longer game. Instead he chose the war against the pirates as his first campaign post-Consulship, a riskier option but one with greater rewards. The pirate problem had been plaguing the Mediterranean for the last century, an indirect consequence of Rome destroying the old Hellenistic order, with the Seleucid and Ptolemaic Empires being reduced in influence, along with lesser powers such as Rhodes. The first Roman campaign against the pirates was in 102 BC and was commanded by M. Antonius, grandfather of the Triumvir, and was perhaps sponsored by C. Marius. However, it had brought few practical results, other than drawing Cilicia into becoming a quasi-Roman protectorate.

A subsequent campaign launched in 74 BC led by another M. Antonius (son of the first commander and father of the Triumvir) had been more noted for the extraordinary scope of the command – Mediterranean-wide and superior to other Roman commanders – than its result; a dismal defeat on Crete. A lesser campaign by Q. Caecilius Metellus 'Creticus' had been successful in conquering Crete, but the wider problem remained.

The command against the pirates held two advantages over the Eastern War: the constitutional scope of the command itself (supreme general of the Mediterranean) and the impact back in Rome, securing the food supply of Italy and the People of Rome and saving the Republic, as opposed to defeating some foreign ruler in a faraway eastern place.

Pompeius therefore prioritized war with the pirates but kept one eye on the Eastern War, and consequently we saw the Tribune A. Gabinius[3] (using powers restored to him by Pompeius) transferring command of the Eastern War to one of Pompeius' subordinates, acting as a caretaker. It is interesting to speculate how far back Pompeius was planning this seizure of the eastern command. Lucullus' control of Asia was removed in 69 BC, with P. Cornelius Dolabella taking charge, and more importantly Cilicia – the original basis of Lucullus' command – was stripped from him in 68 BC (see Chapter Six) and handed over to the Consul Q. Marcius Rex. As we have already commented upon (see previous chapter), Marcius was probably another of Pompeius' supporters and thus by 66 BC Pompeius had at least two men – Acilius Glabrio and Marcius Rex – in command of Rome's military forces in Asia Minor.

Whilst Gabinius' first bill transferred command away from Lucullus, his second gave Pompeius supreme control of the Mediterranean and all lands within 50 miles of the coast, including the majority of major cities of the Roman world. That Pompeius was already thinking of the command after the war with the pirates speaks highly of the man's faith in his own abilities, or his arrogance, depending upon your point of view. The problem had plagued Rome for nearly a century and had seen major military failures time and again, but he believed it could be resolved within three years.

Furthermore, Rome was notoriously uncomfortable at fighting naval battles, though it could do when the need arose. Yet Metellus Creticus had shown that the war need not be simply one with naval engagements, having combined war at sea with conquest on land, reducing the island of Crete and all its pirate bases. Thus Pompeius had a model to follow, and one which he executed with ruthless efficiency.

Though the details of the war fall out of the scope of this work, Pompeius carved the Mediterranean up into various sectors, each with its own commander and forces, thereby conducting simultaneous campaigns Mediterranean-wide, denying the pirate fleets the chance to flee to another sector unchallenged or reinforce another under attack. Furthermore, naval victories were followed up by land campaigns to destroy the pirate bases.

To undertake this task, the Lex Gabinia gave Pompeius three years, which may well have been his initial estimate.[4] It is interesting to contemplate how the Eastern War would have gone with Glabrio in charge for three years. Yet by the end of 68 BC, Pompeius' simple yet effective policy had destroyed the pirate fleets of the Mediterranean, leaving Pompeius as the hero of the Republic yet again and able to enact the second element of his 'masterplan', being appointed commander of the Eastern War.

Unsurprisingly, early in 66 BC, another Tribune, C. Manilius, proposed to the Assembly – and had it voted through – that Pompeius be given command of the provinces of Pontus, Bithynia and Cilicia, with overall command of the Pontic and Armenian Wars.[5] This ended the commands of two of the caretaker governors, M. Acilius Glabrio in Bithynia and Q. Marcius Rex in Cilicia (along with its three legions). It also removed the final province from Lucullus himself.

There is nothing to state that Pompeius' command of the Mediterranean was removed, as it had been granted for a period of three years and thus the two most likely overlapped, further enhancing his power. A passage of Cicero from this period, though written up later, sums up the mood at Rome over this appointment:

> '... that Lucullus, after having performed great exploits, is departing from that war; that it is not enough that whoever succeeds him should be prepared for the conduct of so important a war; that one general is demanded and required by all men, both allies and citizens, for that war; that he alone is feared by the enemy, and that no one else is.'[6]

The approach taken was clear, and totally hypocritical: Mithridates and Tigranes did not fear Acilius Glabrio, but they would Pompeius, overlooking his role in appointing Glabrio in the first place. Thus command of Rome's Great Eastern War fell to Rome's foremost general, Cn. Pompeius Magnus, who was to expand its remit far beyond that envisaged by anyone at Rome, more than matching the ambition of Lucullus.

The Pompeian Campaign – Transfer of Command

Unlike Glabrio upon his appointment, Pompeius was already in Cilicia at the head of Roman forces when news of his new command reached him. From there he could easily take charge of Marcius' three legions, conveniently placed there the previous year, so already possessed a Roman army before moving to Galatia to meet Lucullus. Before leaving Cilicia, Pompeius wasted no time in proclaiming that the war was now under his charge, immediately sending word to all Roman commanders and allied kings:

'For he sent out edicts in all directions calling the soldiers to his standard and summoned the subject potentates and kings into his presence.'[7]

Having established his position, he marched with his forces to Galatia to meet (and confront) his predecessor-but-one, Lucullus, the man whose command he had so successfully undermined. Any thoughts of a reconciliation between these two former allies – both men having served under Sulla during the First Civil War – were soon dispelled by Pompeius' actions as he travelled across Asia Minor:

'Moreover, as he traversed the country, he left nothing undisturbed that Lucullus had done, but remitted punishments in many cases, and took away rewards, and did everything, in a word, with an eager desire to show the admirers of that general that he was wholly without power.'[8]

As was to be expected, the meeting between these two men in Galatia, at the town of Danala,[9] started badly, then went downhill quickly:[10]

'When he was now in Galatia, Lucullus met him and declared the whole conflict over, claiming there was no further need of an expedition, and that for this reason, in fact, the men sent by the Senate to arrange for the government of the districts had arrived. Failing to persuade him to retire, Lucullus turned to abuse, stigmatising him as officious, greedy for war, greedy for office, and so on. Pompeius, paying him but slight attention, forbade anybody longer to obey his commands and pressed on against Mithridates, being eager to join issue with him as quickly as possible.'[11]

'However, their conference resulted in no equitable agreement, but they left it still more estranged from one another. Pompeius also annulled the ordinances of Lucullus and took away all but sixteen hundred of his soldiers. These he left to share his triumph, but even these did not follow him very cheerfully.'[12]

Lucullus was summarily dismissed and sent back to Rome, though Pompeius' belittling of him did not stop there, with attacks on him continuing when he reached Rome (see below). Pompeius took control of the Roman legions stationed in Galatia, though we are not told the number, and must have added them to the three legions from Cilicia. The most commented upon of Pompeius' actions was the reintegration of the Fimbrian legions, which had mutinied under Lucullus and done so much to undermine his final campaign. Despite being released from service under the Lex Gabinia of 67 BC, we are told that they happily signed on for Pompeius' campaigns, giving him none of the problems that Lucullus had experienced:

> 'The proof of this is that Pompeius took these same men, for he enrolled the Valerians again, and kept them without the slightest show of revolt. So much does one man differ from another.'[13]

The Pompeian Campaign – Tactics

Despite the optimism brought about by Pompeius taking command in the East, and even without the issues of a mutinous army, he still faced the same basic conundrum that Lucullus had; namely, how to turn military superiority on the battlefield into a permanent victory. Having spent so much political capital to acquire this command, Pompeius clearly had to deliver, and this meant securing the person of Mithridates, dead or alive. He also had to show to the Senate and People of Rome that this war was being won and would not drag on endlessly. Thus he needed to deliver a quick win and to secure Mithridates.

The Mithridatic and Tigranean Campaign – Tactics

Naturally, given the fact that the bulk of our surviving sources are Roman – and here we must lament the loss of Memnon – we have little detail as to what Mithridates and Tigranes were doing during this Roman hiatus. Certainly, they would not have wasted such an opportunity. For Mithridates, the priority would have been to resecure as much of Pontus as he could. We are not told whether Roman garrisons were still left in key Pontic cities or withdrawn, nor if they were left when Mithridates chose to attack them. A key goal would have been rebuilding the Pontic armies and securing as much control over mainland Pontus as he could. His Black Sea Empire, centred on the Crimea, was still under the control of his son Machares, who had allied to Rome (see Chapter Five).

For Tigranes, the key aim would have been to re-establish his authority over his Armenian Empire, which had seen Roman armies roaming it for the last two years. Central to this would have been ensuring that newly conquered territory, such as the Seleucid provinces, did not rebel again, and that Parthia did not take advantage of his weakness. The secondary consideration would have been to rebuild the Armenian army for a potential renewed Roman onslaught, though there must have been the possibility for a diplomatic solution. As we have seen, both monarchs certainly felt strong enough to invade Cappadocia and remove the pro-Roman client king, bringing more territory into their sphere of influence. Bithynia still seems to have retained Roman forces, while Galatia was the winter quarters of the main Roman army, ruling those out for easy annexation.

In terms of tactics, here the two kings may well have diverged. Mithridates could well expect a renewed Roman invasion of Pontus but knew that Pompeius, for all his political manoeuvrings at Rome, still faced the same fundamental problem as Lucullus: whilst Rome may win battles, the war would not be over until Mithridates was dead or captive. Thus for Mithridates, the key to his strategy would be to elude set-piece battles with Rome, and avoid capture at all costs.

Tigranes had more options; the first being whether to fight at all. Although Rome coveted his Armenian Empire, Lucullus' attack had been a major escalation of the war and there was always the possibility that he could seek separate terms with Pompeius, as his own defeat and capture was not an issue in Rome, especially given the relative ease (at least in Roman minds) of his recent defeats. Consequently, Tigranes seemed to pose far less of a threat to Rome.

The Pompeian Campaign – The Diplomatic Offensive

As Pompeius was reorganizing his army for the coming campaign, he seems to have gone on a diplomatic offensive, sending emissaries to both Mithridates and Phraates, the Parthian Emperor, though strangely no mention is made of Tigranes. Whilst both Lucullus and Mithridates had courted the Parthian ruler, Pompeius seems to have changed tactic slightly and encouraged Phraates to launch a second front against Tigranes, invading the Armenian Empire to reoccupy the lands taken by Tigranes during the previous decades.

Such a tactic would ensure that Tigranes was tied down in the south and in no position to bring his forces to bear to the west. However, it is far from clear whether Phraates did invade as quickly as Pompeius wanted or merely paid lip service to another Roman general, as he had with Lucullus. Clearly Phraates wanted to recover the lost Parthian territories, but he still seemingly faced a rival in Parthia in the ongoing civil war (see Appendix Two).

The second emissary, who went to Mithridates himself, was a man named Metrophanes.[14] We are not told the content of the message Pompeius sent, but the eventual terms he named for an end to the war were the return of all Roman deserters (for punishment) and the king to hand himself over. With neither of these conditions likely to be met, we must question what Pompeius was trying to achieve here. While he clearly intended that the war should be finished on the battlefield, with a display of his martial prowess, he cannot have seriously expected Mithridates to accede to his demands.

In the short term, however, he had time to kill whilst he rebuilt the Roman army, and it was worth testing Mithridates' resolve. Furthermore, it may have been the case that Pompeius was not intending his message to solely be to Mithridates, but to set out to the wider audience of Pontic and Armenian commanders the terms that he would end the war on – the person of Mithridates himself and the Roman deserters – and thus hopefully encourage any disaffected elements amongst Mithridates' supporters to turn on their master.

It is the lack of any reference to Tigranes that is perhaps the most interesting. Any analysis of the previous stages of the war reveals that it was only with Tigranes' assistance that Mithridates was able to continue to persecute the conflict, having exhausted (at the time) the military resources of Pontus. Furthermore, Tigranes had been reluctant to get involved in the war against Rome, needing to focus his efforts on defending his new empire, and only did so when Lucullus invaded. Of all Mithridates' allies, it was Tigranes who was the most valuable and thus the most important one for Pompeius to persuade to change sides.

Again, whilst we have no surviving sources to point to a diplomatic exchange between the two men, it would seem odd that Pompeius sent emissaries to both Mithridates and Phraates, but not Tigranes. Furthermore, as events soon proved, we see a marked change in Tigranes' stance towards his father-in-law – no doubt chastened by the two major military defeats – and it is worth speculating that there was diplomatic activity between Pompeius and Tigranes, with an offer to refrain from attacking the Armenian Empire if Tigranes stopped his support of Mithridates. If this was the case, then this was a major Roman diplomatic and tactical triumph.

The Pompeian Campaign – The Invasion of Pontus (66 BC)

However, as Pompeius would have hoped, the diplomatic mission came to nought and thus war could be resumed. For the Pompeian campaigns we have the surviving narratives of Plutarch, Appian and Dio. Prior to any land invasion, Plutarch informs us that Pompeius deployed his considerable naval resources –

a legacy of the pirate war – in an arc from Phoenicia and the Bosphorus, though with the loss of his Pontic fleet between 73 and 71 BC and the loss of his Black Sea Empire to his son Machares, Mithridates would have had little in the way of naval resources. Nevertheless, the main thrust would be a Roman advance from Galatia into southern Pontus, the region referred to as Armenia Minor.

As detailed above, Mithridates was always going to sit back to await any renewed Roman onslaught and try to avoid battle. Both Plutarch and Appian state that Mithridates had been able to assemble a new Pontic army of 30,000 infantry and 2,000–3,000 cavalry.[15] Unfortunately, we are not told the size of Pompeius' army. We can assume that it would have been larger than that of Lucullus, having retained all of Lucullus' army (bar 1,600 men) and with the possible addition of a portion of the legions from Cilicia (see below) along with any additional forces he may have recruited from Asia Minor. An educated estimate could place Pompeius' army at around six legions – or roughly 24,000–30,000 infantry – along with an unknown number of cavalry and allied units, including slingers.

As expected, Mithridates did not advance to meet Pompeius' invasion, for fear of losing in open battle, and thus held back. Interestingly, Appian refers to desertions from the Mithridatic armies over a lack of provisions. He again refers to the Lucullan activity seemingly over the winter of 67/66 BC:

> '[Mithridates] had an army selected from his own forces, of 30,000 foot and 3,000 horse, stationed on his frontier; but since Lucullus had lately devastated that region there was a scant supply of provisions, and for this reason many of his men deserted. The deserters whom he caught he crucified, or put out their eyes, or burned them alive. But while the fear of punishment lessened the number of deserters, the scarcity of provisions weakened him.'[16]

Mithridates withdrew from his position and retreated eastwards, frustrating Pompeius in a game of cat and mouse and hoping to draw his adversary into the same issues that he himself was having with insufficient supplies. If there was not enough food and fodder for his own army, then there would not be enough for Pompeius and he would have to rely on his supply lines from Galatia, which would be increasingly stretched and open to harassment as he pursued Mithridates. Appian states that Pompeius anticipated this and had his supplies sent ahead of the intended route of his army, though Dio's account disputes this and details the issues the Romans had with foraging (see below).[17] Nevertheless, for Pompeius it was imperative that he bring Mithridates to battle and end the chase, and hopefully the war.

The First Battle (66 BC)

Pompeius sent his cavalry ahead to harass the Pontic rearguard and hopefully provoke them into battle. Appian provides details of the first clash between the two armies:

> 'Then Pompeius placed a cavalry force in ambush and sent forward others to harass the king's outposts openly and ordered them to provoke the enemy and then retreat, as though vanquished. This was done until those in ambush attacked the enemy in the rear and put them to flight. The Romans might have broken into the enemy's camp along with the fugitives had not the king, apprehending this danger, led forward his infantry. Then the Romans retired. This was the result of the first trial of arms and cavalry engagement between Pompeius and Mithridates.'[18]

Pompeius scored an early victory over Mithridates in this limited encounter, being able to draw first blood. Nevertheless, Mithridates was able to limit the damage this attack caused and keep the Roman army at bay.

Clashes and Tactical Manoeuvres

All three main sources provide details for the further clashes and manoeuvrings between the two armies before they eventually met in battle. Yet all three vary in certain ways, which could either be different accounts of the same events or even differing events. Nevertheless, the key ones are outlined below. Appian describes Pompeius using a tactic of sending men ahead of Mithridates' army and trying to encircle him, provoking a further clash:

> '[Pompeius] passed around to the eastward of Mithridates, established a series of fortified posts and camps extending a distance of 25 kilometres, and drew a line of circumvallation around him which made foraging still difficult for him. The king did not oppose this work, being either afraid or mentally paralysed, as often happens on the approach of calamity. Being again pressed for supplies he slaughtered his pack animals, keeping only his horses. When he had scarcely fifty days' provisions left, he fled by night, in profound silence, by bad roads.'[19]

Plutarch provides details of an incident at an unnamed mountain and then a clash between the two forces where Mithridates again escapes from a Roman siege:

'To begin with, the king was strongly encamped on a mountain which was difficult to assault, but abandoned it, supposing it had no water. Pompeius took possession of this very mountain and judging by the nature of the vegetation and by the channels in the slopes that the place had springs, ordered his men to sink wells everywhere. At once, then, his camp was abundantly supplied with water, and men wondered that in all the time of his encampment Mithridates had been ignorant of this possibility.

'Next, he invested the king's camp and walled him in. But after enduring a siege of forty-five days, Mithridates succeeded in stealing off with his most effective troops; the sick and unserviceable he killed.'[20]

Finally, Dio has an account of the incident of the 'mountain' and skirmishes between the two forces:

'[Mithridates] seized a strong hill opposite the Romans and there rested with his entire army, hoping to exhaust them by the failure of their provisions, while he could secure an abundance from many quarters, being among his own subjects. But he kept sending down some of his cavalry into the plain, which was bare, and attacking those who fell in with them, as a result of which he was receiving large numbers of deserters.

'Pompeius did not dare to assail them in that position but moved his camp to another spot where the surrounding country was wooded and where he would be troubled less by the foe's cavalry and archers, and there he set an ambuscade where an opportunity offered.

'Then with a few troops he openly approached the camp of the barbarians, threw them into disorder, and luring them to the point he wished, killed a large number. Encouraged by this success, he also sent men out in various directions over the country after provisions.

'Mithridates became frightened and no longer kept his position, but immediately set out unobserved in the night.'[21]

These three accounts present some interesting details, but also have quite different perspectives. In Appian's account, the Romans are on the front foot, with supplies being sent ahead of them and being able to encircle Mithridates' army with a series of forts, entrapping him. Plutarch's account also seems to be in this vein, with Mithridates being trapped, primarily due to his own bizarre behaviour, and having to break his way out of a Pompeian siege. By contrast, Dio has the Romans on the back foot, suffering issues with foraging supplies, under Pontic cavalry attacks and suffering desertions. We find further short supporting passages in Frontinus and Orosius:

'Mithridates, when he was blockaded by Pompeius and planned to retreat the next day, wishing to conceal his purpose, made foraging expeditions over a wide territory, and even to the valleys adjacent to the enemy. For the purpose of further averting suspicion, he also arranged conferences for a subsequent date with several of his foes; and ordered numerous fires to be lighted throughout the camp. Then, in the second watch, he led out his forces directly past the camp of the enemy.'[22]

'Pompeius surrounded the king's camp in Lesser Armenia by Mount Dastracus. The king made a sally with all of his troops by night.'[23]

Thus we can see at some point during the chase that Mithridates did indeed take a fortified position on a mountain or hilltop as a base of operations from which to harry Pompeius' forces. It seems that some form of siege and encirclement then ensued, which Mithridates was able to break out of. Thus once again, Mithridates continued his flight eastwards, with Pompeius giving chase.

The Mysterious Campaign of Q. Marcius Rex

Perhaps the most telling passage comes from Dio when he refers to the arrival of Roman reinforcements, which seemingly tip the balance in favour of Pompeius:

'When Pompeius continued to procure these [supplies] in safety and through certain men's help had become master of the land of Anaïtis, which belongs to Armenia and is dedicated to a certain goddess of the same name, and many others as a result of this kept revolting to him, while the soldiers of Marcius were added to his force, Mithridates became frightened and no longer kept his position, but immediately set out unobserved in the night, and thereafter by night marches advanced into the Armenia of Tigranes.'[24]

This is a wonderfully frustrating paragraph as it is the only reference to the legions under the command of Q. Marcius Rex and their activities separate from those of Pompeius. As we have seen, Marcius had three legions at his disposal when he was commanding in Cilicia, but it seems from this passage that they did not all transfer to Pompeius when he marched to Galatia to take up the command of the Eastern War. It seems that whilst Pompeius invaded

Pontus, Marcius and a portion of his forces held an independent command in the early months of the year which seemingly involved conquering or securing fresh territories for the Romans and then, when this had been accomplished, he joined up with the main Roman army.

Interestingly, a passage of the near contemporary source Sallust, when referring to later events, states that Marcius Rex (in 63 BC) was at Rome being prevented from celebrating a Triumph by his political enemies. As we have no other references to military action taken by Marcius during the war, the most logical assumption is that his demand for a Triumph related to this campaign.[25] Dio is frustratingly vague on what territories fell to the Romans, saying they secured the 'land of Anaïtis' and 'many others'. Dio later refers to Pompeius wintering in the land of Anaïtis, near the River Cyrnus, on land which bordered the Albanian tribes (near the Caspian Sea).[26] Dio does not directly refer to the Marcian legions conquering the lands of Anaïtis, which would have meant that in a few months they had crossed the length of the Armenian Empire, conquered a region near the Caspian and then returned to eastern Pontus.

Ultimately, we will never make clear sense of this passage other than as proof that Marcius was operating an independent campaign during the early months of 66 BC, with at least some of his three legions, for which he felt qualified for a Triumph and so involved meeting the enemy in battle, and then rejoined Pompeius in Pontus. It is most likely that his efforts were subduing territories far nearer to Pontus, given the distance he travelled and the time he took, and thus may have been in Pontus itself or even recapturing Cappadocia.

Nevertheless, the outcome was that Pompeius' forces had been reinforced and were once more giving chase to Mithridates, who again seems to be making for the territories of the Armenian Empire and his son-in-law Tigranes. For Pompeius, it was important that he be prevented from doing so and once again escalate the war, though Pompeius probably had high hopes that Tigranes would not take to the field again.

The Battle of Nicopolis (66 BC)

To that end it seems that Pompeius spurred his men and was able not only to catch the Pontic army, but get ahead of it and lie in wait. Plutarch places this as being near the Euphrates, close to the Armenian border.[27] It is only Dio that provides any detail of this process (though Plutarch refers to it):

'Pompeius followed after him, eager to engage in battle; yet he did not venture to do so either by day, for they would not come out of their camp, or by night, since he feared his ignorance of their country, until they got near the frontier. Then, knowing that they were about to escape, he was compelled to fight by night. Having decided on this course, he eluded the barbarians while they were taking their noonday rest and went on ahead by the road along which they were to march. And coming upon a defile between some hills, he stationed his army there on the higher ground and awaited the enemy. When the latter had entered the defile confidently and without any precaution, in view of the fact that they had suffered no injury previously and now at last were gaining safety, insomuch that they even expected the Romans would no longer follow them, he fell upon them in the darkness; for there was no illumination from the sky, and they had no kind of light with them.'[28]

It appears that Pompeius finally gained the tactical advantage over Mithridates by force-marching his own army whilst the Pontic army was at rest. It did of course mean that Mithridates' soldiers would be the fresher, having not been marching in the noonday sun. However, not only did Pompeius gain the tactical advantage of being able to lie in wait ahead of his opponent, and secure the high ground, but he further chose to attack at night, albeit one illuminated by a full moon. Plutarch adds a passage about the Roman discussion of the dangers and benefits of fighting at night:

'... he put his army in battle array and led it against him at midnight.

'But when Pompeius perceived their preparations to meet him, he hesitated to hazard matters in the dark, and thought it necessary merely to surround them, in order to prevent their escape, and then to attack them when it was day, since they were superior in numbers. But his oldest officers, by their entreaties and exhortations, prevailed upon him to attack at once; for it was not wholly dark, but the moon, which was setting, made it still possible to distinguish persons clearly enough; indeed, it was this circumstance that brought most harm to the king's troops.'[29]

It seems that Pompeius himself favoured waiting until the next day to give battle, but was persuaded by his veteran commanders that it was better to attack now, especially as they had the moon at their backs to further confuse the enemy:

'For the Romans came to the attack with the moon at their backs, and since her light was close to the horizon, the shadows made by their bodies were thrown far in advance and fell upon the enemy, who were thus unable to estimate correctly the distance between themselves and their foes, but supposing that they were already at close quarters, they hurled their javelins to no purpose and hit nobody.'[30]

Thus Pompeius gave the order to attack the enemy at night, a tactic that we must assume Mithridates was not expecting, thus further catching his forces off-guard. It is Dio who provides a detailed description of the battle which followed:

'The course of the battle was as follows: first, all the trumpeters together at a signal sounded the attack, then the soldiers and all the multitude raised a shout, while some clashed their spears against their shields and others struck stones against the bronze implements. The mountains surrounding the valley took up and gave back the din with most frightful effect, so that the barbarians, hearing them suddenly in the night and in the wilderness, were terribly alarmed, thinking they had encountered some supernatural phenomenon.

'Meanwhile the Romans from the heights were hurling stones, arrows, and javelins upon them from every side, inevitably wounding some by reason of their numbers; and they reduced them to the direst extremity. For the barbarians were not drawn up for battle, but for the march, and both men and women were moving about in the same place with horses and camels and all sorts of baggage; some were riding on chargers, others in chariots or in the covered waggons and carriages, in indiscriminate confusion; and as some were being wounded already and others were expecting to be wounded they were thrown into confusion, and in consequence the more easily slain, since they kept huddling together.

'This was what they endured while they were still being assailed from a distance. But when the Romans, after exhausting their long-distance missiles, charged down upon them, the outermost of the enemy were slaughtered, one blow sufficing for their death, since the majority were unarmed, and the centre was crushed together, as all by reason of the danger round about them moved thither.

'So they perished, pushed about and trampled upon by one another without being able to defend themselves or show any daring against the enemy. For they were horsemen and bowmen for the most part and were unable to see before them in the darkness and unable to carry out any manoeuvre in the narrow space. When the moon rose, the barbarians rejoiced, thinking that in the light they would certainly beat back some of the foe.

'And they would have been benefited somewhat, if the Romans had not had the moon behind them and as they assailed them, now on this side and now on that, caused much confusion both to the eyes and hands of the others. For the assailants, being very numerous, and all of them together casting the deepest shadow, baffled their opponents before they had yet come into conflict with them. The barbarians, thinking them near, would strike vainly into the air, and when they did come to close quarters in the shadow, they would be wounded when not expecting it. Thus many of them were killed and fewer taken captives. A considerable number also escaped, among them Mithridates.'[31]

Thus, the Roman army destroyed the Pontic one, utilizing the element of surprise, the dark and the advantage of having secured the high ground. Having opened with a volley of distance weapons – using slingers, archers and the pilum – the Romans then sent in the infantry and attacked at close quarters, again on an enemy that had been caught unawares and at night, with the Romans having the advantage of the moon behind them. Given these advantages, it is not surprising that the Romans were victorious. Some credit for the victory must go to Pompeius for his forced march, getting his army ahead of the Pontic force and securing the height advantage. However, credit must be shared with Pompeius' unnamed veteran legates who advised him to attack at night, when Mithridates least expected it. Plutarch only has a small sentence on the battle, which merely adds a total for the number of the Pontic army killed:

'The Romans, seeing this, charged upon them with loud cries, and when the enemy no longer ventured to stand their ground, but fled in panic fear, they cut them down, so that many more than ten thousand of them were slain, and their camp was captured.'[32]

There are a number of lesser sources who discuss the battle, with Orosius and Festus representing a variant tradition that has the Pontic army suffering over 40,000 casualties, suggesting that the Pontic army was far larger than the figures we find in Plutarch and Appian. Orosius and Eutropius also provide some figures for the number of Roman dead and injured:

'And so battle was joined at night. The Moon had risen and was at the Romans' backs. The king's men, seeing the length of the enemies' shadows, thought that they were closer to them and threw all their javelins in vain. After this the Romans advanced upon them when they were almost unarmed and easily defeated them. 40,000 of the royal army were captured of killed, whilst 1,000 Romans were wounded and scarcely 40 killed.'[33]

'[Pompeius] overcame Mithridates in Armenia Minor in a battle by night, and plundered his camp, killing at the same time forty thousand of his troops, while he lost only twenty of his own men, and two centurions.'[34]

'Cn. Pompeius, of proven good fortune, after he had been dispatched to a Mithridatic War, having attacked Mithridates in Armenia Minor, prevailed in a night battle and, when forty-two thousand of the enemy had been killed, he occupied his camp.'[35]

'The engagement took place at night, and the moon took sides in it; for when the goddess, as if fighting on Pompeius' side, had placed herself behind the enemy and facing the Romans, the men of Pontus aimed at their own unusually long shadows, thinking that they were the bodies of their foes.'[36]

'Cnaeus Pompeius, desiring to check the flight of Mithridates and force him to battle, chose night as the time for the encounter, arranging to block his march as he withdrew. Having made his preparations accordingly, he suddenly forced his enemy to fight. In addition to this, he so drew up his force that the moonlight falling in the faces of the Pontic soldiers blinded their eyes, while it gave his own troops a distinct and clear view of the enemy.'[37]

'In Cappadocia Cnaeus Pompeius chose a lofty site for his camp. As a result the elevation so assisted the onset of his troops that he easily overcame Mithridates by the sheer weight of his assault.'[38]

Interestingly, Frontinus places the battle in Cappadocia rather than Pontus (Armenia Minor), which may tie in with the campaigns of Marcius Rex (mentioned above) in terms of a confusion arising over two different campaigns being fought at once.

The Battle of Nicopolis (66 BC) – Appian's Version

In contrast to all these sources, Appian seems to be describing a totally different battle, which is worth examining in its own right:

'At daybreak both commanders put their forces under arms. The outposts began skirmishing along the defile, and some of the king's horsemen, without their horses and without orders, went to the assistance of their advance guard. A larger number of the Roman cavalry came up against them, and the horseless Mithridateans rushed back to their camp to mount their horses and thus to make themselves a more equal match for the advancing Romans.

'When those who were still arming on the higher ground looked down and saw their own men running toward them with haste and outcries, but did not know the reason, they thought that they had been put to flight. They threw down their arms and fled as though their own camp had already been captured on the other side. As there was no road out of the place, they fell afoul of each other in the confusion, until finally they leaped down the precipices.

'Thus the army of Mithridates perished through the rashness of those who caused a panic by going to the assistance of the advance guard without orders. The remainder of Pompeius' task was easy, in the way of killing and capturing men not yet armed and shut up in a rocky defile. About 10,000 were slain and the camp with all its apparatus was taken.'[39]

In Appian's account, not only does the battle take place at daybreak, but the battle is determined by a self-inflicted rout caused by the Pontic army, whose cavalry chose to rush to support their advance guard, under attack by the Roman cavalry, albeit forgetting to use their own horses, then seemingly remembering they were meant to be a cavalry unit and returning to remount. This amazingly sparked a full-scale (and possibly comedic) rout of the rest of the Pontic army, who (in Appian's version) are the ones on the high ground, and then fell or were driven over the edge into precipices that cannot be found in Dio's account. The only detail which tallies with the other accounts is the number of Pontic dead (10,000). To say that this is a bizarre account of the battle would be an understatement, and we would dearly love to know what source he was using.

The Collapse of the Mithridatic Alliance

Despite the comprehensive nature of the Roman victory and the destruction of the Pontic army, albeit with only a third killed – 10,000 out of 33,000 – Pompeius suffered from the same problem that had confounded Lucullus before him; once again Mithridates escaped from a comprehensive defeat and fled to keep the war alive. Mithridates thus kept up his remarkable record of managing to escape from a losing battle, initially leading a breakout of Pontic forces numbering between less than 1,000 and 5,000 men, depending on the various sources:

'Mithridates made his escape through the cliffs with his attendants only and fled. He fell in with a troop of mercenary horse and about 3,000 foot who accompanied him directly to the castle of Simorex, where he had accumulated a large sum of money. Here he gave rewards and a year's pay to those who had fled with him.'[40]

'Mithridates himself, however, at the outset, cut and charged his way through the Romans with eight hundred horsemen; but the rest were soon dispersed, and he was left with three companions.'[41]

'Mithridates fled with his wife and two attendants.'[42]

Though the Pontic army had been soundly defeated again, a considerable force remained. If we accept the main sources for their casualty numbers (Plutarch and Appian), then 10,000 of them were killed, leaving another 20,000 to account for. Dio has the following:

'Thus many of them were killed and fewer taken captives. A considerable number also escaped, among them Mithridates.'[43]

This would imply that the Romans did not take many prisoners, possibly due to the chaotic situation of an army being routed at night and in hilly territory. This meant that the bulk of the army dispersed, with natives going back to their homes and mercenaries looking for another paymaster. Mithridates consequently found himself without an army and quite shortly, if we are to believe Plutarch and Eutropius, was reduced to just three travelling companions: his wife and two attendants. On the one hand, he was defenceless, but on the other, he could travel quickly and possibly incognito. With the Romans occupying Pontus in the west and his son Machares in the Bosphorus to the north, having allied to Rome, there was only one obvious escape route: eastwards to the court of his son-in-law Tigranes, following a route he had taken in 71 BC. Yet unlike in 71–70 BC, on this occasion Mithridates found no welcome in Armenia:

'From thence he set out towards Armenia on his way to Tigranes; but that monarch forbade his coming and proclaimed a reward of a hundred talents for his person; he therefore passed by the sources of the Euphrates and continued his flight through Colchis.'[44]

Mithridates thereby suffered a second and more damaging blow. Since his defeat at Cabira and the loss of Pontus and the Bosphorus, Mithridates' war against the Romans had only been sustained thanks to the support provided by

Tigranes and his Armenian Empire; support which had now been withdrawn. We can see a combination of reasons for Tigranes' decision. The first and most obvious was the losses suffered by Tigranes at Tigranocerta and Artaxata, which had clearly shown the weakness of the Armenian forces in a set-piece battle with the Roman army. As Mithridates had shown, picking a fight with the Romans would lead to the destruction of his dynasty and empire. In 69 BC, Lucullus had forced Tigranes' hand by invading Armenia, leaving him with no option but to fight, and furthermore the two sides had not met before on the battlefield. By 66 BC, this was no longer the case.

Secondly, as both Dio and Plutarch report, the Armenian Empire had succumbed to the curse of civil war, with Tigranes' son (also named Tigranes) having risen against his father for control of the empire. Thus, Tigranes was in no position to aid Mithridates, but rather had to concentrate his efforts on securing his throne. Thirdly, we have the possibility that Tigranes and Pompeius had reached an agreement during the winter or spring of 66 BC, whereby Tigranes withdrew support from Mithridates in return for an end to the Romano-Armenian War.

Mithridates had lost his only regional ally and could find no haven in Armenia. Though a severe blow, Mithridates seems to have been undaunted and immediately came up with a fresh strategy, making his way to the Bosphoran Kingdom, the heartland of his former Black Sea Empire, now controlled by his pro-Roman son Machares. He must have calculated that if he could regain control of his former empire, then he could use it as a base to continue his war with Rome, as Appian relates:

'Mithridates wintered at Dioscurias in Colchis, which city, the Colchians think, preserves the remembrance of the sojourn there of the Dioscuri, Castor and Pollux, with the Argonautic expedition. Mithridates here made no small plans, nor yet plans suitable for a fugitive, but conceived the idea of making the circuit of the whole Pontic coast, passing from Pontus to the Scythians around the Sea of Azov and thus arriving at the Bosphorus. He intended to take away the kingdom of Machares, his ungrateful son, and confront the Romans once more; wage war against them from the side of Europe while they were in Asia.'[45]

He set off for the Crimea overland – having no fleet and his son controlling the Bosphoran fleet – through the Caucasus and around the eastern coast of the Black Sea. His initial destination was the region around Colchis, which formed part of his former Bosphoran Kingdom (see Map 5). Soon enough, Pompeius learned of Mithridates' plan and sent a force in pursuit.

Back in Rome: An Inglorious Return – Prosecutions and Persecutions

For the two former commanders of the Eastern War, their return to Rome was not as glorious as they may have hoped. Though both M. Aurelius Cotta and L. Licinius Lucullus returned to Rome a few years apart (*c.*70 and 66 BC, respectively), they both met a similar reception, with neither man being allowed to bask in their victories:

'When Cotta arrived at Rome, he was honoured by the Senate with the title of "Ponticus imperator", because he had captured Heracleia. But then the accusation reached Rome, that he had destroyed the great city merely for his personal gain, and his enormous wealth aroused envy, so that he became an object of public hatred. In an attempt to avoid the jealousy which his wealth provoked, he handed over much of the plunder from the city to the treasury, but this did not mollify the others, who assumed that he was giving up just a little and keeping the most part for himself.'[46]

'Now when Lucullus had returned to Rome, he found, in the first place, that his brother Marcus was under prosecution by Caius Memmius for his acts as Quaestor under the administration of Sulla. Marcus, indeed, was acquitted, but Memmius then turned his attack upon Lucullus, and strove to excite the people against him. He charged him with diverting much property to his own uses, and with needlessly protracting the war, and finally persuaded the People not to grant him a Triumph.'[47]

Thus, both Cotta and Lucullus faced charges, both of corruption and in Lucullus' case one of extending the war. Whilst such political score-settling was commonplace, in the case of Lucullus we can perhaps detect the hand of Pompeius, clearly wanting the Roman People to only associate his victories with the war in the East and not those of the commanders who preceded him. Of the two men, it was Cotta who suffered the most, having the weaker power base in Rome. He was put on trial soon after his return for corruption – namely the booty seized from Heracleia – duly convicted and expelled from the Senate. Lucullus, with the far larger powerbase amongst the oligarchy, fared better and was not only able to brush off the charges, but eventually forced the awarding of his Triumph in 63 BC (see Chapter Ten).

Summary

During 66 BC, the balance of the war swung decisively in favour of Pompeius, both with the overwhelming military victory at Nicopolis and in the breaking of the alliance between the two kings. In one respect this formed a clean break with the phase of the war that had gone before it, as Mithridates was now without regional allies and was truly on the run, having fled the Near East. Yet in another respect, the war was still following the same pattern as before. Mithridates had been defeated in battle by the Romans yet again and lost control of his kingdom of Pontus yet again. However, once more the Romans had failed to capture or kill him, and he was at liberty and planning a fresh campaign.

Though Pompeius sent men after him, Mithridates had a head start and was able to far outpace them, given the small party he was travelling with, as opposed to a larger force travelling though potentially hostile territory, far further than any Roman army had reached before. Pompeius, as with Lucullus before him, now found the matter quite out of his hands, having to rely on Machares not losing control of the Bosphoran Kingdom and hopefully killing or capturing his father, or Mithridates being killed or captured en route. Thus, the war continued into another year, and Pompeius turned his attention to the wider issues of establishing Roman control of the region, unveiling his blueprint for a new Eastern empire.

Part IV

The Rise of Rome's Eastern Empire (66–62 BC)

Chapter 8

Forging an Eastern Empire: Armenia and the Caucasus (66–65 BC)

ith Mithridates having fled Asia Minor and Roman forces in pursuit, Pompeius seems to have turned his efforts towards transforming the Roman victories on the battlefield into a lasting dominance in the region, and as such again went beyond the original remit of the war. Bithynia had been recovered, Pontus had been annexed and the allied kingdom of Cappadocia had been restored. Yet Pompeius, as Lucullus had before him, turned his thoughts to the creation of a new empire in the East.

As detailed in Chapter One, in the century-and-a-half since Rome had first engaged in warfare with the Hellenistic powers with the First Romano-Macedonian War of 214–205 BC, Rome had barely extended its influence beyond the Mediterranean. The only territories Rome held in Asia Minor were coastal ones: Asia (bequeathed to Rome) and Cilicia, recently secured. Now the Senate and People of Rome found themselves holding Bithynia (bequeathed) and Pontus (annexed in war). With the new powers of the Pontic and Armenian Empires clearly posing a threat to Roman interests – at least in Rome's view – many amongst the ruling elite would have taken the view that now was the time to extend Roman control into the Near East.

As is common, the three main surviving sources for these events – Plutarch, Appian and Dio – disagree on the details and sequence of events that took place in late 66 and early 65 BC. Nevertheless, there were two clear theatres of operation: Armenia and the Caucasus.

The End of the Romano-Armenian War and the Fall of the Armenian Empire (66 BC)

As has been detailed before, prior to the outbreak of this interlocking series of Eastern wars, it was the Armenian Empire that had been the pre-eminent power of the region, having defeated the Parthian and Seleucid Empires. Yet Lucullus had inflicted two heavy defeats on the Armenians, at Tigranocerta and Artaxata, which had clearly shattered the myth of Tigranes' military prowess and jeopardized his whole empire. Threats soon emerged both from within and without.

The external threats were obviously Pompeius and his Roman army, but also the new Parthian Emperor, Phraates III. If being encircled by two powers eager to dismember his new empire were not bad enough, he faced a challenge from within in the form of a son, also named Tigranes, who was the surviving son from his marriage to Mithridates' daughter (and thus a grandson of Mithridates). A passage of Appian – if accurate – provides us with an insight into the issues which Tigranes had already faced with his offspring:

'[Tigranes] had had three sons by the daughter of Mithridates, two of whom he had himself killed – one in battle, where the son was fighting against the father, and the other in the hunting field because he had neglected to assist his father who had been thrown, but had put the diadem on his own head while the father was lying on the ground. The third one, whose name was Tigranes, had seemed to be much distressed by his father's hunting accident, and had received a crown from him, but, nevertheless, he also deserted him after a short interval, waged war against him.'[1]

Thus, Tigranes found himself challenged for the Armenian throne by his remaining son of that marriage. Yet the young man seems to have been no match for his more experienced father, and was soon defeated. At this point the sources diverge, with Appian having the younger Tigranes fleeing to the Parthian court first and then being sent by Phraates to Pompeius, whilst Plutarch has the prince fleeing straight to Pompeius. Plutarch also places these events in late 66 BC, before the Caucasus campaign, whilst Appian has them take place in 65 BC after that campaign. Dio has the prince fleeing to Phraates, who then invades Armenia himself (as Pompeius has probably encouraged him to do so earlier):

'While Pompeius was thus engaged, Tigranes, the son of Tigranes, fled to Phraates, taking with him some of the foremost men, because his father was not ruling to suit them; and though Phraates, in view of the treaty made with Pompeius, hesitated about what he ought to do, he was persuaded to invade Armenia.

'So they came as far as Artaxata, subduing all the country before them, and even assailed that place too, for Tigranes the elder in fear of them had fled to the mountains. But when it appeared that time was required for the siege, Phraates left a part of the force with the young Tigranes and retired to his own land. Thereupon the father took the field against his son, who was now left alone, and conquered him.

'The latter, in his flight, set out at first to go to Mithridates, his grandfather; but when he learned that he had been defeated and was rather in need of aid than able so assist any one, he went over to the Romans. Pompeius, employing him as a guide, made an expedition into Armenia against his father.'[2]

In all three narratives, prince Tigranes is defeated by his father and ends up seeking shelter with Pompeius, who now had a perfect opportunity to place a puppet ruler on the Armenian throne. Clearly, in Pompeius' mind – and that of Lucullus – the power of the Armenian Empire had to be crushed, to safeguard Roman interests in the region. Thus the Roman army invaded Armenia for a third time.

Once again, Tigranes was faced with the dilemma of whether to fight or negotiate. When Lucullus invaded Armenia in 69 BC, Tigranes was at the height of his power and chose to fight. The result had been the two defeats of Tigranocerta and Artaxata and the clear message that Armenian military might, whilst dominant in the Near East, was no match for Rome. When faced with the same scenario just three years later, he chose to negotiate. The price of peace which Pompeius set was high; Tigranes would retain control of Armenia itself, which would become a Roman ally, but the Armenian Empire was to be dismantled, as various sources attest:

'Now on the following day, when Pompeius had heard the claims of both [Tigranes], he restored to the elder all his hereditary domain; but what he had acquired later (chiefly portions of Cappadocia and Syria, as well as Phoenicia and the large district of Sophene bordering on Armenia) he took away, and demanded money of him besides. To the younger he assigned Sophene only.'[3]

'Pompeius pardoned him [Tigranes] for the past, reconciled him with his son, and decided that the latter should rule Sophene and Gordyene (which are now called Lesser Armenia), and the father the rest of Armenia, and that at his death the son should succeed him in that also. He required that Tigranes should at once give up the territory that he had gained by war. Accordingly he gave up the whole of Syria from the Euphrates to the sea; for he held that and a part of Cilicia, which he had taken from Antiochus, surnamed Pius.'[4]

'Pompeius caught him [Tigranes] by the hand and drew him forward, and after giving him a seat near himself, and putting his son on the other side, told him that he must lay the rest of his losses to Lucullus, who had robbed him of Syria, Phoenicia, Cilicia, Galatia, and Sophene; but that what he had kept up to the present time he should continue to hold if he paid six thousand talents to the Romans as a penalty for his wrongdoing; and that his son should be king of Sophene.'[5]

Pompeius and Tigranes therefore came to a pragmatic solution which ended the Romano-Armenian War and abolished the Armenian Empire. Tigranes kept his throne and Armenian independence. Though he became a client king of Rome, his new overlords were on the far side of the Mediterranean and would hopefully soon return there, leaving him with a free hand to deal with the more immediate threat, Parthia. We must remember that when Tigranes came to the Armenian throne (c.95 BC), Armenia was a de-facto part of the expanding Parthian Empire, so he had come out of this disastrous war with his independence intact, which Pontus had not.

For Pompeius, this too was a rational solution. The Armenian Empire had been dismembered and so posed no threat to Rome, and Armenia was now a Roman client state, ruled by an experienced military leader who could act as a bulwark for Roman interests in the Near East. Pompeius could certainly have placed the younger Tigranes on the throne, but he had shown himself to be a Parthian ally and not a very capable military leader, both of which may well have opened the region to renewed Parthian expansion. Furthermore, this may well have simply reignited the Armenian Civil War, with Tigranes or his allies rejecting the imposition of the prince and continuing fighting.

Pompeius could have annexed Armenia, as had happened to Pontus, but again, this would have led to continued warfare, with Tigranes taking to the hills and rebuilding the Armenian military, prolonging an already long conflict and distracting Pompeius from ending the Mithridatic threat. Furthermore, when the Romans eventually did win, they would be left with administering a landlocked state, far from their Mediterranean heartland, and bounded by the tribes of the Caucasus to the north-east and the Parthian Empire to the south-east.

Both Bithynia and Pontus had been annexed, but they could easily be reached by sea through the Bosphorus and both had been urbanized Hellenistic states. Furthermore, neither could be allowed to fall into the hands of Mithridates, who unlike Tigranes had long passed the point of accommodation. In addition, the 6,000 talents of war reparations would fund Pompeius' eastern campaigns nicely, a sum which the younger Tigranes clearly did not have at his disposal. As both Appian and Dio point out, this allowed Pompeius to reward his army, which had been so rebellious under Lucullus:

'[Pompeius] was overjoyed and promised to give each soldier half a mina of silver, to each Centurion ten minas, and to each Tribune a talent.'[6]

'... for the army fifty drachmas to each soldier, 1,000 to each Centurion, and 10,000 to each Tribune.'[7]

Thus, Tigranes held onto his throne and changed overnight from Roman enemy to Roman ally. In the place of the Armenian Empire would stand a patchwork of independent (and weak) Hellenistic kingdoms, including a reborn Seleucid state (see below), none of which would be a threat to Rome and all of whom would become Roman clients. The clear loser out of this accommodation was prince Tigranes, who emerged with only the consolation prize of the Kingdoms of Sophene and Gordyene.[8] His sense of injustice soon caused his falling out with Pompeius and unwisely plotting against his decision, which quickly led to his imprisonment:

'Those Armenians who deserted Tigranes on the road, when he was going to Pompeius, because they were afraid, persuaded his son, who was still with Pompeius, to make an attempt upon his father. Pompeius seized him and put him in chains. As he still tried to stir up the Parthians against Pompeius, he was led in the latter's triumph and afterward put to death.'[9]

'From Tigranes he received plenty of everything and far more money than had been agreed upon. It was for this reason particularly that he shortly afterwards enrolled the king among the friends and allies of the Roman People and brought his son to Rome under guard.'[10]

Ironically, it was the prince Tigranes that was led away to Rome in captivity and paraded during Pompeius' triumph, whilst his father – who had fought against Rome in two battles and supported their enemies – became an ally of the Romans. With matters in Armenia settled and still with time left in the year, Pompeius marched the Roman army north towards the Caucasus and Colchis, the last known destination of Mithridates. A legate, L. Afranius (Consul in 60 bc), was left behind in Armenia, along with an unknown number of troops, to ensure Tigranes' compliance with the new arrangements.

The Caucasus Campaigns (66–65 bc) – the Albanian and Iberian Wars

It is far from clear what Pompeius' objectives were in moving the army from Armenia late in 66 bc. We know that Mithridates was wintering in Colchis, but was this solely a move to put pressure on Mithridates or was it a show of Roman aggression determined to bring the whole region under Roman influence? Plutarch sums up the situation:

'Pompeius himself proceeded against Mithridates, and of necessity passed through the peoples dwelling about the Caucasus mountains. The greatest of these peoples are the Albanians and the Iberians, of whom the Iberians extend to the Moschian mountains and the Euxine Sea, while the Albanians lie to the eastward as far as the Caspian Sea.'[11]

'For the Iberians had not been subject either to the Medes or the Persians, and they escaped the Macedonian dominion also, since Alexander departed from Hyrcania in haste.'[12]

Pompeius was deliberately marching into hostile territory, home to the mountainous tribes of the Iberians and Albanians, who had resisted all efforts to subdue them, from the Persians to Alexander the Great. In short, did these tribes present too tempting a challenge for a commander of Pompeius' ego? He had only fought the one battle this year, an ambush and destruction of the Pontic army, and thus probably craved a fresh challenge, with Armenia having fallen by negotiation. Nevertheless, it must be acknowledged that marching a Roman army into mountainous territory populated by aggressive tribes with the onset of winter was a risk, though Appian does state that Pompeius was accompanied by a number of other (presumably lesser) tribes, who could act as guides.[13]

Pompeius sent envoys to the Albanian tribes demanding passage through their territory, which initially seems to have been granted. This acquiescence, however, appears to have been a tactic on the part of the Albanian King Oroeses, who wanted to lure the Roman forces into a trap and destroy them.

The Battle of Cyrnus River (66 BC)
The Roman army by then had broken into three forces, one led by Pompeius himself and two others led by legates Q. Caecilius Metellus Celer (Consul in 60 BC) and L. Valerius Flaccus. Each, it seems, had camped separately from the others. Oroeses had mustered over 40,000 men (according to Plutarch[14]), and likewise broke his force into three to attack each of the Roman camps. Dio and Plutarch state that this attack took place at the time of the Roman festival of the Saturnalia (mid-December[15]). Dio preserves the most detailed account of the attacks.

'Oroeses himself marched against Metellus Celer, in whose charge Tigranes was, and sent some against Pompeius and others against

Lucius [Valerius] Flaccus, the commander of a third of the army, in order that all might not assist one another.

'And yet, in spite of all, he accomplished nothing at any point. Celer vigorously repulsed Oroeses. Flaccus, being unable to save the whole circuit of his entrenchments by reason of their size, constructed another line inside. This fixed in his opponents' minds the impression that he was afraid, and so he was able to entice them inside of the outer trench, whereby making an unexpected charge upon them he slaughtered many in the conflict and many in flight.

'Meanwhile Pompeius, having already learned of the attempt which the barbarians had made on the others, came, much to their surprise, to meet the detachment that was proceeding against him, conquered it, and at once hurried on just as he was against Oroeses. He did not overtake him, however, since Oroeses had fled after being repulsed by Celer and learning of the failures of the others; but he seized and destroyed many of the Albanians near the crossing of the Cyrnus. He then made a truce at their request; for although on other accounts he was extremely anxious to invade their country out of revenge, he was glad to postpone the war because of the winter.'[16]

Plutarch has a condensed version.

'To do this, they crossed the river Cyrnus, which rises in the Iberian mountains, and receiving the Araxes as it issues from Armenia, empties itself by twelve mouths into the Caspian. Although Pompeius could have opposed the enemy's passage of the river, he suffered them to cross undisturbed; then he attacked them, routed them, and slew great numbers of them.'[17]

We can see that the Albanians chose to strike at the static Roman camps rather than make better use of the mountainous terrain and attack the Romans on the march. Unsurprisingly, the defences of Metellus' and Flaccus' camps held – though in the case of Flaccus, only just – and both attacks were beaten off with heavy Albanian casualties. The attacks do not seem to have been successfully coordinated, as Pompeius had already received word of the other two attacks and was on the march when he intercepted the force sent against him.

Thus, Pompeius had defeated an Albanian attack, but had been unable to press home his advantage, given that he was operating in the mountains in the depths of winter. It appears that the conflict was suspended until the new year, when Pompeius went on the offensive. Clearly Pompeius had determined to subdue the region and impress on them the power of Rome, rather than just fight his way through to Colchis, which he could have done. By choosing to winter in the valleys of the Caucasus, rather than push on to Colchis and meet up with the Roman fleet (which he eventually did), Pompeius was making a clear statement of his intent. He was also delaying his pursuit of Mithridates, which allowed the king time to enact his plans.

The Invasion of Iberia (65 BC)

Again Dio preserves the most detailed account of the subsequent campaigns. It seems that, having witnessed the defeat of the Albanians, the king of the neighbouring Iberians, Artoces, sent emissaries to Pompeius over the winter to establish cordial relations. Dio states that this was a ruse, simply to buy time, and Pompeius was aware of this. Despite the opening of diplomatic contact, Pompeius launched a pre-emptive attack on the Iberian territory:

> 'Pompeius, learning of this also in good season, invaded the territory of Artoces before the other had made sufficient preparations or had secured the pass on the frontier, which was well-nigh impregnable. In fact he had advanced as far as the city called Acropolis before Artoces became aware that he was at hand.
>
> 'This fortress was right at the narrowest point, where the Cyrnus flows on the one side and the Caucasus extends on the other and had been built there in order to guard the pass. Thus Artoces, panic-stricken, had no chance to array his forces, but crossed the river, burning down the bridge; and those within the fortress, in view of his flight and also of a defeat they sustained in battle, surrendered. Pompeius, after making himself master of the pass, left a garrison in charge of it, and advancing from that point, subjugated all the territory this side of the river.'[18]

Pompeius had stolen a march on Artoces and forced entry into Iberian territory, forcing the king to retreat and costing him a border fortress.

Battle of Pelorus (65 BC)

Having been taken by surprise, King Artoces again turned to diplomacy, as Dio relates:

> 'But when he [Pompeius] was on the point of crossing the Cyrnus also, Artoces sent to him requesting peace and promising to yield the bridge to him voluntarily and to furnish him with provisions. Both of

these promises the king fulfilled as if he intended to come to terms but becoming afraid when he saw his enemy already across, he fled away to the Pelorus, another river that flowed through his domain. Thus he first drew on, and then ran away from, the enemy whom he might have hindered from crossing.'[19]

With Artoces having lost his nerve for a second time, Pompeius set off in pursuit, seemingly determined to bring him to battle:

'Upon perceiving this Pompeius pursued, overtook, and conquered him. By a charge he came to close quarters with the enemy's bowmen before they could show their skill, and very promptly routed them. Thereupon Artoces crossed the Pelorus and fled, burning the bridge over that stream too; of the rest some were killed in conflict, and some while fording the river. Many others scattered through the woods and survived for a few days, while they shot their arrows from the trees, which were exceedingly tall; but soon the trees were cut down under them and they also were slain.'[20]

Plutarch only mentions the campaign in passing, but does provide us with casualty figures for the Iberians:

'Pompeius routed this people also in a great battle, in which nine thousand of them were slain and more than ten thousand taken prisoners.'[21]

Pompeius was victorious once again, but the king fled once more and again opened up negotiations. The matter, however, was not apparently concluded until the summer of 65 BC:

'Artoces, however, delayed for a time, until in the course of the summer the Pelorus became fordable in places, and the Romans crossed over without any difficulty, particularly since no one hindered them; then at last he sent his children to Pompeius and concluded a treaty.'[22]

The Invasion of Colchis

It would seem that Pompeius, having defeated the Iberians, pushed on to the Black Sea coast in pursuit of Mithridates, presumably leaving behind either Metellus or Flaccus to deal with finishing the negotiations with Artoces. A Roman army had for the first time pushed through the Caucasus to the eastern coast of the Black Sea. His destination was the Greek coastal city of

Phasis, where he was joined by the Roman Black Sea fleet commanded by a Servilius. Moving on to Colchis, Pompeius spent some little time subduing the region and thus denying it to Mithridates as a base of operations. Dio and Appian, however, skirt over the details of the campaigns:

> 'He advanced as he intended, traversing the territory of the Colchians and their neighbours, using persuasion in some quarters and fear in others.'[23]
>
> 'Pompeius pursued Mithridates in his flight as far as Colchis, but he thought that his foe would never get around to Pontus or to the Sea of Azov or undertake anything great even if he should escape. He advanced to Colchis in order to gain knowledge of the country visited by the Argonauts, Castor and Pollux, and Heracles, and especially he desired to see the place where they say that Prometheus was fastened to Mount Caucasus.'[24]

Having subdued at least the coastal elements of Colchis, Pompeius gave up on his pursuit of Mithridates and turned back. As he had no doubt been made aware, Mithridates was no longer in Colchis, but was making his way northwards around the northern-eastern coast of the Black Sea. Pompeius faced a choice: continue the pursuit or return to Asia Minor. Dio summarizes the problems he faced if he continued the pursuit.

> 'But, perceiving at this point that the route on land led through many unknown and hostile tribes, and that the voyage by sea was still more difficult on account of the lack of harbours in the country and on account of the people inhabiting the region, he ordered the fleet to blockade Mithridates so as to see that he did not sail away anywhere and to prevent his importing provisions, while he himself directed his course against the Albanians.'[25]

Plutarch adds the following:

> 'Now, the pursuit of Mithridates, who had thrown himself among the peoples about the Bosporus and the Maeotic Sea, was attended with great difficulties; besides, word was brought to Pompeius that the Albanians had again revolted.'[26]

It must be admitted that Pompeius' pursuit of Mithridates had been half-hearted at best, as seen by his wintering in the Caucasus and preferring to wage war on the Albanians and Iberians. The campaign to date had been a relatively short thrust from Roman-controlled Asia Minor through the edge of the Caucasus to the Greek south-eastern coast of the Black Sea, where he met up with the Roman Black Sea fleet. It had been limited in its scale, with relatively short supply lines.

To continue to pursue Mithridates would have meant the Roman army having to cross the Caucasus and march to the edge of Scythia, with no guarantee that they would catch Mithridates. The Roman supply lines would have been stretched, and they would have set off deeper into tribal territory with no clear strategic goal, other than chasing a rumour. For these reasons, and with the Albanians still unsubdued to his south, Pompeius gave up the chase, at least by land, and retraced his route, to finish the task of vanquishing the Albanians. It seems that on the way back, Pompeius lost several hundred men to a local tribe, the Heptacometae, but other than that returned to Armenia successfully:

> 'The Heptacometae cut down three maniples of Pompeius' army when they were passing through the mountainous country; for they mixed bowls of the crazing honey which is yielded by the tree-twigs, and placed them in the roads, and then, when the soldiers drank the mixture and lost their senses, they attacked them and easily disposed of them.'[27]

Mithridates' Black Sea Campaigns (65 BC)

Whilst the Romans gave up the pursuit of Mithridates, the man himself had been busy with his own campaigns. Although he had certainly wintered in Colchis, he soon left that region in early 65 BC – as Pompeius was fighting the Iberians – and continued his northward circuit of the Black Sea in order to reach his former empire in the Crimea. Whilst he reached Colchis a fugitive, he seems to have left it at the head of a force of men he had recruited over the winter, though no numbers are given. This force, which was probably bolstered by men from the local tribes, was clearly not able to stand against the Romans, but it did allow him to progress northwards at the head of a military body rather than as a refugee. Appian is the only surviving source to provide us with details of his campaigns, though we do have an excerpt from Strabo:

> 'He pushed on through strange and warlike Scythian tribes, partly by permission, partly by force, for although a fugitive and in misfortune he was still respected and feared. He passed through the country of the Heniochi, who received him willingly. The [Scythian] Achaeans, who resisted him, he put to flight.'[28]

'For instance, the Heniochi had four kings at the time when Mithridates Eupator, in flight from the country of his ancestors to the Bosporus, passed through their country; and while he found this country passable, yet he despaired of going through that of the Zygi, both because of the ruggedness of it and because of the ferocity of the inhabitants; and only with difficulty could he go along the coast, most of the way marching on the edge of the sea, until he arrived at the country of the Achaei; and, welcomed by these, he completed his journey from Phasis, a journey not far short of four thousand stadia.'[29]

Mithridates, having travelled around the Black Sea coast, reached his former kingdom in the Crimea through a combination of utilizing existing friendships with the tribes of the region or fighting his way through when necessary. Reached the Crimea, ruled by his son Machares, who had betrayed him and allied with the Romans, he was able to retake it without even needing force. The arrival of the man who had forged the empire – and a man of near mythical exploits – saw all the local rulers defect to him, forcing his son to flee and soon afterwards commit suicide. Mithridates then purged the Bosphoran Kingdom of all Macharen supporters:

'Mithridates finally reached the Azov country, of which there were many princes, all of whom received him, escorted him, and exchanged presents with him, on account of the fame of his deeds, his empire, and his power, which were still not to be despised.

'When his son, Machares, learned that he had made such a journey in so short a time among savage tribes, and through the "Scythian Gates", which had never been passed by any one before, he sent envoys to him to defend himself, saying that he was under the necessity of conciliating the Romans. But, knowing his father's inexorable temper, he fled to the Pontic Chersonesus, burning the ships to prevent his father from pursuing him. When the latter procured other ships and sent them after him, he anticipated his fate by killing himself. Mithridates put to death all of his own friends whom he had left here in places of authority when he went away, but those of his son he dismissed unharmed, as they had acted under the obligations of private friendship. This was the state of things with Mithridates.'[30]

Thus, against all the odds, Mithridates, who had fled Pontus as a fugitive with just a wife and two slaves, had now reconquered his Black Sea Empire, having travelled, and fought, his way around the Black Sea. No longer a fugitive, he now had the resources to rebuild his armies and continue his war with Rome. Furthermore, large swathes of tribal territories acted as a buffer between Roman territory and his own, on both sides of the Black Sea. For Pompeius, as with Lucullus before him, the failure to kill or capture Mithridates ensured that the Romano-Pontic War continued. Pompeius' hopes that Mithridates would either be killed or fail to retake control of the Black Sea Kingdom had been dashed. Appian includes a story which shows how much Mithridates preyed on the Roman mind:

'[Mithridates] formed alliances with them in contemplation of other and more novel exploits, such as marching through Thrace to Macedonia, through Macedonia to Pannonia, and passing over the Alps into Italy.'[31]

The Romano-Albanian Campaign (65 BC)

Whilst Mithridates was re-establishing control of the Black Sea, Pompeius had returned southward to fight the Albanian tribes once more and establish Roman control over the Caucasus. Although the Iberian tribes had been defeated and had come to terms, King Oroeses of the Albanians had not, and despite being defeated in his attack on the Romans during the winter of 66 BC, had taken to the field once more.

Again Dio provides the most detailed account, with Pompeius not directly retracing his route and attacking the Albanians but travelling straight from Colchis to Armenia (see Map 9), presumably to resupply his army, and then swinging back round to the Caucasus to confront them. On this occasion he had to penetrate deeper into Albanian territory than before, presumably with Oroeses hoping to draw him further in. The Romans crossed the River Cyrnus and then the Cambyses. At one stage Oroeses' plan appeared to be working, with the Roman soldiers suffering from thirst and being taken on circuitous routes by guides taken from native prisoners.

Battle of the River Abas (65 BC)

Nevertheless, the Romans penetrated as far as the River Abas, where the Albanian army was apparently waiting for them. Plutarch and Dio preserve accounts of the battle which followed:

'[Pompeius] found them drawn up on the river Abas, sixty thousand foot and twelve thousand horse, but wretchedly armed, and clad for the most part in the skins of wild beasts. They were led by a brother of the king, named Cosis, who as soon as the fighting was at close quarters, rushed upon Pompeius himself and smote him with a javelin on the fold of his breastplate; but Pompeius ran him through the body and killed him.

'In this battle it is said that there were also Amazons fighting on the side of the Barbarians, and that they came down from the mountains about the river Thermodon. For when the Romans were despoiling the Barbarians after the battle, they came upon Amazonian shields and buskins; but no body of a woman was seen.'[32]

'Accordingly he marshalled his cavalry in front, giving them notice beforehand what they should do; and he kept the rest behind them in a kneeling position and covered with their shields, causing them to remain motionless, so that Oroeses should not ascertain their presence until he came to close quarters.

'Thereupon the barbarian, in contempt for the cavalry, whom he supposed to be alone, joined battle with them, and when after a little they purposely turned to flight, he pursued them at full speed. Then the foot-soldiers suddenly rose and by extending their front not only afforded their own men a safe means of escape through the ranks but also received within their lines the enemy, who were heedlessly bent on pursuit, and surrounded a number of them.

'So these troops cut down those caught inside the circle; and the cavalry, some of whom went around on the right and some on the other side of them, assailed in the rear those who were on the outside. Each force slaughtered many there and burned to death others who had fled into the woods, crying out the while, "Aha, the Saturnalia!" with reference to the attack made on that occasion by the Albanians.'[33]

Even though the Albanians outnumbered the Romans, they fell into an ambush, as Pompeius had concealed the presence of his infantry behind his cavalry, leading Cosis to rashly attack the Roman force. Having fallen into the ambush and with their general dead – apparently at the hands of Pompeius himself – the Albanian force was destroyed. No numbers are given for their casualties, and Oroeses seems to have survived. Having been defeated, the Albanians came to terms with Pompeius, as did, according to Dio, other smaller tribes.[34]

The defeat of the Albanian tribes, like that of the Iberians before them, ensured that the near Caucasus region was now dominated by Rome. Yet although this meant that the north-eastern flank of Rome's extended sphere of influence was now secure, and Roman influence extended to the Caspian Sea, it added little to the overall war itself, with Mithridates back in charge of the Bosphoran Kingdom and arming for a fresh war with Rome.

With the tribes of the region subdued, Pompeius set off eastwards, hoping to reach the Caspian Sea. At the time, most scholars believed that the Caspian Sea linked to the greater ocean which surrounded the Eurasian landmass (see illustrations section). Pompeius quite literally believed that he was marching his Roman army to the ends of the earth. In any event, the attempt was cut short just three days from the Caspian when the army encountered what Plutarch describes as 'a multitude of deadly reptiles'.[35] Nevertheless, Pompeius had extended Roman power virtually to the shores of the Caspian Sea, brought the Caucasus region under Roman influence and extended Roman power further eastwards than it had ever been. Having accomplished all this, he returned to Armenia to continue the development of a new eastern empire.

Rome and Parthia – The Beginnings of the Rivalry

By the time Pompeius and the army had returned to Armenia, there was another more pressing matter that required his attention, namely relations with the Parthian Empire. As has been detailed (see Chapter One), just as Rome had risen in the West at the expense of the post-Alexandrian Hellenistic powers, so Parthia had risen in the East. Similarly, just as Rome had collapsed into civil war in 91 BC, Parthia too suffered internecine conflict around this time. Whilst Mithridates had exploited this opportunity to carve out a new empire at Rome's expense, Tigranes had done the same at Parthia's expense and gone from vassal state to King of Kings.

Whilst Parthia was emerging from its own civil war (see Appendix Two), it was the Romans who had destroyed the Armenian Empire, firstly by Lucullus in battle and then Pompeius by diktat. Furthermore, both Lucullus and Pompeius had encouraged Parthia to invade Armenia when it was at war with Rome. Now, however, having removed the main obstacle to Parthian expansion and encouraged its aggression, it was the Romans (and Pompeius) who had to face the effects of this policy.

As we have seen, in 66 BC the Parthian Emperor Phraates III had intervened in the Armenian Civil War and invaded Armenia. Though that civil war had been quelled by Pompeius, his absence in the Caucasus offered the Parthians a fresh opportunity to regain the lands that they had lost to Tigranes. In Pompeius' absence, it seems that Phraates dispatched Parthian forces into the former Parthian territory of Gordyene. In theory, this move was in line with Pompeius' twin policies of encouraging Parthian aggression against Armenia and removing from Tigranes any territory he had conquered during the expansion of the Armenian Empire over the previous two decades. Phraates clearly felt it was within his rights to reoccupy that territory.

Unfortunately for him, however, he had misjudged the Roman character, and in particular that of Pompeius. Firstly, Pompeius had encouraged Parthian aggression against Armenia when Armenia was Rome's enemy, but now it was Rome's ally and the new eastern bulwark in Rome's (Pompeius') new eastern empire. Thus, Phraates was now in fact attacking a Roman ally. Secondly, Pompeius had decreed the end of the Armenian Empire, and the loss of its territories, but that was for Rome to liberate them in a show of Roman power and then munificence. Such a display would not tolerate being undermined by the Parthians retrieving by force what Rome may have chosen to gift them. In short, to Roman eyes this was a clearly provocative act by the Parthians and a challenge to the newly established Roman supremacy in the East.

Therefore, Pompeius had no hesitation in ordering his legate L. Afranius, who held command in Armenia, to drive the Parthians out of the province of Gordyene. Thus, 65 BC was the year that Rome determined upon military action against Parthia for the first time, though strictly limited in its aims. Such an action could easily have led to the First Romano-Parthian War a decade before it actually came to pass. Plutarch and Dio relate what occurred:

'... but against the Parthian king, who had burst into Gordyene and was plundering the subjects of Tigranes, he sent an armed force under Afranius, which drove him out of the country and pursued him as far as the district of Arbela.'[36]

'[Phraates] accomplished nothing, however; for Pompeius, in view of the present situation and the hopes which it inspired, held him in contempt and replied haughtily to the ambassadors, among other things demanding back the territory of Gordyene, concerning which Phraates was quarrelling with Tigranes. When the envoys made no answer, inasmuch as they had received no instructions on this point, he wrote a few words to Phraates, but instead of waiting for a reply sent Afranius into the territory at once, and having occupied it without a battle, gave it to Tigranes. Afranius, returning through Mesopotamia to Syria, contrary to the agreement made with the Parthian, wandered from the way and encountered many hardships by reason of the winter and the lack of supplies. Indeed, his troops would have perished, had not the Carrhaeans, Macedonian colonists who dwelt somewhere in that vicinity, received him and helped him forward.'[37]

War was averted only by the Parthians withdrawing in the face of Afranius' advance and not contesting the province of Gordyene. Phraates had no wish to provoke a war against Rome, especially with Pompeius and his legions stationed only across the border in Armenia. The Parthian Empire was still recovering from its own civil war, elements of which may still have been ongoing, and having seen the Armenian army destroyed by Rome on two occasions, discretion was clearly the better part of valour. We have to speculate whether Pompeius was hoping to provoke a reaction from the Parthians and thus spark a Romano-Parthian war. As events of the following year showed (see Chapter Nine), Pompeius was clearly in an expansive frame of mind. With Phraates not rising to the bait, Pompeius had lost his opportunity for now, but had still asserted Roman dominance over Parthia.

Afranius drove southwards and then turned west through northern Mesopotamia, the second Roman army to do so, but penetrating further south than any Roman commander to date. In the same year, Roman armies had marched further east than ever before, through the Caucasus to within a few days' march of the Caspian Sea, and further south than ever before and crossed the Tigris. The year ended with Afranius in Mesopotamia, wintering near the town of Carrhae coincidentally – site of the famous Roman defeat some twelve years later – and with Phraates sending further ambassadors to Pompeius demanding a settlement to the issue.

Other Military and Diplomatic Activity

Prior to the Afranius expedition, we have two other interesting brief notes relating to Roman military and diplomatic activity in the region, one from Dio and another from Plutarch:

> 'Pompeius' success, and the fact that his legates were also subjugating the rest of Armenia and that part of Pontus, and that Gabinius had even advanced across the Euphrates as far as the Tigris, filled him with fear of them, and he was anxious to have the truce confirmed.'[38]
>
> 'Here the kings of the Elymaeans and the Medes sent ambassadors to him, and he wrote them a friendly answer.'[39]

Thus, we have references to campaigns undertaken by the Romans in both Armenia and Pontus whilst the main Roman army was campaigning in the Caucasus. Those in Armenia must have been commanded by Afranius, but it is not clear whom he was fighting, as Tigranes had accepted Roman terms. There may have been a hard core of Armenians who did not accept the surrender to Rome, or perhaps elements of the forces loyal to the younger Tigranes chose to fight on.

The campaigns in Pontus were commanded by another legate, A. Gabinius, who would return to the region a decade later as the first commander of the

Romano-Parthian War (see Appendix One). Again we have no details as to the enemy he faced, but they must have been elements of the Pontic forces of Mithridates who had remained in southern Pontus and chose to fight on. As Dio points out, Gabinius marched as far westwards as the River Tigris, though Afranius seems to have been the first one to cross it.

On the diplomatic front, it is interesting that Pompeius received an embassy from the Medes – most likely Media-Atropatené – and from Elymais, both of which kingdoms had traditionally fallen under Parthian influence, though latterly must have been dominated by the Armenian Empire. Media-Atropatené lay to the south of Armenia proper, whilst Elymais was at the mouth of the Persian Gulf (see Map 2). With Rome in the ascendant, both kingdoms saw an opportunity to free themselves from Parthian domination and become clients of Rome, a much more distant power.

Aside from this brief mention, however, we have no further details; both kingdoms ultimately remained in Parthia's orbit until the 30s BC and the Second Romano-Parthian War.[40] With the year drawing to a close, Pompeius and the Roman army returned to Pontus to complete the reduction of the kingdom in preparation for converting it into a Roman province:

> 'Pompeius passed this winter likewise in Aspis, winning over the districts that were still resisting, and taking also Symphorion, a fort which Stratonice betrayed to him. She was the wife of Mithridates, and in her anger against him because she had been left there, she sent out the garrison, ostensibly to collect supplies, and then let the Romans in.'[41]

Not only does this show that resistance to Roman rule was continuing, some seven years after Lucullus first invaded, but we must assume that by now, news had reached the kingdom that Mithridates had taken control of the Bosphoran Kingdom and was continuing the war against Rome. This must have had a galvanizing effect on the Mithridatic loyalists and again showed that although Rome was seemingly unstoppable on the battlefield, this could not always be converted into lasting rule.

The Roman Annexation of Crete and Attempted Roman Annexation of Egypt (66–65 BC)

Pompeius was not the only Roman determined to expand Rome's influence and empire in the East. Though the Lex Gabinia had given Pompeius overall command of the war against the pirates of the Mediterranean, the war's previous commander, Q. Caecilius Metellus 'Creticus', scion of one of Rome's most powerful political families, had continued in his command of the campaign on Crete, which continued when Pompeius transferred to the Pontic and Armenian Wars. Metellus continued his campaigns against the pirates, but went further and turned it into a war of conquest. We have no further details, but we must assume that the locals could do little to resist the Roman advance.

The move made strategic sense, both in the long and short term. Pompeius' campaigns had destroyed the pirate problem in the Mediterranean, but the question that must have occupied those in the Roman oligarchy interested in such matters would have been what would happen when Roman forces withdrew. The concern must have been that when that happened, then the problem would emerge once more. Cilicia, another hotbed of pirate activity, was already in the process of being converted into a Roman province; that left the independent island of Crete, which had formerly been part of the Ptolemaic Empire. Thus the easiest solution would have been to conquer and turn it into a Roman province to ensure that such a problem never arose again. A passage of Cicero confirms as much:

'... moreover, that Crete, owing to the valour of Metellus, is ours; that the pirates have now no ports from which they can set out and none to which they can return; that all the bays, and promontories, and shores, and islands, and maritime cities, are now contained within the barriers of our empire.'[42]

As we have seen, after the devastation caused by the First Roman Civil War, Rome's rulers had adopted a more aggressive attitude towards the rest of the Mediterranean and Eurasian territories. Roman armies had ranged further north than ever before to the Danube, and now further east to the Caspian. After over sixty years of not expanding eastwards – since the annexation of the Kingdom of Pergamum (in 133–129 BC) – the Roman oligarchy now seemed to be fused with a new imperialist spirit. Both the pirate problem and that of the rise of the Pontic and Armenian Empires seemed to be leading the Roman oligarchy to the conclusion that only conquest and Roman rule would stop these threats reoccurring. Thus, throughout 66 BC and probably into 65 BC, Metellus Creticus continued with the annexation of Crete.

In the same vein, 65 BC saw a more audacious move on the part of the Republic, and one man in particular, M. Licinius Crassus. Crassus had been the other half of the Duumvirate which had reshaped the constitution of the Roman Republic, having seized control of Rome in 70 BC in partnership with his rival Pompeius. Though a notable general in his own right, Crassus chose to immerse himself in the heart of Roman political life and not absent himself from the centre of power by going on campaign.

Nevertheless, this did not stop his eye for conquest and personal accomplishment. It was 65 BC that saw Crassus reach the pinnacle of the official Roman *cursus honorum*, when he was elected as one of the Censors, the other being Q. Lutatius Catulus. The main duty of the post, which had been resurrected by Pompeius and Crassus, concerned the organization the Roman census to register all eligible Roman citizens for the dual purpose of military recruitment and voter registration.

Yet just as Pompeius had used the resurrected Tribunate to further his own career, Crassus now proposed to extend the power of the Censorship in an extraordinary way, by proposing the annexation by Censorial decree of the Ptolemaic Empire (now reduced to Egypt) to Roman control, thus proposing conquest by administration rather than force of arms. Details on this major proposal are few, and the main ones come from Plutarch's life of Crassus, which are substantiated by vague references in Cicero:[43]

'… but they say that when Crassus embarked upon the dangerous and violent policy of making Egypt tributary to Rome, Catulus opposed him vigorously, whereupon, being at variance, both voluntarily laid down their office.'[44]

Suetonius has a similar story, but here it was Caesar – who was sponsored by Crassus – who attempted to use the Tribunes to accomplish this:

'Caesar made an attempt through some of the Tribunes to have the charge of Egypt given him by a decree of the Assembly, seizing the opportunity to ask for so irregular an appointment because the citizens of Alexandria had deposed their king, who had been named by the senate an ally and friend of the Roman People, and their action was generally condemned.'[45]

This proposal was blocked by the rest of the oligarchy, notably Q. Lutatius Catulus, his Censorial colleague, aided, it seems, by Cicero. Nevertheless, this incident does show the ambition of men such as Crassus and the expansionist spirit that had gripped the Roman oligarchy, not to mention the weakness of the other powers of the Near East.

Summary

Once again we can see that 65 BC was a year of mixed fortunes for the key participants of the war. On the one hand, Pompeius had begun to implement the key foundations for the creation of Rome's new eastern empire, with the dismantlement of the Armenian Empire, the humbling of the Parthian Empire, victories over the tribes of the Caucasus and stretching Roman influence from Colchis on the Black Sea to the Caspian. Furthermore, he had ended one of the two ongoing conflicts, the Romano-Armenian War, with the total submission of Armenia, the loss of its empire and it becoming a Roman client state.

Yet although the Romano-Armenian War was of greater strategic significance, it was the Romano-Pontic War that Pompeius would be judged against back in Rome, both in the Senate and amongst the People, and here Pompeius' record began to look tarnished. Not only had Mithridates escaped the Roman pursuit, but he had regained control of the northern half of the Pontic Empire and now had the resources of the Crimea and its surrounding regions to call on to continue the war. Thus, not only was the war to drag on into another year, but it looked to all intents and purposes like it would be escalating once more.

Furthermore, Mithridates basing himself in the Crimea presented Pompeius with a major strategic headache. His legions were in Armenia and Asia Minor and could not easily reach Mithridates to engage him in battle. To do so he would have to march them around the eastern or western coast of the Black Sea, or transport them across the Black Sea and land them in the Crimea, and all three routes would be contested to varying degrees. Added to this was the fact that Pompeius himself seemed to prefer remaining in the Near East to continue his work in building Rome's new empire. Pompeius had some clear thinking ahead of him, facing the same problem that had plagued Lucullus: how to bring the Pontic war to an end.

Chapter 9

Forging an Eastern Empire:
Syria and Judea (64–62 BC)

The Romano-Pontic War – Stalemate

Pompeius continued with his campaign to fully bring mainland Pontus back under Roman control, notably taking the Mithridatic fortress of Caenum. In wider strategic terms however, the war continued to be in abeyance, with the Romans occupying the southern half of the Pontic Empire and Mithridates the northern part, and neither side seemingly making a move towards the other. We know that Pompeius had deployed at least a portion of the extensive Roman fleet, which he had used to clear the Mediterranean of pirates, to the Black Sea, but they do not seem to have been used in an offensive capacity against the Bosphoran Kingdom. We unfortunately do not know the size of the Pontic fleet, but the majority seems to have been destroyed in the early phases of the war off the coast of Asia Minor (see Chapters Three and Four).

Despite this apparent naval superiority, it seems Pompeius had no plans to take the offensive against Mithridates and launch a naval invasion of the Bosphorus. The land route, around either the eastern or western coasts, would need to be secured against the native tribes of the region first, even with the groundwork done by M. Lucullus in the west and Pompeius himself in the east. Thus neither route would have been an easy endeavour. Nevertheless, Plutarch does report that Pompeius deployed the Roman fleet, not to attack the Bosphorus Kingdom, but to starve it into submission:

> '[Pompeius] stationed ships to keep guard against the merchants sailing to Bosporus; and death was the penalty for such as were caught.'[1]

Whilst Pompeius placed the Bosphorus Kingdom under a blockade, at least from the Black Sea, this still left the land routes available to Mithridates. Furthermore, the kingdom was a known exporter of grain. All of which reduced the effectiveness of Rome's action. Nevertheless, it would stop fresh supplies coming to Mithridates quickly and denied him the use of the Black Sea to launch any attack on Asia Minor. Mithridates was apparently in the process of rebuilding his army, which had been defeated by both Lucullus and Pompeius in Asia. Having lost the manpower of Pontus and Armenia, he would need to enlist the various tribes that occupied the Black Sea region, and these would take time to forge into a coherent force.

Pompeius remained content to continue his twin policies of completing the reduction of Pontus proper whilst implementing his plan for an eastern Roman empire, all the while waiting for Mithridates' next move. In the Romano-Pontic War at least, Pompeius seemed content to cede the initiative to Mithridates. The war was now entering its tenth year and Rome had still not ended the threat posed by the Mithridates. As we have seen, it was this failure to end the war that had done so much to undermine the command of Lucullus. Yet not only was Pompeius in a stronger political situation back in Rome, especially after his victories in the Mediterranean, but he had driven Mithridates from Asia and into exile in what Romans would have considered the edge of the civilized world.

Furthermore, as we saw with Lucullus to a certain degree, the continued freedom of Mithridates provided Pompeius with an opportunity to keep his command in the East and use it to forge a new regional empire for Rome. Unlike Lucullus, there were no setbacks to report to the Roman Senate and People, only tales of empires and kingdoms in the East paying homage to Rome (and Pompeius) and barbarians being subdued. It seems that Pompeius was in no hurry to end the Mithridatic threat, instead using the time to complete his eastern masterplan.

Pompeius' Eastern Settlement – Asia Minor (64 BC)

Having completed the reduction of the remaining Mithridatic resistance in Pontus itself to his satisfaction, and reduced Armenia and the Caucasus the previous year, Pompeius turned his attention first to Asia Minor and then further south, to the former Armenian Empire. The kingdoms of Bithynia and Pontus were confirmed as Roman provinces, though the Kingdom of Paphlagonia, which lay between the two, became an independent client kingdom under a restored dynasty.[2]

Two other kingdoms were given their independence in Asia Minor under restored dynasties, and in both cases Pompeius went further and gave them territory taken from the defeated powers. The first of these was Galatia, which Eutropius states was enhanced with former Pontic territory.[3] Similarly, Cappadocia regained its (nominal) independence under the rule of a restored dynasty and its territory too was actually enlarged:

'To Ariobarzanes he gave back the Kingdom of Cappadocia and added to it Sophene and Gordyene, which he had partitioned to the son of Tigranes, and which are now administered as parts of Cappadocia. He gave him also the city of Castabala and some others in Cilicia. Ariobarzanes entrusted his whole kingdom to his son while he was still living.'[4]

Pompeius did not only restore Cappadocia, but bolstered it with former Parthian lands taken from the Armenian Empire. Originally these had been intended for a new independent kingdom ruled by the son of Tigranes, but his fall from grace required a new plan. An enlarged Roman-backed Cappadocia would form a buffer between Roman Pontus and the allied kingdom of Armenia and the Parthian Empire. In reality, this was not much of a bulwark as Cappadocia had been frequently overrun, whether by Pontus or Armenia, and would pose no physical barrier to either a renewed Armenia or an expanding Parthia. Yet whilst it was a poor physical barrier to expansion, it was a strong psychological one. Both Armenia and Parthia now faced a large Roman allied state on their borders. As Mithridates had found, invading a Roman ally such as Cappadocia would bring Roman intervention.

Pompeius clearly hoped that adding Sophene and Gordyene to Cappadocia would defuse the situation, an assessment which was soon proved to be wrong (see below).

Nevertheless, Asia Minor had been carved up between the Roman provinces of Asia, Bithynia, Pontus, Cilicia and the Roman allied states of Paphlagonia, Galatia and Cappadocia. This was supported by the Roman client kingdom of Armenia to the east and the (temporarily) subdued Caucasus tribes of the Iberians and Albanians. This was further bolstered by Pompeius granting independence to the Black Sea Kingdom of Colchis – formerly part of the Pontic Empire – which also became a Roman client kingdom, having a new dynasty appointed.[5] Pompeius had by now created a new system of Roman provinces and client kingdoms that stretched from the Aegean to the Caspian Sea (see Map 10), a massive expansion of Roman territory and Roman power.

Pompeius' Eastern Settlement – the Romano-Commagene War (64 BC)

Having settled Asia Minor and the Caucasus, Pompeius turned his attention to the south and the former Armenian and Seleucid Empires. The first two kingdoms that felt his attention were those of Commagene and Osrhoene (see Map 2), both small kingdoms buffered between Roman Asia Minor and the Parthian Empire. The first of these was Commagene, which was taken by force:

'Pompeius then passed over Mount Taurus and made war against Antiochus, the king of Commagene, until the latter entered into friendly relations with him.'[6]

Other than this brief note, we have no other details for the Roman conquest of Commagene. Frustratingly, we do not know why Commagene fought the Romans, especially as the other rulers of the region had established friendly relations with Pompeius. Commagene had previously been part of the Seleucid and Armenian Empires, and we will never know why this short war broke out. The result was hardly in doubt, though the native ruler, Antiochus, retained his throne and the Roman system of client kings was further expanded. This expansion continued with the Kingdom of Osrhoene, which occupied northern Mesopotamia and had traditionally been a Parthian client kingdom. Again we only have a later passing reference in Dio:

> 'Nevertheless, the greatest injury was done to them by Abgarus of Osrhoene. For he had pledged himself to peace with the Romans in the time of Pompeius.'[7]

So the Roman client system now extended into northern Mesopotamia and up to the borders of the Parthian Empire.

The Romano-Median War (65/64 BC)

It seems that the reach of Rome stretched even further eastwards into Media-Atropatené (see Map 2). There was one other conflict referred to in the sources, but only in passing, and we have no clear idea when the clash took place. In the valedictory inscription Pompeius set up to record his achievements in these wars, we find the following: 'He subjugated Dareius king of the Medes.'[8] The problem we have is that nowhere in the surviving sources is there a description of a war between Pompeius and a King Darius, although Appian does make a similar passing reference to Pompeius having defeated the Medes.[9]

The Medes in question must have been those of Media-Atropatené, who were former vassals of Parthia and then the Armenian Empire. We know that the king of Media-Atropatené was heavily involved in the fighting of the war, being present at Tigranocerta in 69 BC – on what proved to be the crucial right wing – and leading an army in Pontus to support Tigranes in 67 BC (see Chapters Five and Six). The problem we have is that this invading army was commanded by King Mithridates I, the son-in-law of Tigranes himself, though he is not named at Tigranocerta.

After this incursion into Roman territory, we hear no more of Mithridates or his army, in Pompeius' campaigns in either Pontus or Armenia. It is likely that they withdrew from Pontus during the winter of 67/66 BC. This reference has led many to speculate that Darius succeeded Mithridates soon afterwards. It is also clear that Darius did not come to terms with the Romans for his predecessor's actions, and that a clash between the two took place in which the Medians lost, after which Darius is referenced no more. This clash may well have proved fatal to Darius, or he was overthrown soon after by Artavasdes I, who was to play a role in the later Romano-Parthian Wars. We are further in the dark whether this victory brought Media-Atropatené into the wider circle of Roman client states, though this seems unlikely as the subsequent Romano-Parthian Wars found them as part of the wider Parthian Empire.

We do not know in what year this clash took place: was it in 65 BC during Pompeius' first invasion of Armenia, 64 BC as part of the Partho-Armenian War or later as part of the wider 'mopping up' campaigns against Armenian allies, such as the Romano-Commagene War? Furthermore, we do not know if Roman armies invaded Media-Atropatené itself, or whether Darius had invaded Armenia. If nothing else, this war shows two important aspects: the breadth of the Roman victories, which now encompassed Media-Atropatené, and just how little detail of these wars we have with the loss of so many ancient sources.

Pompeius and the Annexation of the Seleucid Empire

Up until this point, Pompeius' eastern system had been built on recreating a system of Roman client kingdoms in the region and ensuring the destruction of the aggressive power of the Pontic and Armenian Empires. Yet the greatest of the Armenian conquests had been the remnants of the Seleucid Empire, once the mightiest of the successor kingdoms to Alexander the Great. During the third century BC, the empire had stretched from India in the east to the Aegean in the west, and at its height under Antiochus III (222–187 BC) had extended into mainland Greece itself.

As previously discussed (see Chapter One), the beginning of its downfall came at the hands of the Romans when they defeated Antiochus at the Battles of Thermopylae (191 BC) and Magnesia (190 BC). Under the terms of the subsequent Treaty of Apamea, the Seleucid Empire was expelled from Asia Minor, leading to the creation of the patchwork of independent kingdoms which ultimately gave rise to the empires of Pontus and Armenia. Of far greater consequence to the Seleucids was the rise of the Parthian Empire in the east, which by the 140s–130 BC had annexed their Mesopotamian heartlands. Thus caught between the expanding Roman and Parthian Empires, by the 80s BC the Seleucid Empire had been reduced to the province of Syria and Phoenicia, both of which fell to the Armenian Empire during the late 80s BC.[10]

Unsurprisingly, given our paucity of surviving sources, the details surrounding the annexation of the Seleucid Empire by the Armenian Empire are not well understood. Whilst the bulk of the provinces seem to have fallen to Tigranes in the 80s BC, he was again fighting the Seleucid Queen Cleopatra II Selene in 69 BC when Lucullus invaded. Whilst this forced Tigranes to break off his campaigns, some Armenian military presence remained, and Cleopatra Selene was captured and subsequently executed:

'When the Roman general, Lucullus, was pursuing Mithridates, who had taken refuge in the territory of Tigranes, Magadates went with his army to Tigranes' assistance. Thereupon Antiochus, the son of Antiochus Pius, entered Syria clandestinely and assumed the government with the consent of the people. Nor did Lucullus, who first made war on Tigranes and wrested his newly acquired territory from him, object to Antiochus exercising his ancestral authority.'[11]

'After Tigranes was conquered by Lucullus, Antiochus, the son of Cyzicenus, was made king of Syria by his authority.'[12]

Thus it seems that in 69 BC, the newly crowned Antiochus XIII established an independent Seleucid state, a move that in the short term at least seemingly had the approval of Lucullus. At this point, any destabilization of the Armenian Empire would have been welcome. Pompeius' abolition of the Armenian Empire must have given the Seleucids hope that they too would maintain their independence, albeit as a Roman client.

Throughout the latter stages of its existence, the Seleucid Empire had been beset by internal conflict, which seemingly increased in proportion to the amount of territory the Seleucids lost.[13] By c.65 BC, a cousin of Antiochus, Philip II, seems to have emerged as a rival claimant to the throne. At some point, Pompeius had seemingly dispatched the Proconsul Q. Marcius Rex (Consul in 68 BC), the Governor of Cilicia, to the Seleucid capital of Antioch to open discussions with the rival claimant Philip:[14]

'The old hippodrome and the old palace were originally built from his own funds by Quintus Marcius Rex, when he visited Antioch in Syria to force Philippus Barypus, the Macedonian king of Antioch, to pay tribute to the Romans.'[15]

It appears that Antiochus appealed to Pompeius to be confirmed as Seleucid Emperor, in the same way as the other kings of the region had, especially if he had been confirmed by Lucullus. Yet he was to be disappointed. At some point during his eastern campaigns, Pompeius had determined not to restore the Seleucid Empire, but to annex it to Rome as a province. There are a number of sources which refer to this, the most detailed being Justin and Dio:

'But what Lucullus gave, Pompeius soon after took away; telling him [Antiochus], when he made application for the crown, that he would not give Syria, even if it was willing to accept him, and much less if unwilling, to a king, who for eighteen years, during which Tigranes had governed Syria, had lain hid in a corner of Cilicia, and now, when Tigranes was conquered by the Romans, asked for the reward of other men's labours.'[16]

'[Pompeius] advanced against, and brought under Roman rule without fighting, those parts of Cilicia that were not yet subject to it, and the remainder of Syria which lies along the Euphrates, and the countries called Coele Syria, Phoenicia, and Palestine, also Idumea and Ituraea, and the other parts of Syria by whatever name called; not that he had any complaint against Antiochus, the son of Antiochus Pius, who was present and asked for his paternal kingdom, but because he thought that since he had dispossessed Tigranes, the conqueror of Antiochus, it belonged to the Romans by the law of war.'[17]

'Coele-Syria and Phoenicia, which had lately rid themselves of their kings and had been ravaged by the Arabians and Tigranes, were united by him. Antiochus had dared to ask them back, but did not secure them; instead, they were combined into one province and received laws so that they were governed in the Roman fashion.'[18]

'[Pompeius] himself went down into Syria, and since this country had no legitimate kings, he declared it to be a province and possession of the Roman People.'[19]

Interestingly, a number of the later sources – such as Eusebius and Jerome – present different versions, mostly accounted for by their mixing up of their various kings named Antiochus. Thus we have stories of Antiochus fleeing to the Parthians and the provinces being annexed in the 90s BC, of them being willed to Rome, of even Caesar annexing the kingdom; all of which present an excellent example of how the reporting of a key historical event can change over time:

'And then two others began to fight over the kingdom: Philippus, the brother of Seleucus and son of Antiochus Grypus, and Antiochus, the son of Antiochus Cyzicenus. Starting from the third year of the 171st Olympiad, they fought against each other for possession of Syria with substantial armies, each controlling part of the country. Antiochus was defeated and fled to the Parthians. Later he surrendered to Pompeius, in the hope of being restored to Syria. But Pompeius, who had received a gift of money from the inhabitants of Antioch, ignored Antiochus and allowed the city to be autonomous.'[20]

'After taking refuge with the Parthians, Antiochus surrendered to Pompeius. Later, Philippus was captured by Gabinius.'[21]

'When king Antiochus, the son of Dionices, was about to die, he left his kingdom and all his possessions to the Romans. After king Antiochus died, Antioch the great came under Roman rule, together with all the land of Syria, Cilicia, and the other dominions of the Macedonians.'[22]

'Philippus was the last of the kings, and with him the kingdom of the Syrians came to an end. Caius Iulius Caesar, the Roman Emperor, brought it under Roman control. The kingdom of the Syrians had lasted for 221 years before it came to an end.'[23]

The surviving sources provide us with little detail on the annexation. It is interesting that later sources bring the Parthians into the narrative. Initially, Antiochus had been sent to Rome to seek the Senate's support for his restoration (c.75 BC), but soon returned with only vague assurances. Following Tigranes' subsequent campaigns in Syria and Phoenicia, Dio states that Antiochus had hidden in Cilicia, but this does raise the possibility that he had indeed fled from the Armenian Empire altogether and sought shelter at the Parthian court. This was not the first time that the Parthians had entertained a Seleucid ruler to be used as a puppet,[24] and although Antiochus was seemingly back on the throne in 69 BC, there may have been a suspicion in Pompeius' mind that he was a Parthian stooge.

Even if there was no truth in the story, and Antiochus was not a Parthian puppet, had he been confirmed in his restoration then Pompeius would be placing a strategically key region in the hands of a perpetually weak dynasty. None of the other client kingdoms of the region held the significance of Syria and Phoenicia, controlling the majority of the eastern coast of the Mediterranean and thus the coastal outlets for the overland trade routes from the East (the other route being through the Red Sea and controlled by Ptolemaic Egypt). Thus the region was strategically important and economically prosperous.

Furthermore, acquisition of Syria had been a long-term Parthian goal, to facilitate access to the Mediterranean. Had Parthia gained control of the region, then its fleets would be able to ply the Mediterranean. Having just cemented Roman control of the Mediterranean, and annexed Cilicia to ensure its control, it made total strategic sense to continue this process and secure the rest of the coastline, adding its resources to Rome and ensuring that Parthia did not gain access. It would also allow Rome to place legions in Syria, within striking distance of the lower Euphrates and the Parthian Empire. Aside from the practical considerations, Plutarch ascribes grander notions to Pompeius' actions:

'Moreover, a great and eager passion possessed him to recover Syria, and march through Arabia to the Red Sea, in order that he might bring his victorious career into touch with the Ocean which surrounds the world on all sides; for in Africa he had been the first to carry his conquests as far as the Outer Sea, and again in Spain he had made the Atlantic Ocean the boundary of the Roman dominion, and thirdly, in his recent pursuit of the Albanians, he had narrowly missed reaching the Hyrcanian [Caspian] Sea. In order, therefore, that he might connect the circuit of his military expeditions with the Red Sea, he put his army in motion.'[25]

Whilst the strategic and economic arguments clearly dominated, they may well have been supported by a more 'romantic' notion of going further than any Roman had before and reaching the ends of the earth (as the ancients believed). Furthermore, he would have been walking in the footsteps of Alexander the Great, a concept that appealed to most Romans of the time.[26]

Plutarch provides some details as to Pompeius' campaign, which set off from the Pontic coastal city of Amisus. Moving southwards, Plutarch notes that Pompeius came across the remains of the Roman force commanded by Valerius Triarius, defeated by Mithridates early in 67 BC (see Chapter Six):

'Then taking the great mass of his army, he set out on his march, and when he came upon the still unburied bodies of those who, led by Triarius, had fallen in an unsuccessful combat with Mithridates, he gave them all an honourable and splendid burial.'[27]

Moving further south, the Roman army crossed the Amanus Mountains, separating Cilicia from Syria, with Pompeius' legate L. Afranius in the lead. After defeating some of the local tribes, the Roman army pushed through and invaded Syria, making for the Seleucid capital of Antioch.[28] Again, due to the paucity of our sources, there does not seem to have been much resistance in the region to Roman annexation, and many would have welcomed the peace and stability that such a move brought, especially those engaged in trade. As Plutarch points out, once the capital had been secured and the Roman declaration had been made, Pompeius spent the majority of his time in administration:

'But most of his time he spent in judicial business, settling the disputes of cities and kings, and for those to which he himself could not attend, sending his friends.'[29]

The immediate fates of the two Seleucid Emperors, Antiochus XIII and Philip II, is also far from clear. A fragment of Dio reports that an Antiochus was seemingly killed by an Arabian chieftain, but this does not easily fit in with the existing (and already fragmented) narrative.[30] Philip II appears to have survived at least until the 50s BC (see Appendix One). Whilst securing Antioch was the clear priority for Rome, it seems that Roman armies were sent further south to secure the whole of the province. Josephus records that Pompeius dispatched two legates, L. Lollius and Q. Caecilius Metellus Nepos (Consul in 57 BC), to secure Damascus:

'… so Scaurus came to Damascus, which had been lately taken by Metellus and Lollius, and caused them to leave the place.'[31]

'In the meantime Pompeius sent Scaurus into Syria, while he was himself in Armenia, and making war with Tigranes; but when Scaurus was come to Damascus and found that Lollius and Metellus had newly taken the city …'[32]

We can see that Pompeius swiftly occupied the whole of Seleucid Syria, though the city of Tyre remained autonomous.[33] Thus, the second of the great Hellenistic successor kingdoms of Alexander the Great fell to Rome, whose rule was now extended as far south as Judea and as far east as the Euphrates. Yet whilst it made perfect strategic and economic sense to annex the kingdom, it did expose Roman borders to new threats and instabilities, notably the independent Kingdom of Judea to the south and the Arabian Nabataean kingdom to the south and east. With Pompeius installed in Syria, the other independent kingdoms of the region soon sent ambassadors bearing gifts to the new (temporary) ruler of the region:

'A little afterward Pompeius came to Damascus, and marched over Coele Syria; at which time there came ambassadors to him from all Syria, and Egypt, and out of Judaea also, for Aristobulus had sent him a great present, which was a golden vine of the value of five hundred talents. Now Strabo of Cappadocia mentions this present in these words: "There came also an embassy out of Egypt, and a crown of the value of four thousand pieces of gold; and out of Judaea there came another, whether you call it a vine or a garden; they call the thing Terpole, the Delight.

However, we ourselves saw that present reposited at Rome, in the temple of Jupiter Capitolinus, with this inscription, "The gift of Alexander, the king of the Jews." It was valued at five hundred talents; and the report is, that Aristobulus, the governor of the Jews, sent it."[34]

Clearly, Ptolemaic Egypt and the Kingdom of Judea both feared that they too would fall to Rome's – and Pompeius' – new eastern empire.

The Partho-Armenian War (64 BC)

With Pompeius and the Roman army tied down in Pontus for the winter, and then moving south into Syria in the spring (see below), it seems that the Parthian Emperor Phraates decided once again to attack Armenia to restore the lands previously lost to him. Whilst this was a potentially risky move, given that he had been chased out of Gordyene the previous year by the Roman army commanded by Afranius, we do not know what sort of pressure Phraates was under domestically. His grip on the throne was far from secure, with Parthia having collapsed into a civil war. Although he had inherited the throne from his father Sinatruces, there may well have been one other challenger still in the empire (see Appendix Two).

Therefore, although Phraates would have wanted to avoid a war with Rome at all costs, he may have been under pressure to (re)assert Parthian military pride, especially having been chased out of Gordyene – which the Parthians considered to be theirs – the year before. Though the exact timing is unclear, Phraates possibly received word that Gordyene was being gifted to Cappadocia. Again, details of this war are far from clear. Only Appian and Dio mention it, and Appian's account (as is common) is vague. Dio presents us with the following:

'Phraates immediately began a campaign in the spring against Tigranes, being accompanied by the latter's son, to whom he had given his daughter in marriage. This was in the Consulship of Lucius Caesar and Caius Figulus. In the first battle Phraates was beaten, but later was victorious. And when Tigranes invoked the assistance of Pompeius, who was in Syria, Phraates again sent ambassadors to the Roman commander, bringing many charges against Tigranes, and making many insinuations against the Romans, so that Pompeius was both ashamed and alarmed.'[35]

If it were not for the clear assertion by Dio that these events took place in the Consulship of Caesar and Figulus (64 BC), there would be the temptation to take this account as a duplicate from the previous year. The most striking aspect is that Dio states that Phraates had a son of Tigranes with him (now his son-in-law). Here we have two options, one being that this is indeed a duplicate of the events of 65 BC, which ended with a treasonous son of Tigranes – also named Tigranes – in Roman custody, where he remained until he was shipped to Rome. The alternative is that Phraates found another son of Tigranes to be the figurehead of his invasion. If so, this would be the fourth son of Tigranes to turn against his father.

We are not given any details as to where Phraates invaded Armenia; if it was again the Kingdom of Gordyene, this would have been a direct affront to the Roman action of a few months previously and the Roman settlement of Cappadocia. It is possible that this action was intended to force a Roman rethink. If Phraates did avoid Gordyene, then the only other invasion route would have been through Media-Atropatené (see Map 2).

Given that Dio is clear on the date and that by the time of Phraates' victory some months had elapsed, and Pompeius was by then in Syria, the balance of evidence does favour this clash being a further one and not a duplicate. This is supported by Appian, who also has two different accounts of the war between Armenia and Parthia, the second of which did take place whilst Pompeius was in Syria. Thus Phraates, though defeated at first, triumphed over Tigranes, though we are given no figures for the scale of the defeat Tigranes suffered nor what lands the Parthians occupied. Both parties then sent ambassadors to Pompeius, Tigranes appealing for military aid from his new patron, whilst Phraates presented his grievance against Armenia (not Rome) and reaffirmed Romano-Parthian friendship.

For Pompeius, the timing of the war was awkward to say the least. Having thought that he had settled affairs in the north, he had marched south into Syria to oversee the annexation of the Seleucid Empire. Now he faced not only a Parthian attack on a Roman ally, but the potential reopening of his whole settlement of territories. Yet despite the Romans' apparent overwhelming military superiority, the question Pompeius was faced with was a similar one which faced Lucullus before him; namely, could he afford to get involved in a war with Parthia?

Pompeius' campaigns to date had all been short, sharp ones, supported by a clear supply chain from Roman territory. To attack Parthia itself would have been a major logistical undertaking, and the Parthians could simply fall back eastwards, drawing him further into hostile territory. Furthermore, it would distract from the major issue of entrenching Roman rule in the Near East and offer a clear opportunity for Mithridates to attack Asia Minor once more. Even Pompeius had to take note of the mood of the Senate and People. Attacking the Parthian Empire whilst Mithridates was in the Crimea was clearly going to raise questions and whilst his powerbase was much stronger than that of Lucullus, he was far from unchallenged. Crassus may indeed have used this opportunity to attack him.

Consequently, Pompeius overlooked the attack on a new and not very reliable Roman ally and sent mediators to negotiate a settlement between the two parties, rather than reinforce Tigranes as he had requested:

'As for the barbarian's [Phraates'] complaints, he made light of them, offering no answer, but asserting that the dispute which the prince had with Tigranes concerned some boundaries, and that three men should decide the case for them. These he actually sent, and they were enrolled as bona fide arbitrators by the two kings, who then settled all their mutual complaints. For Tigranes was angry at not having obtained the desired aid, and Phraates wished the Armenian ruler to survive, so that in case of need he might someday have him as an ally against the Romans. For they both well understood that whichever of them should conquer the other would simply help along matters for the Romans and would himself become easier for them to subdue. For these reasons, then, they were reconciled.'[36]

Phraates came out of the matter with at least his prestige enhanced as he had stood up to Rome and forced it to negotiate. We are not told what outcome the commissioners reached, but it seems to have been a face-saving solution that Phraates could take back to the Parthian court, having upheld Parthian honour. It appears highly unlikely that they saw the return of Gordyene, thus leaving a long-standing grievance between the parties.

The Romano-Pontic War – Waiting For Mithridates

With Pompeius' focus being on Syria, this gave Mithridates time to consolidate his control of the Bosphoran Kingdom and plan his next campaigns against Rome. Appian provides a detailed account of the king's activities in this period.[37] Throughout the account, we can see both the preparations he made for the next campaign and the setbacks he suffered. In terms of preparations, Appian provides us with the following details:

'When he [Mithridates] had recovered from his illness and his army was collected (it consisted of sixty picked cohorts of 6,000 men each and a great multitude of other troops, besides ships and strongholds that had been captured by his generals while he was sick) he sent a part of it across the strait to Phanagoria, another trading place at the mouth of the sea, in order to possess himself of the passage on either side while Pompeius was still in Syria.'[38]

As always, we have to treat Appian's troop numbers with a significant degree of scepticism, and it seems that though Mithridates was for a time able to gather a fresh army of tribesmen from the region, he could not hold them together (see below). In terms of his plans for his next campaign, he conceived his boldest move yet; an attack on Italy itself:

'Mithridates did not give way himself under his misfortunes but relying more on his will than on his power, he planned, especially as Pompeius was now tarrying in Syria, to reach the Ister through Scythia, and from there to invade Italy.'[39]

'He proposed to turn his course to the Gauls, whose friendship he had cultivated a long time for this purpose, and with them to invade Italy, hoping that many of the Italians themselves would join him on account of their hatred of the Romans; for he had heard that such had been Hannibal's policy after the Romans had waged war against him in Spain, and that he had become in this way an object of the greatest terror to them.

'He knew that almost all of Italy had lately revolted from the Romans by reason of their hatred and had waged war against them for a very long time, and had sustained Spartacus, the gladiator, against them, although he was a man of no repute.'[40]

Although this may sound implausible, there was no Roman territory between the Italian Alps and the Crimea, and no Roman armies. The main barriers to such a move were geographical ones – rivers such as the Dniester and Danube, and mountains such as the Carpathians – and the native tribes in-between. As we have seen, Mithridates had carved out an empire from the tribes of the region and many others may have welcomed an attack on the expanding power of Rome, including the recently defeated Thracian tribes (see Chapter Four). Had he been able to achieve such a feat, it would have exceeded that of Hannibal. Yet, for all his grand schemes and tribal armies, Mithridates faced a number of challenges and setbacks, some of which are described by Dio:

'Among other things the greatest earthquake ever experienced destroyed many of their cities; the soldiery also mutinied, and some of Mithridates' sons were kidnapped and conveyed to Pompeius.'[41]

Furthermore, Appian informs us, Mithridates had to execute another son, Xiphares, when his concubine mother betrayed a coastal fortress to Pompeius.[42] Appian also provides more detailed information on the mutinies and revolts that Mithridates suffered:

> 'Castor of Phanagoria, who had once been maltreated by Trypho, the king's eunuch, fell upon the latter as he was entering the town, killed him, and summoned the citizens to revolt. Although the citadel was already held by Artaphernes and other sons of Mithridates, the inhabitants piled wood around it and set it on fire, in consequence of which Artaphernes, Darius, Xerxes, and Oxathres, sons, and Eupatra, a daughter, of Mithridates, in fear of the fire, surrendered themselves and were led into captivity.'[43]

So Mithridates lost another four sons to captivity, and they were soon handed to the Romans. We can see that despite his grand plans and the raising of another army, support for Mithridates was ebbing away. We can also perhaps see the subtle hand of Pompeius in these events. Whilst Pompeius and the bulk of the Roman army were indeed in Syria, there was a Roman naval presence in the Black Sea blockading the Crimea, which was in itself a very visible statement of Rome's power and whose effects would have been impacting on the local elites, who relied on the two-way naval trade across the Black Sea for their prosperity. Furthermore, we cannot rule out Pompeius having instructed his legates in the Black Sea to actively seek out those who would betray the Mithridatic cause. It was at some point during the year that this Roman pressure erupted into a full-scale revolt:

> 'All the neighbouring castles that had been lately occupied by Mithridates now revolted from him in emulation of the Phanagoreans, namely, Chersonesus, Theodosia, Nymphaeum, and others around the Euxine which were well situated for purposes of war.
>
> 'Mithridates, observing these frequent defections, and having suspicions of the army itself, lest it should fail him because the service was compulsory and the taxes very heavy, and because soldiers always lack confidence in unlucky commanders, sent some of his daughters in charge of eunuchs to be married to the Scythian princes, asking them at the same time to send him reinforcements as quickly as possible.
>
> 'Five hundred soldiers accompanied them from his own army. Soon after they left the presence of Mithridates they killed the eunuchs who were leading them (for they always hated these persons, who were

all-powerful with Mithridates) and conducted the young women to Pompeius.'[44]

Having suffered such setbacks, it is no surprise that Mithridates' campaign across Eastern Europe did not materialize this year. Appian's account, which had so recently stated the great size of Mithridates' army, then provides the following statement:

> 'Although bereft of so many children and castles and of his whole kingdom, and in no way fit for war, and although he could not expect any aid from the Scythians.'[45]

Thus, it seems Mithridates' plan had come to nought and he was unable to muster an army for a fresh campaign to challenge Rome, so sat in the Crimea on the defensive. It is at this point that he opened up negotiations with Pompeius by sending ambassadors to Syria:

> 'And now he sent ambassadors to Pompeius, who was still in Syria and who did not know that the king was at that place. They promised that the king would pay tribute to the Romans if they would let him have his paternal kingdom. When Pompeius required that Mithridates should come himself and make his petition as Tigranes had done, he said that as long as he was Mithridates he would never agree to that, but that he would send some of his sons and his friends to do so.'[46]

Mithridates well knew that Pompeius would not grant him the freedom to remain at liberty and in charge of a kingdom. The success of Pompeius' whole eastern campaign rested on Mithridates being dead or in captivity, to allow Pompeius to return to Rome and clearly demonstrate that it was he who had ended the war and the threat was no more. With the Scythian tribes having revolted and the Gallic alliance proving illusive, Mithridates was reduced to enrolling slaves and freedmen into a force to defend the Bosphorus:

> 'Even while he [Mithridates] was saying these things he was levying an army of freedmen and slaves, manufacturing arms, projectiles, and machines, helping himself to timber, and killing plough-oxen for the sake of their sinews. He levied tribute on all, even those of the slenderest means. His ministers made these exactions with harshness to many.'[47]

Having failed to muster an army to challenge Rome, and facing so many defections and treachery, Mithradates finished the year in a far weaker position, barely holding onto power in the Bosphoran Kingdom and having to rely on even harsher methods to ensure his rule, which would only have increased the opposition against him. It seems that it was Pompeius who was winning this 'Cold War'.

Defending Syria – Judea and Nabataea

Pompeius, meanwhile, was continuing his campaigns to secure Rome's new empire in the East. Whilst Syria itself had not proved difficult to annex, his thoughts then turned to securing its borders. In the north, Syria bordered Roman allied kingdoms, but in the north-east was the Euphrates, across which lay the Kingdom of Osrhoene. As we have seen, Pompeius had already drawn this traditional Parthian client state into Rome's orbit, so that border was for now a secure one. However, this was not the case to the south and east of Syria, where lay the kingdoms of Judea and the Nabataean Arabs.

Of the two, it was the Nabataean Kingdom, under King Aretas III (*c.*87–62 BC), that posed the greatest threat, having been used to expanding at the expense of its weaker Seleucid and Judean neighbours. The Nabataeans were an Arabic people who controlled an arc of territory from the Euphrates to the Red Sea (see Map 10). As recently as 82 BC, the Nabateans had defeated and killed the Seleucid Emperor Antiochus XII at the Battle of Cana and overrun eastern Syria.

By contrast, the Judean Kingdom was far weaker. Having once been part of the Seleucid Empire, Judea revolted against Antiochus IV in 168/167 BC, an event known as the Maccabean Revolt,[48] which was in part caused by the Roman intervention against Antiochus IV and his invasion of Egypt (see Chapter One). Having been repulsed in attacking Egypt, Antiochus tried to secure his rule in Judea, which sparked the revolt. By 141 BC, Judea had gained autonomy within the Seleucid Empire, ruled by its own native Hasmonaean dynasty, a status which was endorsed by the Roman Senate. The collapse of the Seleucid Empire allowed Judea to gain full independence by *c.*110 BC, a status which it maintained even in the face of Armenian expansion.[49] Unfortunately for Judea, a civil war erupted in 66 BC between the two brothers Hyrcanus II and Aristobulus II, with the former being overthrown by the latter. By *c.*64 BC, Hyrcanus and his advisor Antipater (father of King Herodes) had fled to the Nabataeans and the court of Aretas III, who was persuaded to invade Judea at the head of a 50,000-strong army to restore Hyrcanus.

Unfortunately for all parties concerned, this civil war and the full-scale Nabataean invasion brought matters to the attention of Pompeius, who decided that the disruption was of such magnitude that it threatened Roman interests. In particular, Pompeius would have been worried about the creation of a rival power in the region in the form of the expansionist Nabataeans. Pompeius dispatched his Quaestor M. Aemilius Scaurus and a Roman army (of unknown size) to intervene in the matter. As detailed in Josephus, by the time Scaurus reached Judea, Aretas (along with Hyrcanus and Antipater) were laying siege to Aristobulus in the city of Jerusalem:[50]

> 'As soon, therefore, as he was come into the country, there came ambassadors from both the brothers, each of them desiring his assistance; but Aristobulus's three hundred talents had more weight with him than the justice of the cause; which sum, when Scaurus had received, he sent a herald to Hyrcanus and the Arabians, and threatened them with the resentment of the Romans and of Pompeius, unless they would raise the siege. So Aretas was terrified, and retired out of Judaea to Philadelphia, as did Scaurus return to Damascus again.'[51]

Thus, Scaurus ordered Aretas to break off the siege, which the king did, unwilling to risk a war with Rome over Judea. Though Aristobulus may well have bribed Scaurus, Josephus was overlooking the likely possibility that those were Scaurus' orders anyway. Pompeius would have been far more concerned about a pro-Nabataean puppet being placed on the Judean throne and the expansionist tendencies of Aretas, than being concerned with which man was the rightful king. The siege was lifted and Aristobulus was confirmed as King of Judea, with tacit Roman backing. For Scaurus, the matter had been totally successful, with the Nabataean army withdrawing on his word and a large donation from the Judean king for following Pompeius' orders anyway.

Though Scaurus returned to Roman Syria, the matter did not end there. Aristobulus took the initiative, and once the siege of Jerusalem had been lifted, he quickly gathered his force and gave chase to the Nabateans, ambushed and defeated them:

> '... nor was Aristobulus satisfied with escaping, but gathered all his forces together, and pursued his enemies, and fought them at a place called Papyron, and slew about six thousand of them, and, together with them Antipater's brother Phalion.'[52]

Thus, by the end of 64 BC, Rome had intervened in the Judean Civil War to support Aristobulus on the throne and ensure the humbling of Aretas and the Nabataeans. Yet though this had been accomplished on Rome's part without any fighting, the fundamentals of the two problems remained: of Rome's two new neighbours, Judea was still weak and vulnerable, and the Nabateans were still strong and expansionist. Furthermore, Aretas would have certainly harboured two grudges against Rome; for being ordered out of Judea and being ambushed by a now Roman ally. For the Roman conquest of Syria to be secured, both problems would need to be addressed. However, with the year drawing to a close, Pompeius and Rome had much to be satisfied with in their new empire in the East.

Summary

By the end of the year, the Roman Republic had annexed the remnants of the Seleucid Empire – the second of the former great Hellenistic powers – and expanded its empire to the Euphrates and the borders of Judea. Aside from territories they directly ruled, the whole of the Near East was now clearly under Roman control, with only the Parthian Empire showing any independence. Whilst technically the Romano-Pontic War was going to enter its second decade, Mithridates' position was the least secure it had ever been: confined to the Crimea, under blockade, seemingly unable to raise an army and facing rebellions and treason at every turn. Consequently, Pompeius had every reason to be satisfied through the winter of 64/63 BC.

Chapter 10

The Final Years: The Judean and Nabataean Wars (63–62 BC)

The End of the Romano-Pontic War – The Death of Mithridates (63 BC)

It was at the early point of this year – the exact date is not given in our surviving sources – that the original conflict, the clash between Rome and the Pontic Empire, came to a conclusion. The last full-scale clash of arms between the two empires had come in 66 BC, when Pompeius defeated Mithridates at the Battle of Nicopolis (see Chapter Seven.). In the years that followed, the Romans had completed their conquest of Pontus, separated Colchis from the Pontic Empire and placed the Bosphoran Kingdom under a naval blockade. As we have seen, this blockade, and the increasing inevitability of Roman victory and domination of the region, had taken its toll on the nobles and soldiers of the kingdom, and on the family of Mithridates himself. We do not know how many children Mithridates had in total, but in recent years he had executed two sons for treachery and seen another four sons captured and handed over to the Romans.

The most senior surviving son of Mithridates seems to have been Pharnaces, though the surviving sources have little mention of him prior to this period. He seemed to have shared the widely held outlook that Mithridates' fight was hopeless, and that it would consume the whole kingdom and Mithridates' whole family. As we have seen, as far back as 71 BC, his elder (half) brother, Machares, had struck a deal with the Roman commander Lucullus and been confirmed as ruler of an independent Bosphoran Kingdom. This independence had been terminated by Mithridates himself in 65 BC when he retook the kingdom, but nevertheless a precedent had been set.

Appian preserves the fullest surviving account of the Pharnacean conspiracy, which was originally detected and crushed by Mithridates.[1] On this occasion, however, Mithridates chose to exercise leniency when it came to Pharnaces himself, having already murdered two of his sons. As Appian states, this may not have been a matter of sentiment on Mithridates' part but for fear of Pharnaces' murder provoking an even bigger rebellion. However, Pharances used this unexpected reprieve to try once more, this time changing tactics and turning to corrupting the seemingly large number of Roman deserters who were in the Bosphoran Kingdom in Mithridates' employ:

'After Pharnaces had persuaded them [the Roman deserters], he sent emissaries the same night to other camps nearby and won them over. Early in the morning the first deserters raised a shout, and those next to them repeated it, and so on. Even the naval force joined in the cry, not all of them having been advised beforehand perhaps, but eager for a change, despising failure, and always ready to attach themselves to a new hope. Others, who were ignorant of the conspiracy, thought that all had been corrupted, and that if they remained alone, they would be scorned by the majority, and so from fear and necessity rather than inclination joined in the shouting.'[2]

Thus, ironically, a Roman force was eventually responsible for overthrowing Mithridates, even if a force of Roman deserters. Mithridates' position was further undermined by the treachery of a number of his own bodyguard, who ensured that on this occasion he would not be able to flee, as he had successfully done on so many occasions:

'When Mithridates heard this he went out to reason with them. A part of his own guard then ran to join the deserters, but the latter refused to admit them unless they would do some irreparable deed as a proof of their fidelity, pointing at the same time to Mithridates. So they hastened to kill his horse, for he himself had fled, and at the same time saluted Pharnaces as king, as though the rebels were already victorious, and one of them brought a broad papyrus leaf from a temple and crowned him with it in place of a diadem.'[3]

So Mithridates was overthrown by his own son in a palace coup, supported by a force of Roman deserters. With flight no longer an option, Mithridates made the only choice he had left (as he saw it) and committed suicide. When poison failed, due to a well-documented built-up tolerance for poisons, he asked a Gallic officer to kill him. Mithridates clearly preferred death over being a prisoner and then a trophy in Pompeius' triumph. Appian sums up the remarkable career of Mithridates:

'He lived sixty-eight or sixty-nine years, and of these he reigned fifty-seven, for the kingdom came to him when he was an orphan. He subdued the neighbouring barbarians and many of the Scythians and waged a formidable war against the Romans for forty years, during which he frequently conquered Bithynia and Cappadocia, besides making incursions into the Roman province of Asia and into Phrygia,

Paphlagonia, Galatia, and Macedonia. He invaded Greece, where he performed many remarkable exploits, and ruled the sea from Cilicia to the Adriatic until Sulla confined him again to his paternal kingdom after destroying 160,000 of his soldiers.

'Notwithstanding these great losses he renewed the war without difficulty. He fought with the greatest generals of his time. He was vanquished by Sulla, Lucullus, and Pompeius, although several times he got the better of them also. Lucius Cassius, Quintus Oppius, and Manius Aquilius he took prisoners and carried them around with him. The last he killed because he was the cause of the war. The others he surrendered to Sulla. He defeated Fimbria, Murena, the Consul Cotta, Fabius, and Triarius.'[4]

Pharances, now king of the rump Pontic Empire, dispatched emissaries to Pompeius to inform him of Mithridates' death and open up negotiations to bring an end to the long Romano-Pontic War and secure the future of the Bosphoran Kingdom as a Roman ally.

The Romano-Nabatean War (63 BC)

Whilst these events were taking place in the Crimea, Pompeius was on campaign once more. With the Pontic War still dragging on, and as yet to yield a positive outcome – as far as he was aware – he continued with his policy of cementing Roman control of the region. As stated previously, there were now only two regional powers completely outside of Roman control: the Parthian Empire and the Nabatean Kingdom (with both Judea and Ptolemaic Egypt being Roman 'allies').

As we have also stated, a war against the massive Parthian Empire was clearly out of the scope of his command and, given the distances involved, would require a multiple-year campaign. As powerful as Pompeius was, he could not be sure of his position in Rome, having been away from the centre of politics now for a fifth year. Furthermore, with the blockade of the Crimea, he must have assumed that it was only a matter of time before events in the Pontic War came to a head one way or another, with either a Mithridatic attack, a Mithridatic surrender or a revolt against him. Pompeius could not afford to be distracted by a war in Parthia and be too far away from the situation in the Near East.

With Parthia off-limits, the greatest threat to Rome's new empire in the East, therefore, was the Nabataean Kingdom and its expansionist ruler, King Aretas. Thus, at the start of 63 BC, Pompeius mounted a punitive expedition, effectively marking time until the situation in the Crimea resolved itself one way or the other. We find as much in Plutarch:

'… an expedition which was not a little censured by most of his followers. For they thought it an evasion of the pursuit of Mithridates and demanded that he should rather turn against that inveterate enemy, who was again kindling the flames of war and preparing, as it was reported, to march an army through Scythia and Paeonia against Italy. Pompeius, however, thinking it easier to crush the king's forces when he made war than to seize his person when he was in flight, was not willing to wear out his own strength in a vain pursuit, and therefore sought other employment in the interval of the war and thus protracted the time.'[5]

The sources do provide some details of his movements. First came a move to Damascus, which became the Roman base for preparations for the campaign. Josephus provides some additional details:

'… in the beginning of the spring, he brought his army out of their winter quarters, and marched into the country of Damascus; and as he went along he demolished the citadel that was at Apameia, which Antiochus Cyzicenus had built, and took cognisance of the country of Ptolemaeus Mennaeus, a wicked man, and not less so than Dionysius of Tripoli, who had been beheaded, who was also his relation by marriage; yet did he buy off the punishment of his crimes for a thousand talents, with which money Pompeius paid the soldiers their wages. He also conquered the place called Lysias, of which Silas a Jew was tyrant. And when he had passed over the cities of Heliopolis and Chalcis, and got over the mountain which is on the limit of Coele Syria, he came from Pella to Damascus.'[6]

So Pompeius even managed to pay for the campaign by eliciting 1,000 talents from one of the local rulers. Whilst he was at Damascus, he received envoys from many of the rulers of the region, both major and minor. The most significant were ambassadors from the two claimants for the Judean throne – Aristobulus and Hyrcanus – both offering substantial rewards for Pompeius' backing. At the time, Pompeius seems not to have come to a decision on the matter, but marched the Roman army into Nabatean territory, with the aim of capturing the city of Petra. We have few details of the campaign itself, with conflicting accounts of whether Pompeius actually captured Petra. The fullest accounts are those of Dio and Plutarch:

'When, then, the regions in that quarter had been subdued, and Phraates remained quiet, while Syria and Phoenicia had become tranquil, Pompeius turned against Aretas. The latter was king of the Arabians, now subjects of the Romans, as far as the Red Sea. Previously he had done the greatest injury to Syria and had on this account become involved in a battle with the Romans who were defending it; he was defeated by them, but nevertheless continued the war at that time. Pompeius accordingly marched against him and his neighbours, and, overcoming them without effort, left them in [the] charge of a garrison.'[7]

'But fortune resolved the difficulty. For when he was come within a short distance of Petra and had already pitched his camp for that day and was exercising himself on horseback nearby, dispatch-bearers rode up from Pontus bringing good tidings.'[8]

We also have a line of Orosius, which contradicts Plutarch and states that Pompeius did indeed capture Petra: 'He first subdued the Ituraeans and Arabs and captured their city which they call Petra.'[9]

All we can say for certain is that there seem to have been no major battles in this campaign, with Aretas seemingly happy to fall back further into the desert than stand and face the Roman army. As for the end of the campaign, we have two possible alternatives. If we follow Plutarch, then the campaign was called off when Pompeius received the news of Mithridates' death:

'Then Pompeius, having brought his achievements and expeditions to such an unexpectedly easy completion, straightway withdrew from Arabia.'[10]

However, Josephus states that Pompeius heard the news during his subsequent Judean campaign (see below). This would fit in with Orosius' account of Petra being captured by Pompeius. To further complicate matters, Dio's account has Pompeius hearing the news before he started the Nabataean campaign. Of the three versions, it seems reasonable that Pompeius would not start a fresh campaign after hearing of the death of Mithridates, which brought the Romano-Pontic War to a conclusion and thus allowed him to return to Rome triumphant, re-establishing and enhancing his political standing. He would have been well aware of the manoeuvrings of his long-time rival – and sometime ally – Crassus, not to mention the various other factions.

That being the case, it seems more logical that we follow Josephus and that Pompeius received the news of Mithridates' death after the completion of the Nabatean campaign and during the Judean one. We thereby conclude that

Pompeius did indeed capture Petra, but with Aretas refusing to give battle, cut the campaign short in favour of settling matters in Judea.

The Romano-Ituraean War (63 BC)

Several sources refer to a Roman victory against the Ituraean Kingdom.[11] This was another small Arabian kingdom, to the south of Damascus and bordering Judea (see Map 10). Orosius states that Pompeius first moved against the Ituraeans before attacking Petra, and given their proximity to Damascus this is more than possible. Unfortunately, aside from these passing references, no source dwells long enough on these events to provide any detail.

This campaign would certainly fit in with the overall narrative of the Nabataean campaign, to subdue the various Arab tribes and kingdoms that bordered on Rome's new Syrian province. As with the Nabataeans, the Ituraeans – under their ruler Ptolemy – had a history of raiding their weaker neighbours, Judea and Syria, and in particular Damascus. Thus, a short campaign against the Ituraeans would have taught them that such behaviour would no longer be tolerated. It seems that Ptolemy kept his throne and became another Roman client king.

The Romano-Judean War (63 BC)

If we accept that Pompeius had not yet heard the news of Mithridates' death (for which we have no secure chronology), then it can be argued that Pompeius put aside the Nabataean campaign after capturing Petra for a more lucrative proposition, the reduction of the Kingdom of Judea. The Roman intervention the previous year had seen Rome back the usurper Aristobulus against his cousin Hyrcanus, but only due to the invasion of the Nabataeans supporting Hyrcanus. With that invasion defeated, Aristobulus remained on the throne, but the major stumbling block to supporting Hyrcanus – his Nabataean allies – had been removed. As we have seen, both men sent emissaries to Pompeius whilst he was at Damascus.

For Pompeius, it was hardly a matter of the rights and wrongs of the usurpation, but rather which man would suit Rome best as a client (puppet) king. There was also the matter of which man made the most lucrative offer, especially if Pompeius had one eye on returning to Rome. Josephus presents us with the following.

'Aristobulus had sent him a great present, which was a golden vine of the value of five hundred talents.'[12]

'In a little time afterward came ambassadors again to him, Antipater from Hyrcanus, and Nicodemus from Aristobulus, which last also accused such as had taken bribes; first Gabinius, and then Scaurus, the one three hundred talents, and the other four hundred, by which procedure he made these two his enemies, besides those he had before.'[13]

It appears that both men sent suitable bribes to the various Roman commanders to support their cause. As detailed earlier, Rome had long taken a passing interest in Judean affairs and had recognized the de facto independence of Judea as far back as 139 BC. Yet Roman interest had been far from altruistic, and had used an independent Judea as a counterweight to the Seleucid and Ptolemaic Empires. Now Rome was the dominant power in the region, Judea would become a client kingdom once more; the only question was: under which ruler? It seems that Pompeius initially deferred the matter until after his Nabatean campaign, confirmation of which can be found in both Dio and Josephus:

'While Pompeius was staying near Damascus in Syria, he was approached by Aristobulus the king of the Jews and his brother Hyrcanus, who were in dispute over who should be king. The most eminent of the Jews, more than two hundred in number, met the imperator and explained that their ancestors, when they rebelled from Demetrius, had sent envoys to the senate. In response, the senate granted them authority over the Jews, who were to be free and autonomous, under the leadership not of a king but of a high priest. But their current rulers, who had abolished their ancestral laws, had unjustly forced the citizens into subjection; with the help of a large number of mercenaries, they had procured the kingship through violence and much bloodshed.

'Pompeius postponed a decision about their dispute until later; but he strongly rebuked Hyrcanus and his associates for the lawless behaviour of the Jews and the wrongs they had committed against the Romans. He said that they deserved a stronger and harsher reprimand, but in conformity with the traditional clemency of the Romans, if they were obedient from now onwards, he would grant them forgiveness.'[14]

'... he then spoke civilly to them, and sent them away; and told them, that when he came again into their country, he would settle all their affairs, after he had first taken a view of the affairs of the Nabataeans.'[15]

As we have seen, Pompeius broke off the Nabataean campaign shortly after capturing Petra and turned his attention to Judea. At some point during this campaign, Pompeius had decided which candidate to back and actually reversed the decision he had made the previous year and found in favour of

Hyrcanus. The Roman army then invaded Judea for the first time. None of the surviving sources detail why Pompeius made such a decision and changed which claimant Rome would support.

Both men would have offered up substantial bribes, though only Aristobulus was actually in a position to pay out on that, being in possession of Judea. It is clear that Pompeius chose the more difficult option, backing the candidate not in power rather than the one on the throne. By doing so, Hyrcanus would be more in debt to Pompeius than Aristobulus would be if he had merely been confirmed in the position that he himself had secured. Furthermore, of the two men, Hyrcanus seemed to be the weakest and thus the less threat to Rome. Finally, it gave Pompeius the chance to invade Judea and take the Roman army further south than it had ever been in the Near East, right up to the Red Sea (and again to the edge of the known world – see illustrations section).

Thanks to Josephus, we have detailed accounts of the campaign which followed, though interestingly, Plutarch's biography of Pompeius passes over the campaign, only giving it half a sentence, writing that 'he also subdued Judaea and made a prisoner of Aristobulus the king'.[16] Faced with losing his crown, naturally Aristobulus chose to resist, but fell back rather than face the Roman army in battle, eventually retreating to his capital Jerusalem. It was whilst Pompeius was at Jericho that, according to Josephus, Pompeius received the emissaries from Pharnaces, revealing that Mithridates had been overthrown and killed:

'A little after this, certain persons came out of Pontus, and informed Pompeius, as he was on the way, and conducting his army against Aristobulus, that Mithridates was dead, and was slain by his son Pharnaces.'[17]

'... he was also obliged to make haste in his attempt, by the death of Mithridates, of which he was informed about at Jericho.'[18]

The timing of this news would have placed Pompeius in something of a quandary. Whilst certainly it was the news he had been awaiting for nearly two years, he was in the middle of a military campaign, which he would need to conclude swiftly to see Mithridates' body and end the war which had been the very reason he had been sent to the East. Pompeius therefore broke camp and marched towards Jerusalem.

It was at this point that Aristobulus made an attempt to come to terms, and went to meet Pompeius in person and agreed to hand over Jerusalem along with a substantial monetary donation. The timing was probably not a coincidence, with Aristobulus realizing that Pompeius would want to end the war quickly and return to the north to conclude the Pontic War. He may have been hoping that once the Romans withdrew from Judea and Pompeius returned home, he could try once again to usurp the throne.

However, Aristobulus' plan backfired when Pompeius dispatched a legate, A. Gabinius, to Jerusalem to secure both the city and the money, and Gabinius found his way barred by Aristobulus' supporters. Angered when Gabinius delivered this news, Pompeius had Aristobulus arrested and determined to take Jerusalem by siege, though the endeavour did not seem an easy one:

> '[Pompeius] came himself to the city, which was strong on every side, excepting the north, which was not so well fortified, for there was a broad and deep ditch that encompassed the city and included within it the temple, which was itself encompassed about with a very strong stone wall.'[19]

As it was, the city fell without a siege, being riven by the supporters of the two rival candidates for the throne. Faced with the Roman army outside the walls, the majority of the population saw no reason to hold out, whilst Aristobulus' hard-core supporters were too few to defend the whole city. They retreated to the Temple of Solomon on the Temple Mount and prepared to defend it, whilst the supporters of Hyrcanus and the neutrals opened the city gates to Pompeius:

> '... but the others admitted Pompeius's army in and delivered up both the city and the king's palace to him. So Pompeius sent his lieutenant Piso with an army, and placed garrisons both in the city and in the palace, to secure them, and fortified the houses that joined to the temple, and all those which were more distant and without it.'[20]

Thus, Jerusalem fell and Pompeius set about besieging the great Temple of Solomon, a bastion in its own right. Josephus provides some details of the following siege, which took three months to complete:

> '... but even on that side there were great towers, and a ditch had been dug, and a deep valley around it, for on the parts towards the city were precipices, and the bridge on which Pompeius had got in was broken down. However, a bank was raised, day by day, with a great deal of labour, while the Romans cut down materials for it from the places round about.

'And when this bank was sufficiently raised, and the ditch filled up, though but poorly, by reason of its immense depth, he brought his mechanical engines and battering-rams from Tyre, and placing them on the bank, he battered the temple with the stones that were thrown against it.'[21]

Josephus goes on to note that the Romans took advantage of the Jewish sabbath to capture the temple:

'And had it not been our practice, from the days of our forefathers, to rest on the seventh day, this bank could never have been perfected, by reason of the opposition the Jews would have made; for though our law gives us leave then to defend ourselves against those that begin to fight with us and assault us, yet does it not permit us to meddle with our enemies while they do anything else.

'Which thing when the Romans understood, on those days which we call Sabbaths they threw nothing at the Jews, nor came to any pitched battle with them; but raised up their earthen banks, and brought their engines into such forwardness, that they might do execution the next day.'[22]

Finally, after a three-month siege, the temple was stormed, with the loss of between 12,000 and 13,000 of the Jewish defenders:

'But when the battering-engine was brought near, the greatest of the towers was shaken by it, and fell down, and broke down a part of the fortifications, so the enemy poured in apace; and Cornelius Faustus, the son of Sulla, with his soldiers, first of all ascended the wall, and next to him Furius the centurion, with those that followed on the other part, while Fabius, who was also a centurion, ascended it in the middle, with a great body of men after him.

'But now all was full of slaughter; some of the Jews being slain by the Romans, and some by one another; nay, some there were who threw themselves down the precipices, or put fire to their houses, and burnt them, as not able to bear the miseries they were under.

'Of the Jews there fell twelve thousand, but of the Romans very few.'[23]

Thus, the Temple Mount fell, with Pompeius famously violating the inner sanctuary, the Holy of Holies, and carrying away a number of items as loot, though not the famous Menorah, which Josephus states was left.[24] Another source tells us:

'Pompeius the Great captured Jerusalem and despoiled the temple. He took away the Holy Scriptures, the vessels, the golden engravings, the golden vine, the couch of Solomon and many other holy objects.'[25]

Pompeius also took away 10,000 talents in money. The city walls of Jerusalem were razed to the ground, and Aristobulus and his family were taken as captives back to Rome. Hyrcanus was restored to the position of High Priest, but of a semi-independent Roman client kingdom. Judea also lost a number of cities, which were either granted their independence or joined to Roman Syria:

'[Pompeius] restored the rest of the cities, Hippos, and Schoolish, and Pella, and Dios, and Samaria, as also Marissa, and Azotus, and Jamneia, and Arethusa, to their own inhabitants. These were in the inland parts. Besides those that had been demolished, and also of the maritime cities, Gaza, and Joppa, and Dora, and Strato's Tower, which last Herodes rebuilt after a glorious manner, and adorned with havens and temples, and changed its name to Caesarean. All these Pompeius left in a state of freedom and joined them to the province of Syria.'[26]

Pompeius had gained the final piece for the Roman system in the Near East, adding Judea as a client kingdom whilst taking Roman control to the Red Sea and the very borders of the decaying Ptolemaic Empire. Nevertheless, it must be said that it was at the cost of three months, time in which he could have been finalizing matters in the East and preparing to return to Rome, which as detailed below was in the midst of a political crisis that led to the outbreak of the Second Civil War (63–62 BC).

With matters settled, Pompeius returned north to Asia Minor to formally end the Romano-Pontic War and prepare for his return home. In just three years, he had conquered the whole Near East, from the Black Sea to the Red Sea; the greatest expansion of Roman territory since the conquest of Greece in the 140s BC. Only two independent powers remained, the Ptolemaic and Parthian Empires, both considered to be weak, and both only being left alone due to matters of politics in Rome. Command in Syria was turned over to Pompeius' Proquaestor, M. Aemilius Scaurus, who was left with two legions. Pompeius himself returned to Pontus.

Pompeius & Ptolemaic Egypt (63 BC)

Prior to leaving Judea to return north, Pompeius it seems received an offer from Pharaoh Ptolemy XII to invade Egypt and suppress a revolt, as recorded by Appian:

> 'But he did not advance into Egypt, although the king of that country invited him there to suppress a revolt and sent gifts to himself and money and clothing for his whole army.'[27]

As Appian records, though Pompeius declined the opportunity, Ptolemy still provided monies that financed the Judean campaign. Although Egypt was a tempting target for any empire builder, Pompeius knew that the Senate would never allow him to march his army against a Roman ally, even if was to support a monarch that had been confirmed by the Senate and People. Just two years previously, the various factions within the Senate had united to thwart Crassus' proposal to annex Egypt, and Pompeius knew he would face a similar backlash. So Pompeius declined the opportunity to invade, but kept the scheme at the back of his mind and revisited it some years later, when his powerbase in Rome was stronger, thanks to a fresh alliance with Crassus (see Appendix One).

Pompeius' Eastern Campaigns – A Summary

In summing up the Pompeian campaigns, we can do no better than to quote the man himself. Dio provides us with an inscription which Pompeius raised, detailing his campaign:

> 'This is a copy of the inscription that Pompeius set up, recording his achievements in Asia.
>
> 'Pompeius Magnus, son of Gnaeus, imperator, freed the coasts of the world and all the islands within the Ocean from the attacks of pirates. He rescued from siege the kingdom of Ariobarzanes, Galatia and the territories and provinces beyond there, Asia, and Bithynia. He protected Paphlagonia, Pontus, Armenia, and Achaia, also Iberia, Colchis, Mesopotamia, Sophene and Gordyene.
>
> 'He subjugated Dareius king of the Medes, Artoles king of the Iberians, Aristobulus king of the Jews, and Aretas king of the Nabataean Arabs, also Syria next to Cilicia, Judaea, Arabia, the province of Cyrenaica, the Achaei, Iozygi, Soani and Heniochi, and the other tribes that inhabit the coast between Colchis and Lake Maeotis, together with the kings of

these tribes, nine in number, and all the nations that dwell between the Pontic Sea and the Red Sea.

'He extended the borders of the empire up to the borders of the world. He maintained the revenues of the Romans, and in some cases, he increased them. He removed the statues and other images of the gods, and all the other treasure of the enemies, and dedicated to the goddess, 12,060 pieces of gold and 307 talents of silver.'[28]

The End of the Romano-Pontic War – The Peace Treaty (63 BC)

It is hard to determine what Pompeius would have thought when news reached him of Mithridates' death. The first emotion would likely have been relief that finally, the elusive king was dead and the war would drag on no longer. This may well have been tinged with regret that the king was dead and not by Pompeius' hand. Nevertheless, for Pompeius this was the final objective, the end of the man who had plagued Rome for nearly thirty years and whom only the great Pompeius could subdue (at least in his mind). This was also finishing something that his former father-in-law and patron, Sulla, had been unable to complete.

As we have stated above, there are differing records of when Pompeius heard of Mithridates' death and the events that followed it. If he was in Jericho at the time, then it is unclear whether he stayed until the siege had ended (three months) or left the siege in the command of a subordinate, such as A. Gabinius, whilst he went to see Mithridates' body. Given the length of the siege and the importance of confirming the death of his legendary foe, the balance of probability suggests that Pompeius left the siege of Jerusalem to see the body for himself.

Again, the various surviving sources provide differing accounts of where Pompeius saw the body of his fallen foe. Plutarch has it at Amisus, whilst Appian says it was Sinope, both Pontic ports.[29] However, it is clear that Pharnaces sent the body across the Black Sea to what was now Roman territory, along with various gifts and hostages. Though the corpse had been embalmed, it would have made a grizzly trophy for any Triumph, so Pompeius ordered it to be interned in the Pontic royal tombs at Sinope, with his ancestors.[30]

As for Pharnaces, Pompeius resurrected Lucullus' solution, whereby the Pontic Empire was abolished and the Bosphoran Kingdom became an independent allied client governed by a son of Mithridates. In 71 BC it was Machares, now it was Pharnaces, who was confirmed as a friend and ally of the Roman Senate and People:

'Pharnaces, for delivering Italy from much trouble, was inscribed as a friend and ally of the Romans, and was given Bosphorus as his kingdom.'[31]

Thus, the Romano-Pontic War came to an end in 63 BC, after more than a decade, with the destruction of the Pontic Empire, half of which became a Roman province, the other half becoming part of Pompeius' network of client states in the East. Roman rule now crossed the Black Sea into the Crimea, extending the network of Roman control from the Crimea to the Caspian Sea, from the Euphrates to the Red Sea. It was possibly the greatest shift in the geopolitical situation in the Near East since Alexander himself.

Naturally, Pompeius wasted no time in sending the Senate and People of Rome the good news that finally, Mithridates, the long-time 'scourge' of Rome, was dead, and that it was under his command that this had been achieved. We have a first-hand account of this event, from the narrative of Cicero himself, who was Consul during 63 BC, and naturally wasted no opportunity in ensuring his name was attached to the glory:

'And in respect of that, I, who as Consul brought forward the motion, first, for decreeing a supplication of ten days to Cnaeus Pompeius after Mithridates had been slain and the Mithridatic war been ended. I, in compliance with whose opinion it was that the ordinary number of days that a supplication in honour of a Consul lasted was doubled (for you all agreed with me when, having had the letters of that same Pompeius read, and knowing that all wars both by sea and land were happily terminated, you decided a supplication of twelve days). I admired the virtue and greatness of mind of Pompeius in that, when he himself had hitherto been preferred to all other men in every sort of honour, he now was giving a more ample honour to another than he himself had received. Therefore, in that supplication which I proposed, the honour was paid to the immortal gods, and to the established usages of our ancestors, and to the welfare of the Republic.'[32]

With Mithridates dead, it really was a case of 'mission accomplished' for Pompeius, who could now return to Rome having ended both the pirate menace of the Mediterranean and the threat posed by the man who had been an enemy of Rome for a generation. Not only had he 'saved' the Republic, but he had extended Roman rule further than at any time since the conquest of Greece in the 140s BC.

Pompeius wintered in Pontus, finalizing his settlement of the Near East and converting Pontus itself into a Roman province.[33] These matters appear to have taken him until the summer of 62 BC, when he made a leisurely return to Italy, via the Greek islands of Mitylene and Rhodes and the Greek mainland itself, stopping off at Athens along the way. By the time he reached Italy in late 62 BC, dismissing his army at Brundisium, the Republic was recovering from a Second Civil War in which he was to play no part, but with his arrival eagerly anticipated by friends and enemies alike.[34]

Pompeius and the Second Civil War (63–62 BC)

During the latter stages of 63 BC, the New Republic – which Pompeius and Crassus had helped forge – saw the outbreak of a Second Civil War, details of which have been covered elsewhere.[35] This conflict is commonly referred to – somewhat erroneously – as the 'Catiline Conspiracy', a label that has helped to downplay the gravity of the matter and misdirect attention from the underlying causes to the somewhat tragi-comical figure of L. Sergius Catilina himself. This process was no doubt helped at the time, and ever since, by the influence of Cicero, who used the change of focus onto Catilina himself, his long-term rival, to claim that he had 'saved' the Republic.

Catalina was merely one of a group of former Sullan supporters, headed by P. Cornelius Lentulus Sura (Consul in 71 BC), who had attempted to mastermind a coup in Rome in response to what had been a growing number of attacks on ex-Sullans. These included prosecutions headed by two young aspiring politicians, one being C. Iulius Caesar (the most prominent surviving relative of C. Marius) and the other M. Porcius Cato, scion to a noble Plebeian lineage. These prosecutions had seen a number of lesser Sullan supporters convicted of 'crimes' committed during the Sullan regime (which were legal at the time), but naturally had not touched the leading ex-Sullans, men such as Lucullus, Crassus and Pompeius. This backlash against the Sullan faction culminated in 65 BC with the unprecedented overturning of the election of Sulla's nephew, himself named P. Cornelius Sulla, on a charge of bribery, a common-enough practice at Roman elections.

These aristocratic conspirators were joined by a significant number of Sullan army veterans, led by a C. Manlius. These veterans had been settled on land in Italy confiscated from local communities that had been judged to have backed the opposing faction in the civil war, but many had lost their new estates and been left destitute. The third element to this plot were other disaffected communities in Italy, many of whom had been impoverished by Sulla's victories and thus were still being affected by the First Civil War and its outcomes.[36] These many disparate elements came together in an attempt to overthrow the Pompeian-Crassan settlement and restore their varying fortunes. In Rome, the plot itself was a shambles and soon betrayed, with many conspirators rounded up, but the survivors raised several armies within Italy and plunged the Republic into a Second Civil War, this time confined to Italy itself.

Never one to let a crisis go unexploited, in early 62 BC we find one of the Tribunes, Q. Caecilius Metellus Nepos, a known supporter of Pompeius, proposing two laws. The first was to recall Pompeius himself to Italy to defend the Republic, while the second was to let him stand for Consul *in absentia*. We can see that this collapse into internecine strife, which had defined Pompeius' early career, offered him the chance of a glorious return to a new command, this time in Italy.

Naturally enough, the various other factions in the Senate – including, we must assume, that of Crassus – united to oppose and then defeat the proposals. In their view, the one way to make the current crisis worse was to let Pompeius loose in Italy with a battle-hardened army. Metellus' proposals were duly vetoed by a fellow Tribune, none other than M. Porcius Cato. Unwilling to let the matter drop, especially given the rewards he would reap from Pompeius if it passed, Metellus fell back on the tried and tested method of using armed support to drive the opposing Tribune – and his veto – from the Assembly.

The opposing factions in the Senate combined and threatened to issue the *senatus consultum ultimum* (the final decree of the Senate) and charge the Consuls with the defence of the city. Whenever this decree had been used in the past, the Tribune in question had ended up murdered, and the threat was enough for Metellus not only to withdraw the proposals, but flee from Rome (and break the sacred vow of his office not to leave the city during its term) and head to Pompeius in the East.

The major clash of the Second Civil War took place in January 62 BC at Pistoria, where the army of Manlius (along with Catilina) was crushed by the Consul C. Antonius.[37] Nevertheless, fighting continued across Italy and spread into Gaul throughout 62 BC. Though perhaps annoyed that his scheme had failed, Pompeius clearly did not rush to return to Rome, perhaps wanting to see how events unfolded throughout the year whilst he made a leisurely return. Metellus returned with him, and far from suffering from his actions, prospered politically, being rewarded for his loyalty to Pompeius with a Praetorship in 60 BC, followed by a Consulship in 57 BC.

The Triumph of Lucullus (63 BC)

Ironically, prior to the outbreak of the Second Civil War, Rome saw the much-delayed triumph of Lucullus for his success against Mithridates and

Tigranes. As we have seen (see Chapter Seven), Lucullus' return to Rome was hardly a triumphant one, with both he and his brother being prosecuted by his enemies. Lucullus' powerbase was strong enough to avoid the fate of his fellow Consul M. Aurelius Cotta and fight off the prosecution, and attention turned to his expected Triumph. Although the details in the surviving sources are far from clear, it seems that opposition within the Senatorial oligarchy prevented Lucullus from being awarded his Triumph until 63 BC.

Under normal circumstances, a commander would celebrate a Triumph for his victories in battle whilst the war continued. However, on this occasion we must assume that it was opposition from Pompeius' faction within the Senate that had organized this obstruction. The most logical assumption is that Pompeius did not wish his predecessor to claim – or steal – the glory for defeating Mithridates whilst he was still fighting the campaign. It is perhaps no coincidence that once news of Mithridates' death reached Rome, having been announced by Pompeius, opposition to Lucullus' Triumph vanished and he was able to celebrate it in 63 BC.

By blocking the granting of the Triumph, Pompeius would have put Lucullus in an awkward position politically. Under Roman law and tradition, no general could pass through the sacred boundary of Rome (the Pomerium) whilst holding his command (his imperium). Thus, the act of crossing the Pomerium meant the expiration of a general's imperium. Without his imperium, a commander could not celebrate a Triumph. This meant in practice that no returning general could enter Rome until he had celebrated his Triumph. If he did so, then he forfeited his right to a Triumph. By blocking the awarding of a Triumph, Pompeius was not merely being spiteful, but ensuring that his rival could not enter the Senate or take part in public political life, and thus not be physically present to stir up trouble for him.

It is perhaps no coincidence that Lucullus was not the only commander who suffered such a delay. The other prominent general similarly humiliated was Q. Caecilius Metellus 'Creticus', whose Triumph for his pirate campaign was also blocked. Again we are not given any details, but it can hardly be a coincidence that he too wanted a Triumph for a campaign more associated with Pompeius. As it was, Creticus was not granted his Triumph until 62 BC.

The third commander whose Triumph was delayed was Q. Marcius Rex, who was briefly Proconsul of Cilicia in 67 BC and a presumed supporter of Pompeius. We know that he returned to Rome and claimed a Triumph for the campaign he undertook in 66 BC, of which little detail remains (see Chapter Seven). As a supporter of Pompeius, we do not know why his request for a Triumph was blocked, but again perhaps he incurred Pompeius' ire by wanting a Triumph for a Pontic campaign before Pompeius returned. We know that by late 63 BC, when the Second Civil War broke out, he was still waiting and became a commander in the civil war campaign of 62 BC. There is no record of him celebrating a Triumph before his subsequent death in 61 BC.

In Lucullus' case, seemingly by mid-63 BC, and presumably after news of Mithridates' death reached Rome, opposition to his Triumph disappeared and it was finally granted.[38] Plutarch describes his Triumph:

'[Lucullus] decorated the circus of Flaminius with the arms of the enemy, which were very numerous, and with the royal engines of war; and this was a great spectacle in itself, and far from contemptible.

'But in the procession, a few of the mail-clad horsemen and ten of the scythe-bearing chariots moved along, together with sixty of the king's friends and generals. A hundred and ten bronze-beaked ships of war were also carried along, a golden statue of Mithridates himself, six feet in height, a wonderful shield adorned with precious stones, twenty litters of silver vessels, and thirty-two litters of gold beakers, armour, and money.

'All this was carried by men. Then there were eight mules which bore golden couches, fifty-six bearing ingots of silver, and a hundred and seven more bearing something less than two million seven hundred thousand pieces of silver coin.

'To crown all, Lucullus gave a magnificent feast to the city, and to the surrounding villages called Vici.'[39]

The Nabatean Campaign of Scaurus (62 BC)

Just because Pompeius had left for Rome and Mithridates had died, this did not automatically mean the end of the wider Eastern Wars, as many tend to assume. De-facto command of the war to secure Rome's new eastern empire now fell to M. Aemilius Scaurus, operating under Pompeius' imperium, and there was one further campaign the following year. As stated above, the most immediate threat to the security of Rome's new empire in the region was the Arab Nabatean Kingdom and its expansionist King Aretas. As we have also seen, Pompeius' campaign of 63 BC was aborted, either by a desire to conquer Judea or the news of Mithridates' death. There is further uncertainty over whether Pompeius actually took the Nabatean city of Petra or not.

What is clear is that, in Scaurus' mind, the Nabataeans in general – and Aretas in particular – were not sufficiently bowed to Roman rule, so a further campaign was required to bring about their acceptance of the new world order in the Near East. The only accounts we have for this campaign come from Josephus, with the surviving Roman and Greco-Roman sources seemingly eager to follow Pompeius and cover events at Rome instead:

'In the meantime, Scaurus made an expedition into Arabia, but was stopped by the difficulty of the places about Petra. However, he laid waste the country about Pella, though even there he was under great hardship; for his army was afflicted with famine. In order to supply which want, Hyrcanus afforded him some assistance, and sent him provisions by the means of Antipater; whom also Scaurus sent to Aretas, as one well acquainted with him, to induce him to pay him money to buy his peace. The King of Arabia complied with the proposal and gave him three hundred talents; upon which Scaurus drew his army out of Arabia.'[40]

'Scaurus made now an expedition against Petra, in Arabia, and set on fire all the places round about it, because of the great difficulty of access to it. And as his army was pinched by famine, Antipater furnished him with corn out of Judaea, and with whatever else he wanted, and this at the command of Hyrcanus.

'And when he was sent to Aretas, as an ambassador by Scaurus, because he had lived with him formerly, he persuaded Aretas to give Scaurus a sum of money, to prevent the burning of his country, and undertook to be his surety for three hundred talents. So Scaurus, upon these terms, ceased to make war any longer, which was done as much at Scaurus' desire, as at the desire of Aretas.'[41]

Therefore, the second Roman expedition against the Nabataeans fared little better than the first and again ended with a Roman withdrawal, the Nabataeans paying a large bribe for them to do so. The Nabataean Kingdom retained its nominal independence, relying on its inhospitable terrain to protect it from Roman retaliation. Nevertheless, its era of westward expansion did come to an end, but they remained a regional (pro-Roman) power until their eventual annexation by the Emperor Trajan in AD 106.

Scaurus was recalled to Rome in 61 BC, where his political career continued, aided by marrying the recently divorced wife of Pompeius. A Praetorship followed in 56 BC, but his bid for the Consulship ended in a corruption trial and exile, though he was acquitted.[42] His replacement in the East as Governor of Syria was L. Marcius Philippus, who was appointed by the Senate, rather than Pompeius, thus marking the transition from Syria being a theatre in Pompeius' campaign to a regular Senatorial command.

Scaurus' Nabataean campaign was to be the last of the Great Eastern War, which ended with Rome in complete control of the Near East. With the Nabataeans buying their freedom, the only powers that remained outside of Roman control were the Ptolemaic Empire – by now reduced to Egypt – and the Parthian Empire. Within a decade, both would come to the attention of Pompeius once again, both collapsing into internal conflict, allowing the Romans an opportunity to install puppet kings (see Appendix One).

The Final Act – Ratification of the Eastern Settlement (62–59 BC)

Though Pompeius had undertaken a comprehensive restructure of the Near East, using his powers as Proconsul, he still needed to have this ratified by the Senate and People of Rome. Under normal circumstances, such confirmation of a commander's settlement was a simple matter, yet Pompeius found this ratification consistently blocked in the Senate. Though he held significant patronage amongst the Senate and the People, and returned to Rome as the conqueror of Mithridates and a new Alexander, if anything this galvanized his opponents, who may have included his old partner and rival Crassus, the only man whose political influence rivalled his own.[43] Whilst no one in Rome objected to the annexation of Bithynia, Pontus and Syria, and the monies this brought to the Roman exchequer, many took the view that having all those foreign kings beholden to one man, rather than the Republic, was a dangerous precedent.

Pompeius' influence extended to securing at least one of the Consuls each year in 61 and 60 BC – M. Pupius Piso Frugi Calpurnianus and L. Afranius respectively, both former legates of his. Yet this and the splendid Triumph he held for his victories over Mithridates, Tigranes and the pirates were not enough to overcome the opposition in the Senate and Assemblies.[44] It was only when he reformed the Duumvirate with his long-time partner and rival Crassus that his eastern settlement was ratified,[45] though with much dubious legality.[46] Thus, the political settlement that formally redrew the map of the Near East and was the last act of Rome's Great Eastern War, fell to Pompeius' (and Crassus') latest agent in the Consulship: a rising politician named C. Iulius Caesar.[47]

Appendix I

Between the Wars – Rome's Eastern Campaigns (61–58 BC) and the Duumviral Masterplan (57–55 BC)

Though 59 BC saw the final political act of the Great Eastern War, with Caesar's law ratifying the whole of Pompeius' political settlement of the East, Rome's (and Pompeius') attention soon returned to that arena.

Syria and the Romano-Nabatean War (61–59 BC)

Between Scaurus' recall to Rome and Gabinius' appointment, there were two men who held the Governorship of Syria: L. Marcius Philippus (61–60 BC) and Cn. Cornelius Lentulus Marcellinus (59–58 BC). Our assumption is that both men would have been acceptable to Pompeius, if not outright his choices, to ensure that neither did anything to destabilize his eastern settlement and his future plans for Rome's empire in the East. Of the two, we know that Lentulus Marcellinus was indeed a legate of Pompeius during his pirate war of 67 BC, though we know nothing of Philippus prior to this appointment.[1] Coincidentally – or perhaps not – both men held the Consulship of 56 BC, though Marcellinus chose to oppose Pompeius and the Triumvirate.

In terms of their governorships, we only have Appian to provide us with any detail as to their activities, but they must primarily have been concerned with ensuring that Pompeius' eastern settlement was embedded, and that Syria continued its conversion into a Roman province:

'Much of the biennial term of each was consumed in warding off the attacks of the neighbouring [Nabataean] Arabs. It was on account of these events in Syria that Rome began to appoint for Syria Proconsuls, with power to levy troops and engage in war like Consuls. The first of these sent out with an army was Gabinius.'[2]

It seems that with Pompeius and Scaurus both returning to Rome, the Nabataean Arabs still posed issues for the security of Rome's new empire, in terms of border raids. We have no other details for Philippus' and Marcellinus' campaigns against the Nabataeans, but apparently the issues were still unresolved by 58 BC, leading to the appointment of a Proconsul to lead the campaign, though this did give Pompeius (and perhaps Crassus) the excuse they needed to mount another major campaign in the region.

Duumviral Recognition of Ptolemy XII (59 BC)

That very same year, Caesar passed another bill – again at the behest of his two political masters – concerning the Ptolemaic monarch of Egypt, Ptolemy XII (Auletes). Ptolemy had been ruling Ptolemaic Egypt since 80 BC, having come to the throne during another period of Ptolemaic upheaval, following the murders of Berenice III (81–80 BC) and Ptolemy XI (80 BC). Furthermore, Ptolemy had been a hostage of Mithridates VI, along with his brother, who became King of Ptolemaic Cyprus (see below). Having these two factors in his background, combined with Rome's growing territorial acquisitions in the region, which included the annexation of Cyrene in the 70s BC and Crassus' attempt to annex Egypt itself by censorial decree in 65 BC, meant that Ptolemy sought further assurance of his position from Rome.

As we have seen (see Chapter Ten), Ptolemy XII's position on the Egyptian throne was far from secure, suffering from internal rebellions, and he had already reached out to Pompeius in the late 60s BC for help, which had not borne fruit. This was on account of Egypt being outside of Pompeius' command, and the other factions within the Senate no more amenable to Pompeius gaining influence/control in Egypt than Crassus.

Therefore, in order to gain this security, Ptolemy himself went to Rome in 60 BC to plead his case, and found that Pompeius and Crassus had reformed their partnership and were seizing temporary control of the machinery of government. This clearly represented both an opportunity for Ptolemy and a threat, as both men would have relished the chance to annex Egypt, but perhaps not allowed the other to do so. Thus, Ptolemy promised them 6,000 talents to gain the official recognition of the Senate and People of Rome (in the form of Pompeius and Crassus). Caesar, as their agent in office as Consul, duly passed the law and Ptolemy XII was recognized as King of Egypt, but clearly beholden to the Duumvirate for his survival.[3]

The Annexation of Cyprus (58 BC)

Though Ptolemy XII had bought his survival on the throne of Egypt, his brother Ptolemy of Cyprus was not so lucky. In the eastern Mediterranean, the island of Cyprus now stood out as a bastion of independence in a Roman-controlled world. Cyprus had been ruled by Ptolemy XII's brother since c.80 BC, and he too had been a hostage of Mithridates. Cyprus receives little attention during the pirate campaigns of Metellus and Pompeius, which had seen the island of Crete and the mainland of Cilicia annexed to Rome. Clearly, the Duumvirate's agreement with Ptolemy XII did not include Cyprus, and perhaps that was clear at the time to the men involved.

The very next year, Cyprus was annexed by Tribunician law, proposed by a Tribune named P. Clodius Pulcher. Clodius, who had transferred from the Patrician order to the Plebeian one to become Tribune – an unprecedented act[4] – had originally been sponsored by the Duumvirs to ensure they had tribunician agents the following year to secure their previous legislation. Thus, Clodius presented the Roman Assembly with a watered-down version of Crassus' plan of 65 BC to annex foreign territory by decree, and the last independent island kingdom in the Mediterranean was extinguished and added to Rome's new eastern empire. Despite being offered an accommodation by Rome, King Ptolemy chose to commit suicide, and received no help from his brother. Though following Duumviral orders, Clodius had two other reasons for relishing this annexation. Firstly, there seems to have been a standing grudge between Clodius and Ptolemy, dating from when Clodius had been captured by the pirates of the region and Ptolemy – in Clodius' opinion – had not done enough to ransom him.[5] Secondly, Clodius' law appointed M. Porcius Cato, a known opponent of both him and the Duumvirs, to be the officer (*quaestor pro praetore*) responsible for overseeing the annexation, thereby removing him from Rome (and being able to oppose them) and making him complicit in Clodius' legislation.[6]

Clodius and Gabinius (58 BC)

Clodius was not the only agent of the Duumvirs elected this year. For the fourth year running, Pompeius had a hand in the selection of one of the Consuls, and having dispensed with Caesar's services fell back on his tried and tested method of ensuring the election of one of his legates (the third since his return). In 60 BC, Pompeius had chosen a legate from his eastern campaigns, L. Afranius, and in 58 BC, the choice fell on another, A. Gabinius.[7] It is therefore not a surprise that before the year was out, Gabinius, under a law of Clodius, received the province of Syria, which until this point had been a Propraetorian command (see below).

Furthermore, according to a passage of Cicero, Gabinius received an unlimited command, though what is exactly meant by this is not clear.[8] It seems, however, that Gabinius received a command far wider in scope and power than was usual. Thus, one of Pompeius' agents was sent back to Syria to continue to implement Pompeius' grand design for Rome's new eastern empire. Initially, it appeared that the main campaigns would be against Judea and Nabataea, though as we will see, Egypt and Parthia were drawn into this command.

Clodius and the Eastern Settlement (58 BC)

Towards the end of the year, Clodius apparently turned his attention to Pompeius' eastern settlement, which had only been ratified by the People of Rome the year before. Cicero accuses Clodius of elevating to the kingship of Galatia, a certain Brogitarus, son-in-law of the current King Deiotarus, in some type of joint rule, as the result of a bribe.[9] It is assumed that this came after the falling out between Pompeius and Clodius, and thus Clodius was tampering with Pompeius' settlement of the region.[10]

Gabinius and the Romano-Jewish War (57 BC)

In 57 BC, Gabinius reached his province of Syria. Though Appian states that the Senate upgraded the governorship from a Propraetorian to a Proconsular one to deal with the Nabataean problem, Josephus paints a different picture, namely that Gabinius' first priority was to deal with a renewed outbreak of civil war in Judea, something which Rome must have been aware of.[11] This would merely have increased the importance of sending someone with more power than a Praetor, as with the Nabataeans and Judeans threatening Rome's (and Pompeius') eastern settlement, Rome once again needed to demonstrate its military and political might.

Though Pompeius must have thought that he had ended the Judean Civil War by installing Hyrcanus II on throne and taking Aristobulus II prisoner (and back to Rome, see Chapter Ten), Hyrcanus' rule was challenged once again, this time by a son of Aristobulus II named Alexander. He had used Pompeius' absence and the distraction of the Nabataeans to raise a fresh force opposed to Hyrcanus II and invade Judea:

> 'However, Alexander went over all the country round about, and armed many of the Jews, and suddenly got together ten thousand armed footmen, and fifteen hundred horsemen, and fortified Alexandreium, a fortress near to Corea, and Machaerus, near the mountains of Arabia.'[12]

He was even able to recapture Jerusalem and began to rebuild the city's defences. Seemingly wasting little time, Gabinius invaded Judea once again, commanding the main body of his army, whilst a contingent of cavalry was sent ahead, led by a young nobleman fighting his first campaign, none other than M. Antonius – the future Triumvir) – starting a two-decade (and ultimately fatal) association with the Near East.[13] Fighting alongside Gabinius was a contingent of Jews loyal to Hyrcanus II, including his chief advisor Antipater, father of Herodes I. Initially, Alexander withdrew in the face of the Roman advance, which was a sensible move, but eventually he felt he had no alternative but to give battle near Jerusalem, which quite frankly was not a sensible move.

Battle of Jerusalem (57 BC)

As Josephus does not analyse Alexander's motives, we must only assume that he felt compelled to give battle or face the loss of Jerusalem and the collapse of his whole campaign. However, given the disparity in both the quality and numbers between the two sides, there was only ever going to be one outcome. Alexander may well have been better served to withdraw and fight a guerrilla campaign, until Rome's attention wandered once more:

> '... and as Alexander was not able to sustain the charge of the enemies' forces, now they were joined, he retired. But when he was come near to Jerusalem, he was forced to fight, and lost six thousand men in the battle; three thousand of which fell down dead, and three thousand were taken alive; so he fled with the remainder to Alexandreium.'[14]
>
> 'Hereupon Alexander retired to the neighbourhood of Jerusalem, where they fell upon one another, and it came to a pitched battle, in which the Romans slew of their enemies about three thousand and took a like number alive.'[15]

With Alexander's army crushed, Jerusalem was lost to him and he fled to the fortress of Alexandreium, which Gabinius soon put under siege. After a short period, Alexander opened negotiations and surrendered himself and the fortress to Gabinius. Thereafter, Gabinius once again installed Rome's (and Pompeius') client king, Hyrcanus II, back on the throne. However, as Hyrcanus II had still proved inept in keeping control of his own country, Gabinius reduced the power of the monarchy at the expense of the country's aristocracy:

> 'After this Gabinius brought Hyrcanus to Jerusalem and committed the care of the temple to him; but ordained the other political government to be by an aristocracy. He also parted the whole nation into five conventions, assigning one portion to Jerusalem, another to Gadara, that another should belong to Amathus, a fourth to Jericho, and to the fifth division was allotted Sepphoris, a city of Galilee. So the people were glad to be thus freed from monarchical government and were governed for the future by all aristocracy.'[16]

Yet within the year, civil war broke out once again as Alexander's father, the former ruler Aristobulus II, reappeared in Judea, having fled Rome at some point, presumably spurred by his son's rebellion. By the time Aristobulus reached Judea, it seems Alexander had been defeated, but he nevertheless decided to raise a fresh rebellion himself, rather than wait until Gabinius had departed. Having gathered a scratch army, he chose to pit his forces against those of Rome in open battle, but fared no better than his son.

Unnamed Battle (57 BC)

Once again, we have few details as to the size of the Roman force or the tactics involved in this clash:

> 'And as for the unarmed multitude, he dismissed them, and only marched on with those that were armed, being to the number of eight thousand, among whom was Pitholaus, who had been the lieutenant at Jerusalem, but deserted to Aristobulus with a thousand of his men; so the Romans followed him, and when it came to a battle, Aristobulus's party for a long time fought courageously; but at length they were overborne by the Romans, and of them five thousand fell down dead, and about two thousand fled to a certain little hill, but the thousand that remained with Aristobulus broke through the Roman army, and marched together to Machaerus.'[17]

Though Aristobulus II – and his other son, also named Aristobulus – escaped the battlefield, they too were soon besieged and captured, and all three men were ferried back to Rome, where the Senate kept Aristobulus II under confinement but sent his sons back to Judea. Josephus states that this was due to an agreement between Gabinius and the wife of Aristobulus II, who handed over a number of fortresses to the Romans.[18] Those of us with more suspicious minds could interpret this as a deliberate move to keep Judea destabilized and thereby requiring an active Roman presence in the region, as soon happened (see below).

Political Turmoil in Egypt and Parthia (58–57 BC)

With Judea restored to the rule of a Roman client king, there may have been the expectation that Gabinius would turn his attention back to the Nabataeans, yet events proved to be more advantageous to Rome – and Pompeius and Crassus – than ever. The end of Rome' Great Eastern War had seen only two other empires remain independent, the Ptolemaic and the Parthian, although acquisitive Roman eyes had been turned towards both recently. The monarchs of the two empires were Ptolemy XII Auletes and Phraates III, both of whom had done much to ensure their countries remained independent of Rome. Yet within a year, both had been ousted from their throne by their own families.

Though Ptolemy had been confirmed as Pharaoh of Egypt by the Senate and People of Rome, at the behest of the Duumvirate, only in 59 BC, he was soon toppled. As Dio points out, the two events were connected:

> 'After this there was further disturbance on account of King Ptolemy. He had spent large amounts upon some of the Romans, part of it out of his own purse and part borrowed, in order to have his rule confirmed and to receive the name of friend and ally; and he was now collecting this sum forcibly from the Egyptians. They were accordingly very angry at him both on this account and also because when they had bidden him to demand back Cyprus from the Romans or else renounce his friendship for them, he had been unwilling to do so. And since he could neither persuade nor yet compel them to be quiet, as he had no foreign troops, he fled from Egypt, and coming to Rome, accused his countrymen of having expelled him from his kingdom.'[19]

Ptolemy was overthrown for trying to raise the money he needed to pay off the Duumvirs, as well as part of a backlash for the loss of Cyprus, the Ptolemies' last imperial possession. He was replaced on the throne by his daughter Berenice IV. Ptolemy fled Egypt – along with another daughter, none other than Cleopatra VII – and made a leisurely progression to Rome and his patrons Pompeius and Crassus, who coincidentally (or not) now had a large Roman army on the borders of Egypt. With Ptolemy being overthrown in 58 BC, it is perfectly possible that the Duumvirs were aware of this and thus ensured that their agent, Gabinius, would be sent to the East with a sufficiently enhanced imperium that would allow him to return Ptolemy to the throne of the region's richest kingdom as Rome's – and the Duumvirs' – puppet king.

However, the Duumvirs' plans were thwarted by a coalition of their enemies in the Senate, who had no wish to see either man secure control of Egypt. This was helped by the Duumvirs having seemingly entered one of their periods of working against each other, and Rome having descended into open street warfare between the armed gangs of Clodius and Milo.[20] Pompeius managed to get as far as having a Tribune propose a law that Pompeius, accompanied by only two lictors – though with a large Roman army in neighbouring Judea – return the king to Alexandria and act as mediator, though the Senate blocked this measure. Ptolemy left Rome in 56 BC, with the plan in abeyance.

If the Duumvirs were able to make a plan to exploit the turmoil in Egypt, we must ask whether the same could be said for the events that occurred in Parthia. Having done so much to stabilize Parthia after decades of civil war (see Appendix Two), Phraates himself was ousted and murdered in a palace coup led by two of his sons, Mithradates and Orodes, with the former taking the throne as Mithradates IV. Interestingly, as with much of Parthian history, especially during this period, we do not have an exact date for this act; all we know is that soon afterwards, the two brothers fell out and Mithradates was then ousted by Orodes, who established himself, on a very shaky throne, as Orodes II. Mithradates managed to avoid his father's fate and fled westwards to Rome and Gabinius.

Given the lack of any detail in our surviving sources, and no recorded length of the rule of Mithradates – and it is entirely possible for Phraates to have been overthrown in either 59 or 58 BC – it could have thus occurred to the Duumvirs that the Parthian Empire was collapsing into at least political turmoil at court and possibly a renewed breakdown into full-scale civil war. It is entirely possible that such an opportunity was again in the minds of the Duumvirs when they arranged for Gabinius to be invested with a superior and wonderfully vague eastern command. As it was, events turned out perfectly for them, and Gabinius had a deposed Parthian monarch in his camp by 56 BC, ripe for installation as a client king.

Gabinius and the End of the Seleucid Dynasty (57/56 BC)

Tied into the political turmoil in Egypt is an interesting note in the chronicles of Eusebius about the last Seleucid monarch, repeated by Jerome:

> 'Philippus whom we mentioned before, the son of Grypus and of Tryphaena the daughter of Ptolemy VIII, was also deposed. He wanted to go to Egypt, because he too had been invited by the inhabitants of Alexandria to rule there, but Gabinius, an officer of Pompeius, who was the Roman Governor of Syria, stopped him from going. And so the royal dynasty in Syria came to an end with Antiochus and Philippus.'[21]
>
> 'Later, Philippus was captured by Gabinius.'[22]

Both sources believe that the Philippus in question was Philip II (Philoromaeus), the last surviving Seleucid Emperor, and that a plan had been drawn up by the new Pharaoh of Egypt, Berenice IV, for them to marry and thus create a new Seleucid-Ptolemaic Dynasty. It seems, however, that his plan was betrayed to Gabinius, who had Philip arrested – and possibly murdered, though that is never stated – and put a stop to such a plan. Had this plan succeeded, it would have challenged two planks of the Pompeian settlement: the removal of the Seleucid Dynasty and having a puppet ruler in Egypt. Interestingly, we find corroboration of parts of this story in Dio, though it is Berenice herself who kills Philip:

'Berenice was at this time ruling the Egyptians, and though she feared the Romans, she took no steps suitable to emergency; instead, she sent for one Seleucus [Philip] who claimed to belong to the royal race that once had flourished in Syria, formally recognized him as her husband, and made him a partner in the kingdom and in the war. When he was seen to be held in no esteem, she had him killed.'[23]

Gabinius and the Aborted Romano-Parthian War (56 BC)

With the Roman sources focusing on the political chaos in Rome itself, we have little detail about Gabinius' activities in 56 BC. Cicero (not a known fan of Gabinius) goes out of his way to label the man with being deficient in his duties in Syria and allowing piracy to flourish once more.[24] Yet Gabinius clearly faced a dilemma. Whilst officially he was Governor of Syria to enforce the will of the Senate and People of Rome, in reality he was there to enforce the will of his patron Pompeius. However, Pompeius was in the midst of the political turmoil at Rome, where he received no support and more than a little opposition from his former Duumviral colleague Crassus. So Pompeius was in no position to secure political support in Rome for an invasion of Egypt or one of Parthia to restore either deposed monarch.

All Gabinius could do was prepare his army for one of the forthcoming wars, and that which is mentioned first in a number of surviving sources is the Parthian one, an endeavour in which he was joined by none other than Ptolemy XII himself (presumably along with Cleopatra):

'Gabinius had harried Syria in many ways, even to the point of inflicting far more injury upon the people than did the pirates, who were flourishing even then. Still, he regarded all his gains from that source as mere trifles and was at first planning and preparing to make a campaign against the Parthians and their wealth.'[25]

'When Gabinius was sent into Syria, Archelaus himself also went there in the hope of sharing with him in his preparations for the Parthian War.'[26]

'Now when Gabinius was making an expedition against the Parthians and had already passed over Euphrates.'[27]

'But now as Gabinius was marching to the war against the Parthians, he was hindered by Ptolemy, whom, upon his return from Euphrates, he brought back into Egypt.'[28]

'As he was in readiness to begin the war, Mithradates, king of the Parthians, who had been driven out of his kingdom by his brother, Orodes, persuaded Gabinius to turn his forces from the Arabs against the Parthians. At the same time Ptolemy, King of Egypt, who likewise had lost his throne, prevailed upon him by a large sum of money to turn his arms from the Parthians against Alexandria.'[29]

Here we must be clear that Gabinius was not hiring out his army to the highest bidder, an accusation which his enemies in Rome liked to tar him with, but would have been training it for the invasion of the Parthian Empire, to install Mithradates IV as a pro-Roman monarch on the Parthian throne, continuing the masterplan laid down by Pompeius during the 60s BC.

We are told that he got as far as the Euphrates, which would have been a sensible launching point for any invasion and good preparation for his army in the conditions of the region. He was certainly not prevented from invading by the plans – and money – of Ptolemy XII, but by the fact he was waiting from orders from Rome (i.e. Pompeius) that the war had been granted its political blessing. Towards those ends, his superior imperium was extended into 55 BC.

Yet when Gabinius' orders did come, they were not those he was expecting, but reflected the new political reality at Rome. Amidst the political chaos and bloodshed, the old rivals of Pompeius and Crassus, along with their new junior partner C. Iulius Caesar, reformed their Duumviral alliance, now technically a Triumviral one – by dint of Caesar's armies in Gaul – and seized control of the Republic, ensuring Pompeius' and Crassus' elections as Consuls for 55 BC. With control of Rome came control of its foreign policy, and with Caesar devoted to the conquest of Gaul and Pompeius determined to oversee Rome itself, Crassus abandoned his ambitions towards Egypt and turned towards the invasion and defeat of Parthia, along with an annexation of its former Seleucid Mesopotamian heartlands. Gabinius therefore found himself removed from command of the prospective Romano-Parthian War, instead receiving orders to install Ptolemy as the Duumvirs' puppet Pharaoh of Egypt.

Gabinius and Romano-Egyptian War (55 BC)

Gabinius, robbed of his chance to be the first Roman commander to invade Parthia – notwithstanding the disputed Parthian provinces in the earlier war – instead became the first Roman commander to invade Egypt. Amongst his retinue were not only the deposed Egyptian Pharaoh, but a certain young M. Antonius and Cleopatra. Clearly, the order arrived too late in 56 BC for a campaign to be mounted, but one was scheduled for early 55 BC, using Judea as a springboard and receiving the full support of the restored King Hyrcanus II:

> '... making use of Hyrcanus and Antipater to provide everything that was necessary for this expedition; for Antipater furnished him with money, and weapons, and corn, and auxiliaries; he also prevailed with the Jews that were there, and guarded the avenues at Pelusium, to let them pass.'[30]

Again, rather than negotiate, the incumbent Pharaoh, Berenice IV, chose to oppose the Roman invasion. Her newest consort was a certain Archelaus, son of a Mithridatic general. The invasion was spearheaded by Antonius:

> 'Antonius was therefore sent with the cavalry, and he not only occupied the narrow pass, but actually took Pelusium, a large city, and got its garrison into his power, thus rendering its march safer for the main army and giving its general assured hope of victory. And even the enemy reaped advantage from Antonius' love of distinction. For Ptolemy, as soon as he entered Pelusium, was led by wrath and hatred to institute a massacre of the Egyptians; but Antonius intervened and prevented him.
>
> 'Moreover, in the ensuing battles and contests, which were many and great, he displayed many deeds of daring and sagacious leadership, the most conspicuous of which was his rendering the van of the army victorious by outflanking the enemy and enveloping them from the rear. For all this he received rewards of valour and fitting honours. Nor did the multitude fail to observe his humane treatment of the dead Archelaus.'[31]

Dio also preserves an account which briefly describes one land battle and a naval engagement:

> 'Thus he [Gabinius] reached Pelusium without encountering any opposition; and while advancing from there with his army in two divisions he encountered and conquered the Egyptians on the same day, and after this vanquished them again on the river with his ships and also on land.'[32]
>
> 'So Gabinius conquered them, and after slaying Archelaus and many others he promptly gained control of all Egypt and handed it over to Ptolemy. The latter put to death his daughter and also the foremost and richest of the citizens, because he had need of much money.'[33]

Thus, Egypt fell to Rome (and the Duumvirs) with Ptolemy XII restored to his throne and with an even larger indemnity to pay to the Duumvirs. Having learned from their earlier mistake, which saw Ptolemy ousted in 58 BC, the Duumvirs, via Gabinius, left behind a garrison of Roman soldiers to support Ptolemy against his own family and people, and installed a Roman businessmen and banker, C. Rabirius Postumius, as *Dioiketes* (chief financial official). Consequently, the Duumvirs assumed temporary control of Egypt's finances, a long-term aim of Crassus.

As it turned out, Rabirius' extraction of money from the Egyptian economy proved so unpopular that there was another revolt, forcing Ptolemy to imprison Rabirius, who subsequently fled back to Rome and was promptly prosecuted, though successfully defended by Cicero. Nevertheless, Ptolemy remained on the throne, backed by his Roman soldiers, one of whom was to play an infamous role in Roman history in the aftermath of the Battle of Pharsalus in 48 BC, when he murdered Pompeius on an Egyptian beach on the orders of the new co-Pharaoh Ptolemy XIII (Ptolemy XII having died in 51 BC). The other co-ruler was Cleopatra VII, promoted to joint successor of Ptolemy XII after the death of Berenice IV.

Gabinius and the Romano-Jewish War (55 BC)

With Roman attention focused on Egypt, the Judean Civil War flared up yet again in the shape of the formerly pardoned Judean prince Alexander, an act which almost everyone would have predicted. Although we have a brief description in Josephus' works,[34] we will never know what possessed Alexander to raise another revolt, with a Roman army having just overrun and occupied neighbouring Egypt and one of the Duumvirs himself due to arrive in the region.

Nevertheless, he managed to raise an impressive force of at least 30,000, overran the country and started butchering any Romans he could find. Retribution was unsurprisingly swift, with Gabinius leading the Roman army out of Egypt and Alexander once again obligingly giving battle, with predictable results.

Battle of Mount Tabor (55 BC)

We only have scant accounts in Josephus of the subsequent clash, and no idea of the Roman numbers or tactics:

'However, thirty thousand still continued with Alexander, who was himself eager to fight also; accordingly, Gabinius went out to fight, when the Jews met him; and as the battle was fought near Mount Tabor, ten thousand of them were slain, and the rest of the multitude dispersed themselves, and fled away.'[35]

'[Antipater] could not restrain Alexander, for he had an army of thirty thousand Jews, and met Gabinius, and joining battle with him, was beaten, and lost ten thousand of his men about Mount Tabor.'[36]

The Romans again restored Hyrcanus II to the throne, though Alexander seems to have again escaped Roman justice and was later to try yet another revolt. Gabinius settled matters in Jerusalem, leaving the aristocracy in power once more, with a growing role for Antipater, the king's advisor. With Judea again quiet, he finally turned his attention to the Nabataeans.

Gabinius and Romano-Nabataean War (55 BC)

We have next to no detail about Gabinius' final campaign against the Nabataeans, with only brief mentions of it in Josephus:

'... thence he [Gabinius] marched, and fought and beat the Nabataeans.'[37]
'... and [Gabinius] went against the Nabataeans, and overcame them in battle.'[38]

All we know is that Gabinius, in his last year of command, having been replaced by Crassus, wanted one final campaign and felt that he could not finish without fighting the Nabataeans. We must assume that the Nabataeans themselves had continued to take advantage of Gabinius' entanglements in Judea and Egypt to persist with their border raids.

There are no details as to where Gabinius marched, presumably on one of their cities, or whether the subsequent clash was a major battle or a small skirmish. All we know is that according to Josephus, Gabinius was victorious and rounded off his campaign, presumably wintering in Syria to await the arrival of Crassus and the next major phase of Roman involvement in the East, the First Romano-Parthian War.

Waiting For Crassus – The Eastern World in 54 BC

This period sat between Rome's Great Eastern War (74–62 BC) and the First Romano-Parthian War (55–50 BC). The campaigns of this intervening period both built on the achievements of the first conflict and laid the foundations for the second. The end of the first war had seen a massive expansion of Roman power in the Near East. Unsurprisingly, the two kingdoms most recently affected by this expansion – Judea and Nabataea – both required further military action before they were brought into accepting Roman rule in the region.

Furthermore, the Duumvirs finally got their respective wishes when a Roman army invaded Egypt for the first time and installed their candidate on the throne, temporarily gaining access to Egyptian wealth. Both men now had their *causus belli* for the inevitable war against what they believed to be a decaying Parthian Empire, which was the final piece of the jigsaw for Roman rule over the Near and Middle East and the fulfilment of inheriting the mantle of Alexander the Great.

In 54 BC, Gabinius departed for Rome, where he was subsequently put on trial for his actions by his – and the Duumvirs' – political enemies, scapegoated for following the orders of his two masters and subsequently exiled.[39] He was later recalled by Caesar and entered his service in the Third Civil War, dying of disease soon afterwards. Gabinius was replaced as Governor of Syria by Crassus himself, who was at the height of his power, having – for the second time – temporarily seized control of the Republic. The stage was set for what Rome believed would be the final war of conquest in the East, a clash with Parthia.[40]

Appendix II

The Parthian Civil War (c.91–64 BC) – An Overview

Throughout this work, reference has been made to the collapse of Parthian power caused by their civil war, which raged over several decades. Yet unlike the other civil wars of the region, especially Rome's, we have little or no detail as to the events that took place, only their wider effects: the collapse of Parthian military power, whose most obvious manifestation was the rise of the Armenian Empire and Tigranes' usurpation of the title of 'King of Kings'.

Furthermore, we cannot with any certainty put an exact year to when the Parthian Civil War started or ended. What we do know is that at its heart, the clash was a dynastic one, with various rival candidates struggling for the throne, and that its catalyst was the old age, and then death, of Mithradates II (the Great). Without any native sources, we have to rely on passing references in much later Greco-Roman sources, and more importantly use the coins that the various competing monarchs minted.

As we have seen throughout the history of this region, the key danger to any Hellenistic empire lay in the death of its monarch. From the Hittites through to the Assyrians, Babylonians and Egyptians, empires rose and fell on the vagaries of genetics, whether it be the health of the monarch or the capacity of his (or her) successor. When we enter the Greek period, we can see this more clearly, with the sources relating the various dynastic feuds of the Persian Empire, which led to its eventual decay and overthrow, and then the sudden collapse of its successor, the Alexandrian Empire, brought about by the unexpected death in his 30s of a monarch without a mature successor.

The Parthians were no different from their Macedonian, Seleucid or Ptolemaic rivals, having suffered similar dips in fortunes upon the death of monarchs. However, we must make clear that Parthia had never suffered a full-blown civil war on this scale. This is perhaps related to the fact that it was under Mithradates II that the Parthian Empire had reached it height. Though his predecessor Mithradates I had invaded and annexed Mesopotamia, and with it snatched the ancient Persian title of 'King of Kings', it was Mithradates II who had secured this acquisition and ensured the perpetual decline of their Seleucid rival. By the 90s BC, the Parthian Empire had advanced up the Euphrates and into the Caucasus, annexing Armenia, and was poised to attack and annex Seleucid Syria. This campaign would have seen the Parthians reach the Mediterranean, with Egypt the next obvious target, which most likely would have brought them into conflict with Rome.

The stakes to succeed Mithradates as Parthian Emperor were far higher than they had ever been. Our fundamental problem is that we do not know who his successor was designated to be. Given the amount of time he ruled – from c.124–c.91 BC – he was not a young man when he died, and therefore we must assume that he fathered many sons.

Furthermore, what we do know is that the ruling Arsacid dynasty had many branches and that over the 150 years of their rule there are indications that different branches claimed the throne at different times. Added to this is the point that the Parthians did not adhere to the rule of primogeniture, so there was no shortage of rival candidates.

Not only can we not reconstruct the events of this period with any certainty, but the last few decades of Parthian scholarship have reinterpreted the coinage of the period and presented alternative versions of long-held or traditional views.

The Written Sources

We only have a handful of written sources which mention the chaos in the Parthian Empire at the time:

'... then, an account of how, after a succession of several kings in Parthia, Orodes came to the throne.'[1]

'... and in the time of Lucullus the Parthian power was not so great as it proved to be in the time of Crassus, nor was it so well united, nay rather, owing to internal and neighbouring wars, it had not even strength enough to repel the wanton attacks of the Armenians.'[2]

Traditional Version

This can be found in works such as Debevoise[3] and has a rival claimant to the throne, Gotarzes I, being crowned as King of Babylon in c.91 BC, whilst Mithradates was still alive. The assumption is that the king was ailing, and a rival – most likely from a cadet branch of the Arsacid dynasty – was proclaimed king, thus splitting the empire in two. With Mithradates dying in c.88 BC, we do not know if a rival was proclaimed in the eastern Parthian Empire or whether Gotarzes took over the whole of Parthia. It was then Gotarzes, defending the western Parthian Empire, who was defeated by Tigranes, possibly dying in the process.

By *c.*80 BC, we see an Orodes proclaimed as king, at least in the western Parthian Empire, but within a few years (*c.*76 BC) he was replaced by a Sinatruces, whom the sources described as an old man when he took the throne, adding that he used Scythian forces from beyond the eastern borders of the empire, as many of his predecessors had done. Sinatruces seems to have ruled the whole Parthian Empire and ended the civil war, successfully passing it on to his son Phraates III, who then faced Rome.

Modern Version[4]
The principal differences found in modern Parthian scholarship can be summed up thus:

- An earlier date for Mithradates' death (*c.*91 BC).
- Gotarzes may well have been Mithradates' son and successor and was ruling Babylon in his name.
- Sinatruces' role as a claimant to the throne can be pushed back to the start of the civil wars.
- More claimants to the throne than just Gotarzes I and Orodes I.

It has been argued by a number of scholars that far from entering the fray in the latter stages of the Parthian Civil War, Sinatruces, who is argued to be a descendant of Mithradates I, actually took part in the early part of the conflict and may well have been a rival claimant to Mithradates II's son Gotarzes. Thus, we have a situation where the descendants of an earlier branch, that had been dispossessed, return to claim the throne back.

Furthermore, new rival claimants have been identified throughout the empire issuing coins claiming to be ruler of the whole or portions of the empire. Arguments have been made for a Mithradates III (87–80 BC), and an unknown Arsaces, labelled as Arsaces XVI (78–61 BC), to join Orodes I (80–75 BC).

We can construct a vague account of Sinatruces challenging Gotarzes' claim to the throne upon the death of Mithradates II, based on a greater lineage (a return to the older line of Arsacid descent) and being of greater age and experience. The disappearance of Gotarzes suggests that he was killed during the conflict and that the Mithradatic II branch then saw further claimants – probably Gotarzes' brothers – in the form of Mithradates III and Orodes I. This first phase of the war lasted until *c.*75 BC, when the last Mithradatic claimants seem to have died out. Where Arsaces XVI fits in is not known, but the above reconstruction is speculative at best.

By 76/75 BC, Sinatruces seems to have been able to secure the Parthian throne, with the help of Scythian tribesmen, and was able to pass it on to his son, establishing his branch as the new prime Arsacid line. It has been argued that it was not until as late as 61 BC that Phraates was able to finally defeat the last challenger, the unknown Arsaces XVI,[5] and finally unify the Parthian Empire. If this was the case, then it meant that during his dealings with the Romans, Phraates still faced a challenger for his throne.

Summary

What we are left with is fundamentally a war between two branches of the Arsacid Dynasty, representing the current (of Mithradates II) and a former (Sinatruces) branch.

Mithradates II (c.121–91 BC)

Gotarzes I (c.91–87 BC)
Mithradates III (c.87–80 BC)
Orodes I (c.80–75 BC)
Arsaces XVI (c.78–61 BC)

Sinatruces (c.91–69 BC)
Phraates III (c.69–58 BC)
Mithradates IV (c.58–55 BC)
Orodes II (57–37 BC)

What we can see is that there were far more claimants to the throne than was previously thought, and that this instability continued into Phraates' reign, when he seems to have been able to finally eliminate all rivals and re-establish central Arsacid authority. However, after nearly thirty years of rival claimants and presumably armed clashes throughout the empire, it appears that the central authority of the Arsacid Emperor was far weaker than it had previously been. We must presume that the leading noble families used this absence of central authority to take power for themselves.[6] Certainly, all subsequent Parthian monarchs seemed to suffer from powerful noble families at court, and the eventual downfall of the dynasty saw it replaced by another noble family from within, in AD 224.

The civil war weakened the Parthian Empire in five critical ways. Firstly, it meant that they were not able to capitalize on the collapse of Roman power in the East and the rise of the Pontic Empire. This inevitably leads to a 'what if?' scenario, with Mithradates living another five years and taking advantage of Rome's absence regarding Seleucid Syria. Aside from the lost opportunity came the second and third factors, namely that this civil war weakened them militarily, actually allowing a rival (Tigranes) to carve out a new empire in the region and achieve the long-term Parthian goal, annexing Seleucid Syria. It also meant that Parthia was in no position to contest the Roman annexation of Syria and domination of the Near East.

Aside from these short-term lost opportunities, there seems to have been two more lasting factors impacting on the Parthian Empire, namely that it weakened the Parthian monarchy, both in terms of a stable succession and of their power over the nobles. Both meant that future Parthian monarchs had to spend more time at court defending their positions, from either their own family or the noble families, than in the field. Phraates III may have ended the Parthian Civil War with the elimination of the last claimant from a rival branch of the dynasty, but almost immediately he was murdered in a palace coup by his own sons, one of whom was subsequently murdered by his brother, and the other by his son. Thus, future Parthian monarchs seemed more inclined to accept the new status quo and less likely to continue the aggressive expansion that had characterized the early centuries of the Parthian Empire, leading to its inevitable stagnation and decline. Though technically the empire collapsed, in reality it remained intact, and it was the ruling dynasty (the Arsacids) that collapsed, being overthrown by a stronger noble family (the Sassanians), who renamed the Parthian Empire as a renewed Persian one.

Appendix III

The Letter of Mithridates to the Parthians

Introduction

As stated earlier, the fragments of Sallust's *Histories* (4.69) contain a letter which purports to be a Latin translation of the original – though we do not know the original language – from the exiled Pontic King Mithridates VI to the Parthian Emperor (either Sinatruces or Phraates III) requesting his military assistance in fighting the Romans. The letter purports to be dated from the time of Mithridates' exile in Armenia, after fleeing from his own kingdom of Pontus, following his defeat at the hands of Lucullus in 71 BC and before the Roman invasion. The letter, if true, would be from *c.*70 BC.

If the letter is genuine, then it represents a rare original account from the hand of one of Rome's opponents, detailing how they saw the rise of Rome. The obvious issue we have, however, is the question of whether it is genuine, as Roman authors long had the habit of either embellishing historical speeches that were made or simply inventing them.[1]

Nevertheless, given that Sallust was writing in the 40s and 30s BC, and was a contemporary (albeit junior) member of the Senatorial oligarchy in the decades which followed the war, it is entirely possible that he had access to either the original, or more likely a Roman translation of the document which had already been produced. McGushin briefly touches on the sources of Sallust's *Histories*, which may have included accounts of the war written at the time by supporters of both Pompeius and Lucullus, perhaps the most noted being Theophanes of Mytilene, who was part of Pompeius' retinue during the war.[2]

This inevitably leads us to ask where these historians would have got an original copy of the letter. Here we have two possibilities. The first is that the Romans secured copies of Mithridates' correspondence, either by seizing it whilst he was alive, captured in a baggage train or when a fortress fell, or after his death as part of Pharnaces' submission. The second is of course, that the Parthian Emperor himself sent either Lucullus or Pompeius a copy as part of their diplomatic activity, in a demonstration of their lack of hostile intent. Therefore, it is entirely possible that the letter is a genuine one.

Text

'King Mithridates, to King Arsaces, Greeting. All those who in the time of their prosperity are asked to form an offensive alliance ought to consider, first, whether it is possible for them to keep peace at that time; and secondly, whether what is asked of them is wholly right and safe, honourable or dishonourable.

'If it were possible for you to enjoy lasting peace, if no treacherous foes were near your borders, if to crush the Roman power would not bring you glorious fame, I should not venture to sue for your alliance, and it would be vain for me to hope to unite my misfortunes with your prosperity.

'But the considerations which might seem to give you pause, such as the anger against Tigranes inspired in you by the recent war, and my lack of success, if you but consent to regard them in the right light, will be special incentives.

'For Tigranes is at your mercy and will accept an alliance on any terms which you may desire, while so far as I am concerned, although Fortune has deprived me of much, she has bestowed upon me the experience necessary for giving good advice; and since I am no longer at the height of my power, I shall serve as an example of how you may conduct your own affairs with more prudence, a lesson highly advantageous to the prosperous.

'In fact, the Romans have one inveterate motive for making war upon all nations, peoples and kings: namely, a deep-seated desire for dominion and for riches. Therefore they first began a war with Philippus, King of Macedonia, having pretended to be his friends as long as they were hard pressed by the Carthaginians.

'When Antiochus came to his aid, they craftily diverted him from his purpose by the surrender of Asia, and then, after Philippus' power had been broken, Antiochus was robbed of all the territory this side of Taurus, and of ten thousand talents.

'Next Perseus, the son of Philippus, after many battles with varying results, was formally taken under their protection before the gods of Samothrace; and then those masters of craft and artists in treachery caused his death from want of sleep, since they had made a compact not to kill him.

'Eumenes, whose friendship they boastfully parade, they first betrayed to Antiochus as the price of peace; later, having made him the guardian of a captured territory, they transformed him by means of imposts and insults from a king into the most wretched of slaves. Then, having forged an unnatural will, they led his son Aristonicus in triumph like an enemy, because he had tried to recover his father's realm.

'They took possession of Asia, and finally, on the death of Nicomedes, they seized upon all Bithynia, although Nysa, whom Nicomedes had called queen, unquestionably had a son.

'Why should I mention my own case? Although I was separated from their empire on every side by kingdoms and tetrarchies, yet because it was reported that I was rich and that I would not be a slave, they provoked me to war through Nicomedes. And I was not unaware of their design, but I had previously given warning of what afterwards happened, both to the Cretans, who alone retained their freedom at that time, and to King Ptolemy.

'But I took vengeance for the wrongs inflicted upon me; I drove Nicomedes from Bithynia, recovered Asia, the spoil taken from king Antiochus, and delivered Greece from cruel servitude.

'Further progress was frustrated by Archelaus, basest of slaves, who betrayed my army; and those whom cowardice or misplaced cunning kept from taking up arms, since they hoped to find safety in my misfortunes, are suffering most cruel punishment. For Ptolemy is averting hostilities from day to day by the payment of money, while the Cretans have already been attacked once and will find no respite from war until they are destroyed.

'As for me, I soon learned that the peace afforded by civil dissensions at Rome was really only a postponement of the struggle, and although Tigranes refused to join with me (he now admits the truth of my prediction when it is too late), though you were far away, and all the rest had submitted, I nevertheless renewed the war and routed Marcus Cotta, the Roman general, on land at Chalcedon, while on the sea I stripped him of a fine fleet.

'During the delay caused by my siege of Cyzicus with a great army provisions failed me, since no one in the neighbourhood rendered me aid and at the same time winter kept me off the sea. When I, therefore, without compulsion from the enemy, attempted to return into my kingdom, I lost the best of my soldiers and my fleets by shipwrecks at Parium and at Heracleia.

'Then when I had raised a new army at Cabira and engaged with Lucullus with varying success, scarcity once more attacked us both. He had at his command the kingdom of Ariobarzanes, unravaged by war, while I, since all the country about me had been devastated, withdrew into Armenia. Thereupon the Romans followed me, or rather followed their custom of overthrowing all monarchies, and because they were able to keep from action a huge force hemmed in by narrow defiles, boasted of the results of Tigranes' imprudence as if they had won a victory.

'I pray you, then, to consider whether you believe that when we have been crushed you will be better able to resist the Romans, or that there will be an end to the war. I know well that you have great numbers of men and large amounts of arms and gold, and it is for that reason that I seek your alliance and the Romans your spoils. Yet my advice is, while the kingdom of Tigranes is entire, and while I still have soldiers who have been trained in warfare with the Romans, to finish far from your homes and with little labour, at the expense of our bodies, a war in which we cannot conquer or be conquered without danger to you.

'Do you not know that the Romans turned their arms in this direction only after Ocean had blocked their westward progress? That they have possessed nothing since the beginning of their existence except what they have stolen: their home, their wives, their lands, their empire? Once vagabonds without fatherland, without parents, created to be the scourge of the whole world, no laws, human or divine, prevent them from seizing and destroying allies and friends, those near them and those afar off, weak or powerful, and from considering every government which does not serve them, especially monarchies, as their enemies.

'Of a truth, few men desire freedom, the greater part are content with just masters; we are suspected of being rivals of the Romans and future avengers.

'But you, who possess Seleucia, greatest of cities, and the realm of Persis famed for its riches, what can you expect from them other than guile in the present and war in the future?

'The Romans have weapons against all men, the sharpest where victory yields the greatest spoils; it is by audacity, by deceit, and by joining war to war that they have grown great.

'Following their usual custom, they will destroy everything or perish in the attempt ... and this is not difficult if you on the side of Mesopotamia and we on that of Armenia surround their army, which is without supplies and without allies, and has been saved so far only by its good fortune or by our own errors.

'You will gain the glory of having rendered aid to great kings and of having crushed the plunderers of all the nations.

'This is my advice and this course I urge you to follow; do not prefer by our ruin to put off your own for a time rather than by our alliance to conquer.'

Appendix IV

Kings, Consuls and Promagistrates

Section One: Roman Promagistrates of the East

Asia

84–81 BC	L. Licinius Murena
80–79 BC	M. Minucius Thermus
c.77 BC	Terentius Varro
76–75 BC	M. Iunius Silanus
75–74 BC	M (Iunius) Iuncus
73–69 BC	L. Licinius Lucullus (Consul 74 BC)
68 BC	P. Cornelius Dolabella

Bithynia

73–70 BC	M. Aurelius Cotta (Consul 74 BC)
69–67 BC	L. Licinius Lucullus? (Consul 74 BC)
66 BC	M. Acilius Glabrio (Consul 67 BC)
66–62 BC	Cn. Pompeius 'Magnus' (Consul 70, 55 & 52 BC)

Cilicia

80–79 BC	Cn. Cornelius Dolabella
78–74 BC	P. Servilius Vatia 'Isauricus' (Consul 79 BC)
74 BC	L. Octavius (Consul 75 BC)
73–68 BC	L. Licinius Lucullus (Consul 74 BC)
67 BC	Q. Marcius Rex (Consul 68 BC)
66–62 BC	Cn. Pompeius 'Magnus' (Consul 70, 55 & 52 BC)

Crete

68–65 BC	Q. Caecilius Metellus 'Creticus' (Consul 69 BC)

Macedon

80–78 BC	Cn. Cornelius Dolabella (Consul 81 BC)
78–76 BC	Ap. Claudius Pulcher (Consul 79 BC)
75–73 BC	C. Scribonius Curio (Consul 76 BC)
72–71 BC	M. Terentius Varro Lucullus (Consul 73 BC)

Mediterranean

74–71 BC	M. Antonius 'Creticus'
67–65 BC	Cn. Pompeius 'Magnus' (Consul 70 BC)

Pontus

72–67 BC	L. Licinius Lucullus (Consul 74 BC)
66 BC	M. Acilius Glabrio (Consul 67 BC)
66–62 BC	Cn. Pompeius 'Magnus' (Consul 70, 55 & 52 BC)

Syria

62 BC	M. Aemilius Scaurus
61–60 BC	L. Marcius Philippus (Consul 56 BC)
59–58 BC	Cn. Cornelius Lentulus Marcellinus (Consul 56 BC)
57–55 BC	A. Gabinius (Consul 58 BC)
54–53 BC	M. Licinius Crassus (Consul 70 & 55 BC)

Section Two: Roman Consuls (75–55 BC)

75 BC	L. Octavius & C. Aurelius Cotta
74 BC	L. Licinius Lucullus & M. Aurelius Cotta
73 BC	M. Terentius Varro Lucullus & C. Cassius Longinus
72 BC	L. Gellius Publicola & Cn. Cornelius Lentulus Clodianus
71 BC	P. Cornelius Lentulus Sura & Cn. Aufidius Orestes
70 BC	Cn. Pompeius 'Magnus' & M. Licinius Crassus
69 BC	Q. Hortensius Hortalus & Q. Caecilius Metellus 'Creticus'
68 BC	Q. Marcius Rex & L. Caecilius Metellus/(Servilius) Vatia
67 BC	M. Acilius Glabrio & C. Calpurnius Piso
66 BC	M. Aemilius Lepidus & L. Vocatius Tullus
65 BC	P. Cornelius Sulla & P. Autronius Paetus (elected but disqualified)
	L. Aurelius Cotta & L. Manlius Torquatus
64 BC	L. Iulius Caesar & C. Marcius Figulus
63 BC	C. Antinous & M. Tullius Cicero
62 BC	D. Iunius Silanus & L. Licinius Murena
61 BC	M. Pupius Piso Frugi Calpurnianus & M. Valerius Messalla Niger
60 BC	L. Afranius & Q. Caecilius Metellus Celer
59 BC	C. Iulius Caesar & M. Calpurnius Bibulus

58 BC	A. Gabinius & L. Calpurnius Piso Caesoninus
57 BC	P. Cornelius Lentulus Spinther & Q. Caecilius Metellus Nepos
56 BC	Cn. Cornelius Lentulus Marcellinus & L. Marcius Philippus
55 BC	Cn. Pompeius 'Magnus' (2) & M. Licinius Crassus (2)

Section Three: Rulers of the Eastern Kingdoms

Parthian Emperors

Mithradates II (*c*.121–91 BC)
Gotarzes I (*c*.91–87 BC)
Mithradates III (*c*.87–80 BC)
Orodes I (*c*.80–75 BC)
Arsaces XVI (*c*.78–61 BC)
Sinatruces (*c*.91–69 BC)
Phraates III (*c*.69–*c*.58 BC)
Mithradates IV (*c*.58–55 BC)
Orodes II (57–37 BC)

Seleucid Emperors

Philip I	95–83 BC
Antiochus XII	87–82 BC
Seleucus VII	83–69 BC

c.83 BC – Seleucid Empire annexed by Armenia.

Cleopatra II Selene	82–69 BC
Antiochus XIII	69–64 BC
Philip II	65–64 BC

64 BC – Seleucid Empire annexed by Rome.

Ptolemaic Pharaohs

Ptolemy IX	116–107 & 88–81 BC
Ptolemy X	107–88 BC
Ptolemy XI	80 BC
Ptolemy XII	80–58 & 55–51 BC
Berenice IV	58–55 BC

Ptolemy XIII	51–47 BC
Cleopatra VII	51–30 BC

Kings of the Albanians
Oroeses	c.60s BC

Kings of Armenia
Tigranes I	123–95 BC
Tigranes II (Great)	95–55 BC
Artavasdes II	55–34 BC

Kings of Bithynia
Nicomedes III	127–94 BC
Nicomedes IV	94–74 BC

74 BC – Kingdom of Bithynia annexed by Rome

Kings of the Bosphorus
Mithridates I	108–70 BC (Mithridates VI of Pontus)
Machares	71–65 BC
Mithridates I (2)	65–63 BC (Mithridates VI of Pontus)
Pharnaces	63–47 BC

Kings of Cappadocia
Ariarathes VIII	101–96 BC
Ariarathes IX	95 BC
Ariobarzanes I	95–c.63 BC
Ariobarzanes II	c.63–51 BC

Kings of Commagene
Mithridates I	109–70 BC
Antiochus I	70–38 BC

Kings of Cyprus
Ptolemy	80–58 BC

Kings of Galatia
Deiotarus	63–40 BC
Brogitarius	63–50 BC

Kings of the Iberians

Artoces	78–63 BC
Pharnavaz II	63–30 BC

Kings of Judea

Alexander Jannaeus	103–76 BC
Salome Alexandra	76–67 BC
Hyrcanus II	67–66, 63–40 BC
Aristobulus II	66–63 BC

Kings of Media

Mithridates I	67–66 BC
Darius I	*c.*65 BC
Ariobarzanes I	65–56 BC

Kings of Nabataea

Aretas II	110s–96 BC
Obodas I	*c.*96–85 BC
Rabbel I	*c.*85/84 BC
Aretas III	84–*c.*59 BC
Obodas II	*c.*62–*c.*59 BC

Kings of Pontus

Mithridates VI	120–63 BC

Notes

Chapter One

1. J. Champion (2010), *The Tyrants of Syracuse. War in Ancient Sicily Volume I: 480–367 BC* (Barnsley).
2. Liv. 9.17–19
3. See B. Bennett & M. Roberts (2008), *The Wars of Alexander's Successors 323–281 BC, Vol 1: Commanders and Campaigns* (Barnsley), and (2009), *The Wars of Alexander's Successors, 323–281 BC, Vol. 2: Battles and Tactics* (Barnsley). R. Waterfield (2011), *Dividing the Spoils: The War for Alexander the Great's Empire* (Oxford). E. Anson & V. Troncoso (2012), *After Alexander: The Time of the Diadochi (323–281 BC)* (London).
4. P. Garoufalias (1979), *Pyrrhus, King of Epirus* (London). J. Champion, (2009), *Pyrrhus of Epirus* (Barnsley).
5. See R. Beaumont (1936), 'Greek Influence in the Adriatic Sea before the Fourth Century BC', *Journal of Hellenic Studies* 56, pp.159–204.
6. *Ibid.*
7. L. Neatby (1950), 'Romano-Egyptian Relations during the Third Century BC', *Transactions and Proceedings of the American Philological Association*, pp.81, 89–98.
8. See J. Grainger (2010), *The Syrian Wars* (Leiden).
9. See J. Fine (1936), 'Macedon, Illyria, and Rome, 220–219 BC', *Journal of Roman Studies* 26, pp.24–39; E. Badian (1952), 'Notes on Roman Policy in Illyria (230–201 BC)', *Papers of the British School at Rome* 20, pp.72–93; H. Dell (1967b), 'The Origin and Nature of Illyrian Piracy', *Historia* 16, pp.344–58; N. Hammond (1968), 'Illyria, Rome and Macedon in 229-205 BC', *Journal of Roman Studies* 58, pp.1–21; A. Eckstein (1994), 'Polybius, Demetrius of Pharus, and the Origins of the Second Illyrian War', *Classical Philology* 89, pp.46–59; and D. Dzino (2010), *Illyricum in Roman Politics 229 BC–AD 68* (Cambridge).
10. See G. Sampson (2016), *Rome Spreads Her Wings: Territorial Expansion Between the Punic Wars* (Barnsley).
11. See G. Daly (2002), *Cannae; The Experience of Battle in the Second Punic War* (London).
12. See J. Grainger (1999), *The League of Aitolians* (Leiden), and R. Allen (1983), *The Attalid Kingdom. A Constitutional History* (Oxford).
13. See S. Mandell (1989), 'The Isthmian Proclamation and the Early Stages of Roman Imperialism in the Near East', *Classical Bulletin* 65, pp.89–94.
14. See J. Grainger (2010).
15. J. Lerner (1996), 'Seleucid Decline on the Eastern Iranian Plateau', *Berytus* 42, pp.103–12; (1999), *The Impact of Seleucid Decline on the Eastern Iranian Plateau* (Stuttgart); N. Overtoom (2016b), 'The Power-Transition Crisis of the 240s BC and the Creation of the Parthian State', *International History Review* 38, pp.984–1013; (2020), *Reign of Arrows: The Rise of the Parthian Empire in the Hellenistic Middle East* (Oxford).
16. See G. Sampson (2008), *The Defeat of Rome. Crassus, Carrhae and the Invasion of the East* (Barnsley), pp.32–55.
17. See M. Taylor (2011), *Antiochus The Great* (Barnsley), and J. Grainger (2015), *The Seleukid Empire of Antiochus III (223–187 BC)* (Barnsley).
18. See D. Magie (1939), 'The "Agreement" between Philip V and Antiochus III for the Partition of the Egyptian Empire', *Journal of Roman Studies* 29, pp.32–44.

19. See J. Grainger (2002), *The Roman War of Antiochus the Great* (Leiden).
20. See A. McDonald (1967), 'The Treaty of Apamea (188 BC)', *Journal of Roman Studies* 57, pp1–8; A. McDonald & F. Walbank (1969), 'The Treaty of Apamea (188 BC): The Naval Clauses', *Journal of Roman Studies* 59, pp.30–39; E. Paltiel (1979), 'The Treaty of Apamea and the Later Seleucids', *Antichthon* 13, pp.30–41.
21. See G. Sampson (2008), pp.32–55.
22. See Z. Petkovic (2012), 'The Aftermath of the Apamean settlement: early challenges to the new order in Asia Minor', *Klio* 94, pp.357–65.
23. See A. Eckstein (1988), 'Rome, the War with Perseus, and Third-Party Mediation', *Historia* 37, pp.414–44.
24. See R. Syme (1999), *Rome and the Balkans 80 BC–AD 14* (Exeter); and M. Schmitz (2015), *Roman Conquests: The Danube Frontier* (Barnsley).
25. See L. Ballesteros Pastor (2008), 'Cappadocia and Pontus, Client Kingdoms of the Roman Republic from the Peace of Apamea to the Beginning of the Mithridatic Wars (188–89 BC)', in A. Coskun (ed.), *Freundschaft und Gefolgschaft in den auswärtigen Beziehungen der Römer (2 Jh. v. Chr.–1 Jh. n. Chr.)* (Berlin), pp.45–63.
26. Polyb. 10.27–31.
27. See G. Sampson (2010), *The Crisis of Rome: The Jugurthine and Northern Wars and the Rise of Marius* (Barnsley).
28. See N. Overtoom (2019), 'The Power-Transition Crisis of the 160s–130s BC and the Formation of the Parthian Empire', *Journal of Ancient History* 7, pp.111–55.
29. See M. Olbrycht (2011), 'Subjects and Allies: The Black Sea Empire of Mithridates VI Eupator (120–63 BC) Reconsidered', *Pontika 2008: Recent Research on the Northern and Eastern Black Sea in Ancient Times* (Krakow), pp.275–81.
30. See L. Ballesteros Pastor (1999), 'Marius' Words to Mithridates Eupator (Plut. *Mar.* 31.3)', *Historia* 48, pp.506–08; and (2014), 'The Meeting between Marius and Mithridates and the Pontic Policy in Cappadocia', *Cedrus* 2, pp.225–39.
31. The date is disputed. Cases can (and have) been argued for 97/96 or 93/92 BC. This author prefers the earlier date, based on Sulla holding the praetorship in 97, at the normal age, rather than inexplicably delayed. This would also link it to Marius' recent visit to the region and meeting with Mithridates. See E. Badian (1959), 'Sulla's Cilician Command', *Athenaeum* 37, pp.279–303; T. Broughton (1986), The *Magistrates of the Roman Republic Volume 3, Supplement* (Atlanta), pp.73–74; P. Cagniart (1991), 'L. Cornelius Sulla in the Nineties: a Reassessment', *Latomus* 50, pp.285–303; T. Brennan (1992), 'Sulla's Career in the Nineties', *Chiron* 22, pp.103–58; and A. Keaveney (1995), 'Sulla's Cilician Command: The Evidence of Apollinaris Sidonius', *Historia* 44, p.29.
32. See A. Keaveney (1981), 'Roman Treaties with Parthia circa 95 – circa 64 BC', *American Journal of Philology* 102, pp.195–212.
33. See G. Sampson (2013), *The Collapse of Rome: Marius, Sulla and the First Civil War 91–70 BC* (Barnsley); and (2017), *Rome, Blood and Politics. Reform, Murder and Popular Politics in the Late Republic 133–70 BC* (Barnsley).
34. See above.
35. See T. Luce (1970), 'Marius and the Mithridatic Command', *Historia* 19, pp.161–94.
36. See M. Marciak (2017), *Sophene, Gordyene, and Adiabene. Three Regna Minora of Northern Mesopotamia Between East and West* (Leiden).
37. See T. Rice Holmes (1917), 'Tigranocerta', *Journal of Roman Studies* 7, pp.120–38.

Chapter Two

1. See G. Sampson (2017), pp.190–201.
2. Eutrop. 6.4.
3. Oros. 5.23.23.
4. Cic. *Clu.* 97.

5. See Z. Petkovic (2010), 'Notes on the Dardanians, the Scordisci and Roman Macedonia 168–75 BC', pp.11–17.
6. Oros. 5.23.17–19.
7. See Z. Petkovic (2008), 'Sulla and the Liburnian Campaign of Cinna', *Aevum* 82, pp.119–25.
8. Cic. *Pis.* 44.
9. Oros. 5.23.19–20.
10. Liv. *Per.* 91.
11. Fest. *Brev.* 9.2.
12. Eutrop. 6.1.
13. See Z. Petkovic (2014), 'The Bellum Dardanicum and the Third Mithridatic War', *Historia* 63, pp.187–93.
14. Sall. *Hist.* 2.80.
15. Flor 1.39.6.
16. App. *Mith.* 63.
17. Liv. *Per.* 89.
18. Suet. *Caes.* 2.
19. See P. de Souza (2008), 'Rome's Contribution to the Development of Piracy', *Memoirs of the American Academy in Rome Supplementary Volume 6*, pp.71–96.
20. Grandfather of the Triumvir.
21. Cic. *Verr.* 2.1.90.
22. Oros. 5.23.21.
23. Eutrop. 6.3.1.
24. Flor. 1.41.4–5.
25. Strab. 14.671.
26. Fest. *Brev.* 11.1.
27. *Ibid.* 12.3.
28. Cic. *Verr.* 2.5.66.
29. For a fuller description of the campaign, see Magie, pp.289–92.
30. App. *Mith.* 93.
31. See Magie, p.291.
32. See Magie, pp.30220.
33. See R. Evans (2014), *A History of Pergamum: Beyond Hellenistic Kingship* (London).
34. See D. Glew (1987), 'The Cappadocian Expedition of Nicomedes III Euergetes, King of Bithynia', *Museum Notes (American Numismatic Society)* 32, pp.23–55.
35. The surviving sources are vague enough for it to be interpreted as either 75 or 74 BC, not helped by the poor state of the Roman calendar during this period.
36. B. McGing (1984), 'The Date of the Outbreak of the Third Mithridatic War', *Phoenix* 38, pp.12–18.
37. See D. Braund (1984), *Rome and the Friendly King: The Character of the Client Kingship* (London), p.135.
38. Vell. 2.42.3, Gell. 5.13.6.
39. Sall. *Hist.* 4.67.
40. See D. Glew (1981), 'Between the Wars: Mithridates Eupator and Rome, 85–73 BC', *Chiron* 11, pp.109–30; &B. McGing (1996), *The Foreign Policy of Mithridates VI Eupator, King of Pontus* (Leiden).
41. App. *Mith.* 69.
42. See C. Konrad (1994), *Plutarch's Sertorius* (Chapel Hill), pp.191–92.
43. Oros. 6.2.12.
44. Plut. *Sert.* 24.2.
45. App. *Mith.* 68.
46. Cic. *Leg. Man.* 9.
47. App. *Mith.* 70–71.

Chapter Three
1. Plut. *Luc.* 7.
2. Frontin. *Str.* 4.1.43.
3. A. Ward (2016), 'Caesar and the Pirates II: The Elusive M. Iunius Iuncus and the Year 75/4', *American Journal of Ancient History 2*, pp.26–36.
4. Plut. *Luc.* 6.1.
5. *Ibid.*
6. Plutarch and the short *de viris illustribus*. For more modern works, see J. Van Ooteghem (1959), *L. Licinius Lucullus* (Brussels); A. Keaveney (1992), *Lucullus; A Life* (London); G. Wylie (1994), 'Lucullus Daemoniac', L'Antiquité Classique 63, pp.109–19; L. Fratantuono (2017), *Lucullus: The Life and Campaigns of a Roman Conqueror* (Barnsley).
7. See G. Sampson (2017), pp.190–201.
8. *Ibid.*, pp.202–16.
9. Vell. 2.33.1.
10. Memm. 27.1.
11. Plut. *Luc.* 5.4.
12. This led both Garofalo and Pais to argue whether Cethegus too was tribune this year. See M. Ziegler, (1903), *Fasti Tribunorum Plebis 133 – 70* (Ulm), p.30; & E. Pais (1918), 'I fasti dei tribuni della plebe', *Ricerche sulla storia e sul diritto pubblico di Roma Volume III* (Pisa), p.219.
13. Plut. *Luc.* 6.4.
14. Memm. 27.2–4.
15. *Ibid.*, 27.5.
16. Plut. *Luc.* 7.5.
17. Plut. *Sert.* 24.3–4.
18. App. *Mith.* 71.
19. Plut. *Luc.* 8.1.
20. Oros. 6.2.13.
21. Memm. 27.7.
22. App. *Mith.* 71.
23. Plut. *Luc.* 8.2.
24. Oros. 6.2.13.
25. The modern chapters 71 and 72.
26. Plut. *Luc.* 9.1.
27. *Ibid.*, 8.5–7.
28. Eutrop. 6.6.1.
29. Plut. *Luc.* 7.5–6.
30. Sall. *Hist.* 2.44.7.
31. App. *Mith.* 72.
32. Plut. *Luc.* 8.5.
33. Plut. *Luc.*7.3–4.
34. Strab. 12.575.
35. *Ibid.*
36. Plut. *Luc.* 9.3.
37. Plut. *Luc.* 8.5.
38. App. *Mith.* 72.
39. *Ibid.*
40. App. *Mith.* 73–74.
41. Plutarch provides the story that Mithridates attempted to bluff the defenders into thinking that Lucullus' army was actually his own reinforcements until the Romans were able to send messengers to the city to inform them otherwise. See Plut. *Luc.* 9.3–4. Also see Front. *Str.* 3.13.6.

42. Plut. *Luc.* 11.1.
43. Flor. 1.40.17.
44. Plut. *Luc.* 11.2.
45. Plut. *Luc.* 11.2–3.
46. App. *Mith.* 75.
47. Memm. 28.1.
48. Oros. 6.2.16.
49. Plut. *Luc.* 11.5.
50. Flor. 1.40.18.
51. Memm. 28.3.
52. Memm. 28.4.
53. *Ibid.*
54. Oros. 6.2.20.
55. Plut. *Luc.* 11.6.
56. Flor. 1.40.17.
57. App. *Mith.* 75.
58. Oros. 6.2.18.
59. Liv. *Per.* 94.
60. Suet. *Caes.* 4.4.
61. Plut. *Luc.* 11.6.
62. Oros. 6.2.19.

Chapter Four
1. He had been adopted into a different Roman family, a standard practice at the time. This was the second year in a row that a brother had replaced a brother as consul, with C. Aurelius Cotta in 75 BC being replaced by M. Aurelius Cotta in 74 BC.
2. App. *Mith.* 76.
3. Memm. 28.4.
4. Eutrop. 6.6.3.
5. Plut. *Luc.* 3.3–4.1, App. *Mith.* 52, Oros. 6.2.10.
6. App. *Mith.* 77.
7. Memm. 33. Though Cicero, with his usual hyperbole, states that it was an attempted invasion of Italy (Cic. *Mur.* 33).
8. See T. Broughton (1986), p.34.
9. Memm. 28.5.
10. See T. Broughton (1986), pp.214–15.
11. App. *Mith.* 77.
12. Memm. 28.5–8.
13. Believed by many, from ancient times to today, to be the city of Troy.
14. Plut. *Luc.* 12.2.
15. App. *Mith.* 77.
16. *Ibid.*
17. Plut. *Luc.* 12.2–5.
18. Oros. 6.2.21.
19. Memm. 29.1.
20. Cic. *Mur.* 33.
21. Cic. *Arch.* 21.
22. Memm. 29, 33.
23. Plut. *Luc.* 13.4.
24. *CIL.* 11.1832.
25. *de. vir. ill.* 74.4.
26. Memm. 29.

27. Plut. *Luc.* 13.1.
28. *Ibid.*, 13.2.
29. App. *Mith.* 78.
30. Memm. 29.3–4.
31. Plut. *Luc.* 14.
32. Memm. 29.5.
33. *Ibid.*, 33.
34. Memm. 32, 34–36.
35. Plut. *Luc.* 14.2.
36. App. *Mith.* 78.
37. *Ibid.*
38. Eutrop. 6.7.
39. Amm. *Marc.* 27.4.11.
40. Dio 36.9.3.
41. Eutrop. 6.10.
42. Strab. 7.6.1.
43. See G. Sampson (2013), pp.197–211.
44. See G. Sampson (2008), pp.62–68.
45. App. *Mith.* 79.
46. Plut. *Luc.* 15.1, App. *Mith.* 78.
47. Memm. 29.8.
48. Plut. *Luc.* 15.2.
49. App. *Mith.* 79.
50. *Ibid.*
51. App. *Mith.* 79. Also see Plut. *Luc.* 15.3.
52. App. *Mith.* 80.
53. Plut. *Luc.* 15.5–7.
54. Memm. 29.8.
55. Plut. *Luc.* 17.1.
56. Ibid. 17.1–2.
57. App. *Mith.* 81.
58. Plut. *Luc.* 17.3.
59. App. *Mith.* 82.
60. Memm. 29.9.
61. Eutrop. 6.8.

Chapter Five

1. Cn. Pompeius Strabo died of a pestilence (or possibly even a lightning strike) during the siege of Rome, whilst P. Licinius Crassus died during the Sack of Rome, as did his eldest son of the same name.
2. Memm. 30. Also see Plut. *Luc.* 19.1–4.
3. Memm. 37.
4. *Ibid.*
5. Memm. 36.
6. Plut. *Luc.* 19.1.
7. Eutrop. 6.8.3.
8. Plut. *Luc.* 20.3.
9. Plut. *Luc.* 14.5.
10. See Livy 9.17–19.
11. Plut. *Luc.* 21.
12. *Ibid.*, 21.6.
13. Plut. *Luc.* 21.7.

14. *Ibid.*
15. Memm. 38.
16. *Ibid.*
17. Plut. *Luc.* 24.1–3.
18. Memm. 38.2.
19. App. *Mith.* 84.
20. Sall. *Hist.* 4.60.
21. Plut. *Luc.* 24.4.
22. App. *Mith.* 84.
23. Plut. *Luc.* 25.1.
24. Joseph. *BJ* 1.116 & *AJ* 421.
25. Plut. *Luc.* 25.2.
26. Ibid. 25.3–4.
27. App. *Mith.* 84.
28. Plut. *Luc.* 25.5–6.
29. Memm. 38.3.
30. App. *Mith.* 84–85.
31. Dio 36.9.3.
32. Plut. *Luc.* 25.3.
33. *Ibid.*, 25.5–6.
34. App. *Mith.* 85.
35. Plut. *Luc.* 24.3.
36. See G. Sampson (2019), pp.31–46.
37. Plut. *Luc.* 26.6.
38. App. *Mith.* 85.
39. Memm. 38.4.
40. Plut. *Luc.* 26.4.
41. Plut. *Luc.* 26.6.
42. See G. Sampson (2020), *Rome and Parthia: Empires at War: Ventidius, Antony and the Second Romano-Parthian War, 40–20 BC* (Barnsley).
43. See G. Sampson (2008), pp.114–38.
44. Plut. *Luc.* 26.3, App. *Mith.* 85.
45. Plut. *Luc.* 27.4.
46. *Ibid.*, 27.6.
47. Plut. *Luc.* 28.1–6.
48. App. *Mith.* 85.
49. Frontin. *Str.* 2.1.14.
50. *Ibid.*, 2.2.4.
51. Memm. 38.5.
52. Oros. 6.3.6.
53. Fest. *Brev.* 15.3.
54. Eutrop. 6.9.1.
55. App. *Mith.* 86.
56. Plut. *Luc.* 29.2–3.
57. Dio 36.2.3–4.
58. Memm. 38.6.

Chapter Six
1. Dio 36.2.2.
2. Plut. *Luc.* 29.5–6.
3. Dio 36.2.5.
4. Oros. 6.3.7.

5. Memm. 38.6.
6. App. *Mith.* 87.
7. Plut. *Luc.* 30.2.
8. Dio 36.5.4.
9. Plut. *Luc.* 31.2.
10. *Ibid.*, 30.3.
11. Plut. *Luc.* 31.2.
12. Dio 36.5.4.
13. Named after Q. Fabius Maximus Cunctator, who faced Hannibal in the aftermath of the major Roman defeat at the Battle of Cannae in 216 BC.
14. Plut. *Luc.* 31.4–8.
15. Dio 36.5.5.
16. The legend being that it was Hannibal who helped the Armenian King Artaxas found the city. See Plut. *Luc.* 31.3.
17. Plut. *Luc.* 32.3.
18. Dio 36.6–8.
19. *Ibid.*, 36.8.
20. App. *Mith.* 88.
21. Dio 36.9.1.
22. *Ibid.*, 36.9.3–5.
23. App. *Mith.* 88.
24. Dio 36.10.1–2.
25. *Ibid.*, 36.10.2–3.
26. App. *Mith.* 88.
27. See R. Williams (1984), 'The Appointment of Glabrio ("cos". 67) to the Eastern Command', *Phoenix* 38, pp.221–34; & L. Hayne (1974), 'The Politics of M. Glabrio, Cos. 67', *Classical Philology* 69, pp.280–82.
28. Plut. *Luc.* 33.4–5.
29. Cic. *Leg. Man.* 26.
30. See D. Mulroy (1988), 'The Early Career of P. Clodius Pulcher: A Re-Examination of the Charges of Mutiny and Sacrilege', *Transactions of the American Philological Association* 118, pp.155–78.
31. App. *Mith.* 90.
32. Dio 36.12–13.
33. App. *Mith.* 89.
34. Plut. *Luc.* 35.1.
35. *Ibid.*, 35.2.
36. Dio 36.14.1–2.
37. Plut. *Luc.* 35.3.
38. *Ibid.*, 35.4–5.
39. App. *Mith.* 90.
40. Sall. *Hist.* 5.12.
41. Dio 36.15.1.
42. *Ibid.*, 36.17.2.
43. Cic. *Leg. Man.* 12, App. *Mith.* 91.
44. App. *Mith.* 97.

Chapter Seven
1. Though records for men who held the praetorship are notoriously poor. See T. Brennan (2000), *The Praetorship in the Roman Republic Volumes 1 & 2* (Oxford).
2. See G. Barnett (2017), *Emulating Alexander. How Alexander the Great's Legacy Fuelled Rome's Wars with Persia* (Barnsley).

3. See E. Badian (1959b), 'The Early Career of A. Gabinius (Cos. 58 BC)', *Philologus* 103, pp.87–99.

4. See J. Davison (1930), 'Cicero and the Lex Gabinia', *Classical Review* 44, pp.224–25; W. Loader (1940), 'Pompey's Command under the Lex Gabinia', *Classical Review* 54, pp.134–36; A. Ward (1969), 'Cicero's Support of the Lex Gabinia', *Classical World* 63, pp.8-10; O. Watkins (1987), 'Caesar Solus? Senatorial Support for the Lex Gabinia', *Historia* 36, pp.120–21.

5. See T. Frank (1914), 'The Background of the Lex Manilia', *Classical Philology* 9, pp.191–93. Manilius was subsequently prosecuted for his actions as tribune but defended by Cicero. See E. Phillips (1970), 'Cicero and the Prosecution of C. Manilius', *Latomus* 29, pp.595–607; A. Ward (1970b), 'Politics in the Trials of Manilius and Cornelius', *Transactions and Proceedings of the American Philological Association* 101, pp.545–56; & J. Ramsey (1980), 'The Prosecution of C. Manilius in 66 BC and Cicero's "pro Manilio"', *Phoenix* 34, pp.323–36.

6. Cic. *Leg. Man.* 5.

7. Plut. *Pomp.* 31.1.

8. *Ibid.*

9. Strab. 12.567.

10. See T. Hillman (1991), 'The Alleged Inimicitiae of Pompeius and Lucullus: 78–74', *Classical Philology* 86, pp.315–18.

11. Dio 36.46.1.

12. Plut. *Luc.* 36.4.

13. Dio 36.16.3. Also see Dio 36.46.1, Suda. A.2424.

14. Dio 36.45.2.

15. Plut. *Pomp.* 31.1, App. *Mith.* 97.

16. App. *Mith.* 97.

17. *Ibid.*, 99, Dio 36.47.2.

18. App. *Mith.* 98.

19. *Ibid.*, 99.

20. Plut. *Pomp.* 32.2–3.

21. Dio 36.47.2–4.

22. Frontin. *Str.* 1.1.7.

23. Oros. 6.4.3.

24. Dio 36.48.1.

25. Sall. *Cat.* 30.3.

26. Dio 36.52.5.

27. The site of the battle is unnamed in the surviving sources, but Pompeius chose to found the veteran colony of Nicopolis near to the site to mark his victory. See App. *Mith.* 105, 115, Dio 36.50.3, Oros. 6.4.7, Strab. 12.555. See J. Anderson (1922), 'Pompey's Campaign against Mithridates', *Journal of Roman Studies* 12, pp.99–105.

28. Dio 36.48.3–5.

29. Plut. *Pomp.* 32.4–5.

30. *Ibid.*, 32.6.

31. Dio 36.49.1–8.

32. Plut. *Pomp.* 32.7.

33. Oros. 6.4.3–5.

34. Eutrop. 6.12.2.

35. Fest. 16.1.

36. Flor. 1.40.3.

37. Frontin. *Str.* 2.1.12.

38. *Ibid.*, 2.2.

39. App. *Mith.* 100.

40. *Ibid.*, 101.

41. Plut. *Pomp.* 32.7.
42. Eutrop. 6.12.2.
43. Dio 36.49.8.
44. Plut. *Pomp.* 32.9.
45. App. *Mith.* 101.
46. Memm. 39.1.
47. Plut. *Luc.* 37.1–2.

Chapter Eight
1. App. *Mith.* 104.
2. Dio 36.51.1–3.
3. *Ibid.*, 36.53.2.
4. App. *Mith.* 105.
5. Plut. *Pomp.* 33.4.
6. *Ibid.*, 33.5.
7. App. *Mith.* 104.
8. See M. Marciak (2017).
9. App. *Mith.* 105.
10. Dio 36.53.5–6.
11. Plut. *Pomp.* 34.1.
12. *Ibid.*, 34.5.
13. Appian (*Mith.* 103) states that 'All the neighbouring tribes accompanied Pompeius on his exploring expedition.' If we are to believe this, then they may have acted as guides.
14. Plut. *Pomp.* 34.2. Appian (*Mith.* 103) states 70,000, but has the Iberians involved as well.
15. Though this was before the Julian reforms to the calendar, which means we cannot date it as securely as we might think.
16. Dio 36.54.2–5.
17. Plut. *Pomp.* 34.2–3.
18. Dio 37.1.1–4.
19. *Ibid.*, 37.2.1–2.
20. Dio 37.2.3–5.
21. Plut. *Pomp.* 34.5.
22. Dio 37.2.7.
23. *Ibid.*, 37.3.1.
24. App. *Mith.* 103.
25. Dio 37.3.2–3.
26. Plut. *Pomp.* 35.1.
27. Strab. 12.549. 'Crazing honey' was a poisonous brew with toxins from native rhododendron plants, which caused intestinal problems and delirium.
28. App. *Mith.* 102.
29. Strab. 11.2.13.
30. App. *Mith.* 102.
31. *Ibid.*
32. Plut. *Pomp.* 35.2–3.
33. Dio 37.4.2–4.
34. Dio 37.5.1. See L. Patterson (2002), 'Pompey's Albanian Connection at Justin XLII, 3,4', *Latomus* 61, pp.312–25.
35. Plut. *Pomp.* 36.1.
36. *Ibid.*, 36.2.
37. Dio 37.5.2–5.
38. *Ibid.*, 37.5.2.
39. Plut. *Pomp.* 36.2.

40. See G. Sampson (2020).
41. Dio 37.6.5.
42. Cic. *Flacc.* 30.
43. Cic. *Leg. Agr.* 2.44, *Schol. Bob.* 91–93.
44. Plut. *Crass.* 13.1.
45. Suet. *Caes.* 11.

Chapter Nine
 1. Plut. *Pomp.* 39.1.
 2. Fest. 11.4. Also see K. Wellesley (1953), 'The Extent of Territory Added to Bithynia By Pompey', *Rheinisches Museum für Philologie* 96, pp.293–318; A. Marshall (1968), 'Pompey's Organization of Bithynia-Pontus: Two Neglected Texts', *Journal of Roman Studies* 58, pp.103–09, J. Hojte (2006), 'From Kingdom to Province – Reshaping Pontus after the Fall of Mithridates VI', in T. Bekker-Nielsen (ed.), *Rome and the Black Sea Region* (Aarhus), pp.15–30.
 3. Eutrop. 16.14. Also see F. Adcock (1937), 'Lesser Armenia and Galatia after Pompey's Settlement of the East', *Journal of Roman Studies* 27, pp.12–17.
 4. App. *Mith.* 105.
 5. Eutrop. 16.14.
 6. App. *Mith.* 106.
 7. Dio 40.20.1.
 8. Diod. 40.4.
 9. App. *Mith.* 114.
10. See J. Grainger (2015b), *The Fall of Seleukid Empire 187–75 BC* (Barnsley), pp.181–207.
11. App. *Syr.* 49.
12. Just. 40.2.
13. See O. Hoover (2007), 'A Revised Chronology for the Late Seleucids at Antioch, 121/0–64 BC', *Historia* 56, pp.280–301.
14. See G. Downey (1937), 'Q. Marcius Rex at Antioch', *Classical Philology* 32, pp.144–51. Also see A. Bellinger (1949), 'The End of the Seleucids', *Connecticut Academy of Arts and Sciences* 38, pp.51–102.
15. Malal. 225.
16. Justin. 40.2.3.
17. App. *Mith.* 106.
18. Dio 37.7.
19. Plut. *Pomp.* 39.2.
20. Euseb. 261.
21. Jerome. *Chron.* 1924.
22. Malal. 212–213.
23. *Exc. Barb.* 46.
24. Seleucus II, Demetrius II, Seleucus V, Antiochus X, Demetrius III. See J. Nabel (2017), 'The Seleucids Imprisoned: Arsacid-Roman Hostage Submission and its Hellenistic Precedents', in J. Schlude and B. Rubin (eds), *Arsacids, Romans and Local Elites. Cross-Cultural Interactions of the Parthian Empire* (Oxford), pp.25–50.
25. Plut. *Pomp.* 38.2–3.
26. See G. Barnett (2017).
27. Plut. *Pomp.* 39.1.
28. *Ibid.*, 39.2.
29. *Ibid.*, 39.3.
30. Diod. 40.1b.
31. Joseph. *BJ.* 1.127.
32. Joseph. *AJ.* 14.29.

33. Strab. 16.757.
34. Joseph. AJ. 14.34.
35. Dio 37.6.4–6.
36. *Ibid.*, 37.7.2–4.
37. App. *Mith.* 107–10.
38. *Ibid.*, 108.
39. Dio 37.11.1.
40. App. *Mith.* 109.
41. Dio 27.11.4.
42. App. *Mith.* 107.
43. *Ibid.*, 108.
44. *Ibid.*, 108.
45. *Ibid.*, 109.
46. App. *Mith.* 107.
47. *Ibid.*
48. See J. Grainger (2011), *The Wars of the Maccabees* (Barnsley).
49. See S. Rocca (2014), 'The Late Roman Republic and Hasmonean Judea', *Athenaeum* 102, pp.47–78; K. Atkinson (2018), *The Hasmoneans and Their Neighbours: New Historical Reconstructions from the Dead Sea Scrolls and Classical Sources* (London); E. Dabrowa (2019), 'The Seleukids, Rome and the Jews (134–76 BC)', in A. Coskun & D. Engels (eds), *Rome and the Seleukid East Selected Papers from Seleukid Study Day V* (Brussels), pp.389–99.
50. Joseph. *BJ.* 126–127.
51. *Ibid.*, 128–129.
52. *Ibid.*, 130.

Chapter Ten

 1. App. *Mith.* 110–111.
 2. *Ibid.*, 110.
 3. *Ibid.*, 111.
 4. *Ibid.*, 112.
 5. Plut. *Pomp.* 41.
 6. Joseph. *AJ.* 38–40.
 7. Dio 37.15.1–2.
 8. Plut. *Pomp.* 41.3.
 9. Oros. 6.6.1.
10. Plut. *Pomp.* 42.1.
11. Orosius (6.6.1) is the most explicit. See E. Myers (2010), *The Ituraeans and the Roman Near East: Reassessing the Source* (Cambridge).
12. Joseph. *AJ.* 14.34.
13. *Ibid.*, 14.37.
14. Dio 40.2.
15. Joseph. *AJ.* 46.
16. Plu. *Pomp.* 39.2.
17. Joseph. *AJ.* 53.
18. Joseph. *BJ.* 138.
19. Joseph. *AJ.* 14.57.
20. *Ibid.*, 14.59.
21. Joseph. *AJ.* 14.61–62.
22. *Ibid.*, 14.63–64.
23. Joseph. *AJ.* 14.69–71.
24. *Ibid.*, 14.72.
25. *Chron. Pasc.* 453.

26. Joseph. *AJ.* 14.75.
27. App. *Mith.* 114.
28. Diod. 40.4.
29. Plut. *Pomp.* 42.1, App. *Mith.* 113.
30. See J. Hojte (2009), 'The Death and Burial of Mithridates VI', in J. Hojte (ed.), *Mithridates VI and the Pontic Kingdom* (Aarhus), pp.121–30.
31. App. *Mith.* 113.
32. Cic. *Prov. Con.* 27.
33. See A. Marshall (1968).
34. See G. Sampson (2019), pp.87–114.
35. *Ibid.*, pp.58–86.
36. See I. Harrison (2008), 'Catiline, Clodius, and Popular Politics at Rome during the 60s and 50s BC', *Bulletin of the Institute of Classical Studies* 51, pp.95–118.
37. See G. Sampson (2019), pp.80–85.
38. See T. Hillman (1993), 'When Did Lucullus Retire?', *Historia* 42, pp.211–28.
39. Plut. *Luc.* 37.
40. Joseph. *BJ.* 1.159.
41. Joseph. *AJ.* 14.80–81.
42. See G. Bucher (1995), 'Appian BC 2.24 and the Trial "de ambitu" of M. Aemilius Scaurus', *Historia* 44, pp.396–421.
43. See E. Parrish (1973), 'Crassus' New Friends and Pompey's Return', *Phoenix* 27, pp.357–80.
44. See R. Williams & B. Williams (1988), 'Cn. Pompeius Magnus and L. Afranius. Failure to Secure the Eastern Settlement', *Classical Journal* 83, pp.198–206, & T. Rising (2013), 'Senatorial Opposition to Pompey's Eastern Settlement. A Storm in a Teacup?', *Historia* 62, pp.196–221.
45. See G. Stanton & B. Marshall, (1975), 'The Coalition between Pompeius and Crassus 60–59 BC', *Historia* 24, pp.205–19.
46. See G. Sampson (2019), pp.103–11.
47. See R. Smith (1964), 'The Significance of Caesar's Consulship in 59 BC', *Phoenix* 18, pp.303–13.

Appendix I

1. See J. Reynolds (1962), 'Cyrenaica, Pompey and Cn. Cornelius Lentulus Marcellinus', *Journal of Roman Studies* 52, pp.97–103.
2. App. *Syr.* 51.
3. See I. Shatzman (1971), 'The Egyptian Question in Roman Politics (59–54 BC)', *Latomus* 30, pp.363–69, & M. Siani-Davies (1997), 'Ptolemy XII Auletes and the Romans', *Historia* 46, pp.306–40.
4. See E. Gruen (1966), 'P. Clodius: Instrument or Independent Agent?', *Phoenix* 20, pp.120–30, T. Hillard (1982), 'P. Clodius Pulcher 62–58 BC: Pompeii Adfinis et Sodalis', *Papers of the British School at Rome* 50, pp.34–44, & W. Tatum (1999), *The Patrician Tribune: Publius Clodius Pulcher* (Chapel Hill).
5. App. *BC.* 2.23, Strab. 14.684.
6. See E. Badian (1965), 'M. Porcius Cato and the Annexation and Early Administration of Cyprus', *Journal of Roman Studies* 55, pp.110–21, & J. Bellemore (1995), 'Cato the Younger in the East in 66 BC', *Historia* 44, pp.376–79.
7. See E. Sanford (1939), 'The Career of Aulus Gabinius', *Transactions and Proceedings of the American Philological Association* 70, pp.64–92, & R. Williams (1978), 'The Role of "Amicitia" in the Career of A. Gabinius (Cos. 58)', *Phoenix* 32, pp.195–210.
8. Cic. *Dom.* 23.
9. Cic. *Sest.* 56.
10. See G. Sampson (2019), pp.117–42.

11. App. *Syr.* 51, Joseph. *AJ.* 14.82.
12. Joseph. *AJ.* 14.83.
13. See G. Sampson (2020).
14. Joseph. *BJ.* 163.
15. Joseph. *AJ.* 14.85.
16. Joseph. *BJ.* 169–170.
17. *Ibid.*, 172.
18. Joseph. AJ. 14.90.
19. Dio 39.12.1–3.
20. See G. Sampson (2019), pp.117–42.
21. Euseb. *Chron.* 261; Hieron. *Chron.* 1924.
22. Hieron. *Chron.* 1924.
23. Dio 39.57.1.
24. Cic. *Prov. Con.* 9.
25. Dio 39.56.1.
26. Strabo. 12.3.34; also see 17.1.11.
27. Joseph. *AJ.* 14.98.
28. Joseph. *BJ.* 175.
29. App. *Syr.* 51.
30. Joseph. *BJ.* 175.
31. Plut. *Ant.* 3.4–6.
32. Dio 39.58.1.
33. Dio 39.58.3.
34. Joseph. *AJ.* 92–95.
35. Joseph. *BJ.* 1.177.
36. Joseph. *AJ.* 14.102.
37. Joseph. *BJ.* 1.178.
38. Joseph. *AJ.* 14.103.
39. See E. Fantham (1975), 'The Trials of Gabinius in 54 BC', *Historia* 24, pp.425–43, & R. Williams (1985), 'Rei Publicae Causa: Gabinius' Defence of His Restoration of Ptolemy Auletes', *Classical Journal* 81, pp.25–38.
40. This war is covered in G. Sampson (2008).

Appendix II

1. Justin. 42.
2. Plut. *Luc.* 36.6.
3. N. Debeviose.(1938), *A Political History of Parthia* (Chicago).
4. See D. Sellwood (1962), 'The Parthian Coins of Gotarzes I, Orodes I, and Sinatruces', *The Numismatic Chronicle and Journal of the Royal Numismatic Society* 2, pp.73–89; K. Dobbins (1975) 'Mithradates II and his Successors; A Study of the Parthian Crisis 90–70 BC', *Antichthon* 5, pp.63–79; (1975b), 'The Successors of Mithradates II of Parthia', *Numismatic Chronicle* 15, pp.19–45; G. Assar (2005), 'The Genealogy of the Parthian King Sinatruces', *Journal of the Classical and Medieval Numismatic Society* 6, pp.16–33; & (2006b), 'A Revised Parthian Chronology of the Period 91–55 BC', *Parthica* 8, pp.55–104.
5. See G. Assar (2006b), pp.82–87.
6. See E. Dabrowa (2013), 'The Parthian Aristocracy: its Social Position and Political Activity', *Parthica* 15, pp.53–62.

Appendix III

1. See F. Ahlheid (1988), 'Oratorical Strategy in Sallust's Letter of Mithridates Reconsidered', *Mnemosyne* 41, pp.67–92.
2. See B. Gold (1985), 'Pompey and Theophanes of Mytilene', *American Journal of Philology* 106, pp.312–27.

Bibliography

Adcock, F. (1937), 'Lesser Armenia and Galatia after Pompey's Settlement of the East', *Journal of Roman Studies* 27, pp.12–17.

Ahlheid, F. (1988), 'Oratorical Strategy in Sallust's Letter of Mithridates Reconsidered', *Mnemosyne* 41, pp.67–92.

Allen, R (1983), *The Attalid Kingdom. A Constitutional History* (Oxford).

Anderson, J. (1922), 'Pompey's Campaign against Mithridates', *Journal of Roman Studies* 12, pp.99–105.

—— (1937), 'Two Anatolian Notes: (ii) Pompey's Treatment of Pontus', in W. Calder and J. Keil. (eds), *Anatolian Studies Presented to William Hepburn Buckler* (Manchester), pp.3–7.

Anson, E. and Troncoso, V. (2012), *After Alexander: The Time of the Diadochi (323–281 BC)* (London).

Arnaud, P. (1991), 'Sylla, Tigrane et les Parthes. Un nouveau document pour la datation de la propréture de Sylla: Sidoine Apollinaire Paneg. Aviti, 79–82', *Revue des Études Anciennes* 93, pp.55–64.

—— (1998), 'Les Guerres Parthiques de Gabinius et de Crassus et la politique occidentale des Parthes Arsacids entre 70 et 53 av. J.-C.', in E. Dabrowa (ed.), *Ancient Iran and the Mediterranean World* (Krakow), pp.13–34.

Assar, G. (2005), 'The Genealogy of the Parthian King Sinatruces', *Journal of the Classical and Medieval Numismatic Society* 6, pp.16–33.

—— (2006a), 'A Revised Parthian Chronology of the Period 165–91 BC', *Electrum* 11, pp.87–158.

—— (2006b), 'A Revised Parthian Chronology of the Period 91–55 BC', *Parthica* 8, pp.55–104.

Atkinson, K. (2018), *The Hasmoneans and Their Neighbours: New Historical Reconstructions from the Dead Sea Scrolls and Classical Sources* (London).

Badian, E. (1952), 'Notes on Roman Policy in Illyria (230–201 BC)', *Papers of the British School at Rome* 20, pp.72–93.

—— (1956), 'Q. Mucius Scaevola and the Province of Asia', *Athenaeum* 34, pp.104–23.

—— (1958), *Foreign Clientelae (264–70 BC)* (Oxford).

—— (1959), 'Sulla's Cilician Command', *Athenaeum* 37, pp.279–303.

—— (1959b), 'The Early Career of A. Gabinius (Cos. 58 BC)', *Philologus* 103, pp.87–99.

—— (1965), 'M. Porcius Cato and the Annexation and Early Administration of Cyprus', *Journal of Roman Studies* 55, pp.110–21.

—— (1967), 'The Testament of Ptolemy Alexander', *Rheinisches Museum für Philologie* 110, pp.178–92.

—— (1968), *Roman Imperialism in the Late Republic* (Ithaca).

—— (1970), *Titus Quinctius Flamininus; Philhellenism and Realpolitik* (Cincinnati).

—— (1976), 'Rome, Athens and Mithridates', *American Journal of Ancient History* 1, pp.105–28.

Ball, W. (2000), *Rome in the East* (London).

Ballesteros, Pastor. L. (1999), 'Marius' Words to Mithridates Eupator (Plut. *Mar.* 31.3)', *Historia* 48, pp.506–08.

—— (2008), 'Cappadocia and Pontus, Client Kingdoms of the Roman Republic from the Peace of Apamea to the Beginning of the Mithridatic Wars (188–89 BC)', in A. Coskun (ed.), *Freundschaft und Gefolgschaft in den auswärtigen Beziehungen der Römer (2 Jh. v. Chr.–1 Jh. n. Chr.)* (Berlin), pp.45–63.

—— (2014), 'The Meeting between Marius and Mithridates and the Pontic Policy in Cappadocia', *Cedrus* 2, pp.225–39.

—— (2016), 'The Satrapy of Western Armenia in the Mithridatid Kingdom', in V. Cojocaru and A. Rubel (eds), *Mobility in Research on the Black Sea Region* (Cluj-Napoca), pp.273–87.

—— (2017), 'Pharnaces II and his Title "King of Kings"', *Ancient West and East* 16, pp.297–303.

Bammel, E. (1961), 'The Organisation of Palestine by Gabinius', *Journal of Jewish Studies* 12, pp.15–162.

Bar-Kochva, B. (1976), *The Seleucid Army: Organization and Tactics in the Great Campaigns* (Cambridge).

Barnet, G. (2017), *Emulating Alexander. How Alexander the Great's Legacy Fuelled Rome's Wars with Persia* (Barnsley).

Beaumont, R. (1936), 'Greek Influence in the Adriatic Sea before the Fourth Century BC', *Journal of Hellenic Studies* 56, pp.159–204.

Bellemore, J. (1995), 'Cato the Younger in the East in 66 BC', *Historia* 44, pp.376–79.

Bellinger, A. (1949), 'The End of the Seleucids', *Connecticut Academy of Arts and Sciences* 38, pp.51–102.

Bennett, B. and Roberts, M. (2008), *The Wars of Alexander's Successors 323–281 BC, Vol 1: Commanders and Campaigns* (Barnsley).

—— (2009), *The Wars of Alexander's Successors, 323–281 BC, Vol. 2: Battles and Tactics* (Barnsley).

—— (2011), *Twilight of the Hellenistic World* (Barnsley).

Bispham, E. (2007), *From Asculum to Actium: The Municipalization of Italy from the Social War to Augustus* (Oxford).

Boak, A. (1918), 'The Extraordinary Commands from 80 to 48 BC: A Study in the Origins of the Principate', *American Historical Review* 24, pp.1–25.

Braund, D. (1983a), 'Gabinius, Caesar and the Publicani of Judea', *Klio* 65, pp.241–44.

—— (1983b), 'Royal Wills and Rome', *Papers of the British School at Rome* 51, pp.16–57.

—— (1984), *Rome and the Friendly King: The Character of the Client Kingship* (London).

Brennan, T. (1992), 'Sulla's Career in the Nineties', *Chiron* 22, pp.103–58.

Brodersen, K. (1986), 'The Date of the Secession of Parthia from the Seleucid Kingdom', *Historia* 35, pp.378–81.

Broughton, T. (1946), 'Notes on Roman Magistrates. I. The Command of M. Antonius in Cilicia. II. Lucullus' Commission and Pompey's Acta', *Transactions and Proceedings of the American Philological Association* 77, pp.35–43.

—— (1948), 'More Notes on Roman Magistrates', *Transactions and Proceedings of the American Philological Association* 79, pp.63–78.

—— (1952), *The Magistrates of the Roman Republic Volume II 99 BC–31 BC* (New York).

—— (1960), *The Magistrates of the Roman Republic; Supplement* (New York).

—— (1986), *The Magistrates of the Roman Republic Volume 3, Supplement* (Atlanta).

Brown, T. (1964), 'Polybius' Account of Antiochus III', *Phoenix* 18, pp.124–36.

Bucher, G. (1995), 'Appian BC. 2.24 and the Trial "de ambitu" of M. Aemilius Scaurus' *Historia* 44, pp.396–421.

Cagniart, P. (1991), 'L. Cornelius Sulla in the Nineties: a Reassessment', *Latomus* 50, pp.285–303.

Cary, M. (1924a), 'Is It the Lex Gabinia?', *Classical Review* 38, p.60.

—— (1924b), 'The Lex Gabinia Once More', *Classical Review* 38, pp.162–64.

Casuleus, N. (2012), 'In Part a Roman Sea: Rome and the Adriatic in the Third Century BC', in C. Smith and L. Mariah Yarrow (eds), *Imperialism, Cultural Politics, and Polybius* (Oxford), pp.205–29.

Champion, C. (2007), 'Empire by Invitation: Greek Political Strategies and Roman Imperial Interventions in the Second Century BC', *Transactions of the American Philological Association* 137, pp.255–75.

—— (2017), 'Conquest, Liberation, Protectionism, or Enslavement? Mid-Republican Rome from a Greek Perspective', in T. Naco del Hoyo and F. Sanchez. (eds), *War, Warlords, and Interstate Relations in the Ancient Mediterranean* (Leiden), pp.254–65.

Champion, J. (2009), *Pyrrhus of Epirus* (Barnsley).

—— (2010), *The Tyrants of Syracuse. War in Ancient Sicily Volume I: 480–367 BC* (Barnsley).

—— (2012), *The Tyrants of Syracuse. War in Ancient Sicily Volume II: 367–211 BC* (Barnsley).

Chrubasik, B. (2016), *Kings and Usurpers in the Seleukid Empire: The Men who would be King* (Oxford).

Cobban, J. (1935), *Senate and Provinces, 78–49 BC* (Cambridge).

Coello, J. (1995–96), 'C. Flavivs Fimbria, Consular y Legado en la Provincia de Asia (86/84 a. de C.)', *Studia historica historia Antigua* 13–14, pp.257–75.

Coskun, A. and Engels, D. (eds) (2019), *Rome and the Seleukid East: Selected Papers from Seleukid Study Day V* (Brussels).

Coudry, M. (2016), 'Cassius Dio on Pompey's Extraordinary Commands', in C. Lange and J. Madsen, (eds), *Cassius Dio. Greek Intellectual and Roman Politician* (Leiden), pp.33–50.

Dabrowa, E. (2003) (ed.), *The Roman Near East and Armenia* (Krakow).

—— (2011), *Studia Graeco-Parthica: Political and Cultural Relations Between Greeks and Parthians* (Wiesbaden).

—— (2013), 'The Parthian Aristocracy: its Social Position and Political Activity', *Parthica* 15, pp.53–62.

—— (2015), *Central Asia and Iran: Greeks, Parthians, Kushans and Sasanians* (Krakow).

—— (2019), 'The Seleukids, Rome and the Jews (134–76 BC)', in A. Coskun and D. Engels (eds), *Rome and the Seleukid East Selected Papers from Seleukid Study Day V* (Brussels), pp.389–99.

Daly, G. (2002), *Cannae: The Experience of Battle in the Second Punic War* (London).

Darbyshire, G, Mitchell, S. and Vardar, L. (2000), 'The Galatian Settlement in Asia Minor', *Anatolian Studies* 50, pp.75–97.

Davison, J. (1930), 'Cicero and the Lex Gabinia', *Classical Review* 44, pp.224–25.

Debeviose, N. (1938), *A Political History of Parthia* (Chicago).

del Hoyo, N., Antela-Bernardez, B., Arrayas, I. and Busquets, S. (2009), 'The Impact of the Roman Intervention in Greece and Asia Minor Upon Civilians', in B. Antela-Bernárdez and T. Ñaco del Hoyo (eds), *Transforming Historical Landscapes in the Ancient Empires* (Oxford), pp.35–51.

—— (2011), 'The Ultimate Frontier between Rome and Mithridates: War, Terror and the Greek Poleis (88–63 BC)', in O. Hekster and T. Kaizer (eds), *The Frontiers of the Roman World* (Leiden), pp.291–304.

Dell, H. (1967a), 'Antigonus III and Rome', *Classical Philology* 62, pp.94–103.

—— (1967b), 'The Origin and Nature of Illyrian Piracy', *Historia* 16, pp.344–58.

—— (1970), 'Demetrius of Pharos and the Istrian War', *Historia* 19, pp.30–38.

Derow, P. (1979), 'Polybius, Rome and the East', *Journal of Roman Studies* 69, pp.1–15.

—— (1991), 'Pharos and Rome', *Zeitschrift für Papyrologie und Epigraphik* 88, pp.261–70.

—— (2003), 'The Arrival of Rome; From the Illyrian Wars to the Fall of the Macedon', in A. Erskine (ed.), *A Companion to the Hellenistic World* (London), pp.51–70.

—— (2014), *Rome, Polybius, and the East* (Oxford).

de Souza, P. (2008), 'Rome's Contribution to the Development of Piracy', *Memoirs of the American Academy in Rome Supplementary Volume* 6, pp.71–96.

Dmitriev, S. (2006), 'Cappadocian Dynastic Rearrangements on the Eve of the First Mithridatic War', *Historia* 55, pp.285–97.

Dobbins, K. (1975a), 'Mithradates II and his Successors; A Study of the Parthian Crisis 90–70 BC', *Antichthon* 5, pp.63–79.

—— (1975b), 'The Successors of Mithradates II of Parthia', *Numismatic Chronicle* 15, pp.19–45.

Dobiás, J. (1931), Les premiers rapports des romains avec les parthes et l'ocuptaion de la syria', *Archiv Orientalni* 3, pp.215–56.

Downey, G. (1937), 'Q. Marcius Rex at Antioch', *Classical Philology* 32, pp.144–51.

—— (1951), 'The Occupation of Syria by the Romans', *Transactions and Proceedings of the American Philological Association* 82, pp.149–63.

Drogula, F. (2015), *Commanders and Command in the Roman Republic and Early Empire* (Chapel Hill).

Dueck, D. (2006), 'Memnon of Herakleia on Rome and the Romans', in T. Bekker-Nielsen (ed.), *Rome and the Black Sea Region* (Aarhus), pp.43–62.

Dyson, S. (1985), *The Creation of the Roman Frontier* (Princeton).

Dzino, D. (2005), 'Late Republican Illyrian Policy of Rome 167–60 BC: The Bifocal Approach', *Studies in Latin Literature and Roman History* 12 (Brussels), pp.48–73.

—— (2010), *Illyricum in Roman Politics 229 BC–AD 68* (Cambridge).

Eckhardt, B. (2016), 'The Hasmoneans and their Rivals in Seleucid and Post-Seleucid Judea', *Journal for the Study of Judaism in the Persian, Hellenistic, and Roman Period* 47, pp.55–70.

Eckstein, A. (1987), *Senate and General: Individual Decision Making and Roman Foreign Relations 264–194 BC* (Berkeley).

—— (1988), 'Rome, the War with Perseus, and Third-Party Mediation', *Historia* 37, pp.414–44.

—— (1994), 'Polybius, Demetrius of Pharus, and the Origins of the Second Illyrian War', *Classical Philology* 89, pp.46–59.

—— (1999), 'Pharos and the Question of Roman Treaties of Alliance in the Greek East in the Third Century BC', *Classical Philology* 94, pp.395–418.

—— (2006), *Mediterranean Anarchy, Interstate War, and the Rise of Rome* (Berkeley).

—— (2008), *Rome Enters the Greek East. From Anarchy to Hierarchy in the Hellenistic Mediterranean, 230–170 BC* (London).

—— (2013), 'What is an empire and how do you know when you have one? Rome and the Greek States after 188 BC', in P. Burton (ed.), *Culture, Identity and Politics in the Ancient Mediterranean World. Papers from a Conference in Honour of Erich Gruen* (Canberra), pp.173–90.

—— (2017), 'Rome, Empire, and the Hellenistic State-system', in T. Naco del Hoyo and F. Sanchez (eds), *War, Warlords, and Interstate Relations in the Ancient Mediterranean* (Leiden), pp.231–53.

Edwell, P. (2013), 'The Euphrates as a boundary between Rome and Parthia in the late Republic and Early Empire', *Antichthon* 47, pp.191–206.

Ehrenberg, V. (1953), 'Imperium Maius in the Roman Republic', *American Journal of Philology*, pp.113–36.

Erickson, K. (2018), *The Seleukid Empire 281–222 BC* (Swansea).

Erickson, K. and Ramsey, G. (eds) (2011), *Seleucid Dissolution: The Sinking of the Anchor* (Wiesbaden).

Errington, A. (2008), *A History of the Hellenistic World, 323–30 BC* (Oxford).

Errington, R. (1971), 'The Alleged Syro-Macedonian Pact and the Origins of the Second Macedonian War', *Athenaeum* 49, pp.336–54.

—— (1972), *Dawn of Empire: Rome's Rise to World Power* (London).

Erskine, A. (2013), 'The View from the East', in J. Prag and J. Quinn (eds), *The Hellenistic West. Rethinking the Ancient Mediterranean* (Cambridge), pp.14–43.

Evans, R. (2011), *Roman Conquests: Asia Minor, Syria, and Armenia* (Barnsley).

—— (2014), *A History of Pergamum: Beyond Hellenistic Kingship* (London).

—— (2016), 'Pompey's Three Consulships; The End of Electoral Competition in the Late Roman Republic', *Acta Classica* 59, pp.80–100.

Facella, M. (2010), 'Advantages and Disadvantages of an Allied Kingdom; The Case of Commagene', in T. Kaizer and M. Facella (eds), *Kingdoms and Principalities in the Roman Near East* (Stuttgart), pp.181–97.

Fantham, E. (1975), 'The Trials of Gabinius in 54 BC', *Historia* 24, 425-443.

Fine, J. (1936). 'Macedon, Illyria, and Rome, 220-219 BC', *Journal of Roman Studies* 26, pp.24–39.

Fletcher, W. (1939), 'The Pontic Cities of Pompey the Great', *Transactions and Proceedings of the American Philological Association* 70, pp.17–29.

Fowler, R. (2010), 'King, Bigger King, King of Kings: structuring power in the Parthian World', in T. Kaizer and M. Facella (eds), *Kingdoms and Principalities in the Roman Near East* (Stuttgart), pp.57–77.

Frank, T. (1914), 'The Background of the Lex Manilia', *Classical Philology* 9, pp.191–93.

Fratantuono, L. (2017), *Lucullus: The Life and Campaigns of a Roman Conqueror* (Barnsley).

Freeman, P. (1994), 'Pompey's Eastern Settlement: A Matter of Presentation?', *Studies in Latin Literature and Roman History VII*, pp.143–79.

Frendo, D. (2003), 'Roman Expansion and the Graeco-Iranian World: Carrhae, Its Explanation and Aftermath in Plutarch', *Bulletin of the Asia Institute* 17, pp.71–81.

Gabba, E. (1976), *Republican Rome, The Army, and the Allies* (Berkeley).

Garoufalias, P. (1979), *Pyrrhus, King of Epirus* (London).

Gatzke, A. (2013), 'The Propaganda of Insurgency: Mithridates VI and the "Freeing of the Greeks" in 88 BC', *Ancient World* 44, pp.66–79.

Glew, D. (1977a), 'Mithridates Eupator and Rome: A Study of the Background of the First Mithridatic War' *Athenaeum* 55, pp.380–405.

—— (1977b), 'The Selling of the King: A Note on Mithridates Eupator's Propaganda in 88 BC', *Hermes* 105, pp.253–56.

—— (1981), 'Between the Wars: Mithridates Eupator and Rome, 85–73 BC', *Chiron* 11, pp.109–30.

—— (1987), 'The Cappadocian Expedition of Nicomedes III Euergetes, King of Bithynia', *Museum Notes (American Numismatic Society)* 32, pp.23–55.

Gold, B. (1985), 'Pompey and Theophanes of Mytilene', *American Journal of Philology* 106, pp.312–27.

Grainger, J. (1999), *The League of Aitolians* (Leiden).

—— (2002), *The Roman War of Antiochus the Great* (Leiden).

—— (2010), *The Syrian Wars* (Leiden).

—— (2011), *The Wars of the Maccabees* (Barnsley).

—— (2013a), *Roman Conquests: Egypt and Judaea* (Barnsley).

—— (2013b), *Rome, Parthia, and India: The Violent Emergence of a New World Order 150–140 BC* (Barnsley).

—— (2014), *The Rise of the Seleukid Empire (323–223 BC): Seleukos I to Seleukos III* (Barnsley).

—— (2015a), *The Seleukid Empire of Antiochus III (223–187 BC)* (Barnsley).

—— (2015b), *The Fall of Seleukid Empire 187–75 BC* (Barnsley).

—— (2016), *Great Power Diplomacy in the Hellenistic World* (London).

—— (2017), *Kings and Kingship in the Hellenistic World 350–30 BC* (Barnsley).

—— (2020), *The Galatians: Celtic Invaders of Greece and Asia Minor* (Barnsley).

Graham, D. (2013), *Rome and Parthia: Power, Politics and Profit* (North Charleston).

Grajetzki, W. (2011), *Greeks and Parthians in Mesopotamia and Beyond 331 BC–224 AD* (London).

Green, P. (1990), *From Alexander to Actium. The Historical Evolution of the Hellenistic Age* (Berkeley).

Greenhalgh, P. (1980), *Pompey. The Roman Alexander* (London).

Gregoratti, L. (2017), 'Sinews of the other Empire: Parthian Great King's rule over Vassal Kingdoms', in H. Teigen and E. Seland (eds), *Sinews of Empire: Networks in the Roman Near East and Beyond* (Oxford), pp.95–104.

Grimal, P. (ed.) (1968), *Hellenism and the Rise of Rome* (London).

Gruen, E. (ed.) (1970), *Imperialism in the Roman Republic* (New York).

—— (1974), *The Last Generation of the Roman Republic* (Berkeley).

—— (1976), 'Rome and the Seleucids in the Aftermath of Pydna', *Chiron* 6, pp.73–94.

—— (1984), *The Hellenistic World and the Coming of Rome Volumes I & 2* (Berkeley).

—— (1996), *Studies in Greek Culture and Roman Policy* (Berkeley).

Hall, J. (1997), 'The Roman Province of Judea: A Historical Overview', *Brigham Young University Studies* 36, pp.319–36.

Hammond, N. (1968), 'Illyria, Rome and Macedon in 229–205 BC', *Journal of Roman Studies* 58, pp.1–21.

Hardy, E. (1917), 'The Catilinarian Conspiracy in Its Context: A Re-Study of the Evidence', *Journal of Roman Studies* 7, pp.153–228.

Harris, W. (1979), *War and Imperialism in Republican Rome 327–70 BC* (Oxford).

—— (ed.) (1984), *The Imperialism of Mid-Republican Rome* (Rome).

Harrison, I. (2008), 'Catiline, Clodius, and Popular Politics at Rome during the 60s and 50s BC', *Bulletin of the Institute of Classical Studies* 51, pp.95–118.

Hayne, L. (1974), 'The Politics of M. Glabrio, Cos. 67', *Classical Philology*, 69, pp.280–82.

Hekster, O. (2010), 'Trophy Kings and Roman Power: A Roman perspective on Client Kingdoms', in T. Kaizer and M. Facella (eds), *Kingdoms and Principalities in the Roman Near East* (Stuttgart), pp.45–55.

—— (2012), 'Kings and Regime Change in the Roman Republic', in C. Smith and L. Mariah Yarrow (eds), *Imperialism, Cultural Politics, and Polybius* (Oxford), pp.184–202.

Hillman, T. (1991), 'The Alleged Inimicitiae of Pompeius and Lucullus: 78–74', *Classical Philology* 86, pp.315–18.

—— (1993), 'When Did Lucullus Retire?', *Historia* 42, pp.211–28.

—— (1996), 'Pompeius ad Parthos?' *Klio* 78, pp.380–99.

Hölb, G. (2000), *A History of the Ptolemaic Empire* (London).

Hojte, J. (2006), 'From Kingdom to Province – Reshaping Pontos after the Fall of Mithridates VI', in T. Bekker-Nielsen (ed.), *Rome and the Black Sea Region* (Aarhus), pp.15–30.

—— (2009), *Mithridates VI and the Pontic Kingdom* (Aarhus).

Holt, F. (1999), *Thundering Zeus: The Making of Hellenistic Bactria* (Berkeley).

Hoover, O. (2007), 'A Revised Chronology for the Late Seleucids at Antioch, 121/0–64 BC', *Historia* 56, pp.280–301.

Jameson, S. (1970), 'Pompey's Imperium in 67: Some Constitutional Fictions', *Historia* 19, pp.539–60.

Kaizer, T. and Facella, M. (2010) (eds), *Kingdoms and Principalities in the Roman Near East* (Stuttgart).

Kallet-Marx, R. (1995), *Hegemony to Empire; The Development of the Roman Empire in the East from 148 to 62 BC* (Berkeley).

Keall, E. (1994), 'How many Kings did the Parthian King of Kings rule?', *Iranica Antiqua* 29, pp.253–72.

Keaveney, A. (1981), 'Roman Treaties with Parthia circa 95–circa 64 BC', *American Journal of Philology* 102, pp.195–212.

—— (1982), 'The King and the War-Lords: Romano-Parthian Relations circa 64–53 BC', *American Journal of Philology* 103, pp.412–28.

—— (1992), *Lucullus; A Life* (London).

—— (1995). 'Sulla's Cilician Command: The Evidence of Apollinaris Sidonius', *Historia* 44, pp.29–36.

Kennedy, D. (1996), 'Parthia and Rome; Eastern perspectives', in D. Kennedy (ed.), *The Roman Army in the East* (Michigan), pp.67–90.

Konrad, C. (1994), *Plutarch's Sertorius* (Chapel Hill).

Koon, S. (2010), *Infantry Combat in Livy's Battle Narratives* (Oxford).

Kosmin, P. (2014), *The Land of the Elephant Kings: Space, Territory, and Ideology in the Seleucid Empire* (Harvard).

Kryśkiewicz, H. (2017), 'The Parthians in the 1st Century BC – a worthy enemy of Rome? Remarks on the issue of Roman-Parthian political conflict in the ending period of existence of the Roman Republic, and on its influence on Roman imperial ideology', *Shidnyj Svit* 3, pp.60–72.

Kuhrt, A. and Sherwin-White, S. (1987), *Hellenism in the East* (London).

—— (1993), *From Samarkhand to Sardis* (London).

Kuin, I. (2017), 'Rewriting Family History: Strabo and the Mithridatic Wars', *Phoenix* 71, pp.102–118.

Larsen, J. (1935), 'Was Greece Free between 196 and 146 BC', *Classical Philology* 30, pp.193–214.

Leach, J. (1978), *Pompey the Great* (London).

Lerner, J. (1996), 'Seleucid Decline on the Eastern Iranian Plateau', *Berytus* 42, pp.103–12.

—— (1999), *The Impact of Seleucid Decline on the Eastern Iranian Plateau* (Stuttgart).

Lewis, T. (1728), *The history of the Parthian Empire, from the foundation of the monarchy by Arsaces, to its final overthrow by Artaxerxes the Persian; contained in a succession of twenty-nine kings* (London).

Loader, W. (1940), 'Pompey's Command under the Lex Gabinia', *Classical Review* 54, pp.134–36.

Lomas, K. (1993), *Rome and the Western Greeks, 350 BC–AD 200: Conquest and Acculturation in Southern Italy* (London).

Lozinski, B. (1959), *The Original Homeland of the Parthians* (Hague).

Luce, T. (1970), 'Marius and the Mithridatic Command', *Historia* 19, pp.161–94.

Madsen, J. (2009), *Eager to be Roman: Greek Response to Roman Rule in Pontus and Bithynia* (London).

Magie, D. (1939), 'The "Agreement" between Philip V and Antiochus III for the Partition of the Egyptian Empire', *Journal of Roman Studies* 29, pp.32–44.

—— (1950), *Roman Rule in Asia Minor Volumes I & II* (Princeton).

Manandyan, H. (2007), *Tigranes II and Rome: A New Interpretation Based on Primary Sources* (Mazda).

Mandell, S. (1989), 'The Isthmian Proclamation and the Early Stages of Roman Imperialism in the Near East', *Classical Bulletin* 65, pp.89–94.

—— (1991), 'Did the Maccabees Believe that They Had a Valid Treaty with Rome?', *Catholic Biblical Quarterly* 53, pp.202–20.

Marciak, M. (2017), *Sophene, Gordyene, and Adiabene. Three Regna Minora of Northern Mesopotamia Between East and West* (Leiden).

Marshall, A. (1968), 'Pompey's Organization of Bithynia-Pontus: Two Neglected Texts', *Journal of Roman Studies* 58, pp.103–09.

Marshall, B. (1984), 'Faustus Sulla and Political Labels in the 60s and 50s BC', *Historia* 33, pp.199–219.

Mattern-Parkes, S. (2003), 'The Defeat of Crassus and the Just War', *Classical World* 96, pp.387–96.

Matyszak, P. (2008), *Mithridates the Great: Rome's Indomitable Enemy* (Barnsley).

—— (2009), *Roman Conquests: Macedonia and Greece* (Barnsley).

—— (2019), *The Rise of the Hellenistic Kingdoms 336–250 BC* (Barnsley).

—— (2020), *Greece Against Rome: The Fall of the Hellenistic Kingdoms 250–31 BC* (Barnsley).

Mayor, A. (2009), *The Poison King: The Life and Legend of Mithridates, Rome's Deadliest Enemy* (Oxford).

—— (2014), 'Common Cause versus Rome: The Alliance between Mithridates VI of Pontus and Tigranes II of Armenia, 94–66 BC', in M. Metin (ed.), *Tarihte Turkler ve Ermeniler* (Ankara), pp.99–119.

McDonald, A. (1967), 'The Treaty of Apamea (188 BC)', *Journal of Roman Studies* 57, pp.1–8.
—— (1970), 'Rome and Greece 196–146 BC', in B. Harris (ed.), *Auckland Classical Essays* (Oxford), pp.113–31.
McDonald, A. and Walbank, F. (1969), 'The Treaty of Apamea (188 BC): The Naval Clauses', *Journal of Roman Studies* 59, pp.30–39.
McGing, B. (1984), 'The Date of the Outbreak of the Third Mithridatic War', *Phoenix* 38, pp.12–18.
—— (1986), 'The Kings of Pontus: Some Problems of Identity and Date', *Rheinisches Museum für Philologie* 129, pp.248–59.
—— (1996), *The Foreign Policy of Mithridates VI Eupator, King of Pontus* (Leiden).
Millar, F. (2006), *The Greek World, the Jews, and the East* (Chapel Hill).
Morell, K. (2017), *Pompey, Cato, and the Governance of the Roman Empire* (Oxford).
Morello. R. (2002), 'Livy's Alexander Digression (9.17–19): Counterfactuals and Apologetics', *Journal of Roman Studies* 92, pp.62–85.
Muller, S. and Wiesehofer, J. (eds) (2017), *Parthika. Greek and Roman Authors' Views of the Arsacid Empire* (Wiesbaden).
Mulroy, D. (1988), 'The Early Career of P. Clodius Pulcher: A Re-Examination of the Charges of Mutiny and Sacrilege', *Transactions of the American Philological Association* 118, pp.155–78.
Myers, E. (2010), *The Ituraeans and the Roman Near East: Reassessing the Sources* (Cambridge).
Nabel, J. (2017), 'The Seleucids Imprisoned: Arsacid-Roman Hostage Submission and its Hellenistic Precedents', in J. Schlude and B. Rubin (eds), *Arsacids, Romans and Local Elites. Cross-Cultural Interactions of the Parthian Empire* (Oxford), pp.25–50.
Neatby, L. (1950), 'Romano-Egyptian Relations during the Third Century BC', *Transactions and Proceedings of the American Philological Association* 81, pp.89–98.
Newell, E. (1925), *Mithradates of Parthia and Hypaosines of Characene* (New York).
Olbrycht, M. (2009), 'Mithridates VI Eupator and Iran', in J. Hojte (ed.), *Mithridates VI and the Pontic Kingdom* (Aarhus), pp.163–90.
—— (2010), 'The Early Reign of Mithradates II the Great in Parthia', *Anabasis* 1, pp.144–58.
—— (2011), 'Subjects and Allies: The Black Sea Empire of Mithridates VI Eupator (120–63 BC) Reconsidered', in *Pontika 2008: Recent Research on the Northern and Eastern Black Sea in Ancient Times* (Krakow), pp.275–81.
Oost, S. (1954), *Roman Policy in Epirus and Acarnania in the Age of the Roman Conquest of Greece* (Dallas).
Orian, M. (2015), 'Hyrcanus II versus Aristobulus II and the Inviolability of Jerusalem', *Jewish Studies Quarterly* 22, pp.205–42.
Ormerod, H. (1925), 'The So-Called Lex Gabinia', *Classical Review* 39, pp.15–16.
Osgood, J. (2010), 'Caesar and the Pirates; Or How to Make (and Break) an Ancient Life', *Greece & Rome* 57, pp.319–36.
Overtoom, N. (2016a), 'The Rivalry of Rome and Parthia in the Sources from the Augustan Age to Late Antiquity', *Anabasis* 7, pp.137–74.
—— (2016b), 'The Power-Transition Crisis of the 240s BC and the Creation of the Parthian State', *International History Review* 38, pp.984–1013.
—— (2017a), 'The Parthians' Unique Mode of Warfare: A Tradition of Parthian Militarism and the Battle of Carrhae', *Anabasis* 8, pp.95–122.
—— (2017b), 'The Parthian Rival and Rome's Failure in the East: Roman Propaganda and the Stain of Crassus', *Acta Antiqua Academiae Scientiarum Hungaricae* 57, pp.415–35.
—— (2019), 'The Power-Transition Crisis of the 160s–130s BC and the Formation of the Parthian Empire', *Journal of Ancient History* 7, pp.111–55.
—— (2020), *Reign of Arrows: The Rise of the Parthian Empire in the Hellenistic Middle East* (Oxford).

Paltiel, E. (1979a), 'The Treaty of Apamea and the Later Seleucids', *Antichthon* 13, pp.30–41.

—— (1979b), 'Antiochos IV and Demetrios I of Syria', *Antichthon* 13, pp.42–47.

Papazoglu, F. (1979), *The Central Balkan Tribes in Pre-Roman Times* (Amsterdam).

Parrish, E. (1973), 'Crassus' New Friends and Pompey's Return', *Phoenix* 27, pp.357–80.

Patterson, L. (2002), 'Pompey's Albanian Connection at Justin XLII, 3,4', *Latomus* 61, pp.312–25.

Petkovic, Z. (2008), 'Sulla and the Liburnian Campaign of Cinna', *Aevum* 82, pp.119–25.

—— (2010), 'Notes on the Dardanians, the Scordisci and Roman Macedonia 168–75 BC', pp.11–17.

—— (2012), 'The Aftermath of the Apamean settlement: early challenges to the new order in Asia Minor', *Klio* 94, pp.357–65.

—— (2014), 'The Bellum Dardanicum and the Third Mithridatic War', *Historia* 63, pp.187–93.

Phillips, E. (1970), 'Cicero and the Prosecution of C. Manilius', *Latomus* 29, pp.595–607.

—— (1976), 'Catiline's Conspiracy', *Historia* 25, pp.441–48.

Primo, A. (2010), 'The Client Kingdom of Pontus between Mithridatism and Philoromanism', in T. Kaizer and M. Facella (eds), *Kingdoms and Principalities in the Roman Near East* (Stuttgart), pp.159–79.

Raditsa, L. (1969–70), 'Mithridates' View of the Peace of Dardanus in Sallust's Letter of Mithridates', *Helikon* 9–10, p.632.

Ramsey, J. (1980), 'The Prosecution of C. Manilius in 66 BC and Cicero's "pro Manilio"', *Phoenix* 34, pp.323–36.

——, (1999), 'Mithridates, the Banner of Ch'ih-Yu, and the Comet Coin', *Harvard Studies in Classical Philology* 99, pp.197–253.

Rea, C. (2013), *The Rise of Parthia in the East. From the Seleucid Empire to the Arrival of Rome* (Milton Keynes).

—— (2014), *Leviathan vs. Behemoth: The Roman-Parthian Wars 66 BC–217 AD* (Milton Keynes).

Regling, K. (1907), 'Crassus' Partherkrieg', *Klio* 7, pp.357–94.

Reynolds, J. (1962), 'Cyrenaica, Pompey and Cn. Cornelius Lentulus Marcellinus', *Journal of Roman Studies* 52, pp.97–103.

Rice-Holmes, T. (1917), 'Tigranocerta', *Journal of Roman Studies* 7, pp.120–38.

Ridley, R. (1981), 'The Extraordinary Commands of the Late Republic: A Matter of Definition', *Historia* 30, pp.280–97.

—— (2006), 'Antiochus XIII, Pompeius Magnus and the Unessayed Coup', *Ancient Society* 36, pp.81–95.

Rising, T. (2013), 'Senatorial Opposition to Pompey's Eastern Settlement. A Storm in a Teacup?', *Historia* 62, pp.196–221.

Rizzo, F. (1963), *Le fonti per la storia della conquista Pompeiana della Sira* (Palermo).

Rocca, S. (2014), 'The Late Roman Republic and Hasmonean Judea', *Athenaeum* 102, pp.47–78.

Rosenstein, N. (2012), *Rome and the Mediterranean 290 to 146 BC: The Imperial Republic* (Edinburgh).

Rostovtseff, M. (1916/17), 'Pontus, Bithynia and the Bosporus', *Annual of the British School at Athens* 22, pp.1–22.

Rowland, R. (1966), 'Crassus, Clodius, and Curio in the Year 59 BC', *Historia* 15, pp.217–23.

Sampson, G. (2008), *The Defeat of Rome. Crassus, Carrhae and the Invasion of the East* (Barnsley).

—— (2010), *The Crisis of Rome: The Jugurthine and Northern Wars and the Rise of Marius* (Barnsley).

—— (2013), *The Collapse of Rome: Marius, Sulla, and the First Civil War 91–70 BC* (Barnsley).

—— (2016), *Rome Spreads Her Wings: Territorial Expansion Between the Punic Wars* (Barnsley).

—— (2017), *Rome, Blood and Politics. Reform, Murder and Popular Politics in the Late Republic 133–70 BC* (Barnsley).

—— (2019). *Rome, Blood and Power: Reform, Murder and Popular Politics in the Late Republic 70–27 bc* (Barnsley).

—— (2020). *Rome and Parthia: Empires at War: Ventidius, Antony and the Second Romano-Parthian War, 40–20 bc* (Barnsley).

Sanford, E. (1939), 'The Career of Aulus Gabinius', *Transactions and Proceedings of the American Philological Association* 70, pp.64–92.

—— (1950), 'Roman Avarice in Asia', *Journal of Near Eastern Studies* 9, pp.28–36.

Santangelo, F. (2007), *Sulla, the Elites, and the Empire* (Leiden).

—— (2014), 'Roman Politics in the 70s bc: A Story of Realignments?', *Journal of Roman Studies* 104, pp.1–27.

Sartre, M. (2005), *The Middle East under Rome* (London).

Schlude, J. (2013), 'Pompey and the Parthians', *Athenaeum* 101, pp.163–81.

—— (2020), *Rome, Parthia, and the Politics of Peace: The Origins of War in the Ancient Middle East* (London).

Schlude, J. and Rubin, B. (2017) (eds), *Arsacids, Romans and Local Elites: Cross-Cultural Interactions of the Parthian Empire* (Oxford).

Schmitz, M. (2015), *Roman Conquests: The Danube Frontier* (Barnsley).

Sellwood, D. (1962), 'The Parthian Coins of Gotarzes I, Orodes I, and Sinatruces', *The Numismatic Chronicle and Journal of the Royal Numismatic Society* 2, pp.73–89.

Shatzman, I. (1971), 'The Egyptian Question in Roman Politics (59–54 bc)', *Latomus* 30, pp.363–69.

Sheldon, M. (2010), *Rome's Wars in Parthia: Blood in the Sand* (London).

Sherwin-White, A. (1976), 'Rome, Pamphylia and Cilicia, 133–70 bc', *Journal of Roman Studies* 66, pp.1–14.

—— (1977a), 'Ariobarzanes, Mithridates, and Sulla', *Classical Quarterly* 27, pp.173–83.

—— (1977b), 'Roman Involvement in Anatolia, 167–88 bc', *Journal of Roman Studies* 67, pp.62–75.

—— (1984), *Roman Foreign Policy in the East 168 bc to ad 1* (Oklahoma).

Siani-Davies, M. (1997), 'Ptolemy XII Auletes and the Romans', *Historia* 46, pp.306–40.

Simonetta, A. (1966), 'Some Remarks on the Arsacid Coinage of the Period 90–57 bc', *The Numismatic Chronicle* 6, pp.15–40.

—— (2001), 'A Proposed Revision of the Attributions of the Parthian Coins Struck During the So-called "Dark Age" and its Historical Significance', *East and West* 51, pp.69–108.

Simpson, A. (1938), 'The Departure of Crassus for Parthia', *Transactions and Proceedings of the American Philological Association* 69, pp.532–41.

Smallwood, E. (1967), 'Gabinius' Organisation of Palestine', *Journal of Jewish Studies* 19, pp.89–92.

—— (1981), *The Jews under Roman Rule: From Pompey to Diocletian: A Study in Political Relations* (Leiden).

Smith, R. (1964), 'The Significance of Caesar's Consulship in 59 bc', *Phoenix* 18, pp.303–13.

Stanton, G. and Marshall, B. (1975), 'The Coalition between Pompeius and Crassus 60–59 bc', *Historia* 24, pp.205–19.

Sordi, M. (1973), 'La legatio in Cappadocia di C. Mario nel 99–98 a.C.', *Rendiconti Dell'Instituto Lombardo* 107, pp.370–79.

Southern, P. (2002), *Pompey the Great* (Stroud).

Stark, F. (1966), *Rome on the Euphrates* (London).

Sullivan, R. (1990), *Near Eastern Royalty and Rome 100–30 bc* (Toronto).

Swain, S. (1992), 'Plutarch's Characterisation of Lucullus', *Rheinisches Museum für Philologie* 135, pp.307–16.

Syme, R. (1995), *Anatolica: Studies in Strabo* (Oxford).

—— (1999), *Rome and the Balkans 80 bc–ad 14* (Exeter).

Tatum, W. (1999), *The Patrician Tribune: Publius Clodius Pulcher* (Chapel Hill).

Taylor, L. (1941), 'Caesar,s Early Career', *Classical Philology* 36, pp.113–32.

Taylor, M. (2011), *Antiochus The Great* (Barnsley).

van Ooteghem, J. (1954), *Pompée le grand, bâtisseur d'Empire* (Brussels).

—— (1959), *L. Licinius Lucullus* (Brussels).

Walbank, F. (1963), 'Polybius and Rome's Eastern Policy', *Journal of Roman Studies* 53, pp.1–13.

Ward, A. (1969), 'Cicero's Support of the Lex Gabinia', *Classical World* 63, pp.8–10.

—— (1970a), 'Cicero and Pompey in 75 and 70 BC', *Latomus* 29, pp.58–71.

—— (1970b), 'Politics in the Trials of Manilius and Cornelius', *Transactions and Proceedings of the American Philological Association* 101, pp.545–56.

—— (1972), 'Cicero's Fight against Crassus and Caesar in 65 and 63 BC', *Historia* 21, pp.244–58.

—— (1975), 'Caesar and the Pirates', *Classical Philology* 70, pp.267–68.

—— (1977), 'Caesar and the Pirates II: The Elusive M. Iunius Iuncus and the year 75/4', *American Journal of Ancient History* 2, pp.26–36.

Waterfield, R. (2011), *Dividing the Spoils: The War for Alexander the Great's Empire* (Oxford).

—— (2014), *Taken at the Flood. The Roman Conquest of Greece* (Oxford).

Watkins, O. (1987), 'Caesar Solus? Senatorial Support for the Lex Gabinia', *Historia* 36, pp.120–21.

Wellesley, K. (1953), 'The Extent of Territory Added to Bithynia by Pompey', *Rheinisches Museum für Philologie* 96, pp.293–318.

Wheeler, E. (2002), 'Roman Treaties with Parthia: Völkerrecht or Power Politics', in P. Freeman (ed.), *Limes XVIII: Proceedings of the XVIIIth International Congress of Roman Frontier Studies held in Amman, Jordan* (Oxford), pp.287–92.

Williams, R. (1978), 'The Role of "Amicitia" in the Career of A. Gabinius (Cos. 58)', *Phoenix* 32, pp.195–210.

—— (1984), 'The Appointment of Glabrio (Cos. 67) to the Eastern Command', *Phoenix* 38, pp.221–34.

—— (1985), 'Rei Publicae Causa: Gabinius' Defence of His Restoration of Ptolemy Auletes', *Classical Journal* 81, pp.25–38.

Williams, R. and Williams, B. (1988), 'Cn. Pompeius Magnus and L. Afranius. Failure to Secure the Eastern Settlement', *Classical Journal* 83, pp.198–206.

Wolski, J. (1956/8), 'The Decay of the Iranian Empire of the Seleucids and the Chronology of the Parthian Beginnings', *Berytus* 12, pp.35–52.

—— (1999), *The Seleucids, The Decline and Fall of Their Empire* (Krakow).

—— (2003), *Seleucid and Arsacid Studies: A Progress Report on Developments in Source Research* (Krakow).

Wylie, G. (1994), 'Lucullus Daemoniac', *L'Antiquité Classique* 63, pp.109–19.

Index